William Blackstone

William Blackstone

LAW AND LETTERS IN THE EIGHTEENTH CENTURY

WILFRID PREST

OXFORD
UNIVERSITY PRESS

OXFORD
UNIVERSITY PRESS

Great Clarendon Street, Oxford OX2 6DP

Oxford University Press is a department of the University of Oxford.
It furthers the University's objective of excellence in research, scholarship,
and education by publishing worldwide in

Oxford New York

Auckland Cape Town Dar es Salaam Hong Kong Karachi
Kuala Lumpur Madrid Melbourne Mexico City Nairobi
New Delhi Shanghai Taipei Toronto

With offices in

Argentina Austria Brazil Chile Czech Republic France Greece
Guatemala Hungary Italy Japan Poland Portugal Singapore
South Korea Switzerland Thailand Turkey Ukraine Vietnam

Oxford is a registered trade mark of Oxford University Press
in the UK and in certain other countries

Published in the United States
by Oxford University Press Inc., New York

British Library Cataloguing in Publication Data
Data available

Library of Congress Cataloging in Publication Data
Data available

Typeset by Newgen Imaging Systems (P) Ltd., Chennai, India
Printed in Great Britain
on acid-free paper by
CPI Antony Rowe, Chippenham, Wiltshire

ISBN 978-0-19-955029-6

1 3 5 7 9 10 8 6 4 2

To Sabina, with all my love

Contents

Contents

Acknowledgements

This book was written on the other side of the world from its archival and manuscript sources. So I am more than usually indebted to those staff of the various institutions listed in the Bibliography who not only made my physical visits more productive than they could otherwise have been, but also answered multiple emailed questions and supplied images of the uniquely valuable material in their care. Closer to home, I gladly acknowledge a continuing obligation to the dedicated and friendly personnel of the University of Adelaide's Barr Smith Library and Sir John Salmond Law Library, the State Library of South Australia, and the National Library of Australia, especially the Petherick Room. Funding as an Australian Research Council Discovery Project, with additional support from the Law School and the School of History and Politics of the University of Adelaide, has among other things enabled me to benefit from the research assistance of Mark Bode, Irene Cassidy, Alasdair Hawkyard, Maaike Knottenbelt, Matthew Kilburn, Martin McElroy, Vida Russell, and William Woods. For all this I am exceedingly grateful, as I am for the support and encouragement of colleagues and friends over the years. It also seems proper to acknowledge the enormous benefits conferred by the new digital technology, including the online scholarly databases which have revolutionized research in the humanities and social sciences, especially so far as this book is concerned A2A (Access to Archives), ECCO (Eighteenth Century Collections Online), the English Short Title Catalogue, and the Royal Historical Society's Bibliography of British History.

When I first worked on Blackstone's life at the National Humanities Center some ten years ago, Eliza Robertson and Alan Tuttle helped me accumulate an invaluable collection of references and photocopies. In Oxford I have benefited immeasurably from bibliographical assistance supplied by Penelope Bulloch and Alan Tadiello of the Balliol College Library, Mary Clappinson and Mike Webb at the Bodleian Library, and Norma Aubertin-Potter and Gaye Morgan of the Codrington Library. I thank them most sincerely, as also those many other kind persons who have helped me sort out various puzzles, or confirmed that they are likely to remain such: among them John Baker (University of Cambridge); Simon Bailey and Alice Millea (Oxford University Archives); Paul Brand (All Souls College, Oxford); Celia Charlton (Inner Temple); Sarah Charlton (Buckinghamshire Record Office); Morris Cohen, John Langbein, Simon

May, and Angus Trumble (Yale University); Mike Davis and Anthony Page (University of Tasmania); Ian Doolittle; Jack P. Greene; Richard P. Heitzenrater (Duke University); Guy Holborn and Jo Hutchings (Lincoln's Inn); Amanda Ingram (Pembroke College, Oxford); Emily Kadens (University of Texas); John Keeler and Dave Lemmings (University of Adelaide); Michael Lobban (Queen Mary, University of London); Lawrence Macintosh; Ann Mitchell (Woburn Abbey); Jonathan Oates (Ealing Local History Centre); Ruth Paley (History of Parliament); David Pedgley; Michael Roberts (Macquarie University); Barry Smith (The Australian National University); John Walsh (Jesus College, Oxford); and Richard Yeo (Griffith University).

Lastly, I am extremely grateful to Paul Langford and Dave Lemmings, who have both read and commented on the final draft, to Robert Phiddian, who helped me make better sense of Blackstone as poet, and to Peter Cane, who clarified my ideas about Blackstone's thought, although none of them is to blame for the outcome. My greatest debt, now and always, is to the dedicatee of this book.

Wilfrid Prest
Adelaide, June 2008

List of Illustrations

Abbreviations

Note: unless otherwise indicated, all works cited here and below were published in London.

AJLH	American Journal of Legal History
Al. Oxon.	*Alumni Oxonienses 1715–1886*, ed. J. Foster, 4 vols. (1887–8)
ASC	All Souls College, Oxford
Baker, *Serjeants*	J. H. Baker, *The Order of Serjeants at Law* (1984)
BB	*Bibliotheca Blackstoneiana. A Catalogue of a Library of 4,500 Volumes...the greater part having been collected by the celebrated Judge Blackstone and Dr Blackstone of Oxford...Sold by Auction, by Mr. Price...10th of Sept., 1845*
BL	British Library, London
Bodl.	Bodleian Library, Oxford
Clitherow	J. Clitherow, 'Preface, Containing Memoirs of his Life', from [W. Blackstone], *Reports of Cases Determined in the Several Courts of Westminster-Hall, from 1746 to 1779*, ed. J. Clitherow (1781), vol. i, pp. i–xxi
CJ	*Journals of the House of Commons* (1742–)
Codrington	Codrington Library, All Souls College, Oxford
Commentaries	W. Blackstone, *Commentaries on the Laws of England*, 4 vols. (Chicago, 1979; Oxford, 1765–9)
Doolittle	I. Doolittle, *William Blackstone: A Biography* (Haslemere, 2001)
Eller	C. S. Eller, *The William Blackstone Collection in the Yale Law Library: A Bibliographical Catalogue* (New Haven CT, 1938)
ER	*English Reports*
HEL	W. S. Holdsworth, *History of English Law*, 16 vols. (1922–66)
H of P 1715–54	R. Sedgwick, *The House of Commons 1715–1754*, 2 vols. (1970)
H of P 1754–90	L. B. Namier and J. Brooke, *The House of Commons 1754–1790*, 3 vols. (1964)

HUO	*The History of the University of Oxford*, ed. T. H. Aston: Volume V: *The Eighteenth Century*, ed. L. S. Sutherland and L. G. Mitchell (Oxford, 1986)
IT	Inner Temple
Lemmings, *Professors*	D. F. Lemmings, *Professors of the Law: Barristers and English Legal Culture in the Eighteenth Century* (Oxford, 2000)
Letters	*The Letters of Sir William Blackstone 1744–1780*, ed. W. R. Prest (2006)
LJ	*Journals of the House of Lords* (1767–)
LL	*A Catalogue of the Law Library of Philip Stanhope... To which is added the Reserved Part of the Library of the Late Justice Blackstone... Leigh, Sotheby, & Son... 1803*
LMA	London Metropolitan Archives
LPL	Lambeth Palace Library
Martin	C. T. Martin, *Catalogue of the Archives in the Muniment Room of All Souls College* (1877)
MT	Middle Temple
MTAdmR	*Register of Admissions to the Honourable Society of the Middle Temple*, ed. H. A. C. Sturgess, 3 vols. (1949)
Newdigate Diary	Diaries of Sir Roger Newdigate, 1750–1780, Warwickshire County Record Office, CR 136
ODNB	*Oxford Dictionary of National Biography*, ed. H. C. G. Matthew and Brian Harrison, 60 vols. (Oxford, 2004)
OUA	Oxford University Archives
Philip	I. G. Philip, *William Blackstone and the Reform of the Oxford University Press in the Eighteenth Century*, Oxford Bibliographical Soc. Publications, n.s., vol. vii (1957 for 1955)
Reports	[W. Blackstone], *Reports of Cases Determined in the Several Courts of Westminster Hall from 1746 to 1779*, 2 vols. (2nd rev. edn., 1828)
RO	Record Office, or Archives
Sainty, *Judges*	J. C. Sainty, *The Judges of England 1272–1990* (1993)
Sainty, *Law Officers*	J. C. Sainty, *A List of English Law Officers, King's Counsel and Holders of Patents of Precedence* (1986)
Simmons List	J. S. G. Simmons, 'List of All Souls Fellowship Candidates 1689–1914' (ts, Codrington)

TNA	The National Archives (formerly Public Record Office)
VCH	*Victoria County History of England*
Wither Family	R. F. Bigg-Wither, *Materials for a History of the Wither Family* (Winchester, 1907)

Notes:

Dates are New Style throughout, with the year beginning on 1 January. Except where indicated, chapter titles are derived from Clitherow.

CHAPTER 1

Introduction

Authors of famous books are liable to be overshadowed by their literary progeny. William Blackstone's *Commentaries on the Laws of England*, a huge publishing success from its first appearance in four volumes between 1765 and 1769, has been continuously reprinted, revised, and re-edited down to the present day. Wherever the founding influence of English common law is acknowledged, Blackstone's name appears on the walls of courthouses, legislatures, and university buildings. At the middle of the last century it was still sufficiently familiar for the comic poet Ogden Nash to inform readers of his 'Lines to Be Embroidered On a Bib Or, the Child is Father of the Man, But Not For Quite A While' (first published on 22 November 1947) that 'Blackstone and Hoyle | Refused cod-liver oil'.[1] We have Blackstone's physical likeness in contemporary portraits by Gainsborough and others, innumerable printed engravings, several marble statues, and at least two Victorian stained-glass windows.[2] Yet the man who wrote the first accessible, authoritative, and comprehensive guide to the common law's complexities, a work characterized by one contemporary enthusiast as the 'most correct and most beautiful outline that ever was exhibited of any human science',[3] has been largely neglected by biographers and historians. There is a vast accumulated scholarly literature on the *Commentaries*, but the author of that 'excellent work'—which the young Edward Gibbon 'considered as a rational System of the English Jurisprudence digested into a natural method, and cleared of the

---

[1] Ogden Nash, Centennial, 'Lines to Be Embroidered On a Bib Or, the Child is Father of the Man, But Not For Quite A While', *The New Yorker*, 5 August 2002, 50 (I owe this reference to Sabina Flanagan).

[2] The windows are at the Marshall-Wythe School of Law, College of William and Mary, Williamsburg, Virginia (see plate 20), and the Great Hall of the University of Sydney.

[3] W. Jones, *Essay on the Law of Bailments* (1781), 3–4.

pedantry and obscurity which rendered it the unknown horror of all men of taste'[4]—remains a distant and elusive figure.

I

This is not a novel observation. As long ago as 1937, an energetic Midwestern lawyer noted the 'Astonishing Fact' that 'There Does Not Exist a Real Biography of the Legal Scholar Whose Name is Unquestionably the Most Familiar to the English-Speaking World'. Using occupational data from the US census, Homer H. Cooper went on to calculate the potential minimum American market for an 'interesting biography' at a minimum of 220,405 lawyer customers.[5] Coincidentally or not, the following year saw the publication in quick succession of two full-length lives of Blackstone. The second and weightier of these was the work of an established academic with a doctorate in history from the University of North Carolina, besides a law degree and several years of legal practice. There seems no reason to doubt Professor David Lockmiller's claim that his book was hastened by the appearance of Lewis Warden's *The Life of Blackstone*, a chatty compilation, of literary rather than scholarly pretensions, by a recent Harvard Law School graduate.[6] Unfortunately, neither would-be biographer showed much interest in relating his subject to the cultural, intellectual, and social worlds of mid-eighteenth-century England. Partly for that reason, and also because they relied on a limited range of printed sources, neither added significantly by way of information or interpretation to the late Victorian memoir produced for the original *Dictionary of National Biography* by the journalist G. P. Macdonnell. There was, however, one notable difference. Macdonnell wrote a condescending and iconoclastic exercise in the orthodox tradition of nineteenth-century legal positivism, dismissing Blackstone as a confused reactionary ('not a mind of much analytical power, nor in any high sense . . . an original thinker'). But Lockmiller's and Warden's books are discursive, uncritical eulogies of 'this eighteenth-century Englishman whose writings continue to exert a great influence throughout the world'.[7] As the legal historian T. F. T. Plucknett commented, 'Blackstone's life can hardly be written by authors

---

[4] *The English Essays of Edward Gibbon*, ed. P. B. Craddock (Oxford, 1972), 63.

[5] H. H. Cooper, 'An Unwritten Biography', *Amer. Bar Assocn. J.*, 23 (1937), 9–15.

[6] D. A. Lockmiller, *Sir William Blackstone* (Chapel Hill NC, 1938), viii; L. C. Warden, *The Life of Blackstone* (Charlottesville VA, 1938).

[7] G. P. Macdonnell, 'Sir William Blackstone (1723–1780)': *Dictionary of National Biography*, ed. S. Lee (1885), v. 133–40. The quotation is from the dust jacket to Lockmiller's *Blackstone*.

who are so incurious about his times . . . There probably ought to be a life of Blackstone, but it is a very difficult life to write.'[8]

The *Commentaries* gradually attracted more appreciative attention from academic lawyers, legal historians, and students of political thought throughout the middle and later decades of the twentieth century. But the next notable monograph on their author did not appear until 2001. It is the work of a former Oxford postgraduate student in Modern History, whose supervisor developed a keen interest in Blackstone during her final major scholarly project.[9] Armed with Dame Lucy Sutherland's encouragement, and her notes, Ian Doolittle published in 1983 a pathbreaking article which foreshadowed a full-scale biography, but then abandoned academe for legal practice.[10] While his recent 112 self-published pages use a wider range of evidence than any previous account, their brevity has necessitated some sacrifices. The emphasis is overwhelmingly public-political, despite succinct comments on Blackstone's family background, Anglicanism, marriage, and intellectual interests. Nevertheless, Doolittle's slim volume now provides an indispensable source of reference and point of departure for all subsequent biographical accounts.

II

How are we to explain the relative paucity and thinness of biographical writing on William Blackstone? Why has the author of the most celebrated and influential law book in the English language, and one of the more notable publications of the eighteenth century, attracted so little interest and attention from biographers and historians? Stanley N. Katz supplied one possible answer in his introduction to a modern facsimile edition of the *Commentaries*: 'Though the list of his honors and activities is long, Sir William Blackstone was undoubtedly a dull man'.[11] Katz wrote these words more than a quarter-century ago. Today we are better placed to appreciate

---

[8] 'Book Notes', *Harvard Law Rev.*, 52 (1939), 721.

[9] *HUO*. Before her death in 1980, Sutherland published a characteristically perceptive study of 'William Blackstone and the Legal Chairs at Oxford' in *Evidence in Literary Scholarship*, ed. R. Wellek and A. Ribiero (1979), 229–40.

[10] I. G. Doolittle, 'Sir William Blackstone and his *Commentaries on the Laws of England* (1765–69): a biographical approach', *Oxford Journal of Legal Studies*, 3 (1983), 99–112; see also his 'William Blackstone and the Radcliffe Camera, 1753', *Bodleian Library Record*, 11 (1982), 47–50 and *idem*, 'Jeremy Bentham and Blackstone's lectures', *Bentham Newsletter*, 6 (1982), 23–5.

[11] *Commentaries*, I. iii. Katz appears to echo the words of Gareth Jones, in his *The Sovereignty of the Law: Selections from Blackstone's Commentaries on the Laws of England* (1973), xii: 'Blackstone's life was conventionally dull'.

the extraordinary breadth and diversity of Blackstone's accomplishments and involvements—as administrator, antiquary, architect and builder, bibliophile, critic, historian, legislator, poet, and politician—not to mention judge, jurist, lawyer, and penal reformer. So while it may be readily admitted that Blackstone's relatively short lifespan was not saturated with drama or sensation, nor was it wholly lacking in action, conflict, or variety. Without denying the personal reticence which led a younger contemporary to refer to Blackstone as 'a guarded man',[12] a degree of introversion, or modesty, is not necessarily equivalent to dullness. That Blackstone has appeared an uninteresting figure says more about the manner in which he has been presented by previous writers than the intrinsic interest which attaches to the man and his life. In particular, as this book seeks to demonstrate, tracing the connections between Blackstone's life and his writings is far from a barren or tedious exercise.

A further, more substantial explanation for the lack of work on Blackstone's life is an apparent lack of sources from which that life might be written. There is no Blackstone archive as such. Indeed, no original contemporary collection of Blackstone's personal, family, or professional papers is known to survive, apart from a small deposit of executors' accounts in the London Metropolitan Archives and two volumes of retained drafts and inward correspondence held by the Bodleian Library and Oxford University Archives.[13] We do not know whether Blackstone himself, his family, or his executors consciously embarked on the destruction of his papers before or after his death in 1780. But whereas his will carefully bequeathed various specified manuscripts, while prescribing that his 'Books of General Antiquities or History', together with the best household furniture, plate, and utensils should be catalogued and preserved, it makes no mention of personal records of any kind.[14] The lack of surviving papers from either of his parents, or their siblings, suggests there was no tradition of archival preservation among Blackstone's immediate kin. Whereas matters were somewhat different among his wife's family, the Clitherows of Boston Manor, Brentford, Blackstone himself evidently never became a sufficiently large-scale landowner to possess a cache of estate deeds and rentals among which his private and professional papers might have been more or less routinely preserved. Judging by the cheerful alacrity with which in 1829 his son James replied to an enquirer seeking 'an autograph of my deceased father . . . out of the variety in my possession',

[12] *The Letters of Sir William Jones*, ed. G. Cannon (Oxford, 1970), ii. 809.
[13] London Metropolitan Archives, ACC 1360/580–587; Bodl. MS Top. Oxon. d 387; OUA, WPα/22/1.
[14] TNA, PROB 11/1061, fos. 102–3.

his immediate descendants seem to have attached little value to whatever of their father's papers did come down to them.[15]

Blackstone's extensive published writings, which did not all appear under their author's name, yield few useful biographical scraps. Much manuscript material in his own hand—correspondence, legal opinions, lecture notes, and other writings—does survive, scattered widely across England and the United States. Tracing and reassembling these dispersed remnants has been a big and often frustrating task.[16] In this respect, strong demand by private collectors for Blackstone manuscripts acts as a two-edged sword. Soaring prices may help bring to light hitherto lost material, but also put at risk Blackstone items in inadequately secured public collections, as for example the manuscript 'Select Poems and Translations Between the Years 1736 and 1755' which has unaccountably disappeared from the law library of the University of California at Berkeley, together with its only known microfilm copy. Other Blackstone manuscripts continue to turn up in auction and dealer's catalogues from time to time. But it seems unlikely, if by no means impossible, that we shall come across a hidden hoard of papers which might fill most remaining gaps in the documentary evidence for Blackstone's life and thought. So, rather than holding fire in anticipation of some such improbable eventuality, the intending biographer must make the most of the large— indeed still growing—body of sources which is available at present.

The unique authority of the earliest surviving contemporary account of Blackstone's life has been a further and perhaps no less effective deterrent, by suggesting that little remains to be said about the man and his career. Blackstone's will directed that 'my Manuscript Reports of Cases determined in Westminster Hall taken by myself . . . be published after my decease . . . and the produce thereof be carried to and considered as part of my personal Estate'.[17] Early in 1780 the task of preparing this substantial body of material for the press fell to James Clitherow, a former Oxford colleague whose younger sister had married Blackstone twenty years before. Clitherow's editorial preface to the first volume of Blackstone's law reports claimed that he had been persuaded by many of the latter's 'Friends . . . to pay a Tribute to the Memory of so respectable a Person, by imparting at the same time to the Public a short Account of his Life and gradual Rise from a posthumous Orphan to the Dignity and

[15] Folger Shakespeare Library, MS Y.c. 162 (1), James Blackstone to Henry Adams, Wallingford, 25 December 1829.
[16] Cf. my 'Reconstructing the Blackstone Archive: or, Blundering After Blackstone', *Archives*, 31 (2006), 108–118.
[17] TNA, PROB 11/1061, fo. 102v.

high Station He at last attained'.[18] This blandly celebratory formula set the tone for what would follow.

Clitherow had hoped, he says, to leave the biographical part of his mission to 'an abler Pen'. But the illness and death of 'the learned and ingenious' Dr Buckler, 'one of Mr Justice Blackstone's oldest and most intimate Friends' forced him, 'though totally unused to writing for the public Eye, to undertake the Task himself'.[19] Fortunately (Clitherow went on), he could call upon his own 'intimate Acquaintance with Mr Justice Blackstone for above Thirty Years', the assistance of others who had known him even longer, and above all, an autobiographical outline compiled by the subject himself: 'a short Abstract of every Circumstance of Consequence in his Life, written by himself with his accustomed Accuracy'.[20] This document, although now known to us only in so far as it is incorporated in the text of Clitherow's 'Memoirs of His Life', constitutes Blackstone's sole surviving attempt at autobiography—and at controlling his own posthumous reputation.

Most of Clitherow's account of his subject's family origins and education must have come directly from Blackstone's own summary 'Abstract', including the description of the affectionate oversight of his fatherless young nephews by the London surgeon Thomas Bigg, and that of Blackstone's schooling at the London Charterhouse. The same may well apply to the picture of his first years at Oxford, where we are told that 'he prosecuted his Studies with unremitting Ardour'. An autobiographical note is also sounded by the candid account of Blackstone's early difficulties at the bar, 'not being happy in a graceful Delivery or a Flow of Elocution (both which he much wanted) nor having any powerful Friends or Connexions to recommend him'.[21] The account and explanation of the resignation of his Oxford chair and headship of New Inn Hall ('finding he could not discharge the personal Duties of the former, consistently with his professional Attendance in London, or the Delicacy of his Feelings as an honest Man') is likewise very much after Blackstone's own style.[22] Finally, Clitherow identifies as direct quotation ('to use his own Expression') Blackstone's characterization of the relief with which he abandoned the House of Commons in 1769, 'where . . . amid the Rage of contending Parties, a Man of Moderation must expect to meet with no Quarter from any Side'.[23] With these few exceptions, authentic Blackstone

---

[18] *Al. Oxon.*, i. 265; Simmons List; Clitherow, i.

[19] Ibid. Benjamin Buckler preceded Blackstone to All Souls; the two became close friends and allies: *ODNB*.

[20] Clitherow, ii.   [21] Ibid., vii.

[22] Ibid., xvii.   [23] Ibid., xx.

gold is not readily distinguishable from a Blackstone–Clitherow amalgam in the twenty-five printed pages which make up the 'Memoirs' proper (the remaining six pages of Clitherow's preface deal with the *Reports* themselves).

That difficulty doubtless bothered contemporary readers less than it concerns later historians. It scarcely weakened the standing of Clitherow's narrative as an authentic, well-grounded account of his distinguished brother-in-law. Indeed, despite initially referring to his text as a 'Tribute', Clitherow subsequently insisted on several occasions that his 'only Intent is to write a faithful Narrative, not a professed Panegyric'.[24] Yet given the circumstances and timing of its appearance, as well as the nature of Clitherow's sources, the 'Memoirs' could hardly avoid the character of an authorized obituary, or memorial. Not merely an act of personal and familial piety carefully prepared for public consumption, Clitherow's narrative incorporates with Blackstone's autobiographical text his subject's view of his own life and its meaning: 'to the rising Generation a bright example of a Man, who without Fortune, Family Interest or Connexions, raised himself by a diligent Attention to his Studies, even from his earliest Youth'.[25]

During the eighteenth century, that 'High Renaissance' in the art of biographical writing, biographers became increasingly prepared to admit to the inevitable mixture of good and bad in all human beings, rather than 'think[ing] it an act of piety to hide the faults or failings of their friends'.[26] So, when introducing the 'Character', which concludes his 'Detail of the Life of this great Man', Clitherow undertook to touch on Blackstone's 'Imperfections (and such the most perfect human Characters have) with Truth and Delicacy'.[27] Yet according to his first biographer and friend, Blackstone's personal shortcomings amounted solely to 'a certain Irritability of Temper'. In conjunction with a strong sense of duty, as well as an intimidating 'Countenance and Figure', this tended to convey 'an Idea of Sternness', even 'the heavy, but unmerited imputation, among those who did not know him, of Ill-Nature; but he had a Heart as benevolent and as feeling as Man ever possessed'. By the same token Blackstone's shyness might appear 'to a casual Observer, though it was only Appearance,

---

[24] Ibid., xix, xx.

[25] Ibid., ii.

[26] D. A. Staufer, *The Art of Biography in Eighteenth-Century England* (Princeton NJ, 1941), 457; S. Johnson, *The Rambler*, no. 60 (13 Oct. 1750), quoted [J. Boswell], *Boswell's Life of Johnson*, ed. R. W. Chapman (Oxford , 1960), 22; S. Howard, 'Biography and the Cult of Personality in Eighteenth-Century England', University of Oxford DPhil thesis, 1989, 68.

[27] Clitherow, xx, xxiv.

like Pride', especially after he became a judge and 'thought it his Duty to keep strictly up to Forms'.

Written at a time when Romantic sensibility and sentiment were burgeoning, these passages might well have struck contemporary readers as pointing to more than trivial defects of character. Nevertheless, Clitherow's final judgement is bland, if not indulgent: 'In short it may be said of him, as the noble Historian said of Mr Selden: "If he had some Infirmities with other Men, they were weighted down with wonderful and prodigious Abilities and Excellences in the other Scale."'[28] There is no suggestion that such personal blemishes in any way affected Blackstone's claims to serve as a role model for the young. That the author of the *Commentaries*, expositor of the laws of a polite and commercial people,[29] could himself behave in a manner less than wholly civil, may indeed seem ultimately inconsequential, however regrettable. But while his subject's shortness of temper was evidently too notorious for Clitherow to ignore altogether, the accusation of ill nature (signifying in this context a generalized unkindness, perhaps even misanthropy), which is raised only to be rather unconvincingly denied, was a far more serious matter. Indeed, it might seem surprising that an ostensibly (and actually) well-disposed biographer, kinsman, and friend could have been so maladroit or tactless as to mention it in the first place. The most likely explanation is that the charge was abroad well before Blackstone's death.

Jeremy Bentham, who first levelled it in print, much later recalled hearing Blackstone's lectures 'with rebel ears' as a precocious Oxford undergraduate.[30] When Bentham's *Fragment on Government* appeared anonymously in April 1776, Blackstone had less than four years to live. He did not choose to answer Bentham's scarifying attack on his book and himself in any public way.[31] After Blackstone's death, Clitherow also maintained a discreet silence, despite discussing earlier critical responses to the *Commentaries* from Joseph Priestley and others. Given the lack of alternative sources, and notwithstanding its brevity and generality, Clitherow's idealized portrayal of the gifted and diligent student rising in the world through virtuous effort supplied a sufficiently circumstantial

[28] Ibid., xxvii. The reference is to Clarendon's portrait of the legal historian John Selden in his *History of the Great Rebellion*.

[29] *Commentaries*, iii. 326, where England is characterized as 'a nation of freemen, a polite and commercial people, and a populous extent of territory'.

[30] J. Bentham, *A Comment on the Commentaries and A Fragment on Government*, ed. J. H. Burns and H. L. A. Hart (1977), 526.

[31] Unless perhaps in the 'Postscript' to the preface of the eighth edition of the *Commentaries* (Oxford, 1778); see below, Chapter 13 pp. 295–6 and Plate 16.

account of Blackstone's career to meet the needs of subsequent biographers well into the twentieth century.[32] But this authorized version could not provide an effective counter to Bentham's persistent and sustained condemnation of the misanthropic enemy of reason and reform, 'everything-as-it-should-be Blackstone',[33] a muddled and shallow apologist for the status quo. Making up in critical acerbity what it lacked in humdrum detail, Bentham's Blackstone replaced the conscientious and upright scholar, judge, and public man with an even more two-dimensional caricature; that of failed barrister turned stodgy Tory academic and confused textbook apologist for the British constitution and unreformed common law. This view of Blackstone as an authoritarian, obscurantist reactionary became widely accepted during the nineteenth century, not least among radicals, reformers, and non-lawyers, and is by no means defunct today.

Neither of these starkly contrasting images, black or white, was calculated to stimulate interest in Blackstone as a biographical subject. But only in the later twentieth century did growing recognition of their inadequacies prompt attempts to construct a more comprehensive, discriminating, and realistic portrait. Sutherland and Doolittle, who led the way, were general rather than legal historians, and Sutherland's attention was focused primarily on Blackstone's administrative and political role in mid-eighteenth-century Oxford. Dame Lucy's disciplinary colleagues, like many of their successors down to the present, by and large shared her relative lack of interest in other—especially legal—aspects of Blackstone's activities and persona. Hence, while historians and other scholars may draw upon the *Commentaries* for summary statements of English law on particular subjects at the beginning of George III's reign, little further attempt has been made to incorporate the book or its author into general accounts of the period.[34] Nor is this altogether surprising. Over the past quarter-century, historians have shown greater willingness to come to terms with the law's various cultural, economic, political, and social dimensions. But Blackstone still tends to be relegated to 'legal history',

---

[32] Clitherow's 'introduction detailing all the incidents of his career . . . from its fairness and impartiality has formed the groundwork of every future memoir', according to E. Foss, *The Judges of England* (1848–64), viii. 250.

[33] *A Comment on the Commentaries*, 13; see also J. H. Burns, 'Bentham and Blackstone: A Lifetime's Dialectic', in *Empire and Revolutions*, ed. G. J. Schochet *et al.* (Washington DC, 1993), 261–78.

[34] Cf. J. B. Owen, *The Eighteenth Century 1714–1815* (1974); G. Holmes and D. Szechi, *The Age of Oligarchy: Pre-Industrial Britain 1722–1783* (1993); F. O'Gorman, *The Long Eighteenth Century: British Political and Social History 1688–1832* (1997); R. Porter, *Enlightenment: Britain and the Creation of the Modern World* (2000); J. Black, *Eighteenth-Century Britain 1688–1783* (2001). Langford's *Polite and Commercial People* is a notable exception.

conceived of as a marginal sub-discipline dominated by antiquarian lawyers and legal academics. So, although a growing body of published research now illuminates particular aspects of eighteenth-century English law in action, to date such specialist knowledge (except in relation to the history of crime and criminal justice) has had relatively little impact on historical interpretation and understanding of the era as a whole.[35]

III

While his authorship of the *Commentaries* undoubtedly remains Blackstone's major claim to fame, neglecting all other aspects of his life makes it difficult, if not impossible, to understand the man and his great work within their historical context. This would be enough to justify a comprehensive biography of an author whose contemporary standing and subsequent influence are entirely comparable to those of such central figures as the historian Edward Gibbon and the political economist Adam Smith. So the following pages discuss for the first time and in some detail Blackstone's entire literary output, ranging from his unpublished early poems, translations, and architectural treatises, his verse essay on comparative religion and his polemical writings on academic, local, and national politics, to his miscellaneous legal writings, scholarly edition of Magna Carta, and extensive critical annotations to Shakespeare's plays. An attempt is also made to trace the stylistic and substantive development of what eventually became the *Commentaries on the Laws of England* from the course of lectures which Blackstone first offered in 1753 and continued to deliver almost every year thereafter until resigning his Oxford positions in 1766. And since Blackstone's activities were by no means confined to the realm of ideas or the pages of a book, this present volume is something more than a standard intellectual or literary biography. In particular, it traces his involvement over more than twenty years in academic administration and government, and for even longer as a legal practitioner with a wide range of clients and business. Attention is also given to Blackstone's somewhat idiosyncratic political behaviour and principles—a significant, if confusing, component of his life story.

One main aim is to restore Blackstone to his own time, by approaching his biography so far as possible without the benefit of hindsight. From Clitherow's 'Memoirs' onwards, accounts of Blackstone have tended to

---

[35] Cf. however *The British and their Laws in the Eighteenth Century*, ed. D. Lemmings (Woodbridge, 2005), 1–26.

present a remarkably static and stereotyped picture of his personality and its trajectory through life, as though the commentator and judge aged in his forties and fifties were merely an inevitable extension or projection of the younger schoolboy, undergraduate, and college fellow. There is an obvious sense in which this is not just true but a truism—the child being father to the man, as Ogden Nash reminded us. But there are dangers in assuming (whether explicitly or not) that Blackstone's attitudes, character, and temperament became fixed at a very early age and thereafter continued essentially unaltered, as also in failing to recognize that alongside the path which led eventually to the *Commentaries* and the bench were other possible routes with quite different destinations which might almost or just as easily have been taken. While much the same could doubtless be said of any human life, Blackstone's previous biographers have generally shown little awareness of the importance of contingency and change in his personal history (except perhaps in crediting at unwarranted face value his self-proclaimed decision to abandon all literary aspirations in favour of a career at the bar). It is true that sheer lack of evidence severely limits what can be recovered of his early years; many aspects of his later emotional life, friendships, and domestic relationships as a husband and father are also more or less hidden from view. Such gaps and silences, frustrating though they undoubtedly are, need not altogether prevent us from at least posing questions about these vital matters, nor indeed from offering answers, however partial, speculative, and tentative they must be. If the missing evidence is in the last analysis irreplaceable, we can at least attempt to ensure that the various cultural, institutional, and social settings within which Blackstone lived and moved are reconstructed as fully as the reader's patience and the state of current scholarship may permit.

Since this book seeks to recover Blackstone's life story as something in the nature of a work in progress, rather than an inevitable and predetermined trajectory, there seems more reason than usual to adopt a conventional chronological structure, instead of a wholly thematic or topical approach. Accordingly, most of the following chapters cover a successive stage in Blackstone's life from childhood to maturity—he could hardly be said to have reached old age. The conclusion glances at the posthumous reputation of Blackstone and his works, and sketches an assessment of his life.

According to Samuel Johnson, 'he that writes the life of another is either his friend or his enemy'.[36] In so far as this characteristically blunt

---

[36] *The Yale Edition of the Works of Samuel Johnson, Volume II: The Idler and the Adventurer*, ed. W. J. Bate *et al.* (1963), 263.

statement of mutually exclusive alternatives applies to the present enterprise, I freely admit that my attitude towards Blackstone is more admiring than hostile, although (I hope) not so blindly enamoured of my subject as to overlook altogether his failings and shortcomings. My initial view of Blackstone was considerably more critical. While recognizing the magnitude of his achievement as the last and most successful in a long line of writers who had struggled to develop a methodical and systematic exposition of the common law, there seemed little reason to doubt the widespread assumption that the values expressed in the formal prose style of the *Commentaries* were those of a complacent, dyed-in-the-wool reactionary. Closer acquaintance with both Blackstone's writings and his times has amply demonstrated the inadequacy of that judgement. I trust that the following pages may contribute to its further discrediting.

CHAPTER 2

'A Young Man of Brilliant Parts'
(1723–38)

I

WILLIAM Blackstone was born on 10 July 1723, 'and baptized the 17th of the same month'[1] in the church of St Vedast, Foster Lane, one of nearly 50 London churches rebuilt under the supervision of Sir Christopher Wren after the Great Fire of 1666. Three Blackstone boys had already been christened at the same font: Charles (named after his father) in August 1719, John (baptized the day he was born, on 11 November 1720, only to be buried 'in the Old Vault' three days later) and Henry, who was born in May 1722. The sequence might well have continued, but for the death and burial of their father, 'Mr Charles Blackstone', in February 1723, five months before William's birth.[2] All these events were recorded in the register of the neighbouring parish of St Michael-le-Quern (also known, more prosaically, as 'at Corn'), which remained an administrative and legal entity even though its burnt-out church had not been restored after the Fire. For within St Michael's long-established boundaries lay the Cheapside silk-draper's shop with house above, 'at the sign of the Blew Boar, near the Conduit', where the young and now fatherless Blackstone family lived.[3] Cheapside, a major east–west thoroughfare and premier shopping centre, was described in 1720 as 'spacious and large', adorned 'with very lofty Buildings . . . well inhabited by Goldsmiths, Linnen Drapers,

---

[1] *The Registers of St. Vedast, Foster Lane, and of St. Michael le Quern, London. Volume i: Christenings*, ed. W. A. Littledale (Harleian Soc., 1902), 267.

[2] Ibid. 266, 267; ii. 346.

[3] Doolittle, 3–4; G. S. Thomson, *The Russells in Bloomsbury 1669–1771* (1940), 260; the trade card illustrated by Thomson cannot now be located in the Woburn Abbey archives, although a photograph does survive (See Plate 1). J. Bedford, *London's Burning* (1966), 86. R. Hyde, *The A to Z of Georgian London* (1982), 12.

Haberdashers, Druggists, and other noted Tradesmen; being one of the chief high Streets in the City'.[4] Its western end, where the Blackstones' shop stood near the Little Conduit at the corner of Paternoster Row, was dominated by the imposing presence of Wren's monumental masterpiece, the recently completed St Paul's Cathedral, eulogized by Daniel Defoe as 'the Beauty of all the Churches in the City, and of all the Protestant Churches in the World . . . a Building exceeding Beautiful and Magnificent'.[5]

So William Blackstone was a true cockney, born at home within the sound of the bells of St Mary-le-Bow, Cheapside, at the heart of Europe's most populous and thriving metropolis, a city now so large that few if any of its half-million inhabitants could have known its whole vast extent.[6] William retained his London connections throughout his life, which indeed ended at most a mile from his birthplace. By the 1720s, thanks in part to the Toleration Act some 30 years before, with its conditional legitimation of the chapels, churches, and meeting houses of Protestant dissenters from the established Church of England, the City's neighbourhoods possibly shared less sense of communal identity than when all its inhabitants had supposedly attended Anglican services in their local parish church. London's traditional occupational topography was also being diluted by continued expansion outside the medieval walls, and the consequent relocation of businesses and housing from within the City proper, much accelerated in the aftermath of the Fire. Yet it is not without significance that William Blackstone was born and brought up in the shadow of London's greatest architectural presence, the soaring cathedral dome which proudly symbolized the durability of the City of London and the Church of England, and close by Stationer's Hall, St Paul's Churchyard, and Paternoster Row, still the centre of the kingdom's booming book and print media trades.[7]

By Blackstone's own account (as incorporated in his brother-in-law's 'Memoirs') his father Charles was 'a London tradesman, not of great Affluence', and the younger son of 'Mr John Blackstone, an eminent Apothecary in Newgate Street'.[8] William did not know his paternal grandfather, who died in 1712, but the latter's friendship with the eminent

---

[4] J. Strype, *A Survey of the Cities of London and Westminster . . . to the Present Time* (1720), i, III. 196.

[5] D. Defoe, *A Tour Thro' the whole Island of Great Britain*, ed. G. D. H. Cole (1927; 1724–7), i. 334. L. Jardine, *On a Grander Scale: the Outstanding Career of Sir Christopher Wren* (2002), 410–28.

[6] V. Harding, 'The changing shape of seventeenth-century London', in *Imagining Early Modern London: Perceptions and Portrayals of the City from Stowe to Strype, 1598–1720*, ed. J. F. Merritt (Cambridge, 2001), 140.

[7] J. Raven, *The Business of Books* (2007), 157–8.

[8] Clitherow, iii.

physician, collector, and natural philosopher Sir Hans Sloane, as well as his benefactions to St Bartholomew's Hospital and prominence in the government of the London Society of Apothecaries, point to something more than nominal intellectual interests and professional involvements.[9] According to William (as relayed by Clitherow), his father and grandfather had 'descended from a Family of that Name in the West of England, at or near Salisbury'.[10] This would seem to point to relatively modest urban origins, as distinct from landed gentry status. Yet instead of being sent to a private teacher or school to learn arithmetic, bookkeeping, modern languages, and other vocational skills directly relevant to commercial life, Charles Blackstone was educated at St Paul's School, one of London's better-known grammar schools, where the curriculum revolved around the study of classical Greek and Latin texts in the original languages. St Paul's was increasingly attracting boarders from outside the City and indeed across the country, besides the citizens' sons like William's father who received a free education as day boys.[11] Further, Charles Blackstone evidently retained sufficiently fond memories of his alma mater to serve in 1716 as steward or organizer of the annual feast attended by former pupils, and in that capacity to make a gift of books to the school library.[12] No doubt he would have sent his sons there had he lived longer, although whether in his own case St Paul's had provided the best available preparation for a shopkeeper's life—even that of a high-class 'silkman'—is another question.

Silkmen bought raw silk and sold it on to the weavers after it had been dyed and thrown or twisted into thread.[13] Charles Blackstone also seems to have traded as a mercer, stocking many varieties of skein silk or thread, and some finished articles like belts, sashes, cord, gloves, and lace, for retail customers. In the land tax assessment books for the northern part of St Michael-le-Quern parish in 1722, he figures as the second-highest rated householder, his status further attested by the title 'Mr' prefixed to his name in the parish register. Here we find entries not only for the christening of his children, but also the burials of two of his servants, who are pointedly listed by name alone: thus 'John Rolfe, servant to

[9] *ODNB, s.v.* Blackstone, John.

[10] Clitherow, iii. H. Gwyn, 'Pedigree of the Blackstone Family', *Gentleman's Magazine* (Sept. 1827), 224.

[11] M. McDonnell, *A History of St Paul's School* (1909); P. Earle, *The Making of the English Middle Class: Business, Society and Family Life in London 1660–1730* (1989), 68; F. Sheppard, *London, A History* (Oxford, 1998), 138.

[12] M. McDonnell, *The Registers of St Paul's School 1509–1748* (1977), 406. This discussion assumes the accuracy of McDonnell's suggested identification of one 'Mr C.B.' with Blackstone's father.

[13] R. Campbell, *The London Tradesman* (1747), 260.

Mr Blackstone'.[14] Retailers, shopkeepers, and manufacturers generally occupied a lower rung on the City's socio-economic ladder than financiers or 'mere merchants' who dealt only wholesale. But silkmen or mercers were often found among the more prosperous citizens in the former category, since their luxury trade required comparatively large amounts of capital, both to acquire an extensive stock and to fit out suitably impressive premises in which to hold and display a rich assortment of wares, domestic and imported.[15] The snapshot impression of Charles Blackstone's material circumstances provided by a post-mortem inventory of his personal property reveals a relatively spacious and elegantly furnished establishment; a three-storied house which he leased for £100 a year, silverware valued at £56, an eight-day clock and no fewer than three watches, two gold, one silver, 'one tea table with china ware' in the dining room, and in the parlour, 'twelve pictures and twenty prints'.[16]

Further indication of the relative economic and social standing of William Blackstone's father, as also of a possible side effect of his gentlemanlike education, is provided by the person of his wife. Charles Blackstone had married Mary Bigg in 1718, a year before the birth of their first child. The Biggs were a family of minor landed gentry of comparatively recent extraction, having apparently migrated from Kent via London to Hampshire and then North Wiltshire in the course of the seventeenth century. Far from enjoying the prestige of a long-settled family estate, the manor house and lands at Chilton Foliat near Hungerford where Mary Bigg grew up had only been purchased by her father in 1689, two years after his eldest daughter's birth.[17] It seems possible that Mary met her future husband through her younger brother Thomas, a surgeon who may have undertaken at least part of his training at St Bartholomew's Hospital, London. Charles's father, the apothecary John Blackstone, had been closely connected with the hospital, although Thomas was only in his early teens when John died.[18] But however the couple became acquainted, we should not suppose that their marriage was regarded as a mismatch by Mary's parents and friends on account of the social distance separating bride and groom. On the contrary, London

[14] Guildhall Library, MS 11,316/70; *Registers . . . of St Michael-le-Quern*, ii. 344.

[15] Earle, *English Middle Class*, 41, 107, 109; N. A. Rothstein, 'The Silk Industry in London, 1702–1766', University of London MA thesis, 1961, 131.

[16] TNA, PROB 3/22/116.

[17] R. F. Bigg-Wither, *Materials for a History of the Wither Family* (Winchester, 1907), 149, and pedigree facing p. 45; *VCH Wiltshire*, xvi. 95. Mary was baptized on 8 May 1687 at Wootton St Lawrence, Hampshire: Hampshire RO, 75M72/PR1.

[18] N. Moore, *The History of St Bartholomew's Hospital* (1918), ii. 636, 716. This plausible hypothesis was first advanced by W. B. Odgers in the *Yale Law Journal*, 27 (1918), 599.

businessmen frequently intermarried with daughters of the landed classes, even if the more well-to-do City men increasingly tended to choose their marital partners from within the commercial community.[19] Indeed the Blackstone–Bigg connection exemplifies the complex web of overlapping interactions between commercial, landed, and professional worlds, as well as those of the provinces and the metropolis, which characterized daily life in early Georgian England.

Rather than any presumed difference in wealth or status, the most striking feature of this marriage was the relatively advanced age of both partners, and especially of Mary Bigg, who was well into her 32nd year on her wedding day. While Charles was perhaps two or three years older than his bride, nearly one-third of a sample of moderately well-to-do male London citizens from the later seventeenth and early eighteenth centuries whose age at first marriage is known were aged in their 30s. But the same is true of fewer than two per cent of the wives in the same sample group. The mean age at first marriage of English women in the first quarter of the eighteenth century seems to have been just under 26 years; in general, the higher a woman's social class, the younger she would wed.[20] We can only guess why Mary (b. 1687) did not marry earlier; there is nothing to suggest that this was not her first marriage. Her matrimonial options may have been restricted by a relatively modest dowry or marriage portion, at a time when the general demographic context, in the form of the gender ratio, was unfavourable to well-born girls seeking suitable husbands. Her two younger sisters, Dorothy (b. 1689) and Alethea (b. 1691), also married in the same year as Mary, two years after the death of their unmarried sister Sarah (b. 1696). The portions bequeathed to Mary's two surviving unmarried younger sisters by their father's will made in November 1723 were £600, plus an annuity of £25, revocable on marriage for an additional £500 lump sum. By contrast, the average marriage portion of a peer's daughter between 1675 and 1729 was over £9,000. Yet Lovelace Bigg, Mary's father, was rumoured to be 'worth thirty thousand Pounds' just before his death in 1725.[21]

If her father's inability or reluctance to provide more competitive dowries did indeed mean that his half-dozen daughters (two of whom

[19] R. Grassby, *Kinship and Capitalism: Marriage, Family and Business in the English-Speaking World, 1580–1740* (Cambridge, 2001), 48–9.

[20] Wiltshire and Swindon Archives 735/5, Chilton Foliat register 1705–64; E. A. Wrigley and R. S. Schofield, *The Population History of England, 1541–1871* (1981), 424; Earle, *English Middle Class*, 182; Grassby, *Kinship and Capitalism*, 60–3.

[21] *Wither Family*, 228; R. B. Outhwaite, 'Marriage as business: opinions on the rise of aristocratic marriage portions in early modern England', in *Business Life and Public Policy*, ed. N. McKendrick and R. B. Outhwaite (Cambridge, 1986), 24. *Remarks and Collections of Thomas Hearne. Vol. VIII. Sept 23 1722–Aug. 9, 1725* (Oxford Historical Soc., 1907), 315.

died unmarried) were not exactly overwhelmed with suitors, perhaps the additional maturity was some compensation in Mary's case, if it helped her cope with her husband's early death. As many as one child in five was likely to be an orphan in early eighteenth-century England, by the strict legal definition of losing their father before reaching adulthood (at 21 years of age). While 'the death of a breadwinner in his prime was . . . the norm in this society', such a commonplace misfortune could plainly have disastrous consequences for the surviving widow and children, dependent on 'earnings which required the dead man's own individual application and knowledge'.[22] In the case of Mary Blackstone and her infant boys, the situation must have looked extremely bleak once the 'bureau desk' in the counting house was opened. Mary later claimed that, having been 'in the life time of her late husband a stranger to his dealings and transactions', on or soon after his decease she discovered 'that he died in very bad circumstances, and that his Estate and Effects would not neere pay and satisfy all his just Debts he having had great Losses'.[23]

As a London-based textile merchant involved in a luxury wholesale import trade, Charles Blackstone was running a relatively high-risk business. His difficulties may well have involved the death of his former business partner Bernard Cotterall, and the general loss of confidence which followed the collapse of the South Sea Bubble in 1720, when the national rate of bankruptcies soared.[24] In July 1724, almost a year after William was born, his mother lodged an answer as executrix to one of several legal actions commenced against her by her former husband's creditors. She alleged that Charles's accumulated business debts totalled around £7,000, of which perhaps a third had been paid off, leaving some £4,500 owing to a total of 104 debtors; further, he had been borrowing large sums over the past ten years from a variety of sources, including his own father-in-law and an apothecary named William Blackstone (presumably another kinsman), who was now among those suing his widow. His personal estate was 'far deficient' to meet these demands, especially since it included around 139 'desperate' or bad debts owed him by a variety of named creditors.[25]

In partnership with one William Hay, Mrs Blackstone preferred to try to trade her way back to solvency by continuing Charles's business from

[22] Earle, *English Middle Class*, 306; Grassby, *Kinship and Capitalism*, 166–8.
[23] TNA, C11/774/46, 74.
[24] J. Hoppitt, *Risk and Failure in English Business 1700–1800* (Cambridge, 1987), 46, 68, 86–7.
[25] TNA, C11/997/20. The death of 'William Blackstone, Esq, of the Temple' was reported by the *Gentleman's Magazine*, 5 (1735), 559; another namesake of East Sheen, Surrey, died the following year: ibid., 6 (1736), 424.

the same premises, rather than looking to the meagre charitable support available from the City and its livery companies in such circumstances. One of their first moves was to slash the shop's inventory, selling off half its stock for just over £1,000. Another was to print a business card advertising their wares.[26] While taking these steps Mary Blackstone was fortunate to have supportive members of her own family close to hand. Besides her sister Dorothy, who had probably already moved to London with her husband Thomas Bethell, she was particularly dependent on her two brothers.[27] The clergyman don Henry Bigg and the surgeon Thomas Bigg both gave vital assistance towards the rearing of her infant sons.

William's two elder brothers, Charles and Henry, aged respectively three-and-a-half years and nine months old at their father's death, would become the particular responsibility of their maternal uncle, Rev Henry Bigg, under whose auspices they first attended Winchester College (where Henry was warden from 1730–40), then New College, its sister institution at Oxford (where Henry had also been fellow and warden for five years before his election to the more lucrative position at Winchester).[28] But in 1723 Henry was 50 miles away in Oxford, while by great good fortune his younger brother Thomas was on the spot in London, and his association with St Bartholomew's Hospital was soon to be formalized by election as assistant surgeon, one of only three such posts in London's oldest hospital.[29] So the orphaned Blackstone brothers, including William ('even from his Birth'), received the 'affectionate, it may be said, the parental, Care' of Thomas Bigg, 'particularly in giving them liberal Educations', which (according to Clitherow), 'supplied the great loss they had so early sustained, and compensated in a great Degree for their want of more ample Fortunes'. Not surprisingly, all three 'always remembered and often mentioned' their uncle's generosity.[30] Indeed, in William's case, his father's death, followed by that of his mother early in 1736 'before he was twelve Years old', turned out to be (by Clitherow's account) anything but 'an Event generally deemed the greatest Misfortune that can befall a Child'.[31] For Thomas Bigg ensured that his youngest nephew's intellectual and literary talents were fostered as they deserved, undertaking 'even from

---

[26] See Plate 1.

[27] *Wither Family*, 227–8; TNA, PROB 11/675/11v–12 (will of Mary Blackstone, proved by Dorothy Bethell, 1736).

[28] T. F. Kirby, *Winchester Scholars* (1888), 236, 238; *New College Oxford 1379–1979*, ed. J. Buxton and P. Williams (Oxford, 1979), 61–2.

[29] Moore, *History of St Bartholomew's*, ii. 636.

[30] Clitherow, iv.

[31] Ibid., iii. However, Mary Blackstone's death occurred on 5 January 1736, six months *after* William's 12th birthday: TNA, PROB 11/675/11v; *Registers . . . of St Michael-le-Quern*, ii. 279

his Birth, the Care both of his Education and Fortune'. Hence William did not end up, as he might otherwise have done, 'in a Warehouse or behind a Counter'.[32]

Clitherow's providentialist and, to our eyes, rather snobbish interpretation of Blackstone's early loss of both his parents almost certainly incorporates his subject's own retrospective view of the matter. Modern readers are perhaps more likely to wonder about the emotional and social effects of Blackstone's bereavement and orphanhood. In many respects his uncle and guardian doubtless served as an adequate substitute for a father whom William never knew, but the psychological impact of his mother's death is now as obscure as almost every other detail of his infancy and childhood.[33] In practical terms, it undoubtedly increased the dependence of all three Blackstone boys on their mother's side of the family. Neither then nor later do they seem to have had any contact with their paternal kin. This may well have been a further consequence of their father's misfortunes, or mismanagement, the after-effects of which were still apparent a decade after his death. Mary Blackstone then wrote a brief paragraph which later became her will:

Not being yet intirely satisfied how strictly justly I might proceed by quite excluding so many of my Husband's creditors from any part of his Estate, it is now my will and pleasure that if I should dye before I have better settled those affairs, then that one thousand pounds of my owne proper money should be distributed among those Creditors (who would otherwise have nothing) in proportion to their debts and I hope the remainder of what I leave will the better prosper with my children. Witness my hand this 27th day of July, 1732. Ma: Blackstone.

On 5 January 1736, 'being the very day she dyed', Mary produced this document, 'owned it to be all of her own proper handwriting', desired it to be read over to her, and 'well approved thereof'.[34] Whether or not her sons were present at her deathbed, they must surely have come to learn of their mother's apparently gratuitous legacy to their late father's creditors, and it would be very surprising if they had not already understood something of the difficulties in which he had left her and them. The ambition, determination, and sense of personal responsibility which henceforth

[32] Clitherow, iii–iv.

[33] Thomas Bigg was described as 'Curator lawfully assigned' to the Blackstone boys when appointed by the Prerogative Court of Canterbury to administer the will of their deceased mother: TNA, PROB 11/675/11.

[34] Ibid. It is not clear by what means Mary could have barred the claims of her late husband's creditors. On the moral and social significance of paying off debts, see M. H. Hunt, *The Middling Sort: Commerce, Gender, and the Family in England 1680–1780* (1996), 41–2.

characterized William's approach to life may also have been part of his mother's legacy.

II

The loss of their mother reinforced the overwhelming masculinity of the immediate emotional and social worlds of the Blackstone boys. In that respect, school must have played at least as large a part as home by 1736, the year William turned 13. Presumably one reason why he did not follow his two elder brothers to board at Winchester College was his uncle's desire to keep a close eye on the welfare of his youngest nephew. The decision to enter him in 1730 'being about seven Years old'[35] at London's Charterhouse (rather than his father's old school, St Paul's) must have been influenced by the location of this former Carthusian monastery, outside the medieval city walls, on the north-eastern boundary of St Bartholomew's Hospital where Thomas Bigg worked, but still less than a mile's walk from the Blackstone home at the western end of Cheapside. The other key consideration was that Charles Wither, a cousin on his mother's side, had managed in 1728 to obtain from Sir Robert Walpole, one of those 'Chief Personages of the State' who acted as governors of Charterhouse, a nomination for William to be admitted as a 'poor Scholar' on the foundation 'in my turn, when it shall fall'—which, as it happened, was not until June 1735.[36]

A further possible attraction was the headmastership of Andrew Tooke, fellow of the Royal Society, professor of geometry at Gresham College, prolific author and translator, who spent most of his life at Charterhouse, as pupil, usher or second master, and finally head. Tooke died in 1732, just two years after Blackstone entered the school, although his memory continued to be celebrated under his less capable successor James Hotchkis, another Charterhouse old boy who had served only one year as usher before becoming head at the age of 30.[37] Blackstone later paid an indirect compliment to his first head teacher by echoing in the title of his own first publication that of Tooke's *The Pantheon* (1698, and

---

[35] Clitherow, iv.

[36] P. Bearcroft, *An Historical Account of Thomas Sutton Esq; And of his Foundation in Charter-House* (1737), v; LMA, ACC1876/PS/04/04/177 (See Plate 3). LMA, Charterhouse Muniments, PS1/6, 117.

[37] R. Congreve, *Panegyrica Oratio Habita in Regio Hospitio Olim Domo Carthusiana* (1733), 6; A. Quick, *Charterhouse: a History of the School* (1990), 28–9.

over 20 subsequent editions), an account of 'the Heathen Gods and most Illustrious Heroes' intended for classroom use.[38]

Charterhouse, founded early in the seventeenth century as a charitable bequest by the enormously wealthy tycoon Thomas Sutton, was both an educational institution and a retirement home. One of the great Victorian public schools, in Blackstone's time it possibly ranked a little behind London's two leading academies—Westminster and St Paul's—despite already recruiting on a national basis. Besides the 40 'gown-boys'—resident scholars aged between 10 and 18 supported from Sutton's endowment—there was a small group of fee-paying day-boys and boarders, but probably well under 100 pupils in all.[39] Nominated by the school's governors, gown-boys were supposedly 'children of poore men that want meanes to bringe them up', specifically excluding heirs to landed estates.[40] In practice the school's intake was dominated by mercantile and professional families, especially parsons' sons. Among Blackstone's near-contemporaries were another future judge (Sir William Ashurst, born in 1725), the High-Church clergyman William Jones of Nayland (1726–1800), and the Whig bishop Edmund Keene (1714–81). His predecessors included the authors Joseph Addison and Richard Steele, and the founder of Methodism, John Wesley, who entered the school as a gown-boy in 1714.[41]

Wesley recalled the Charterhouse regime of his day as bleak and brutal: 'From ten to fourteen, I had little but bread to eat, and not great plenty of that', thanks (it seems) to senior boys raiding the food of their juniors.[42] Blackstone was only seven when he became a fee-paying 'oppidan' (or townie day-boy) in 1730. This was not unusually young to start grammar school, and William could probably count himself lucky to escape the additional privations of boarding-house life during his first five years at Charterhouse. But it seems quite possible that his later self-consciousness, hesitancy in public speaking, and aversion to physical exercise were a partial legacy of unpleasant early experiences at the hands of his fellow students, accentuated by loneliness following his brothers' departure to

[38] See below, pp. 46–8. Tooke also translated an abridgement of Pufendorf's *De Iure Naturae et Gentium Libri Octo* (1672), a work on which Blackstone would later draw; D. Saunders and I. Hunter, 'Bringing the State to England: Andrew Tooke's Translation of Samuel Pufendorf's *De Officio Hominis et Civis*', *History of Political Thought*, 24 (2003), 218–34.
[39] G. S. Davies, *Charterhouse in London* (1921), 247–9; *Rules and Orders relating to Charterhouse* (1748?), 22.
[40] *Rules and Orders*, 19.
[41] J. L. Smith-Dampier, *Carthusian Worthies* (Oxford, 1940).
[42] *The Works of John Wesley. Journals and Diaries V, 1765–75*, ed. W. R. Ward and R. P. Heitzenrater (Nashville TN, 1993), xxii. 237.

Winchester. Yet if Charterhouse life fully justified John Locke's earlier advice that parents should educate children at home with a private tutor, rather than consign them to the harsh and potentially demoralizing pressures of a grammar school, young Blackstone evidently revelled in the academic curriculum.

While most grammar schools paid some attention to the rudiments of English grammar and composition, William must have been able to read and write when he first joined the school.[43] With Latin's cultural and social centrality in continued if still gradual decline, the traditional stipulation that boys spoke only Latin at school was on its last legs by the early eighteenth century.[44] Nevertheless, facility in the language and literature of classical Rome (and, to a lesser extent, Greek and Hebrew) remained the primary aim. Thus at Charterhouse the usher or assistant teacher was responsible for instructing pupils 'to cypher and cast an account, especially those that are less capable of [classical] learning, and fittest to be put to trades'; the head taught only Latin and Greek.[45] There was no standardized curriculum: individual teachers or tutors selected the texts to be studied, which at Charterhouse were supposedly 'approved Authors, Greek and Latin, as are read in the best esteemed Free Schools . . .'.[46] Different schools followed their own traditions; some permitted more or less free versions of whole passages to be rendered into English, others (like Charterhouse in the early nineteenth century) required pupils to translate Latin or Greek sentences word-for-word, before producing an idiomatic English version of the entire passage.[47] After mastering Lily's Latin grammar, Blackstone probably moved on to elementary texts (perhaps Phaedrus's metrical fables and almost certainly Caesar's *Gallic Wars*), before concentrating on the poets, first Ovid and Terence, then Horace and Virgil, perhaps with some selections from the rhetorician Quintilian. Besides memorizing and translating extensive slabs of poetry, students typically produced their own Latin compositions, both prose themes or essays, and verses in a wide variety of different metres and forms. Greek was largely learnt through and translated into Latin, with the poets and dramatists furnishing the main texts for study.[48] At its best such training fostered clarity of expression and sensitivity to words, their use and

---

[43] Davies, *Charterhouse*, 253–5.

[44] M. L. Clarke, *Classical Education in Britain 1500–1900* (Cambridge, 1959), 46–7.

[45] W. H. Brown, *Charterhouse Past and Present* (Godalming, 1879), 98–9, quoted M. Seaborne, *The English School: its architecture and organization 1370–1870* (1971), 46.

[46] *Rules and Orders*, 20.

[47] Ibid., 53–4; S. Rothblatt, *Tradition and Change in English Liberal Education* (1976), 45.

[48] Clarke, *Classical Education*, 50–57.

meaning, in the English vernacular as well as the classical languages. It also provided those who stayed the course with a substantial set of common cultural, historical, and philosophical reference points. These were real virtues, notwithstanding much mechanical and repetitious teaching, emphasis on technical mastery rather than individual creativity, lack of directly vocational content, and the snobbery likely to accompany any form of élite activity.

William Blackstone proved an exceptional pupil. Clitherow tells us that his 'Talents and Industry rendered him the Favourite of his Masters, who encouraged and assisted him with the utmost Attention'.[49] If scarcely a recipe for popularity among his classroom peers, tangible signs of pedagogical approval and favour still survive. In 1736, the year of Mary Blackstone's death, her orphaned son received from William Salisbury, fellow of St John's College, Cambridge, who for 20 years after 1733 combined the post of 'reader' (or preacher) at Charterhouse with a Buckinghamshire rectory, a copy of the third edition of Edward Young's fashionable 'Characteristical' verse satires, *Love of Fame, the Universal Passion*.[50] William Blackstone's literary talents had plainly begun to attract attention; nor can it be entirely coincidental that the earliest material in the (now missing) volume of juvenilia which Blackstone later put together dated from this same year.[51] A still earlier piece of versifying, with a direct Charterhouse link, was apparently not included in that volume. This 30-line set of rhyming couplets celebrates the wedding *c.* 1735 of the Charterhouse headmaster, James Hotchkis, 'in whom', according to his pupil, 'Good nature and sound Learning reign'.[52] Penned in a somewhat immature hand, the addition below the English verses of six lines of Latin summarizing the same hymeneal theme gives the whole piece the character of a school exercise. Even so, the mere fact of its preservation points to contemporary recognition of the unusual promise of the author, who self-deprecatingly styled himself 'a Boy in Praise, unskill'd to tune the Lyre'.[53] Hotchkis showed

[49] Clitherow, iv.

[50] This volume is now Balliol College Library, shelf-mark 1550 f 3; Venn, *Al. Cant.*, iv. 8. For Blackstone's later contact with Salisbury, see *Letters*, 160–3, 166–7.

[51] 'Select Poems and Translations Between the Years 1736 and 1744', as described in Maggs Bros. Catalogue 576 (Autumn 1932), item 843, pp. 9–11.

[52] See Appendix I below. Hotchkis's marriage date is inferred from a memorial in the parish church of Kingsey, Buckinghamshire, where he was vicar from 1726, to Jolly, daughter of James and Mary Hotchkis, who died on 2 September 1736 aged four months: G. Lipscomb, *The History and Antiquities of Buckinghamshire* (1831), i. 303.

[53] Bill Cooper, of Freeman's Auctioneers, Philadelphia, kindly provided a photocopy of this document, seemingly the earliest surviving Blackstone holograph manuscript (listed Freeman Sale 621, 16 December 1993, lot 3; sold on by Baltimore Book Auctions on 20 February 1995). Its present location is unknown.

his own appreciation of such precocious performances in 1737, when he presented Blackstone with the celebrated edition of the works of Horace by the great contemporary classicist Richard Bentley.[54] A more dubious tribute to Blackstone's poetical precocity is a silver medal, one of several commissioned for self-promotional purposes by William Benson, the Whig politician who funded the Westminster Abbey memorial to John Milton by the sculptor Michael Rysbrack. Blackstone's medal, apparently awarded him for Latin verses on Milton which have not survived, depicts the poet's grim-faced head and shoulders, with an obverse legend crediting Benson, the Abbey, and Rysbrack.[55]

Two more traces of Blackstone's Charterhouse days must be briefly mentioned. We are fortunate to have the printed text of a school play performed by the gown-boys on 6 November 1732, the day after the annual celebration of Guy Fawkes' failure to blow up parliament in 1605. Set appropriately enough in the Vatican, its simple plot revolves around the efforts of the Pope, under the direct influence of the Devil, to make Rome once again mistress of the world. An attendant Jesuit reveals in rhyming couplets that 'Albion's Isle' is ripe for the plucking, but then recounts a vision of Britannia escaping from the clutches of Devil and Pope. For while many British 'in Heart revere the Holy See', Rome's chances of a comeback are effectively blocked by the 'Blessings and Glories' flowing from George II and his consort. The Devil's cover is broken, he runs off with the Pope, and another Jesuit finds himself strangely assisted by heavenly powers to discover 'Reason, Truth and Liberty' in Albion's 'blisful Seats'.[56] Since William was just nine years old (and no gown-boy) at the time, it seems unlikely that he would have taken any direct part in this production; but its ultra-patriotic, anti-popish message may well have left a mark.

The other item comes from the latter end of Blackstone's schooling. In a Founder's Day sermon preached by William Salisbury on 12 December 1737 on the text 'thou shalt bless the Lord thy God for the good Land which he hath given thee', Salisbury urged his congregation to appreciate

---

[54] *Q. Horatius Flaccus Ad nuperam Richardi Bentleii editionem accurate expressus* (Cambridge, 1713); this volume, with Blackstone's bookplate and the holograph inscription 'Blackstone, E Dono D[o]mi[ni] J. Hotchkis/1737' is now in the Philadelphia Free Library, Moncure Biddle Collection, HOR/1713/M429.

[55] *ODNB*, s.v. Benson, William; E. Hawkins, *Medallic Illustrations of the History of Great Britain and Ireland* (1885), ii. 524–5. The original medal was presented to Charterhouse School by 'Miss Blackstone, the last representative of that family': *The Carthusian*, July 1885, 83 (my thanks to Ann Wheeler for this information).

[56] LMA, PS1/6, 111; *A Dramatic Piece: By the Charter-House Scholars: In Memory of the Powder-Plot* (1732), 8–29.

the various bounties providentially bestowed upon them. They could make due return by following the philanthropic example of Sutton, whose 'constant Study and Employment' was 'to be doing good'—not least works of 'public Benefit to Mankind; such as, repairing of Bridges, Highways and Churches'.[57] Salisbury's identification of 'industrious Application in the Pursuit of Virtue and Learning' with future 'Preferments and Emoluments', and the state of being 'serviceable to Mankind', was scarcely original.[58] But it is hard to believe that any youthful member of his congregation absorbed and acted upon the message of this sermon more thoroughly than William Blackstone.

By his 15th birthday in July 1738, William's academic achievements and the approval of his teachers had advanced him before all his Charterhouse contemporaries, a pre-eminence marked by his physical elevation to sit at the head or topmost place of the entire school, whether ranked in forms for lessons, or for meals in Gown-boy's Hall. For such a prodigy from such a family, university was the logical next step, notwithstanding the diminished educational and moral reputation of Oxford and Cambridge. There was also the tricky question of William's age. By the 1730s most freshmen at England's two universities were around 17 or 18 years old. Although no fewer than one in five Oxford entrants during the 1630s had been 15 years old or less, a century later such precocious matriculants accounted for only one in 20 of a considerably smaller freshman intake.[59] Whether or not concerns about his relative youth help explain why Blackstone remained at school in London until the end of Michaelmas term 1738, Clitherow notes that doing so also gave him the 'Opportunity of speaking the customary Oration' in praise of Thomas Sutton at the 'Anniversary Commemoration' on 12 December, 'which he had prepared, and which did him much Credit'.[60]

As to how and why William's post-school destination was decided, his Charterhouse teachers, Cambridge graduates to a man, doubtless hoped their star pupil would take the Great North Road to their own alma mater. Yet William's family connections were all with Oxford, where indeed his eldest brother Charles had recently entered New College, a day before his 19th birthday, thus being on the spot to provide oversight and support for

---

[57] W. Salisbury, *A Sermon Preached in Charter-House Chapel, On Monday, Dec. 12, 1737* (1738), 5–6, 17–18.

[58] Ibid. 23–27.

[59] L. Stone, 'The Size and Composition of the Oxford Student Body 1580–1910', in *The University in Society Volume I: Oxford and Cambridge from the 14th to the Early 19th Century* (1974), 57, 97.

[60] Clitherow, v. For an earlier example of such an oration, see n. 37 above.

his gifted sibling.[61] The deciding factor was possibly a newly-instituted scholarship available to former Charterhouse boys at Pembroke College, Oxford. At all events William Blackstone formally joined the University of Oxford by matriculating as a commoner of Pembroke, swearing allegiance to King George II, and subscribing to the 39 articles of the Church of England, on 12 December 1738.

---

[61] *Al. Oxon.*, i.118; besides Henry Bigg's links with New College, Seymour Richmond, another maternal uncle by marriage, matriculated from Queen's College, Oxford, in 1707, and lived not far away in Berkshire: J. Foster, *Alumni Oxonienses 1500–1714* (1891–2), i. 122, iii. 1256.

Chapter 3

'Removed to the University' (1738–43)

I

PEMBROKE COLLEGE, like Charterhouse, was an early seventeenth-century foundation, formed by merging several modest individual benefactions with the land and buildings of Broadgates Hall. This amalgamation was achieved in 1624 under the auspices of the university's then chancellor, the courtier William Herbert, third earl of Pembroke—hence the college's name. Whereas Charterhouse was wealthy enough to subsidize former gown-boys with university exhibitions of £20 per year for up to eight years, the few entrance scholarships offered by Pembroke were mostly 'tied' or restricted to descendants of one of the founders, ex-students of Abingdon grammar school, or residents of the Channel Islands.[1] William hardly fitted any of those categories. But his family and friends may well have noticed the inauguration in 1736 of two Holford exhibitions, each providing a further £20 annually for up to eight years to former Charterhouse scholars elected by the master and fellows of Pembroke College.[2] Given William's demonstrated academic prowess, he was an obvious candidate for one of these awards.

How far the combined Charterhouse and Holford incomes went towards meeting his university expenses is difficult to say. Apart from individual differences in taste, style, and mode of life, costs fluctuated considerably within as well as between colleges. Pembroke students might pay anything from £2–6 a year for their rooms, unless they held a foundation

---

[1] J. Ayliffe, *The Antient and the Present Estate of the University of Oxford* (1714), i. 436–42; *Rules and Orders*, 29.

[2] D. Macleane, *A History of Pembroke College, Oxford, Anciently Broadgates Hall* (Oxford, 1897), 299–300; see also n. 8. below. LMA, PS1/6, 120; PS 2/54. Blackstone was elected to a Holford exhibition at Pembroke College on 22 February. 1739: PS 2/64.

scholarship which provided rent-free accommodation.[3] While a legacy of £40 encouraged the young Samuel Johnson to undertake an Oxford education in the late 1720s, 'failure of pecuniary supplies' had forced him to leave Pembroke before graduating. Ten years later, that same sum possibly represented around two-thirds of the minimum annual outlay of an Oxford undergraduate, even excluding those enrolled in the semi-menial categories of batteler or servitor—in other words, more than sufficient incentive for the talented orphan's guardians to direct him towards Pembroke.[4]

Pembroke had other attractions. A known Whig stronghold earlier in the century, that reputation had not survived the 25-year mastership of Rev Dr Matthew Panting, whom Johnson recalled as 'a fine Jacobite fellow'. Although still in office to receive his new student and allocate him to a tutor in December 1738, Panting died two months later. Little is known of his even longer-serving successor, Rev Dr John Ratcliff, beyond the bare outlines of his career, and the notably cool reception he gave the returning Johnson in 1754.[5] If Pembroke's politico-religious complexion in the late 1730s seems unremarkable in the context of a predominantly High-Church, Tory Oxford, neither was it one of the university's grander or richer societies. Indeed, Pembroke remained 'one of the poorest colleges in Oxford', in marked contrast to Christ Church, its imposing aristocratic neighbour, whose 'magnificent front' with Christopher Wren's impressive Tom Tower dominated the other side of St Aldate's street south of Carfax, the four-way intersection which marked the city of Oxford's traditional centre.[6] An alumnus of Pembroke summed up their relationship in a verse couplet:

The Rival Colleges; or P—mbroke the Humble, to Chr—st Church the Ample:
Truce with thy sneers, thou proud, insulting College
Tho' not much known—we may be men of knowledge.

Cramped, jumbled, and generally undistinguished architecture (dismissed by a contemporary guidebook as 'two small courts of old Buildings . . . there is little that demands our Attention here') reflected a modest endowment

[3] L. S. Sutherland, 'Pembroke College', in *VCH Oxfordshire*, iii. 294.
[4] Stone, 'Size and Composition of the Oxford Student Body', 43; A.D. Godley, *Oxford in the Eighteenth Century* (1908), 130–1; *HUO*, 328; J. C. D. Clark, *Samuel Johnson* (Cambridge, 1994), 116.
[5] *HUO*, 46, 787–8; Godley, *Oxford in the Eighteenth Century*, 285; Boswell, *Life of Samuel Johnson*, ed. Chapman, 53. Macleane, *History of Pembroke*, 342n.
[6] *Oxford in 1710 from the Travels of Zacharias Conrad von Uffenbach*, ed. W. H. and W. J. C. Quarrell (Oxford, 1928), 67. T. Salmon, *The Present State of the Universities* (1743), 28.

and a student body to match.[7] On both economic and prudential grounds Blackstone's guardian uncle may well have approved of such an environment. Although Christ Church also offered Holford exhibitions to Charterhouse scholars, Pembroke attracted fewer aristocratic gentleman-commoners—'smarts' or 'swells'—hence perhaps providing less opportunity for displays of emulative extravagance, and similar undesirable undergraduate behaviour.[8] It was, after all, common knowledge that at university 'many young students miscarry, making little or no progress in their studies, or throwing them entirely aside, and giving themselves up to Idleness and Debauchery'.[9] Finally, Pembroke supplied a receptive setting for literary talents and aspirations: Samuel Johnson, ten years Blackstone's senior, 'was peculiarly happy in mentioning how many of the sons of Pembroke were poets; adding, with a smile of sportive triumph, "Sir, we are a nest of singing birds"'.[10]

It was a very small nest. In terms of human scale, Pembroke College in Blackstone's time might best be thought of as something like a large extended family or clan; indeed the college's founding statutes referred to 'the different members of the society, which is to be constituted as a well-ordered Family in the due subordination and mutual helpfulness of its different parts'.[11] Of course the familial analogy could be partial at best. Women featured only as decorative accessories ('toasts') or functional ancillaries (bed-makers and other domestics) to this formally masculine community. Full membership was confined to males, whose number included both a more or less stable population of fellows, tutors, and college servants on the one hand, and several relatively short-lived undergraduate cohorts on the other. Yet eighteenth-century Pembroke College also seems an almost absurdly minuscule academic institution. During the mid-1730s the college admitted some 13 or 14 new students a year; in 1738 Blackstone was one of a mere 12 freshmen.[12] When his name was added to the buttery book, where battels (charges incurred by college members

---

[7] R. Graves, *Euphrosyne: or, Amusements on the Road of Life* (1780), 269; Salmon, *Present State*, 97.

[8] As did Worcester College and Hart Hall, but they were even smaller, less prestigious, and poorer institutions than Pembroke: Macleane, *History of Pembroke*, 300; E. G. W. Bill, *Education at Christ Church 1660–1800* (Oxford, 1988), 187–8.

[9] D. Waterland, *Advice to a Young Student* (1730), 2; compiled *c.* 1706, for the use of students at Magdalene College, Cambridge, this manual was subsequently published in 1729 and reissued in 1740: C. Wordsworth, *Scholae Academicae Some Account of the Studies at the English Universities in the Eighteenth Century* (Cambridge, 1910), 330.

[10] Boswell, *Life of Johnson*, 55.

[11] Macleane, *History of Pembroke*, 186–7.

[12] Stone, *University in Society*, 106–7; Sutherland, in *VCH Oxon.*, iii. 294; Pembroke College Archives, Buttery Book 9/1/71; dates of entry derived from College Register, 40/5/2.

for food, drink, and other miscellaneous expenditures) were totted up, it joined a total of just over 80 others, not including domestic staff.[13] Only about half these men seem to have been in residence, or at least eating meals in college, for 6 or more of the 12 weeks between 22 September and 12 December 1738. Most of the rest were perhaps only temporarily absent, although some are also noted as having migrated to another college, or indeed 'gone', presumably indicating that they had left Oxford altogether. Eighteenth-century Oxford was not noted for excessively rigorous record-keeping or the enforcement of residential requirements: hence the poet William Shenstone's name still remained on Pembroke's buttery books more than two years after he had left the college for good in August 1739.[14]

The layout of the battel or buttery books reflects the formal structure of a highly stratified community. Names are listed not in alphabetical order, but by descending rank and seniority. Thus during Blackstone's first full term at Pembroke, over the Hilary quarter (which for college accounting purposes extended from 15 December 1738 to 9 March 1739), the hierarchy was headed by the 'Magister Collegi' (master of the college) and 'Mr Vicemgerens' (master vicegerent, or vice-master). These dignitaries are followed successively down the page by the names of 10 fellows, 20 scholars (that is, undergraduates 'on the foundation', supported by scholarships drawing on rental income from the college's endowed property holdings), 4 masters of arts, 2 gentleman-commoners (who dined with the fellows on high table), 13 bachelors of arts, and 27 commoners (Blackstone among them), who ate the standard daily fare provided in hall. The tally concludes with seven battelers or servitors (who served meals and performed other menial tasks around college in return for board, lodging, and tuition), the cook, the butler, and four other college servants.[15] Each of the 25 colleges and halls which collectively constituted the University of Oxford—a whole barely larger than the sum of its constituent parts—encapsulated a similar hierarchical structure of membership, reflecting formal distinctions and gradations which 'ordained privileges and freedoms, disciplines and inhibitions, even social intercourse and the making of friendships'.[16] As an undergraduate commoner, William's standing was clearly signalled to his peers, inferiors, and superiors by his distinctive

[13] Pembroke College Archives, Buttery Book 9/1/71.

[14] *ODNB*, s.v. Shenstone, William. Some graduates paid a nominal fee to keep their names 'on the books' in order to exercise a vote in Convocation, the main academic assembly.

[15] Pembroke College Archives, Buttery Book 9/1/71. A. L. Reade, *Johnsonian Gleanings . . . Part V The Doctor's Life 1728–1735* (1928), 154–5.

[16] G. Midgley, *University Life in Eighteenth-Century Oxford* (1996), 1.

square mortar-board cap or trencher and long black gown, prescribed not just for academic exercises and meals in hall, or the compulsory daily prayers in Pembroke's chapel, but as everyday dress, both within college and outside its walls.[17]

Age was in general a much less significant point of differentiation in Blackstone's Oxford than institutionally-determined dress and decorum, order and precedence, privilege and status. But any fears that William was too young to go to university at the end of 1738 may have been somewhat relieved by the observation that Thomas Tyers, who also entered Pembroke in December 1738, had not then celebrated his 14th birthday.[18] True, the other ten undergraduates already admitted during that year were some-what older, with a median age of just over 18 years, the youngest being 16 at his last birthday before coming up to Oxford, the oldest a ripe 23.[19] It would be anachronistic to impute modern notions about age-specific childrearing and educational practices to Blackstone's contemporaries. Yet they understood that boys from socially elevated backgrounds were likely to have received a better grounding in the classics at an earlier age than their economic and social inferiors, who in general would therefore tend to be somewhat older before they were ready to seek university admission. The previous large age gap between élite and low-status Oxford freshmen had shrunk significantly during the previous century, but some differenti-ation was still apparent at Pembroke College in 1738. For among that year's dozen freshmen, only the two youngest (Blackstone and Tyers) appear in the university's matriculation register as the sons of gentlemen; of the remainder, five had clergyman fathers, with the other (slightly older) half being categorized as plebeians—that is, their fathers were, or were repre-sented to be, shopkeepers, artisans, peasants, and other common folk who worked with their hands.

While Pembroke was a fairly recent addition to the University of Oxford, that university itself proudly claimed King Alfred as foun-der, although its real origins went back only to the twelfth century, when scholars first came to live and teach in the town. The Protestant Reformation of the sixteenth century brought significant changes to the clerical medieval university, including the influx of numerous students seeking a broadly humanistic education for various lay careers, as dis-tinct from the preparation for holy orders which had been its previous major role. It was also then that the colleges, larger and better resourced

[17] *HUO*, 323–4.
[18] See Plate 5.
[19] Data from buttery book and *Al. Oxon.* Stone computed the median age of Oxford under-graduates coming into residence in 1735–6 at 18.2 years: *University in Society*, 97, 249.

as teaching institutions, decisively cemented their ascendancy over the numerous unendowed halls and hostels of medieval Oxford, thereby transforming the university itself into something like a collegiate federation. But this era also saw numerous attacks on the educational role and privileged status of both English universities, especially during the mid-seventeenth-century ferment of radical pamphleteering and theorizing. Critics particularly deplored an outdated academic curriculum, undue emphasis on scholastic Aristotelian philosophy, and lack of attention to modern subjects such as non-classical languages, history, and science, together with Oxford and Cambridge's overall conservatism, élite standing, and privileged alliance with the established Church of England. Such complaints had little discernible impact on the policies and practices of either university, apart from generating defensiveness and a priori resistance to change. But they did tend to reinforce scepticism elsewhere about the value of a university education, hence contributing to the marked slump in undergraduate enrolments which set in around the 1650s and bottomed out a hundred years later.

The English universities of Blackstone's day were frequently depicted as decadent, immoral, insular, priest-ridden institutions. In his notorious *Terrae-Filius* (1721, 1726, and 1754) Nicholas Amhurst highlighted Oxford's pedagogical shortcomings: the colleges 'Nurseries of Pedantry instead of sound Learning', professorships treated as 'pensions and sinecures', college fellows wasting their 'days in luxury and idleness', and students who 'get up by rote' their public disputations, 'or perhaps only read out of their caps, which lie before them with their notes in them'. Amhurst's obvious personal animus (he had been expelled for a satirical attack on the president of his own college and other notables), anticlericalism, and Whig loyalties made it easy for Oxford at large to discount or ignore these matricidal assaults, let alone his calls for 'visitation and Reform'.[20] Blackstone himself would shortly dismiss as 'curious' John Wesley's sweeping public accusations of wholesale academic abuse and corruption. But his own subsequent career reflected a growing realization that all was far from well with the university he had joined in 1738.[21]

Daily life at Pembroke College was theoretically regulated by an extensive framework of rules dating back to the college's foundation in 1624. These statutes prescribed in considerable detail the scholarly activities and spiritual observances of fellows and students alike. Morning and evening

[20] *HUO*, 610–11; [N. Amhurst], *Terrae-Filius: Or, the Secret History of the University of Oxford, in Several Essays* (2nd edition, 1726), i. 51–2, 115–116; ii. 54.
[21] *Letters*, 1–2. See below Chapter 4, p. 57.

prayer (the former commencing at 6:00 in term-time and 7:00 in vacation) were compulsory, with absentees liable to fines (and corporal punishment for those under 18 years old, although Oxford students no longer
suffered this indignity). All members of college had to attend the services held in St Mary's Church to mark the beginning of each term, when
the entire university assembled to hear a public sermon preached before
the vice chancellor seated 'on a kind of a Throne', with the bachelors and
undergraduates crammed into overcrowded 'Galleries' of 'but an indifferent Appearance'.[22] Otherwise Pembroke's statutes make little reference to
university events or functions; there, as at Queen's College in the 1730s,
'academic life seems to have centered primarily around collegiate exercises'.[23]
An elaborate course of lectures, declamations, and disputations in philosophy, natural philosophy, logic, rhetoric, Greek, and 'the sum and foundation of the Christian religion' was set down for fixed times and days of
the week; thus a logic class for all undergraduates convened on Mondays,
Wednesdays, and Fridays after morning prayers, with breakfast at 8:00,
the natural philosophy lecture at 9:00, and disputations following thereafter. Afternoons were usually free, apart from a theological disputation
every other Thursday in term at 4:00 pm; but Saturday was a working day,
indeed the start of the college week, with every student obliged to hand
up a theme, or Latin composition, consisting of a brief essay and verses on
a classical phrase, first thing in the morning after prayers. It was also still
customary on 5 November for Pembroke students to make verses com-
memorating the discovery of the gunpowder plot, presenting one copy
to the master of the college, 'the other to stick up in Hall, and there to
remain until a speech on this occasion is spoken before supper'.[24]

While little direct evidence survives about Blackstone's undergraduate
studies, it seems likely that the liturgical and pedagogical routines laid
down by Pembroke's foundation statutes were still kept up, at least in the
letter, if not necessarily the spirit of the original. We do not even know the
identity of his tutor, one of the college's graduate fellows to whose academic
and moral supervision he would have been allotted by the master. Yet
there is no reason to doubt Clitherow's assertion that William 'prosecuted
his Studies with unremitting Ardour; and although the Classics, and
particularly the *Greek* and *Roman* Poets were his Favourites . . . Logic,
Mathematicks and the other Sciences were not neglected'.[25] As the author

[22] Macleane, *History of Pembroke*, 185–6; Salmon, *Present State*, 34.
[23] R. P. Heitzenrater, *Diary of an Oxford Methodist: Benjamin Ingham, 1733–1734* (Durham NC,
1985), 40.
[24] J. Pointer, *Oxoniensis Academia* (1749), 109–110.
[25] Clitherow, v.

of a contemporary self-help book for undergraduates explained, most university students were intended for careers in the church, and as such had to 'take the Arts in their way. They must be acquainted with Mathematics, Geography, Astronomy, Chronology and other parts of Physicks; besides Logic, Ethics, and Metaphysicks; all which I comprehend under the general name of *Philosophy*.' The other main branch of an arts degree was Greek and Latin, 'Classical Learning . . . the Study of the Languages, and of Oratory, History, Poetry and the like'.[26] This was, of course, the field in which Blackstone had already distinguished himself as a schoolboy; he may well have found that many of the authors and texts he was assigned to read were already familiar from his Charterhouse days. Another recurrent activity was the composition and public declamation of Latin themes, in both prose and verse. While six of Blackstone's handwritten exercises in this genre survive, it is difficult to make much out of their well-turned if somewhat trite reflections on adages or phrases drawn from the works of Horace, Martial, Ovid, and Seneca.[27] For example, on the tag 'Tuta Silentio Merces', Blackstone's 16 lines of prose elaborate the proposition that 'he who reveals secrets, public or private, should be hated and condemned by all', while the accompanying verse couplet observes that even fools may be regarded as astute by the vulgar, so long as they do not open their mouths.[28] One exception to the general blandness is a theme on Horace's celebration of death in the service of one's country, 'Dulce et Decorum est pro Patria mori', now better known as the ironic title of Wilfred Owen's powerful anti-war poem. Although undated, like the rest, this composition embodies and endorses the climate of belligerent mercantile, parliamentary, and popular opinion which eventually pushed Walpole to declare war on Spain in October 1739. Indeed, it specifically praises the honour accrued to 'those who have recently asserted the name of Englishmen and upheld British Liberties with their blood',[29] seemingly a reference to the notorious sufferings of Captain Jenkins and his crew at the hands of Spanish coastguards, or alternatively to Admiral Vernon's much-vaunted capture of Porto Bello in the Spanish Caribbean. However

[26] Waterland, *Advice*, 7.

[27] L. Whibley, 'Dr Johnson and the Universities', *Blackwoods Magazine*, 226 (1929), 371; Sutherland, 'The Undergraduate Curriculum', in *HUO*, 469–81; Pembroke College Archives, 62/1/13/1–5.

[28] 'There is a sure reward for trusty silence': Horace, *Odes*, III. 2. 25–6. Pembroke College Archives, 62/1/13/4.

[29] Horace, *Odes*, III. 2. 13. 'Quanto cum honore a vera posteritate isti afficientur, qui nuper Anglicanum nomen asserierunt, et Britanniae Libertates sanguine vindicarunt!': Pembroke College Archives, 62/1/13/3.

absorbed in his studies, young Blackstone was evidently not wholly oblivious to, or unmoved by, events in the larger world outside Oxford.

The books he owned and read cast some further flickering light on his undergraduate days. While most of Blackstone's extensive personal library was dispersed after his death and cannot now be reconstructed in its entirety, nearly 100 items now at Balliol College bear his book plate, or a flyleaf ownership signature, or both.[30] Some of these inscriptions are dated, while others identify the owner as a commoner of Pembroke College, indicating that they were acquired before Blackstone left that society in November 1743. Additional volumes formerly owned by Blackstone are now scattered in libraries on both sides of the Atlantic, and his name also occurs on various contemporary pre-publication book subscription lists. Admittedly, mere ownership of a book does not necessarily imply possession of its contents in any sense; but while most of the items formerly part of Blackstone's library lack annotations, unlined margins are not equivalent to uncut pages. Finally, the Bodleian, Oxford's university library and supposedly the third largest collection in Europe, maintained a record of manuscripts and printed books produced for readers, as distinct from the chained folios which readers could find for themselves.[31] Bringing these admittedly fragmentary and incomplete sources together gives us at least a suggestive impression of Blackstone's intellectual trajectory during his early undergraduate years.

The results are somewhat unexpected. First, during Blackstone's first five years at Oxford, law books are conspicuously absent, except for one occasion in September 1743 when he consulted the Bodleian's 1567 Spanish edition of Justinian's *Codex*.[32] Second, besides a few standard works in the broad field of philosophy, including Caspar Bartholinus's compendium on physics, first published in the 1690s and still going strong a half-century later, John Keill's somewhat more current mathematical *Introductio ad Veram Physicam* (Oxford, 1705), and Robert Sanderson's truly venerable *Logicae Artis Compendium* (Oxford, 1707; first published 1615), he acquired hot off the press in 1741 the two large and expensive folio

---

[30] Balliol's collection of Blackstone's books came with its annexation of New Inn Hall in 1887; the library holds a typed hand-list of 'William Blackstone's Books at Balliol' compiled by Sutherland. *BB* and *LL* (see list of Abbreviations above) are catalogues of the two auctions of his books not otherwise disposed of, but both sales included other items, among which Blackstone's books are usually indistinguishable.

[31] Salmon, 'Present State of the Universities', 37; I. G. Philip, 'Libraries and the University Press', in *HUO*, 734. Because the Bodleian entry books list shelf-marks rather than titles, positive identification of the text(s) consulted is not always possible, especially where several works were bound up together.

[32] Bodl. MS Lib. Recs. e 554, fo. 29 (17 September 1743).

volumes of the fourth edition of Ephraim Chambers's *Cyclopedia: or, An Universal Dictionary of Arts and Sciences*.[33] As we shall shortly see, this up-to-the-minute example of a relatively new genre of English-language reference works played an important role in one of Blackstone's earliest literary projects. From his first full term at Pembroke he also subscribed to the recently launched omnibus monthly *Gentleman's Magazine* (the first periodical to describe itself explicitly as a magazine, which achieved great commercial success by bridging the cultural gap between metropolitan and rural élites). Blackstone's interests were evidently already wide-ranging, not least in politics and current affairs generally.[34] Third, the bibliographic evidence suggests that Blackstone's preoccupations between 1739 and 1743 were primarily religious or theological in nature. He did acquire John Dryden's translation of Juvenal's *Satires* in a splendid 1697 folio 'Adorn'd with SCULPTURES', as well as the 1730 Tonson edition of Milton's *Paradise Regain'd* (bound up with *Samson Agonistes* and the poet's *Tractate on Education* addressed to Samuel Hartlib). In the Bodleian Library he also read the 1520 Louvain and 1604 Heidelberg editions of the Greek poet Theocritus of Syracuse, Aristotle's *Ars Rhetorica* (Venice, 1579), and the 1614 English translation of a geometrical treatise by Lazarus Schöner. But the largest identifiable element of his pre-1744 book purchases and reading consists of sermons and works of controversial divinity.[35] The authors favoured were orthodox Anglican clergy but not exclusively High-Churchmen, defenders of the established Church of England and Trinitarian Christianity against Arians, Socinians, Deists, Papists, heathens, freethinkers, and miscellaneous sceptics. Thus, having been presented in 1738 by his uncle Thomas Bethell with a copy of the peaceable Tory Bishop George Smalridge's collected sermons, Blackstone bought himself the next year a volume of anti-catholic preaching by Joseph Trapp, one-time Oxford ally of the high-flying Dr Henry Sacheverell. In 1740 he subscribed (alongside another uncle, Rev Henry Bigg) to the posthumous Oxford edition of sermons by Dr Thomas Bisse (1675–1731),

---

[33] Balliol, 1550.a.8 (signed 'e Coll Pemb. Oxon 1740'); 1550.d.26 (signed 'e Coll. Pemb.'); 1550.a.15 (Blackstone's bookplate partially obscures his signature, but Sanderson was still a standard undergraduate text: cf. Bill, *Education at Christ Church*, 264 and Yolton, 'Schoolmen, Logic and Philosophy' in *HUO*, 569–70); 1550.h.1–2 (signed 'Coll. Pembr. Oxon. Comm. 1741'). R. Yeo, *Encyclopaedic Visions* (Cambridge, 2001), 38.

[34] Balliol 1550. 1. 9–17. B. Harris, 'Print Culture' in *A Companion to Eighteenth-Century Britain*, ed. H. T. Dickinson (Oxford, 2002), 287–8; E. A. Reitan, *The Best of the Gentleman's Magazine*, 1731–1754 (Lewiston NY, 1987).

[35] Yale Law School Library, Blackstone Wing J1290, c. 1: *The Satires of Decimus Junius Juvenalis translated into English Verse by Mr Dryden and several Other Eminent Hands* (1697); Balliol, 1550.b.13: J. Milton, *Paradise Regained* (1730); Bodl. MS Lib. Recs. e 554, fos. 20, 20v, 21, 23 (10, 18, 22 February, 7 March, 30 April 1743).

37

while also acquiring the fifth edition (1712) of the non-juror Charles Leslie's *Short and Easie Method with the Deists*, and a weighty doctrinal treatise by the more moderate churchman Laurence Fogg.[36] His acquisitions in 1741 were somewhat more eclectic, and included two volumes of 'moral essays' in English translation by the French Jansenists Pierre Nicole and Blaise Pascal, the Whiggish don John Conybeare's *Defence of Reveal'd Religion* written against the Deist Matthew Tindal's *Christianity as Old as the Creation* (1730), and two sermons delivered in connection with recently-opened charitable institutions at Bristol and Winchester, which probably came from the library of his uncle Henry, who had served on the governing body of Winchester's hospital before his death in 1740.[37] Before leaving Pembroke, Blackstone also collected at least another three weighty volumes on religious topics: Henry Wharton's edition of James Ussher's *Historia Dogmatica Controversiae inter Orthodoxos et Pontificios De Scripturis et Sacris Vernacularis* (1690), Robert Sanderson's *De Obligate Conscientiae* (1682), and Peter Browne's *The Procedure, Extent and Limits of Human Understanding* (1729). To this tally might well be added a number of works Blackstone undoubtedly owned but for which a date of acquisition is lacking; among them are Browne's *Things Divine and Supernatural Conceived by Analogy With Things Natural and Human* (1733), a 1724 Hague edition of Grotius's *De Veritate Religionis Christianae*, Robert Nelson's *Practice of True Devotion* (1722), William King's *Discourse Concerning the Inventions of Men in the Worship of God* (1696), Isaac Barrow's *Of the Love of God and of Our Neighbour* (1680), John Edwards's *Brief Vindication of the Fundamental Articles of the Christian Faith* (1697), and William Laud's *Daily Office of a Christian* (1688).[38]

The character of these early acquisitions is less surprising when we consider Oxford's long-standing role as a seminary for the established Church, the widespread view that all undergraduates should receive some religious education, and Blackstone's previous Charterhouse schooling and clerical connections (two of his Bigg uncles were, as both his brothers

---

[36] Balliol, 1555.h.14, *Sixty Sermons Preached on Several Occasions by the right Reverend George Smallridge* (Oxford, 1724); 1550.b.11, J. Trapp, *Popery Truly Stated, and Briefly Confuted* (1727); 1550.c.2; 1550.d.27, L. Fogg, *Theologiae Speculativae Schema* (1712). T. Bisse, *A Course of Sermons on the Lord's Prayer* (Oxford, 1740), [287]; 1550.e.16, Bisse's *Beauty of Holiness in the Common Prayer* (1716) also came into Blackstone's possession at an unknown date.

[37] Balliol, 1550.b.2; 1550.f.22; 1555.d.1 (A. Clark, *A Sermon Preached in the Cathedral Church of Winchester, before the Governors of the County-Hospital for Sick and Lame . . . to which are added, A Collection of Papers relating to the Hospital . . . for the Management and Conduct of the House* (1736), bound up with C. Reynell, *A Sermon Preached before the Contributors to the Bristol Infirmary* (Bristol, 1738); a mutilated annotation on the front cover includes the words 'Warden of Winchester'.

[38] Balliol, 1550.f.10; 1550.b.1; 1550.b.24; 1550.b.5; 1550.d.3; 1550.d.24; 1550.a.36.

would eventually become, ordained Anglican clergymen).[39] Perhaps more noteworthy is the young student's evident passion for books in general. While he did inherit some texts from kinsmen,[40] and doubtless occasionally bought second-hand for reasons of economy, no such motive satisfactorily explains his purchase in 1742 of a 50-year old almanac, John Playford's *Vade Mecum, Or, the Necessary Pocket Companion* (1692), especially in view of his familiarity with contemporary almanacs, which he customarily distributed as Christmas gifts.[41] Blackstone's interest in old books, rare editions, and fine printing may have been pursued in the library at Pembroke, although there is no record of his having borrowed books from that collection, where borrowing privileges were probably restricted to fellows.[42] However, he was certainly frequenting the university library by February 1743, if not earlier. On this first visit, or at least first occasion when his name is recorded as having placed a book order—using the chained volumes on open shelves left no evidential trace—Blackstone was apparently accompanied by his young Pembroke contemporary and fellow-Londoner Thomas Tyers.[43] Since Tyers had only graduated with the BA during the previous summer, neither held the statutory qualifications for the privilege of admission as a Bodleian reader, theoretically restricted to doctors, masters, BAs of two years standing, and 'Students in the Civil Law, after three years Standing in the University, if Fellows of Colleges'.[44] While curatorial ordinances had modified these original requirements, bachelors and undergraduates were supposedly debarred 'from reading books ill-adapted to their studies', and the library's modern historian informs us that undergraduate admissions remained 'comparatively rare'.[45] In any case, the admission rules cannot have been strictly enforced, since Blackstone did not actually sign the official 'Liber Admissorum' until

---

[39] Sutherland, 'The Curriculum', in *HUO*, 477.

[40] Such items include L. Eachard, *The Gazeteer's Interpreter* (1704) and R. Sanderson, *Logicae Artis Compendium* (Oxford, 1670), both formerly owned by Blackstone's great-uncle Richard Bigg, who matriculated from Corpus Christi College in 1691, and A. Boyer, *A New Methodical French Grammar* (1704), which had evidently belonged to Henry Bigg in 1715: Balliol 1550.a.26, 27; 1550.d.4. *Alumni Oxonienses . . . 1500–1714*, i. 122.

[41] Cf. Doolittle, 5; Balliol, 1550.g.14. *Letters*, 2, 22.

[42] Although most college libraries excluded undergraduates altogether, Johnson evidently had access to the Pembroke library: *HUO*, 749–50; Macleane, *History of Pembroke*, 339.

[43] Bodl. MS Lib. Recs. e 554, fo. 20, lists alongside Blackstone's order that of 'D[ominu]s Tyres of Coll. Pemb.' Further orders by Blackstone are noted on 18, 22 February, 7 March, 30 April, 22 July, 8–9 August, and 17 September 1743 (fos. 20, 20v, 21, 23a, 26, 26v, 29), followed by a gap until 19 June 1744 (fo. 39).

[44] Pointer, *Oxoniensis Academia*, 141.

[45] I. Philip, *The Bodleian Library in the Seventeenth and Eighteenth Centuries* (Oxford, 1983), 20, 34–5.

11 February 1743, the day after he is recorded as putting in his first book order (for the works of Theocritus edited by Daniel Hensius and translated into Latin by, among others, Hugo Grotius).[46] Opening a mere six hours a day, or a little longer in the warmer months, and offering a far from congenial working environment, especially during 'the short Days of Winter', when readers 'must be content to sit without a Fire in a large cold Room', Oxford's university library ran no risk of being overwhelmed by patrons in the early to mid-eighteenth century.[47]

On 9 July 1740, just over 18 months after matriculating, Blackstone formally abandoned his status as an undergraduate preparing for the degree of Bachelor of Arts, on being admitted to study civil (or Roman) law, the only legal code then accorded academic recognition by either English university.[48] Whereas the BA required four years in residence, a bachelor's degree in the 'higher' faculty of Laws took a full seven, of which the first two years were supposedly devoted to a broad course of reading in humane studies. Switching from the BA to the BCL may sometimes have been a means of evading university curricular requirements, especially for students with no intention of taking either degree. And as today, academic law studies, even a law degree, did not necessarily imply either commitment to a legal career or the abandonment of other interests and pursuits. Thus Blackstone's elder brother Charles, who eventually graduated with the BCL alongside William in June 1745, then became an ordained clergyman, able to benefit from the exemption of bachelors of law from prohibitions against holding more than one ecclesiastical benefice with cure of souls. Others again switched into the 'Law Line' precisely in order to avoid the usual requirement for college fellows in arts to take holy orders.[49] But it seems unlikely that his contemporaries viewed Blackstone's change of course as disreputable or improper, even if law was notoriously an even softer academic option than the BA, indeed 'the least exacting alternative open to the undergraduate who desired to complete his statutory exercises with as little trouble as possible'.[50] For that very reason it gave talented students the opportunity to follow their own diverse interests; two leading poets of the era—Edward Young (whose *The Universal Passion* Blackstone already owned), and Pembroke's own William Shenstone—were both enrolled in law as Oxford undergraduates.

---

[46] Bodl. MS Lib. Recs., e 534, fo. 39 and e 554, fo. 20.

[47] Salmon, *Present State*, 37. W. D. Macray, *Annals of the Bodleian Library, Oxford* (Oxford, 1890), 460n.

[48] OUA, SP 70, Book of Admission to Study Civil Law, 1711–1856.

[49] *HUO*, 595.

[50] *HUO*, 478, 595; cf. Doolittle, 5.

More than a year later, on 20 November 1741, 'William Blackston' was admitted a student of the Middle Temple, then the largest of the four London Inns of Court. He thereby began acquiring the seniority or 'standing' which would eventually qualify him for call to the bar and practice as a common lawyer before the central courts.[51] But membership of an Inn no longer involved any residential or educational obligations. Hence many young men joined without any fixed vocational ambition, but 'simply taking up an option on a legal career', an option which might or might not be realized at some later date.[52] Omitting to mention his 1740 switch from arts to law, Clitherow's account lays considerable emphasis on the clarity and fixity of purpose with which Blackstone now settled on a 'future Plan of Life' and 'choice of the Law as a Profession', which is represented as the causal precursor of his admission to the Middle Temple and simultaneous abandonment of 'the more amusing Pursuits of his Youth, for the severer Studies to which he had dedicated himself'.[53] So sharp a break between boyish pleasures and stern manly vocation is integral to Clitherow's version of his subject's life story as the achievement of professional eminence through unremitting diligence and attention to duty. Once he had actually been called to the bar, Blackstone himself, on whose testimony Clitherow must have largely relied, was equally anxious to present himself as a hard-working practitioner with no time for extra-professional diversions. But Blackstone's life course was not quite so neatly bifurcated between youthful flirtation with the arts, followed by mature commitment to the law, if only because he went on writing poetry until at least his mid-30s, while retaining serious antiquarian and literary interests throughout his life. That he had already determined on a legal career as early as July 1740 (when he enrolled for the BCL), or alternatively November 1741 (when he joined the Middle Temple), is also uncertain, given that he remained in residence at Pembroke College, where he pursued and brought to fruition three major literary projects, precisely when he had supposedly moved to London and 'begun his training at the Inns of Court'.[54]

The records of Blackstone's charges for food and drink in the Pembroke college buttery books indicate that after matriculating he did not come

[51] *MTAdmR*, i. 330.
[52] D. Lemmings, *Gentlemen and Barristers: the Inns of Court and the English Bar 1680–1730* (Oxford, 1990), 32.
[53] Clitherow, vi.
[54] Cf. Doolittle, 9. The catalogue of the 1980 Bodleian Library exhibition 'Blackstone and Oxford' states that Blackstone 'left Pembroke in 1741, and moved to London to study at the Middle Temple . . .'. Clitherow, vi.

into residence for a month and a half, until the week beginning 12 January 1739. Thereafter he was present for most or all of every week of the second quarter, all but the first and twelfth weeks of the third quarter (commencing 5th June and 31 August respectively), and the entire fourth quarter.[55] He left Pembroke just before Christmas and stayed away until the week beginning 18 January 1740, but then took meals in college constantly until the end of September, when he missed a fortnight, returning again around 10 October and remaining in residence until Christmas. The following year's pattern was a little less consistent, with a week's break in May 1741 followed by a whole month's holiday in July, and further briefer absences in September (a week or so), October (a week) and November (three weeks). But after his customary Christmas vacation Blackstone apparently spent the entire 12 months of 1742 at Pembroke, except for a week in June and another in late September. Absent from 17 December 1742 until 14 January 1743, he missed a week or slightly more at the beginning of April, before spending the rest of spring and the entire summer in Oxford, apart from a three-week break at the end of August, resuming again until his election to the fellowship of All Souls College early in November.[56] Indeed there is nothing to suggest that from November 1741 onwards he was travelling up to London during the four law terms, either to be in commons at the Middle Temple or to attend court sittings in Westminster Hall.

No one who knew Blackstone as a Pembroke undergraduate appears to have left an account of his student days, nor has any form of autobiographical record survived (other than as transmitted by Clitherow). Nevertheless, the Bodleian's fortuitous glimpse of 'Tom' Tyers as Blackstone's companion on what most probably was the first venture by either into that great library confirms what might otherwise have been inferred: that two young Londoners who entered Pembroke within a few days of each other as the juniors of their year tended to be drawn to each other's company. Unlike Blackstone's other Pembroke contemporaries, Tyers emerges from the relative anonymity of college and university records a distinct and lively character. Son and heir of the cultivated proprietor of London's Vauxhall Gardens, who had successfully transformed a former 'rural brothel' on the south bank of the Thames into a fashionable and financially successful cultural theme park, Tom is pictured in a family group portrait of 1740 dressed in his Oxford student's cap

[55] For elucidation of the Pembroke buttery books, see Reade, *Johnsonian Gleanings Part V*, 154–75.

[56] Pembroke College Archives, Buttery Books 9/1/71–76.

and gown, the first of his family to be so qualified. In later life he was 'inquisitive, talkative, full of notions and quotations' to quote his own self-portrait, and 'having a handsome fortune, vivacity of temper, and eccentricity of mind', according to James Boswell. While such personal qualities seem rather to complement than match those of Blackstone (even if Samuel Johnson later admitted that the well-read 'Tom Restless' could always tell him 'something he did not know before'), the difference doubtless became more pronounced as both men grew older. At Oxford both might have aspired to succeed their seniors William Shenstone and his younger friend Anthony Whistler as a new generation of Pembroke literary men, or songbirds.[57]

We have already seen that Blackstone began writing English verse in his schooldays. The 'small Collection of juvenile Pieces, both Originals and Translations' which according to Clitherow he 'left (but not with a View of Publication)', has once again disappeared from sight.[58] What remains of that 77-page 'Select Poems and Translations Between the Years 1736 and 1744' is little more than a sale catalogue description, although this fortunately includes a table of contents and the facsimile reproduction of one manuscript page.[59] The latter depicts the opening lines of what would become Blackstone's best-known poem, then entitled 'The Lawyer to his Muse'. This first appeared anonymously in the fourth (1755) volume of the leading London literary publisher Robert Dodsley's widely-circulating 'poetic miscellany', *A Collection of Poems By Several Hands*, and was frequently reprinted thereafter.[60] Dodsley's version appends the legend 'Written in the Year 1744' immediately after the title line. Since the whole poem recounts the narrator's largely adverse response to the prospect of being forced to abandon the 'sweet society' of his poetic muse for 'wrangling Courts, and stubborn Law', that date argues strongly against any attempt to push Blackstone's commitment to a career in law, or even a legal education, back to the beginning of the decade.

Reverting to the lost manuscript, on the one page for which a catalogue facsimile has fortunately survived, the item immediately above the opening lines of 'The Lawyer to his Muse' is the final verse and

<hr>

[57] See Plate 5; *ODNB*, s.v. Tyers, Thomas and Whistler, Anthony.
[58] See above, Chapter 1, p. 5.
[59] Maggs Bros. Ltd, Catalogue 576, Autumn 1932, lot 843, and plate III.
[60] M. F. Suarez, 'The Production and Consumption of the Eighteenth-Century Poetic Miscellany', in *Books and their Readers in Eighteenth-Century England: New Essays*, ed. I. Rivers (2001), 217–51. *A Collection of Poems By Several Hands* (1755), 4 vols., iv. 224–8. (My thanks to Michael Suarez for bibliographic assistance.)

a half from what was evidently a reworking of nine pastoral Idylls by Theocritus (whom Blackstone was reading on his first recorded venture into the Bodleian). This is dated 'June 1743', further reason to resist associating the 'The Lawyer to His Muse' with Blackstone's admission to the Middle Temple in 1741. The contents of the missing manuscript appear to be arranged in chronological order. Thus an epilogue to Terence's play 'The Eunuch' (almost certainly a schoolboy effort) is followed by a 'College Exercise', while a poem 'To Mr W[alter] B[igg] on the Birth of his Son' precedes a series of translations from the Greek poetry of Anacreon and Theocritus, the manuscript concluding with the 100 rhyming couplets of 'The Lawyer to His Muse'.[61] In short, Blackstone's corrected fair-copy of his poems and translations evidently included work composed over the full eight-year period indicated by the title which he gave it. And whether or not 77 handwritten pages of verse are adequately characterized as a 'small Collection', we can hardly be sure that Blackstone had ruled out publication when he first brought them together, even if his later views on that subject were just as Clitherow represents them.

In playing down both the duration and intensity of Blackstone's non-legal pursuits, Clitherow also slightly misrepresented his second major student undertaking. This seemingly developed as an offshoot of 'the Mathematicks', for 'he converted that dry Study, as it is usually thought, into an Amusement, by pursuing the Branch of it which relates to Architecture'. The outcome was 'a Treatise, intituled *"Elements of Architecture"*, intended for his own Use only, and not for Publication', completed 'at the early Age of Twenty' and yet 'esteemed by those Judges who have perused it, in no respect unworthy his maturer Judgment, and more exercised Pen'.[62] In fact, the youthful Blackstone actually compiled two architectural treatises. The first, dated from Oxford on 'July 22nd 1743' (less than a fortnight after the author's 20th birthday), is entitled, in Blackstone's distinctive hand, 'An Abridgement of Architecture'. This manuscript book of 40 leaves presents a digest or outline summary of the classical rules held to govern 'the art of building', as originally formulated by the Roman author Vitruvius and subsequently elaborated by his Renaissance followers and commentators. Rather than consulting these authorities directly, Blackstone appears to have relied on two authoritative seventeenth-century texts brought together by the Restoration virtuoso John Evelyn, who added Henry

---

[61] Lovelace, the only child born to Walter Bigg and his wife Jane (*née* Harris), was baptized on 14 August 1741: *Wither Family*, 47.

[62] Clitherow, v.

Wotton's *Elements of Architecture* (first published in 1624) to his own translation of an influential Palladian treatise originally published in French by Roland Fréart in 1650. Besides Evelyn's *Parallel of the Antient Architecture with the Modern,* and possibly Claude Perrault's French translation of Vitruvius, Blackstone drew upon a near-contemporary treatise by the Scottish-born but Italian-trained architect James Gibbs, who was currently in Oxford supervising the construction of his magnificent new domed Radcliffe Library (as it was called until 1860, now known as the Radcliffe Camera) just off the High Street, between the Bodleian and St Mary's Church.[63] Gibbs's *Rules for Drawing the Several Parts of Architecture* (1732) offered a simplified method of calculating the proportional dimensions of the classical architectural orders; Blackstone's treatise also devotes much attention to establishing the ratios of the different parts of columns in the Doric, Ionic, Corinthian, Composite and Tuscan orders, with the aid of detailed numerical tables. For an 'Index of near Seven Hundred terms in Architecture, that are explained in this Abridgement' which rounds off the work, he appears to have relied largely on his own copy of Chambers's *Cyclopaedia.* A tabular 'Analysis of this Abridgement', setting out the various subjects covered in the form of a tree of knowledge which branches out across the page from the most general to the more particular topics handled in its 37 chapters, precedes the text proper.[64] This as we now have it seems to be a working copy, with numerous annotations and crossings-out, as well as a separate series of additions with their own index. The whole appears originally to have been illustrated with 14 'Tables' or drawings, of which only the stubs now remain.

As befitting a didactic work of systematic exposition, the authorial tone throughout remains distant and reserved. So the note of personal engagement struck by the very last sentence is all the more striking: 'Such are the principall Rules laid down by the greatest Masters in this most excellent Art; by the due observation of which a Man may easily acquire a Taste for the Beauties, & perhaps make some Proficiency in the Practice of Architecture: a Science which for its Antiquity, Use, Nobility and Delight has not its equal in the Universe, having had the honour of employing the Divine Majesty itself, in the Temple erected by God's Direction at Jerusalem.'[65] Neither the closing theological reference, nor

[63] I. Guest, *Dr John Radcliffe and His Trust* (1991), 139–44.

[64] See Plate 1. Chambers's *Cyclopaedia* also included a diagrammatic 'View of Knowledge': Yeo, *Encyclopaedic Visions,* 135.

[65] Getty Research Library, Special Collections, MS 89022, 51. C. Matthews, 'Architecture and Polite Culture in Eighteenth-Century England: Blackstone's Architectural Manuscripts', University of Adelaide PhD thesis, 2007, 24–6 and ch. 3, *passim.*

the quasi-vocational aspiration of this statement seem compatible with the contention that Blackstone's early architectural preoccupations amounted to mere 'Amusement'. On the contrary, as we shall see, he continued to interest himself in architectural matters, until—quite literally—the end of his life.

Blackstone's third major undergraduate literary project, and first published book, is not mentioned by Clitherow, although his subject's authorship of *The Pantheon: A Vision* (1747) must have been an open secret at All Souls.[66] Published anonymously by Robert Dodsley, the preface or 'Advertisement' explains that the 'following Piece was written at the University, towards the Close of the Year 1743'. It proceeds to character-ize the author's aim as 'a *Poetical* View of the several Religions, that have prevailed in the World'; or in the words of a phrase from Virgil's *Georgics* which adorns the title page, '*Sanctos ausus recludere fontes*' ('daring to reveal the sacred fountains').[67] Each of these four faiths, or beliefs—Paganism, Judaism, Islam, and Christianity—is 'represented by different Genii resid-ing in their different Temples, with the proper Symbols of their respective Faiths'. The detailed depiction of the built forms housing and symbolizing the various creeds provides ample opportunity for Blackstone to express his religious convictions, or prejudices, in elaborate and sometimes ingeni-ous architectural metaphor. Thus, within the 'the lofty temple' inhabited by a variety of pagan deities,

> Northwards, on slender columns nicely rais'd
> A pointed arch shoots upwards, delicate
> With gothic pride, and lavish ornament.
> Beneath whose narrow bow in giant-state
> Sat mighty Thor, that aw'd the frozen world,
> And stretch'd o'er Saxon hosts his iron sway.

'The South', on the other hand, 'with pointed obelisks was grac'd | And learned Hieroglyphs, divinely dark', while 'Westward an arch, on Dorian columns rais'd | Supports the fabled Gods of antient Greece, | And Rome's proud towers'. Notwithstanding its undeniably formal and mannered

---

[66] In addition to the 1747 letter from Blackstone to George Bingham claiming authorship (now Codrington MS 306; *Letters*, 6–7), see R. Graves, *The Triflers* (1806), 53–4.

[67] *Georgics*, Bk. 2, line 175: Joseph Addison had used lines 173–5 as the epigram for his Whiggish 'Letter from Italy' (1701). Blackstone acknowledges a debt 'for some material Hints, to an Essay of Mr Addison's on a similar Subject, though treated by him in a very different Manner' (sig. A2); the reference is to *The Tatler*, no. 257 (28–30 November 1710), where Addison purports to describe 'a Show at this Time carried up and down in Germany, which represents all the Religions of Great Britain in Wax-work'.

post-Miltonic language, the ambitious scope and imaginative power of this blank verse essay in comparative religion are undeniable.

Blackstone's poem takes the form of a narrator's waking dream, in which he is conducted from a dark wood by a 'rev'rend shape' (later revealed to be his 'guardian Seraph') on a guided tour of 'RELIGION'S sacred fane'. Predictably enough, the 'Pagan dome', 'stately mosque', and Jewish temple are represented in largely negative terms; the latter, for example, while from afar 'a glorious pile, | Of workmanship divine' (that is, as Solomon's Temple at Jerusalem), appears close up with 'nodding walls . . . Majestic, tho' decay'd'. The 'antient Rabbin' seated within has at his feet 'five small, but sacred, books neglected' (the Pentateuch, traditionally ascribed to Moses), while:

> On these uprear'd huge tomes of holy lyes
> Support his leaning arm; his hand behind,
> Grasps the swoln casket, big with gold and gems,
> Spoils of th' uncircumsis'd . . .

Even within the realm of Christianity (where the purple sky 'Glows with serener light'), Blackstone—or at least his poetical persona—has few approving words for 'Rome's grey genius' let alone 'the adverse structure' of non-Anglican Protestantism. Yet popish 'Tyranny', 'Persecution', 'Ignorance', and 'Superstition' are briskly disposed of in a mere 24 lines. More than twice that number are required to delineate the 'jarring crew, in all besides | Dissentient', who naturally 'support with stubborn league the good old cause', together with their progenitors, 'wild Anarchy', 'Enthusiast Zeal', 'Schism', and 'Hypocrisy'. Various stock figures appear, including the 'precisely sour' Presbyterian elder who 'harmonious hymns | Enraptur'd nonsense, and with holy leer | Gloats on the saintly dames that grace his flock'; the whole 'loud-tongu'd dissonance' is followed by a sinister group, initially clad 'in jesuit-weed and monkish cowls', but transformed by 'sable cloaks and puritan disguise' when they 'fire the crowd'.

Hastily departing this scene of chaotic disorder, the narrator and his guide at last reach a 'beauteous dome', with 'chaste Ionic ornaments', surely a reference to Wren's St Paul's Cathedral. These highlight the 'aspect grave, yet chearful, and divine' presented by 'a female-form' on whose 'venerable cheek, | Sat Age and Immortality'. Here is 'pure RELIGION', the Church of England, supported by the 'winning grace' of 'mitred Moderation' (which softens 'fiery rage' with 'Attractive smiles'), 'Gay Liberty, Britannia's darling saint', 'Sweet Piety', and 'Science'. The latter:

> . . . her leaden shackles broke;
> Wide to the world expands a sacred tome,
> Which he that runs may read; On either hand

> She rests, incumbent, on two gentle maids,
> Fair Cam, and Isis crown'd with learned tow'rs.

The poem ends with a vista of the last day and the collapse in 'universal wrack' of all rival creeds and their temples. 'Our sacred structure stood . . . but soon | Grew larger', opening its gates to receive 'torrent-like, in numbers numberless . . . a mighty host, the pride of e'vry clime'. Among this 'zealous throng' the narrator prostrates himself in prayer:

> Accept, great Parent, source of Truth, accept
> These tributary vows, this slender All,
> The last, the meanest of thy sons can pay!
> O may'st thou stand till time itself shall fail,
> Rocklike, tho' papal storms around thee roar,
> Or hollow faction's undermining guile
> In secret plot thy fall! Long mays't thou reign,
> Restor'd to all thy rights, and, greatly just,
> Reform, with due severity, mankind;
> Bid from the dust her head pale Virtue rear,
> From recreant Prelates strip the sullied lawn,
> And teach the Atheist not to scorn his God;
> Then, fill'd with deathless glory, from the world
> Triumphant rise, and fix in heav'n thy throne!

As this closing stanza shows, when not weighted down with over-elaborate language or metaphor, Blackstone's verse has considerable expressive force. But whatever its merits as poetry, there can be no doubt of the author's commitment to a High-Church agenda, for jurisdictional and political resurgence allied with moral reform and castigation of the heterodox (such as the controversial Benjamin Hoadly, now bishop of Winchester). Even accepting the theoretical possibility that not all positions espoused by his poetic persona expressed the poet's personal views, the intensity of his identification with the Anglican Church and its earthly mission can scarcely be equated with a coolly conformist or conventional establishmentarianism.

Besides his architectural, poetical, and theological—or denominational—preoccupations, Blackstone's undergraduate life at Pembroke College presumably involved some study of the civil law, for which purpose he may well have relied to some extent on his brother Charles at New College. There is little or no information about most other aspects of his student existence. Unlike John Wesley at Christ Church in the 1720s,[68] William appears to

---

[68] V. H. H. Green, *The Young Mr Wesley* (1961), 63, 73–6.

havc formed no lasting friendships with his Pembroke contemporaries, including Thomas Tyers. We know nothing of his pastimes or recreations, apart from book-collecting; indeed it may well be that he already exhibited that distaste for physical exercise which eventually produced an unhealthy 'Corpulency of Body'.[69] Nevertheless his expenditure on food and drink as recorded in the Pembroke buttery books does not seem particularly extravagant. It is true that, whereas in the late 1720s Samuel Johnson had run up battels averaging just over eight shillings a week, Blackstone's weekly charges during his first full quarter at Pembroke some ten years later averaged 9/6d, and by the second quarter of 1743 were averaging just over 12 shillings, rising to twice that amount for the second last week of term. Nor can this level of expenditure be attributed to the effects of inflation, since food prices were stagnant or falling throughout the 1730s. Yet Blackstone's charges seem to be more or less in line with those listed against the names of the six other commoners present throughout the first quarter of 1739. As compared with his contemporary Thomas Tyers and the slightly more senior Samuel Pipe, between June 1742 and November 1743 (when he left Pembroke for All Souls) Blackstone's weekly battels were almost always less than those run up by Pipe, and usually below what Tyers incurred. For example, in the six weeks beginning 4 February 1743, Blackstone's highest total was 17 shillings, and his lowest 6, whereas Pipe's never dipped below double figures, and in the last week of the quarter rose to over one pound; Tyers's battels showed the widest fluctuation, ranging from a low of seven shillings and sixpence to three weekly charges of over 20 shillings each.[70]

As for that other perennial student preoccupation, love, or sex, or both; our sources are largely—and predictably—silent. Blackstone's first year at Oxford saw a major scandal involving homosexual activities by the warden of Wadham College; although a 'burlesque poem' on these events does mention Pembroke ('Not Pembroke's Warden: no, tis Wadham | The word, i'faith sounds much like Sodom'), the passing allusion seems driven by the demands of rhyme and otherwise inconsequential.[71] It may be possible to say more on this subject if and when the lost 'Select Poems and Translations' manuscript reappears. For its listed contents include a poem 'To Miss *****', another 'To Miss *** R*** with Pamela' (possibly

---

[69] Clitherow, xxiii.

[70] Reade, *Johnsonian Gleanings*, 158–9; Pembroke College Archives, Buttery Books, 9/1/71–2, 75–6.

[71] Cf. Midgley, *University Life in Eighteenth-Century Oxford*, 90.

addressing his cousin Alethea Richmond,[72] following the publication of Samuel Richardson's popular epistolary novel in 1741), and a third on 'Being ask'd to describe Miss ***'. Paraphrases of Psalms 29 and 95, 'The beginning of ye 2nd Book of Lucretius translated' and the 'Lamentation of Job', are complemented by translations of four odes of the Greek lyric poet Anacreon of Teos, whose verse was preoccupied 'with love and wine' (if not as unrelievedly erotic as Cicero had claimed),[73] besides nine 'idylls' of his major Hellenistic successor Theocritus, the poet who is usually credited with inventing the pastoral genre. It seems reasonable to conclude that the undergraduate Blackstone was not wholly asexual, reclusive, or lacking in romantic interests, even if the precise form and direction of his adolescent appetites remains unknown to us.

One final puzzling reference must be mentioned. In 1739 Nathan Alcock, fresh from medical studies at Edinburgh and Leiden, revitalized the teaching of chemistry at Oxford. Notwithstanding the hostility of the medical faculty and some heads of houses, Nathan's lectures on anatomy and chemistry attracted large audiences. But in 1741 a proposal to grant him the degree of MA in recognition of his Leiden qualification was rejected, partly on religious grounds, for it was rumoured that Alcock's long sojourn in the Netherlands had left him 'not heartily attached to the Church of England'. In the event, Alcock's supporters among Oxford's Convocation, the university parliament of which all MAs and others holding higher degrees were members, staged a voters' strike in which they blocked the granting of every other degree until Alcock's award was approved. A posthumous biography by Alcock's brother lists 'the learned Civilian and Barrister, Doctor Blackstone' among eight other 'principal friends and sticklers for Dr Alcock on this memorable occasion'.[74] Since Blackstone was then still four years from taking his own first degree, his involvement on this occasion seems unlikely, not least in view of his expressed Anglican orthodoxy (although it may be that Alcock's supposed dissenting sympathies were invented by his opponents). Yet besides hinting

---

[72] Alethea was the daughter of Seymour Richmond of Sparsholt, Berkshire, and his first wife Alethea Bigg (d. 1723), whom he married in 1719 (Wither Family, 228); so she was certainly Blackstone's senior by no more than a few years, contrary to a nineteenth-century account of her protracted engagement and subsequent marriage c. 1780: L. Spurrier, 'Eternal Vows: Or a Faithless Old Swain', The Berkshire Echo, 21 (2002), 2.

[73] D. A. Campbell, 'Monody: 4. Anacreon', in The Cambridge History of Classical Literature: I Greek Literature, ed. P. E. Nesterling and B. M. W. Knox (Cambridge, 1985), 216. M. Bowra, Greek Lyric Poetry (Oxford, 1961), ch. 7.

[74] HUO, 663–5; T. Alcock, Some Memoirs of the Life of Dr Nathan Alcock, Lately Deceased (1780), 14, 21.

at an Oxford relationship for which no other evidence has so far materialized, the evident plausibility of associating Blackstone's name with a popular and progressive cause opposed by the university's establishment is suggestive of the high profile he would shortly acquire as an academic reformer.[75]

[75] No other link between Blackstone and Alcock has been identified, although both had friendly relations with Dr William King, the Jacobite principal of St Mary Hall: ibid., 18. The list of Alcock's supporters printed by his brother includes two other distinguished names (those of William Markham, later archbishop of York, and David Durrell, principal of Hertford College 1757–75) who were still undergraduates in 1741: ibid., 20–21.

CHAPTER 4

'Between the University and the Temple' (1744–53)

ACCORDING to his brother-in-law's biographical 'Memoirs', from November 1744 Blackstone 'divided his time' between Oxford and London. In the capital he 'took Chambers [at the Temple] in order to attend the Courts', and 'applied himself closely to his Profession', attempting, not very successfully, to establish a practice in Westminster Hall. But in point of fact the division of time, let alone energy, between London and Oxford was far from equal. As one near-contemporary commentator pointed out, young Blackstone's 'attachment to Oxford commenced early and contin- ued long'. Indeed 'his predilection for the occupations of the University' was clearly a good deal stronger than his initial drive for advancement as a common lawyer at the London bar, and 'may likewise account for, if it did not occasion, the slow progress he made in his profession'.[1]

I

The College of All Souls of the Faithful Departed in Oxford (or as Blackstone himself would later render the original Latin, 'THE COLLEGE OF THE SOULS OF ALL FAITHFUL PEOPLE DECEASED OF OXFORD'),[2] better known as All Souls College, was founded in the late 1430s under a royal charter granted to Henry Chichele, archbishop of Canterbury. In establishing his college, Chichele had two avowed aims: to memorialize and offer prayers for the souls of all those

[1] Clitherow, vii; *Monthly Review*, 67 (July, 1782), 7.
[2] [W. Blackstone], *An Essay on Collateral Consanguinity, Its Limits, Extent, and Duration; More particularly as it is regarded by the Statutes of All Souls College in the University of Oxford* (1750), 1.

Englishmen killed in the Hundred Years War with France, and to furnish the Church of England with learned lawyers and theologians. He laid down that the new corporate institution should consist of a warden and 40 fellows, 16 of whom were to be 'jurists' studying canon or civil law. At an annual election following All Souls' Day (2 November), any vacancies in the fellowship were to be filled by candidates of good character and legitimate birth, aged between 17 and 26, who had been admitted for at least three years to the faculties of arts, or law, or both, and were making good progress in their studies, with first preference given to the founder's kinsmen and descendants.[3] Whereas Pembroke remained one of Oxford's humbler colleges, socially as well as architecturally, All Souls was among its grandest, virtually devoid of undergraduate students but populated by 'smarts and gallant gentlemen', according to a satirical pamphlet of 1733. The clergyman-novelist Richard Graves, who preceded Blackstone from Pembroke to an All Souls fellowship, recalled that in his time 'though there were many very studious young men, there was often a party of loungers in the gateway'. Visiting Oxford in 1769, Samuel Johnson informed the inquisitive James Boswell that 'if a man has a mind to *prance*, he must study at Christ-Church and All-Souls'.[4] By that time fellows of All Souls had endured for more than a century the gibe derived from a free translation of the founder's statutes, that their qualifications consisted of being well born and well dressed, but only indifferently learned (*bene nati, bene vestiti, mediocriter docti*).[5]

No doubt this academic in-joke often carried an envious edge. For fellowships at All Souls had become increasingly desirable prizes, especially now that the founder's original requirement of constant residence in Oxford was no longer strictly enforced.[6] In November 1742, at Blackstone's first attempt, he was among eleven candidates seeking election to the fellowship, of whom only two succeeded. But 12 months later, he was the first elected of four successful applicants from a field of ten; three of those four were, like Blackstone, chosen at their second try.[7]

The exact form then taken by the fellowship selection process is unknown. However it involved an academic examination, partly conducted

---

[3] Ibid; E. F. Jacob, 'All Souls College', in *VCH Oxfordshire*, iii. 173–5.

[4] Godley, *Oxford in the Eighteenth Century*, 91; R. Graves, *Recollections of Some Particulars in the Life of the late William Shenstone, Esq.* (1788), 26n; *Boswell's Life of Johnson*, ed. Chapman, 401n.

[5] H. Colvin and J. S. G. Simmons, *All Souls: An Oxford College and its Buildings* (Oxford, 1989), 47–48n, and Jacob, in *VCH Oxon.*, iii. 173.

[6] C. G. Robertson, *All Souls College* (1899), 28–9, 177–8.

[7] C. W. Oman, 'All Souls College', in *The Colleges of Oxford*, ed. A. Clark (1891), 229–30; Simmons List.

viva voce in the manner of college and university exercises, but also with written components, culminating in a ballot taken by all fellows present at the annual election.[8] Blackstone was fortunate on this occasion not to come up against any candidates able to establish descent from the founder's family. Such 'founder's kin' were now virtually guaranteed a place whenever they stood, thanks to a series of decisions in their favour by successive archbishops of Canterbury, exercising an appellate jurisdiction as the college's *ex officio* visitors. Robert Henley, a later lord chancellor and himself a former fellow, who had been briefed to represent All Souls at the hearing of one such case in 1739, believed that the archbishop's decision on that occasion would henceforth oblige All Souls to 'elect Kinsmen unless they are totally defective in Grammatical rudiments and have not memory sufficient to get by Rote a Scheme of Philosophy': for although 'his Grace was pleased to say he did not take the College for a Hospital, It is plain to see he doth, for a School'.[9] Henley's outrage at this attitude and outcome was fully shared by the civil lawyer and current fellow Thomas Wilbraham, who feared that the archbishop's 'determination . . . in a few years will render All Soules College the most contemptible College in the two Universities', in view of the 'small portion of learning' held sufficient to qualify kinsmen candidates for a fellowship.[10] The vexed issue of founder's kin and the threat they posed to the college's autonomy and academic standing was not least among the numerous All Souls' concerns to which its newest member would shortly apply his formidable energies.

During his first 'year of grace', a probationary 12 months as scholar rather than fellow proper, Blackstone underlined his change of institutional loyalties by reclaiming the £7 'caution money' deposited on his admission to Pembroke College as a good-behaviour bond and security against unpaid college debts. Despite running up a substantial final battels bill of 13 shillings in the first week of November 1743, presumably for the customary drinking and feasting hosted by a successful candidate which still marked academic promotions, there is no evidence that he maintained subsequent contact with his Pembroke contemporaries.[11] Some sign of

---

[8] In 1750 the examination included public disputations in logic and natural philosophy, the composition of a 'Theme' and 'Translations of one of Tully's epistles and a Paragraph from the Spectator': Codrington, Appeals etc., Martin no. 595.

[9] Codrington, Warden's MS 17.

[10] Ibid. Seven of the ten elections between 1733 and 1742 were contested by kinsman candidates, all of whom eventually succeeded, some at the fourth attempt: Simmons List; *Al. Oxon.* iv. 1552.

[11] Codrington, Warden's MS 22/2 (Thomas Wenman's History), p. 188; Pembroke College Archives, 4/4/1, fo. 31, and 9/1/76; H. Rashdall, *The Universities of Europe in the Middle Ages*, ed. F. M. Powicke and A. B. Emden (Oxford, 1936), iii. 436; Macleane, *Pembroke*, 381.

attachment to the college itself is however provided by a handsome lidded silver flagon, inscribed with his coat of arms, presented a decade later as the gift of 'William Blackstone LLD, fellow of All Souls College, commoner of this college for five years, nurtured by Dame Elizabeth Holford and Charterhouse School'.[12]

Like Paul Foley, Charles Wake, and James Yonge, the other three successful candidates of that year, Blackstone went into commons at All Souls immediately after his election. He remained a college resident more or less continuously over the next two years, apart from absences of some two weeks just before Christmas, another five weeks during the summer of 1744, a month the following Christmas, and a break of two months from late June 1745.[13] No doubt this residential pattern was imposed by a mixture of choice and necessity. William evidently found All Souls a congenial place. But then he had no other home to go to, even if he could and did visit relatives from his mother's side of the family for extended periods at Christmas and in the summer. Nor was it until the early months of 1746, during his third year as a member of All Souls, that Blackstone began to spend significant amounts of time in London rather than Oxford.

Although not explicitly stated, Blackstone's satisfaction with his new status and quarters is apparent from his earliest two surviving letters. These were addressed in August and December 1744 to his lawyer uncle Seymour Richmond, who lived in the tiny village of Sparsholt, Berkshire, some fifteen miles southwest of Oxford in the Vale of the White Horse. Richmond, whose yeoman or small gentry family originated from nearby Purton in Wiltshire, entered Queen's College, Oxford in 1707 as the son of a 'plebian', even though his father was busily acquiring land in Berkshire and evidently possessed sufficient means to send two more of his boys to Oxford, the youngest as a gentleman's son. Leaving without a degree, Richmond subsequently set up as an attorney (possibly following the example of his elder brother, who had joined the Middle Temple in 1709 but was never called to the bar), while serving as town clerk of the small

---

[12] Catalogued as no. 253 in the college silver book, this is one of a pair made by John Swift of London in 1755; its twin was given by John Smitheman of Wenlock, Shropshire, marking his honorary MA (conferred 1755): *Al. Oxon.*, iv. 1323.

[13] Codrington, Steward's Book 32, 1742–48. The precise meaning of the various marks and figures used to denote weekly battels and other charges is lost, but comparison of the Steward's Book for 12 months from 25 September 1747 (when the college year began) with the corresponding Commons Book entries (Bodl. MS D.D. All Souls b 114) shows that weeks when Blackstone was absent throughout were listed in the Steward's Book with a numeral '0', usually followed by a 'ii' or 'iiii'.

Thames valley market town of Wallingford, twelve miles downstream from Oxford, between 1713 and 1732.[14]

William was Seymour Richmond's nephew, by virtue of the latter's short-lived marriage to Alethea Bigg, a younger sister of Blackstone's mother. Following Alethea's death, Seymour remarried. His second wife brought him the manor of Sparsholt, where they lived before she in turn died of smallpox in June 1743, leaving Seymour (then aged in his early 50s) with an adolescent son, as well as an older daughter from his first marriage. Yet besides his own two children, his legal practice, and his farming, Seymour Richmond took a keen interest in the welfare of his orphan nephew, being now plainly better placed to do so with William at Oxford than as a London schoolboy. It seems very likely that he encouraged Blackstone's choice of a legal career, while providing considerable moral and practical support during its early stages, assuming in this respect at least something of the quasi-paternal role which his 'Dear Brother', the London-based Thomas Bigg, had played during William's earliest years.[15]

Neither of Blackstone's early letters refers directly to the writer's college life, although both were written from what the first breezily terms 'A.S. Oxon.'. Their focus is rather on the doings of an extended family circle: the Richmonds (Seymour, his daughter Alethea, and son Seymour Jun.), 'my Uncle and Aunt Bigg' (currently visiting Oxford but about to return to Worting, Hampshire, where Rev Walter Bigg held the rectory), and his own two brothers 'Harry' (Henry) and Charles, the former recently graduated with a BA from New College and now 'at Hall' in the parish of Dean, Hampshire, the latter 'soon going into Hampshire to take care of a Church for some months', conveniently located 'about 1 mile from Hall, 4 from Worting, & 3 from Manydown' (where the Biggs also held land). Besides such news and reports of siblings, cousins, uncles, aunts, common acquaintances, and friends, not all of it now or perhaps even then intelligible to those outside the extended family circle, there were domestic favours to be acknowledged and returned: in August a parcel safely come to hand, with 'my thanks for that & all other instances of your Friendship and Kindness by me received'; in December 'two Almanacs of the best Impression to be met with' procured, with assurances that 'as I have no room to doubt of your hearty Friendship, & Goodwill, so I hope I shall leave you none to think me insensible of

[14] Berkshire RO, W/Ac1/1/2, fos. 244v, 297v.

[15] *Alumni Oxonienses . . . 1500–1714*, iii. 1256; *VCH Berkshire*, iv. 257, 312; *Wither Family*, chart facing p. 42. Berkshire RO, W/Ac1/1/2, fo. 244v; Sparsholt parish register 1734–55, entry 13 June 1743; D/EB/E1, Thomas Bigg to Seymour Richmond, 9 July 1743.

the many Obligations I am under to you', capped by an undertaking to 'wait on Yourself & Family at Xmas'. Notwithstanding the early loss of both his own parents, these letters show the young adult Blackstone as far from a lonely outsider, but rather a fully participating member of an extensive network of family and friends.

That general impression is reinforced by the sole intrusion of the larger, non-familial world in these two early letters. This is a strikingly sardonic account of John Wesley's inflammatory sermon on 'Scriptural Christianity', delivered in the university church of St Mary's before the vice chancellor, 'most of the heads of houses, a vast number of gownsmen and a multitude of private people' on St Bartholomew's Day (24 August) 1744.[16] Among 'other equally modest Particulars', Blackstone notes that this 'curious Sermon from Wesley the Methodist . . . informed us 1st That there was not one Christian among all the Heads of Houses' and 'that Pride, Gluttony, Avarice, Luxury, Sensuality & Drunkenness were the general Characteristicks of all Fellows of Colleges, who were useless to a proverbial Uselessness'. His evident lack of sympathy for Wesley's denunciation of the entire university, with its concluding call on the Lord to lay his hand against the city of Oxford (according to another eyewitness, 'words full of such presumption, and seeming imprecation, that they gave an universal shock') may well have been exacerbated by Blackstone's consciousness of their shared Charterhouse background and common status as fellows of colleges.[17] But while his orthodox Anglican principles were bound to be affronted by Wesley's fervent zeal, Blackstone also held an entirely opposite view of the values and worth of the academic institution Wesley had so publicly and vehemently attacked. Hence his evident approval of the vice chancellor's decision to 'punish him by a mortifying neglect', and the implicit assumption that his uncle and any other likely readers of his account would fully endorse these sentiments.[18]

At some point after his November 1743 election to All Souls, quite possibly as late as March 1745, Blackstone completed the slim collection of poetry and translations which he had begun as a Charterhouse schoolboy. Ten years later the last of these works, the poem originally entitled 'The Lawyer to His Muse', appeared anonymously as 'The Lawyer's Farewell to His Muse' in the fourth volume of Robert Dodsley's *Collection of Poems*, the best-selling poetical anthology of the eighteenth century. At the time Dodsley himself claimed not to know its author's identity (presumably because he had received the verses from some third party, possibly the

---

[16] See *Wesley's Standard Sermons*, ed. E. H. Sugden (1961), i. 89, quoting Benjamin Kennicott.
[17] Ibid., i. 110–111.   [18] *Letters*, 1–2.

'gentleman editor' Joseph Spence).[19] But by the last decade of his life
Blackstone's authorship of this 'beautiful little poem' (at just 100 lines,
less than a quarter the length of 'The Pantheon'), seems to have become
widely known, or at least assumed.[20] Clitherow's 'Memoirs' represent this
work as reflecting its author's mental anguish when he 'found it necessary
to quit the more amusing Pursuits of his Youth for the severer Studies
to which he had dedicated himself', once he 'betook himself seriously to
reading Law'.[21] Yet some caution is called for in reading 'The Lawyer's
Farewell to His Muse' as straightforward autobiographical testimony
from a 21-year old facing the unpleasant prospect of abandoning poetry
for the law. Apart from the fact that this poem was evidently subjected
to an unknown amount of authorial revision between its composition
in 1744–45 and first appearance in print ten years later,[22] Blackstone's
personal trajectory scarcely shows a clear disjunction between adolescent artistic dalliance and mature jurisprudential vocation. Further, the
expressed reluctance of the poem's first-person narrator to forsake his
Muse, that 'Companion of my tender age', for 'wrangling courts, and
stubborn Law' plainly owed much to traditional *topoi* positing a mutually
exclusive and wholly antagonistic relationship between the law and polite
letters.[23] Young Blackstone may well have had doubts about dedicating
himself to a career in the common law. But the poet's mental struggle
between letters and the law turns out on closer examination to have been
a one-sided contest. True, the poem's persona is 'pensive', 'with doubtful
mind', 'dreads to go, nor dares to stay', 'Drops a last tear', and bids 'a long,
a last adieu' to his Muse and the pastoral delights (or 'pleasant dream')
they have enjoyed together. But overall the pangs of parting seem notably restrained, and certainly insufficient to bring about any last-minute
career change.

The poem's treatment of legal themes is markedly less conventional.
An initial reference to 'wrangling courts, and stubborn Law' introduces
a ten-line catalogue of assorted urban unpleasantnesses, associated with
'smoak, and crowds, and cities', all these contrasting with the idyllic rustic
scenes previously enjoyed in the Muse's company. Likewise, in place of

---

[19] *The Correspondence of Robert Dodsley 1733–1764*, ed. J. E. Tierney (Cambridge, 1988), 196, 198;
A Collection of Poems by Several Hands, 6 vols., ed. M. Suarez (1782; 1977), i. (94).

[20] T. Spring, *A Familiar Epistle from a Student of the Middle Temple, London, to his Friend in
Dublin* (1771), 25n.

[21] Clitherow, vi.

[22] See below, pp. 59–60.

[23] Cf. my 'Common Lawyers and Culture in Early Modern England', *Law in Context*, 1 (1983),
88–106.

the poets, represented here by Shakespeare, Addison, Waller, Pope, and Milton—whose company and works must now be left to one side—there looms in 'a formal band': these figures:

> In furs and coifs around me stand;
> With sounds uncouth and accents dry
> That grate the soul of harmony,
> Each pedant sage unlocks his store
> Of mystic, dark, discordant lore;
> And points with tott'ring hand the ways
> That lead me to the thorny maze. (ll. 49–57)

This grotesque vision of law as a barbarous, forbidding, and largely inaccessible labyrinth guarded by a repellent cohort of dubiously reliable custodians brilliantly encapsulates long-standing complaints about the difficulties posed for beginning common-law students by the notorious lack of accessible and coherent introductory textbooks. But rather than pursuing that theme, Blackstone (or at least his poetical representative) proceeds to explain the reason for persevering, despite such forbidding obstacles. The goal and motivation is 'Justice', whose 'winding, close retreat' within the law's maze the poet seeks to enter, there to contemplate the 'wisdom of a thousand years', which has been preserved by that 'guardian of Britannia's law'. This worthy ambition is further elaborated via several slightly disconcerting changes of metaphor:

> In that pure spring the bottom view
> Clear, deep, and regularly true,
> And other doctrines thence imbibe
> Than lurk within the sordid scribe;
> Observe how parts with parts unite
> In one harmonious rule of right;
> See countless wheels distinctly tend
> By various laws to one great end;
> While mighty Alfred's piercing soul
> Pervades, and regulates the whole.

These lines foreshadow a personal quest to uncover and reveal the innate reason of the common law, those coherent principles which must—or should—lie beneath the confusing jumble of legal particulars retailed by the 'sordid scribe' (presumably a reference to the dubious motivation and disordered content of the legal 'authorities' already pictured). A somewhat awkward couplet from the original manuscript, not printed in the 1755 version, further characterized his avowed aim, or at least that of his poetical persona, as follows: 'And thence the genuine Maxims draw |

Of unsophisticated Law!'[24] Here 'unsophisticated' is synonymous with original and unadulterated.[25] In chronological terms the reference is to Anglo-Saxon England, as witness the invocation of 'mighty Alfred', king of the West Saxons, no less celebrated in the role of law-giver than for his military exploits against the Danes, or his supposed foundation of Oxford University. That the Saxon 'ancient constitution' was the bedrock of English justice and liberties, notwithstanding subsequent Norman innovations overlaying and subverting its original purity, had long been a staple of legal and political discourse.[26] But in Blackstone's verses the concept derives an added element from the late seventeenth-century Newtonian revolution in natural philosophy. Human law is depicted as a complex mechanism of 'countless wheels', whose diverse ('mix'd, yet uniform') components mesh harmoniously together to achieve the same objective, of right, or justice, as laid down by their original human creator. For Alfred's spiritual presence continues to imbue and oversee their operation, just as the dependence of the entire natural universe on various physical laws determined and still regulated by God was demonstrated by Isaac Newton.

Perhaps the young William Blackstone already saw himself as the common law's Newton, transforming darkness into light, as Alexander Pope famously depicted the great natural philosopher. His poem does set out an extremely ambitious agenda of discovery and reform, since the law's true animating principles and genuine maxims, once properly understood, must supersede the 'mystic, dark, discordant lore' currently on offer.[27] However it is the personal consequences of that commitment to 'unfold the sacred page' with which the poem's last twenty lines deal. They include a mordant sketch of the working lawyer's lot:

> The visage wan, the pore-blind sight,
> The toil by day, the lamp at night,
> The tedious forms, the solemn prate,
> The pert dispute, the dull debate,
> The drowsy bench, the babling Hall . . .

[24] These lines are cited from 'Ms. middle of page 76' in a description of 'Select Poems and Translations' provided by Vernon L. Smith, Law Librarian of the Boalt Hall Law School, University of California at Berkeley, writing to David A. Lockmiller, 11 January 1955: letter on file at Boalt Hall Law School Library, University of California at Berkeley.

[25] Cf. A. O. Lovejoy on 'rationalistic primitivism' in his *Essays in the History of Ideas* (New York, 1960), 86–7.

[26] Cf. C. Hill, 'The Norman Yoke', in *idem, Puritanism and Revolution* (1958), 50–122; J. G. A. Pocock, *The Ancient Constitution and the Feudal Law* (Cambridge, 1987), 318–19.

[27] Cf. Holdsworth's comment: 'Blackstone never lost sight of this resolve to penetrate through legal forms to the principles of the law, and to understand the manner in which those principles united to form an harmonious legal system.' *HEL*, xii. 705.

Yet all these are to be willingly endured as means towards achieving the desired end—that is, 'fair Justice'. Hence, at the close of his working life, this lawyer at least can anticipate a peaceful retirement: 'Untainted by the guilty bribe; | Uncurs'd amid the harpy-tribe; | No ophan's cry to wound my ear; | My honour, and my conscience clear'. These final lines may well embody an element of pious, not to say priggish, platitude. Yet we can also see them as prophetic words of an author who might well have risen even further and a good deal faster than he actually did, but for a certain awkward intractability with regard to what he took to be issues of personal integrity, conscience, and honour.

This poem sufficiently indicates that the prospect of a career in the common law was much on Blackstone's mind during his earliest years at All Souls. At this same time he was also reading for his bachelor's degree in civil law, even if legal texts of any kind are conspicuous by their absence from the (admittedly fragmentary) record of his book purchases and library orders up to and including 1745, the year in which he graduated with the BCL. The one apparent exception occurs in September 1743, when Blackstone evidently consulted the Bodleian's edition of Justinian's *Codex* by the sixteenth-century Spanish humanist scholar Antonio Agustín.[28] As this occasion occurred just over a month before his second attempt at an All Souls fellowship, it is not inconceivable that Blackstone was seeking material to impress the electors with his erudition. More prosaically, he certainly possessed a 1675 Antwerp imprint of Justinian's *Institutes*, although we do not know when he acquired this basic student's text.[29] No doubt he managed to find other civil law material among the chained books in the Bodleian as well as on the shelves of the (old) All Souls college library. He could also have shared resources with his brother Charles at New College; both young men became bachelors of civil law on the same day, Wednesday 12 June 1745.[30] The small collection of his books now at Balliol College also includes a 1665 edition of the 'diffuse and comprehensive' commentary on Justinian by Professor Arnold Vinnius of Leiden, a work which was (according to the Cambridge civilian John Taylor) 'where we commonly set out',[31] together with a 1710 Oxford reprint of

---

[28] Bodl. MS e 554, fo. 29: '8° A 16 Jur. Blackstone e Coll. Pemb. Civilis Jur. Stud.', viz. *Ant. Augustini . . . Constitutionum Graecarum Codices Iustitiani Imp. Collectio, et Interpretatio* (Lérida, 1567).

[29] Balliol, 1550.a.3 (missing title page, colophon 'Approbatio' gives title as *Imperatoris Iustiniani Institutionum Libri IV*). A. Watson, *The Making of the Civil Law* (1981), 62–3.

[30] *The Catalogue of Graduates &c. in the University of Oxford . . . 1735 to October 10. 1747* (Oxford, n.d.), 6.

[31] J. Taylor, *Elements of Civil Law* (Cambridge, 1755), ix; A. Vinnii, *In Quatuor Libros Institutionum Imperialium Commentarius Academicus et Forensis* (Amsterdam, 1665); Balliol, 1555.d.7. Watson, *Civil Law*, 59n, 82.

another Dutch pedagogical standby from the previous century, Theodore Trigland's *Paedia Juris, sive examen Institutionum nova Arte & Methodo Concinnatum* (1671).[32] Two less elementary compilations of civilian learning were the Scot Thomas Craig's *Ius Feudale* in the 1732 Edinburgh edition, and John Cowell's attempt to assimilate English common law to Roman law in his *Institutiones Juris Anglicani* (1605; Oxford, 1676).[33] Unfortunately we cannot say when Blackstone acquired these books. Even greater uncertainty attaches to the nearly 20 pre-1780 canon and civil law titles listed in the catalogues of the auction sales which dispersed the bulk of Blackstone's library, along with the books of two other lawyers, one being his son James. Very probably he was the original owner of most of these items, not least those cited in his first acknowledged publication, the *Essay on Collateral Consanguinity* (1750), but there can be no guarantee that this was indeed the case.[34]

In the last analysis we can do little more than speculate about the nature and detailed content of Blackstone's civil law studies, both at Pembroke and All Souls. Oxford's law faculty was not immune from the general malaise which gripped both English universities in the eighteenth century. Its professors had given up bothering either their students or themselves with lectures, and formal examinations for the bachelor's degree in civil law constituted 'no very serious ordeal'.[35] But it does not follow that Blackstone neglected the subject. The easy familiarity with the concepts and literature of Roman law later displayed in his lectures and published writings points in an entirely opposite direction, as does a casual reference to having 'happened the other day upon a Case in a Civil Law Book'.[36] All Souls could still claim to be Oxford's leading centre of legal studies, for whatever that was worth, and regular scholastic law exercises seem to have continued to be performed in the college throughout the eighteenth century, even if its statutory minority of jurist fellows were now mainly devoted to the study and practice of the common law. Above all, the ideological and professional jealousies which sharply divided civilians from common lawyers in the century after the Reformation lost most of

[32] Balliol, 1550.b.3; Watson, *Civil Law*, 63.

[33] Balliol, 1550.a.23, 1555.f.1.

[34] These include F. Suarez, *Tractatus de Legibus* (1679); J. Calvin, *Lexicon Juridicum* (Geneva, 1683) and W. Lyndwood, *Provinciale, seu Constitutiones Angliae* (Oxford, 1679), cited *Collateral Consanguinity*, 2, 5, 24: *LL*, nos. 579, 595; *BB*, no. 333. Other civilian titles listed in the catalogues include R. Zouch, *Elementa Jurisprudentiae* (Leiden, 1676); G. Gravina, *Origines Juris Civilis* (Leipzig, 1703); J. Domat, *Les Lois Civiles dans Leur Ordre Naturel* (Paris, 1722) and S. Pufendorf, *Law of Nature and Nations* (1729): *LL*, nos. 48, 327, 592; *BB*, no. 280.

[35] *HUO*, 596.

[36] *HUO*, 596–7; *Letters*, 4.

their force in the century following the Glorious Revolution. At the same time, the BCL's relatively modest academic requirements may have made it easier for Blackstone develop and exercise his intellectual talents to a greater extent than would otherwise have been the case.[37] As an Irish participant-observer commented in the 1760s, notwithstanding its notorious shortcomings, Oxford's educational system actually worked very well for that minority of students 'who have Sense to chuse their own Study and Resolution to Pursue it'.[38]

II

But Oxford did not purport to offer any specific qualification or training for common lawyers, whose professional life centred on London. There the four Inns of Court occupied substantial acreages in the City's inner western suburbs, their quasi-collegiate halls and chapels flanked by handsome ranges of professional chambers, attractive courtyards, gardens, and walks, all 'situated in the best Aire [and] free from noyse and disturbance' according to one commentator.[39] Originating in the fourteenth century, the Inns had slightly longer histories than either All Souls or Pembroke College. From humble beginnings as shared hostel-type accommodation rented by groups of lawyers brought to London four times a year for the sittings of the royal courts, they followed the medieval universities in developing an elaborate structure of legal education by means of readings, moots, and other aural 'learning exercises'. These enabled beginners to be inducted by established practitioners into at least some of the mysteries of their craft. As at the universities, much of this system's original rationale was eroded by the advent of the printed book. In the later seventeenth century it effectively collapsed: 'shrunk into mere form, and that preserved only for conformity to rules, that gentlemen by appearance in exercises, rather than any sort of performance, might be entitled to be called to the bar', to quote the Middle Temple lawyer-virtuoso Roger North.[40] Yet despite abandoning any serious attempt to provide legal instruction for their junior members, the self-perpetuating oligarchs who governed each Inn showed no desire

---

[37] *HUO*, 595–6; Doolittle, 43; Robertson, *All Souls*, 177; B. Levack, 'The English Civilians, 1500–1750', in *Lawyers in Early Modern Europe and America* , ed. W. Prest (1981), 123–4; B. P. Levack, 'Law', in *The History of the University of Oxford: Volume IV: Seventeenth-Century Oxford*, ed. N. R. N. Tyacke (Oxford, 1997), 559–68.

[38] Folger MS M. a. 11, 30.

[39] Bodl. MS Rawlinson C 518, 'The Beginner's Advice towards the study of the Common Law', 8.

[40] [R. North], *A Discourse On the Study of the Laws* (1824), 1.

to give up their valuable monopoly control of access to the 'upper branch' of the English legal profession. Hence 'call to the bar' at an Inn of Court remained the indispensable prerequisite for would-be practitioners of the common law, or at least those who envisaged pleading in court and dispensing learned opinions in chambers, rather than undertaking the various routine dealings with courts and clients which typically concerned the more numerous 'lower-branch' of attorneys and solicitors.

No direct assistance with learning the common law was now provided by the Inns, where (as Blackstone himself would later put it, speaking from personal experience), 'all sorts of regimen and academical superintendence, either with regard to morals or studies, are found impracticable and therefore entirely neglected'.[41] So students faced an arduous and lonely form of self-education, involving much private reading, commonplacing of what was read, and attendance at sittings of the courts, sometimes combined with or preceded by placement as a pupil-apprentice in the office of an attorney or other busy practitioner. One educational benefit which the Inns did still offer, even despite the laxness of their residential requirements, was via association with others similarly confronting the 'rude and indigested state, in which the materials of the law have long been suffered to lie'.[42] Such interaction could and did lead to helpful discussion and 'case putting' in which difficult points were clarified: not for nothing had Serjeant Maynard characterized the law as a 'babblative art'.[43] But this hardly made the study itself significantly less 'tedious and intricate', especially for a 'youth of lively genius and liberal learning', who might equally well decide to 'desert his hopeless pursuit' in favour of the various diversions so copiously available in eighteenth-century London.[44]

We do not know why in 1741 Blackstone chose to join the Middle Temple rather than Gray's Inn, the Inner Temple, or Lincoln's Inn. Given the apparent absence of any family connection (other than via an uncle, William Richmond, brother of Seymour, who was admitted as a student of the Middle Temple in 1709),[45] the simplest explanation may well be the best. The topography of London's legal quarter meant that the Middle Temple was the first Inn of Court reached by travellers from Oxford coming in along the Strand, the major thoroughfare linking the medieval walled City with the residential districts and governmental precincts of

---

[41] *Commentaries*, i. 25.

[42] *Monthly Review*, 19 (Nov. 1758), 486 (reviewing Blackstone's *Discourse on the Study of the Law*).

[43] R. North, *The Lives of the Norths*, ed. A. Jessopp (1890), i. 26.

[44] *Monthly Review*, 19 (Nov. 1758), 486.

[45] *MTAdmR*, i. 265.

the increasingly fashionable West End. As well as the former Crusaders' Temple Church, the Middle Temple shared with the neighbouring Inner Temple access to the River Thames at Temple Stairs, providing an alternative route by water between the lawyers' chambers and the courts in Westminster Hall. Middle Temple Hall, the Elizabethan dining hall, with its impressive hammer-beam oak roof, was also the largest public building possessed by any Inn of Court. Besides convenience and architectural distinction, fashion and reputation may also have played some part in a decision on which his guardian Thomas Bigg and uncle Seymour Richmond would certainly have had a major say. For the Middle Temple not only admitted significantly more student members than any other Inn throughout the first half of the eighteenth century, but also accounted for some 40 per cent of the total output of barristers from the four Inns between the 1720s and the first decade of George III's reign.[46]

Blackstone's common-law studies are slightly better documented than his civil-law reading. It seems clear that they did not begin until his return to London in January 1746. On 3 January, after spending Christmas and New Year's Day in Oxford, Blackstone received three months' leave of absence from All Souls, which was extended by a further month in April; these appear to have been the first such periods of leave he had formally requested.[47] His third surviving letter, once again addressed to his uncle Seymour Richmond, but dated from London on 28 January 1746, explains the reason for these long absences.[48] Having occupied for some ten days his 'new Habitation (which is at Mr Stokes's a Limner in Arundel-Street)', William reported that he was now 'tolerably well settled' in congenial, quiet, and well-priced lodgings.[49] Also staying at the same house was 'a young Lady of extraordinary Accomplishments & very ample Fortune'. But he could assure his uncle that, since she possessed 'together with the Riches, the complexion also of a Jew', she was unlikely 'to prove a very formidable Rival to—Coke upon Littleton' (that is, a standard, notoriously challenging introductory law text).[50] Casual anti-Jewish prejudice

---

[46] Lemmings, *Gentlemen and Barristers*, 10; Lemmings, *Professors*, 68–9.

[47] Codrington, Warden's MS 11 [unfoliated].

[48] As with this letter, dated 'Jan. 28. 1745' (that is, 1746 new style), the first law book Blackstone is known to have owned, a copy of *The Law French Dictionary Alphabetically Digested; Very useful for all Young Students in the Common Laws of England* (1718) bears an ownership signature dated '1745' (so was acquired between 25 March 1745 and 24 March 1746, new style). Balliol 1550.f.7.

[49] The *OED* defines 'limner' ('Now *literary* or *arch.*') as 1. An illuminator of manuscripts and 2. A painter, esp. a portrait painter. Mr Stokes has not been further identified, but for the portraitist Thomas Stokes (fl. 1737) see B. Stewart and M. Cutten, *Dictionary of Portrait Painters in Britain* (Woodbridge, 1997), 438.

[50] *Letters*, 3.

and stereotyping had long been part of the national cultural heritage, doubtless aggravated in the young Blackstone's case by a general lack of charity towards all those out of communion with the Church of England. But he also seems anxious on this occasion to reassure his uncle that he would not easily be distracted from the new phase of legal studies on which he had now embarked by what he himself would later term the 'amusements', or 'less innocent pursuits' which London had to offer.[51] (It has been conjectured that Laetitia Pilkington's colourful account in her 1748 *Memoirs* of an extended evening visit to her Fleet Street lodgings by a person identified only as 'the now Lord Chief Justice E_____e, then a Student in Gray's Inn, a fine Gentleman, poetically turned' may refer to 'the promising young scholar and poet William Blackstone'. But apart from other obvious inconsistencies, this alleged encounter appears to have taken place only a year or so after Pilkington reached London from Ireland in 1739.)[52]

Blackstone's letter continued with a jaunty, if properly circumstantial, report on what was plainly his first serious encounter with the common law, even though he had by now accumulated a full five years' standing on the books of the Middle Temple. As British forces under the duke of Cumberland were even now pursuing the Young Pretender's retreating Jacobite army back into Scotland, Blackstone adopted a topically martial turn of phrase; rather than attempting a frontal 'attack' on the formidable *Institutes* and *Reports* of Sir Edward Coke, he had 'stormed one Book of Littleton, and opened my Trenches before the second', and 'can with Pleasure say I have met with no Difficulty of Consequence'.[53] The sole problem he admits to puzzling him in the first book of Littleton's *Tenures*, the fifteenth-century treatise on land law still generally prescribed for common-law novices, is presented as a challenge to Littleton's assertion that 'the writ he produces proves the point he would have it do'. Admittedly, Blackstone continues, this is 'a Point of mere Curiosity':

But I don't love to march into an unknown Country, without securing every Post behind me: and it is a greater Slur upon a General to leave a slight Place untaken, than one more hard of Access. Besides, in my apprehension (and I should be glad to know your Opinion of the matter) the Learning out of use is as necessary to

---

[51] Cf. T. M. Endelman, *The Jews of Georgian England 1714–1830: Tradition and Change in a Liberal Society* (Philadelphia, 1979), esp. ch. 3. *Commentaries*, i. 31.

[52] *Memoirs of Laetitia Pilkington*, ed. A. C. Elias Jr., (1997), i. 178–2, ii. 563–4; *ODNB*, s.v. Pilkington [*née* van Lewen], Laetitia.

[53] *Letters*, 3. On the place of Littleton and Coke in the education of barristers, see Lemmings, *Professors*, 137.

a Beginner as that of every Day's Practise. There seem in the modern Law to be so many References to the antient Tenures and Services, that a Man who would understand the Reasons, the Grounds, and Original of what is Law at this Day must look back to what it was formerly; otherwise his Learning will be both confused and superficial.[54]

The novice common lawyer then launches into a remarkable meditation on the general characteristics of the whole body of knowledge, that 'unknown Country', with which he was now becoming acquainted. In Littleton's day, Blackstone went on, the common law 'resembled a regular Edifice: where the Apartments were properly disposed, leading one into another without Confusion, where every part was subservient to the whole, all uniting in one beautiful Symmetry...'. Now, more than two centuries later, 'altered and mangled by various contradictory Statutes, &c...according to Whim, or Prejudice, or private Convenience of the Builders', the original 'remains a huge, irregular Pile, with many noble Apartments, though awkwardly put together, and some of them of no visible Use at present'. Yet anyone wanting to understand 'why they were built, to what End or Use, how they communicated with the rest, and the like; he must necessarily carry in his Head the Model of the old House, which will be the only Clue to guide him through this new Labyrinth.'[55]

This elaborate architectural-cum-historical metaphor, quoted here only in part, seems entirely of Blackstone's own contriving. Nothing quite comparable in scale or specificity of reference appears in the early modern legal canon. Common lawyers typically referred to the code they professed either in terms of greater abstraction (as derived from custom, statute, judicial learning, and reason, while encompassing or embodying at least to some extent the laws of nature and of nations), or more prosaically as a random assortment of individual procedures and remedies addressing a host of very particular issues.[56] The interest which led to Blackstone's first attempt at expounding the basic rules of classical architecture had clearly continued and deepened in the years since his election to All Souls, an ideal vantage point from which to watch the baroque dome of Gibbs's Radcliffe Library rising in the newly-cleared square bordering Catte Street, just outside the college. As expressed in this 1746 letter it also anticipates what has been termed the 'stock analogy for jurisprudence in the eighteenth century ... the conception of the legal system as a building', shortly to be enunciated in Montesquieu's

[54] *Letters*, 3–4. [55] Ibid., 4.
[56] Cf. my 'Blackstone as Architect: Constructing the Commentaries', *Yale Journal of Law and the Humanities*, 15 (2003), 104–5.

Esprit des Lois (1748), and then further elaborated in Blackstone's own *Commentaries*.[57]

The basis of Blackstone's campaign to master the common law was (as he claimed) the 'Instructions to his Nephew Concerning the Study of the Law' compiled in the 1730s by Sir Thomas Reeve, a former chief justice of common pleas.[58] Numerous documents of this kind were in circulation, recommending what to read and in what order, a natural response to the lack both of formal instruction and satisfactory textbooks providing either an overview of the common law or a coherent account of its various branches. Blackstone may well have followed Reeve's urging to gain a preliminary sense of the 'terms and general meaning of the law' by reading Thomas Woods's *Institute of the Laws of England*, the work of an Oxford civilian and barrister of Gray's Inn, who sought to demonstrate that 'a general and methodical distribution, preparatory to a more large and accurate study of our laws, might now be made, as well as an Institute of the Civil or Canon Law, or of the laws of other nations; which were once too, heap'd up together without beginning or end . . .'. No fewer than four copies of Wood's *Institute*, one in two volumes 'filled with MS notes', were dispersed at the 1803 sale of Blackstone's library.[59]

Reeve's readers were advised to do a good deal of preparatory reading before tackling Coke's commentary on Littleton, and then to compile a detailed alphabetical abridgement, or commonplace book, of its rambling bulk. Blackstone may also have heeded Reeve's suggestion that the next stage of his studies should involve mastering a range of treatises, including Henry Finch's *Law, or a Discourse thereof*, and Matthew Hale's *Analysis of the Common Law*. But while he would later acknowledge a debt to both these earlier attempts at presenting a systematic overview of the common law, it seems less likely that he took much notice of Reeve's warning against premature attendance at the Westminster courts, another traditional activity, since his own posthumously published *Reports* opens with cases heard in the court of King's Bench as early as the Michaelmas or autumn term of 1746. He may well have begun frequenting Westminster Hall even earlier. For the 'five large Note Books, all written with his own Hand', from which Clitherow printed the text of the *Reports*, had themselves been compiled by Blackstone from a much larger body of 'rough

[57] P. Stein, 'Elegance in the Law', in *The Character and Influence of Roman Civil Law* (1988), 15.

[58] *Letters*, 3; Lemmings, *Professors*, 136 and n.

[59] Lemmings, *Professors*, 136–7; *ODNB*, s.v. Wood, Thomas; T. Wood, *An Institute of the Laws of England; or, the Laws of England in their natural order . . . Published for the direction of young beginners, or students in the law; and of others that desire to have a general knowledge of our Common and Statute Laws* (1720; fifth edn., 1734), sig. [b]; *LL*, nos. 114, 350, 629, 655.

Notes', selected according to their interest and general relevance, 'or perhaps, such only (particularly for the first few Years) as he had taken the most accurate Notes of'.[60]

Yet when Michaelmas term began on Monday 20 October 1746 Blackstone was little more than a month from becoming a barrister. As early as June of that year he had been 'proposed for call to the bar by Master Allen', a bencher with antiquarian and literary interests who was a former fellow of King's College, Cambridge, and may well have recognized in Blackstone something of a kindred spirit.[61] Candidates for call were customarily nominated by individual benchers, who supposedly possessed sufficient personal knowledge 'to give some account to their Masterships (if required) of the character, and qualification' of those whom they proposed. Blackstone's call on 28 November would hardly have occurred without Allen's strong support, given that he was one of ten possible candidates nominated in June and had still only accumulated some five years' standing on the Middle Temple's books, one year less than the prescribed minimum. True, this requirement was now far from rigorously enforced. Indeed, none of the other three students called on the same day could claim the statutory six years' standing, nor was Blackstone even the most junior of the quartet, although there were precedents for concessions to bachelors of civil law.[62]

Apart from the few case notes published in his posthumous *Reports*, little record remains of Blackstone's first attempts to establish himself at the London bar. By February 1747, if not before, he had left his Arundel Street lodgings to take rooms in the Middle Temple. While nobody was supposed to be called unless they possessed chambers in the Inn, that requirement could be circumvented by purchasing a three-year lease of 'house chambers' for the relatively modest sum of £8.4/-. Blackstone probably took advantage of this arrangement, since an undated ledger entry made after his call describes him as having house chambers 'four pair of stairs and a half back' on staircase 2 in Garden Court, while also noting that he 'Lives in Pump Court No 3'.[63] It seems likely that the latter reference was to accommodation sublet from its officially-registered tenant,

[60] Clitherow, xxviii–xxix.

[61] *ODNB*, s.v. Allen, Anthony; MT Archives, Parliament Minutes, MT1/MPA/7, p. 545 (13 June 1746).

[62] MT Parliament Minutes, MT1/MPA/7, pp. 342, 456, 548. Richard Vaughan had been admitted in March 1741, Thomas Putt in October of that year, and James Brebner on 5 November 1742, although he may have qualified for special treatment as a member of the Scottish Faculty of Advocates: *MTAdmR*, i. 329, 331. For the previous concessional call of a BCL, see MT Parliament Minutes MT1/MPA/7, 211 (re: Richard Francis, called 15 May 1724).

[63] MT3/BAL/1, p. 49.

whereas the former was his nominated 'house chambers' and perhaps professional office, albeit one not well placed (because it was too high above ground level) to attract passing clients. Alternatively he may have moved chambers at some point between 1746 and 1749, as he certainly had done by February 1751, when he was living at Brick Court No 2.[64] Blackstone did not surrender his house chambers until 28 June 1749, paying £8.19/2 that same day to settle his accounts for commons not kept, and learning exercises forfeited after his call. While he evidently found it worth spending £4 to avoid being assigned to participate in two formulaic moots, the cost of compounding for all his commons and other obligations would have run to nearly £20, an expenditure Blackstone might well have regarded as excessive, and which he avoided by keeping the majority of term and vacation commons during the three years after his call. This was a rather less significant commitment than it might sound, since the obligation to keep term commons, for example, could be satisfied with eight weeks' residence a year.

Thus it was entirely possible for All Souls to remain Blackstone's principal place of residence. Over the five years from 1747 onwards he spent more than half his time there, except during that first year after call, when the college allowed him a total of four and a half months' leave of absence and he actually appeared in commons for only some 22 weeks in all.[65] While the sittings of the central courts during the four terms of the legal year lasted for well under three months in total, he possibly followed an assize circuit, which would have taken him away from Oxford for perhaps a month or two at most. If he elected to follow the Oxford circuit, as one scrap of evidence very faintly suggests,[66] it must have been during the February–March spring vacation between Hilary and Easter terms, rather than in the August or summer vacation, since the All Souls stewards' books show him as a constant resident from late June or early July until Michaelmas term in late October–November. He also usually had at least a month to six weeks before and after Christmas in college, besides another month or so before the end of Trinity term in June. And the initial burst of post-call enthusiasm which kept Blackstone away from

---

[64] See correspondence dated from 'Temple' and 'Middle Temple', 19 February and 15 April 1747: *Letters*, 5–7. Lemmings, *Professors*, 49–50; *idem, Gentlemen and Barristers*, 263; *Master Worsley's Book on the History and Constitution of the Honourable Society of the Middle Temple*, ed. A. R. Ingpen (1910), 30. Newdigate Diary, 24 February 1751.

[65] Codrington, Warden's MS 11 (Absence Book), 25 December 1746, 4 June 1747; Stewards' Books, 1742–48, 1748–54. Blackstone appears to have used only about half of his two leaves of four months each granted on 24 December 1748 and 27 April 1749.

[66] *Letters*, 54 (reference to 'my Brethren on the Circuit', which need not imply his joining them).

Oxford—presumably in London—for some seven months during 1747 was not repeated. By 1750 the pattern was reversed, so that he evidently spent only 18 weeks of the entire 12 months away from All Souls.[67]

Clitherow tells us that Blackstone's early years as a practising lawyer were far from easy; he 'made his way very slowly', acquiring 'little Notice and little Practice'.[68] Such an experience was entirely normal: 'for most barristers, their first attempt at advocacy in Westminster Hall was likely to be succeeded by an anti-climax of prolonged and frustrating unemployment'.[69] Yet Blackstone seems not to have held a single brief on the 'pleas' side of the court of King's Bench, which Lemmings describes as 'the principal tribunal for the mass of practising common lawyers'[70]— especially those newly called to the bar—until the summer of 1748, over eighteen months after his call. Further, his name appears in connection with only six further motions recorded in the court's rule books between that date and November 1751.[71] On the 'Crown' side of the same court, where practice tended to be even more completely dominated by a smaller group of specialist advocates, Blackstone evidently secured no work at all, at least so far as the relevant rule books can tell us.[72] He also enjoyed little success in the court of Chancery, where more eighteenth-century barristers made at least an occasional appearance than in any other central jurisdiction. Only two references to Blackstone moving in Chancery have been identified for each successive Michaelmas term from 1747 to 1752, as well as for Hilary, Easter, and Trinity terms of 1753 (that is, until his announced withdrawal from Westminster Hall in July 1753).[73] True, the densely-packed entries of motions and rules which fill each page of the voluminous Chancery entry books make it difficult to be sure that every single mention of Blackstone's name as counsel has been noted. Further, the practical necessity of proceeding by way of samples drawn from the huge mass of surviving Chancery sources undoubtedly increases the potential margin of error. As it happens, we know from other sources that in Hilary and Easter terms 1752, Blackstone frequently engaged in consultations about

---

[67] MT3/BAL 1, p. 49: 'Chamber surr[endered] 28 June 1749'. While not formally leasing a chamber from the MT after that date, Blackstone could have sub-let rooms from another tenant, leaving no trace on the house records: cf. Lemmings, *Gentlemen and Barristers*, 50–52.

[68] Clitherow, vii.   [69] Lemmings, *Professors*, 156.

[70] Ibid., 169.

[71] Ibid.; TNA, KB21/36–7; KB125/149–153. The cases in which Blackstone was mentioned as moving occurred in June 1748 (*Whickelow on demise of North v Notitle*), June 1749 (*Coventry v Trip*), February 1750 (*Booch v Gould, Coventry v Trip*), April 1750 (*Race v Woodhouses*), May 1750 (*Barton v Morgan*) and November 1751 (*Faulkner v Westall*).

[72] Cf. Lemmings, *Professors*, 165–6, for limitations of these sources.

[73] Ibid., 181–3; TNA, C33/389–402.

Sir Roger Newdigate's Chancery litigation, and appeared as counsel for Newdigate before Lord Hardwicke in Lincoln's Inn Hall on 17 April 1752, speaking 'very short but well enough'.[74] Nevertheless, even granting that Chancery remained in session more or less throughout the year (disregarding the traditional common law vacations), Blackstone could hardly have made more than the most sporadic appearances in that court during his early years as barrister.

Blackstone's singular lack of success in this first venture at the bar was, if anything, overdetermined. He had the bad luck to commence his legal career just as the volume of business handled by the central courts was contracting to what Professor Brooks believes to have been its eighteenth-century nadir. Indeed, Blackstone himself joked about the shortage of work: 'As for Law in the Courts of Westminster', he wrote in December 1751, 'it is grown a perfect Stranger. Not one Determination of any Moment during the whole Term; & the Courts (except the Chancery) not sitting above one hour in the morning. I believe our Clients mistook the Title of an Act that passed last Sessions, & instead of *Abbreviation* read it "An Act for the *Annihilation* of Michaelmas Term".'[75] Moreover Clitherow points out that his brother-in-law laboured under two considerable handicaps. A lack of patronage, or family legal connections (other than through his uncle Seymour) compounded the other major problem, which was that, however fluent on paper, Blackstone was generally a poor public speaker, 'not being happy in a graceful Delivery or a flow of Elocution (both which he much wanted)'.[76]

Many, indeed most, newly-called barristers faced a demanding struggle to survive the first lean years of practice at the bar. But Blackstone's mental attitude and personal circumstances were also less than conducive to persistence in his chosen profession. In November 1747, he informed an All Souls colleague that, although finding the law 'a very dry study', he had '"made myself pretty well master of it". What! In two years, I exclaimed with surprise? "Yes says he; I have reduced it to a system; so that I have only to read new acts of Parliament, and the different authors who have written on our laws".'[77] Such overweening intellectual self-confidence,

---

[74] *Newdigate Correspondence*, 63; Newdigate Diary, 12, 17, 21–22 February, 17, 22 April 1752.

[75] C. W. Brooks, *Lawyers, Litigation and English Society since 1450* (1998), 29; *idem*, 'Litigation, participation, and agency in seventeenth- and eighteenth-century England', in *The British and their Laws*, ed. Lemmings, 155–81; see also the editorial introduction and my own contribution, ibid., 6–7, 19–20, 133–54. *Letters*, 22.

[76] Clitherow, vii.

[77] Graves, *The Triflers*, 54; this exchange evidently occurred 'when [Blackstone] had been about two years at the Temple'.

remarkable enough when expressed in an Oxford common room, might well encounter a considerably more sceptical reception from London attorneys brought up in the 'thorny maze' of particularistic common law learning, the men on whom barristers depended for briefs. Blackstone doubtless guarded his tongue more closely while in the vicinity of Temple Bar, but could hardly have avoided that blinkered professional outlook which earlier in the century had worked against 'some ingenious young men in the Temple that were counsellors but had not much business'. Dudley Ryder then noted that 'it is not the way to get business and have the character of a good lawyer to seem acquainted much with other things'.[78]

As a younger son and orphan, William can have had no illusions about the need to make his own way in the world, perhaps especially after the remarriage of his maternal uncle Thomas Bigg in December 1751.[79] Nevertheless, in point of fact, his prospects were no more limited to the Westminster bar than were his horizons. For, even while in London attending the courts and waiting for briefs, Blackstone found himself still caught up in Oxford business, whether advising how best to deal with refractory tenants on All Souls' estates, or sending news of a 'triumphant Event . . . Victory without a Blow', when the Pelham administration dropped proceedings in King's Bench against the vice chancellor for allegedly failing to punish undergraduates involved in treasonable expressions of Jacobite allegiance.[80] Young Blackstone's special expertise in legal matters relating to the university and its privileges was also becoming apparent to his academic superiors from at least mid-1750, when he served as intermediary between the vice chancellor and the busy Chancery barrister Randle Wilbraham, who thanked him for 'the kind Assistance you have given to the University by your Letter to me' regarding a dispute over the city of Oxford's rights to license traders. This matter dragged on for several years; Blackstone was the junior of three counsel briefed to argue the university's case at the 1753 Oxford summer assizes, and possibly even earlier.[81] Yet another potential distraction from the pursuit of briefs in Westminster Hall was his election as recorder of Wallingford in May 1749, following the resignation of his uncle Seymour Richmond, who had held the position for less than five years. True, in such a relatively small market town with a population not much exceeding 1,500 at mid-century, the recorder's duties were unlikely to be exacting, notwithstanding his role

---

[78] *The Diary of Dudley Ryder 1715–1716*, ed. W. Matthews (1939), 182.

[79] Thomas Bigg took out a special licence on Christmas Eve 1751 to marry Hannah Alexander of Chilton Foliat: *Letters*, 21.

[80] *Letters*, 5–6, 8–9; see further below, Chapter 6, pp. 98–100.

[81] Ibid., 12–13. OUA, CC Papers 1751, pp.14–19; WPα/17/1, fos. 42, 44, 47, 50–51.

as the borough's chief legal officer. Indeed, Blackstone appears to have attended only just over half of the quarter sessions sittings held during his first decade in the post, although he was also very occasionally named to committees hearing appeals against poor-rate assessments, and provided some legal advice on other matters.[82] The recordership of Wallingford was at best a local distinction rather than a sought-after national legal office, while the small trickle of cases going through the town courts could not have generated much fee income to supplement the post's annual £5 stipend. Yet Blackstone was hardly in a position to scorn these modest financial and social benefits, whether on his own account or that of his family, since in addition to Seymour Richmond's connection with the town, his guardian Thomas Bigg held substantial property interests there. Moreover, Wallingford was readily accessible from Oxford.[83] Even if this appointment did not directly hinder Blackstone's efforts to establish a practice at the London bar, its acceptance provides further evidence that his main attention and interests still lay elsewhere, for the moment at least.

[82] Berkshire RO, W/AC1/1/2, fos. 339, 364v; W/JQS/1 (July 1749–October 1759), 17 January 1751, 20 April 1751. I am grateful to David Pedgley for information on Wallingford's population.

[83] The (somewhat irregular) payments of Blackstone's 'sallary' are listed in Berkshire RO W/FA/C/1, pp. 120, 123, 129, 131, etc. Seymour Richmond's connections with Wallingford dated back to 1711; in 1728 he had a house in the town and, despite moving to Sparsholt in the 1730s, maintained links with the borough until at least 1760. Besides holding leases of four houses in the town (Berkshire RO, W/AC/1/1/2, fo. 345v, 348v), Thomas Bigg appears to have owned the property known as Priory Place, where William Blackstone was living by August 1761: Berkshire RO, D/P 139/11/1, January, March, and August 1761. (With thanks again to David Pedgley.)

CHAPTER 5

'Advancing the Interests of the College'
(1744–53)

B LACKSTONE was far from abandoning Oxford during his first attempt at the bar. Even Clitherow's account of the remarkable diversity of matters which engaged his subject's 'Active Mind' between the mid-1740s and his decision to 'retire to his Fellowship and an academical Life' in mid-1753 does not adequately convey the extent and intensity of those continuing involvements, and distractions from the business of Westminster Hall.[1] This chapter turns to Blackstone's collegiate commitments; the next will consider his broader role in university affairs.

I

Blackstone's most visible contribution to All Souls College, and indeed, the University of Oxford, remains the long-delayed completion and fitting out of the great library designed by Nicholas Hawksmoor and named after Christopher Codrington: the wealthy West Indian plantation and slave owner who in 1710 left his former college the huge sum of £10,000 to build a new library and stock it with books. Unfortunately, it then took many years to erect the magnificent shell of the Codrington Library. By the time Hawksmoor died in 1736, money was tighter and disagreements had emerged about the design of the interior. The architect James Gibbs advised in 1740 that the upper gallery of bookshelves envisaged by Hawksmoor should be 'taken intirely away'.[2] Meanwhile another unfinished building

---

[1] Clitherow, viii–x.
[2] E. Craster, *The History of All Souls College Library* (1971), ed. E. F. Jacob, 71–6; Bodl. MS D.D. All Souls c 256/79a.

was attracting at least occasional attention from the warden and fellows of All Souls. The Codrington was part of a larger scheme to develop a new 'Baroque Gothic' quadrangle north of the college's existing medieval buildings, including a common room flanked by twin towers, and a three-storied 'Great Dormitory' linked to the new library and containing sets of fellow's rooms.[3] In 1720 the poet Edward Young, a former All Souls fellow, had persuaded his friend and pupil, the eccentric Whig-Jacobite rake Philip, Duke of Wharton, to guarantee funding for this latter structure. It appears that, before his death in penurious exile ten years later, the duke actually paid for construction of the first two storeys of what became known as the Wharton building.[4] But when his executors refused to forward the balance, the college found itself fighting a protracted Chancery suit, which by 1739 was reported to be 'not in a very forward or favourable stage'.[5] Over five years later, in November 1744, with the litigation still making glacial progress, Dr Wriothesley Digby (doubtless in Oxford for the annual election of fellows on All Souls' Day, and having heard their recently elected young colleague Blackstone deliver the annual Latin oration in praise of the founder and other benefactors) proposed to lend the college £500 'towards finishing duke Wharton's Buildings'.[6] In February 1745 it was agreed to accept this offer, to mobilize an additional £160 from internal funds, and to have the arrangement written up in legal form. As the completed buildings would overlook the warden of New College's garden, further negotiations were necessary. By April 1747, the builders estimated that the third storey could be finished within two months. Just under a year later, a detailed entry in the college minutes, written and signed by William Blackstone, records that the warden and fellows had accepted the proposals of 'Tawney the Carpenter' for fitting out chambers in Wharton's building with 'substantial Doors' and 'a good oaken floor'.[7]

Supporting evidence for Clitherow's claim that 'the Care and Activity of Mr Blackstone' were responsible for bringing the long saga of the Wharton building to a successful conclusion remains largely circumstantial. But it is worth noting that, in 1760, one of the last administrative tasks Blackstone undertook at All Souls was to organize repayment of the

[3] See H. Colvin, 'Hawksmoor and the North Quadrangle' in Colvin and Simmons, *All Souls*.

[4] *ODNB*, s.v. Wharton, Philip; Bodl. MS D.D. All Souls c 255, 19b/15, 19; M. Burrows, *Worthies of All Souls* (1874), 296–7.

[5] Bodl. MS D.D. All Souls c 255, 19b/15, 19; Codrington, Wardens MS 17, R. Henley to S. Niblett, 1 March 1739.

[6] Codrington, Acta in Capitulis 1707–53, fos. 152, 154; Clitherow, vii, mentions Blackstone's 1744 'Anniversary Speech'.

[7] Codrington, Acta in Capitulis 1707–53, fos. 147 (3 August 1743), 159v (24 December 1745), 168v (2 October 1747), 170v (8 March 1748); Bodl. MS D.D. All Souls c 255/19b/20, 58/97.

balance of Dr Digby's loan, expressing the college's and particularly his own thanks 'for your generous & seasonable Assistances, at Times when they stood in the greatest need . . . no Man, as an Individual, entertains a deeper sense of them'.[8] Nor is it irrelevant in this context that Blackstone's intellectual preoccupation with the art and science of building had evidently continued and deepened since the summer of 1743, when he drafted his first attempt at a systematic architectural treatise, the 'Abridgement of Architecture'. For a prefatory note to the manuscript 'Elements of Architecture' (the title of the second version of his text) explains that the earlier draft was 'revised and transcribed, with considerable Additions and Improvements, at leisure hours in the years 1746 & 1747'.[9] So the original working copy with its frequent annotations, interpolations, and deletions became an attractive manuscript, laid out in a clear, flowing hand and illustrated with 23 meticulously executed pen-and-ink drawings.[10] For, not with standing Clitherow's insistence, in deference to a still potent prejudice against mercenary scribblers, that this work was intended solely for its author's personal use, the careful presentation of the surviving text suggests that, on the contrary, 'Elements of Architecture' had been originally envisaged as a fair copy for publication.[11] It did not appear in print because, by the time of the appearance of *The Pantheon* in the spring of 1747, some months after his call to the bar, Blackstone had come to recognize the advisability of dissociating himself from 'such amusements', on account of their perceived incompatibility with 'the Profession I have engaged in'.[12]

Whatever his prudential reservations about publicly-avowed non-legal authorship, Blackstone showed no reluctance to involve himself in the practical business of completing the college's ambitious but dilatory building works. Following a decision during his first year at All Souls to repair the lead flashing on the roof of the new library, there is no hint of further activity on that front until August 1747, when a minute signed 'Will. Blackstone' records the college's agreement 'that Mr Jeremiah Franklyn be immediately employed to finish his work in the new Library according to the terms of his Contract'. But while Jeremiah the joiner did evidently finish off the tall bookcases fitted with wire-meshed wooden

---

[8] Clitherow, viii; *Letters*, 69, 71.

[9] Codrington, MS 333. See also Matthews, 'Architecture and Polite Culture in England', for an annotated transcript.

[10] See Plate 9.

[11] Clitherow, v. In 1858, Butterworth's, the law publishers, issued a prospectus for a limited edition of 'Elements of Architecture': Folger, AP4G3 New Series, v. 6, 1858, pt. 2.

[12] *Letters*, 7.

doors and locks (since in this new library, books would no longer be chained), 'John Franklyn the Carpenter' was evidently making little progress with his work on the gallery running above the bookcases along the north interior wall.[13] Just over a year later, the impasse was tackled by an extensive order entered in Blackstone's hand, providing for the college to pay off Franklyn for 'so much of the Materials prepared by him and now lying in the Library, as will be serviceable in finishing the same, at the Valuation delivered in by Mr Tawney' (that is, the carpenter already employed in fitting out Wharton's building), with the remainder to be 'immediately sent home to his House'. This order, made on Friday 26 August, was to be 'put in Execution next Wednesday'. It was further minuted that 'proper Workmen be employed to finish the Library with all Expedition', with their estimates 'of the expence of compleating the Library according to the new Draughts in the Bursary, marked X' to be procured 'immediately'.[14]

Blackstone may well have taken a personal role in preparing those 'new Draughts' (Clitherow noted that his brother-in-law not only 'hastened the Completion' of the Codrington, but also 'rectified several Mistakes in the Architecture'). He certainly followed closely the subsequent progress of Robert Tawney and his men, who having begun work on New Year's Day 1749, were commissioned in November of that year 'to continue the Pedastal Part of the Ionic Order under the Windows of the library, and make a door and Door Cases according to the Draught this Day produced to the College'. At the same meeting, tenders were called for the 'stucco-work' on the library ceiling 'according to the plans agreed', while 'Mr Blackston when he goes to Town' was commissioned to obtain from the fashionable 'Mr Cheere of Picadilly' (who had already supplied a marble statue of Christopher Codrington dressed 'in a Roman habit') specimens of the busts and vases to be placed atop the (now single) gallery's bookshelves, as previously recommended by Gibbs.[15] These samples proving satisfactory, Blackstone was empowered on 17 January 1750 to contract

[13] Codrington, Acta in Capitulis 1707–53, fos. 150 (1 June 1744), 166 (21 August 1747); Bodl. MS D.D. All Souls c 256/86, 'Account of the Expenses incurred in Building and fitting up the Codrington Library' (in Blackstone's hand) clarifies the different tasks that Jeremiah and John Franklyn were undertaking. See also P. Neill, 'Blackstone, Oxford, and the Law', in *All Souls Under the Ancien Régime*, ed. S. J. D. Green and P. Horden (Oxford, 2007), 273–4.

[14] Codrington, Acta in Capitulis 1707–53, fo. 172v.

[15] Clitherow, viii; Craster, *Library*, 75, 79; Codrington, Acta in Capitulis 1707–53, fo. 179; Bodl. MS D.D. All Souls c 256/86; M. Craske, 'Contacts and Contracts: Sir Henry Cheere and the Formation of a New Commercial World of Sculpture in Mid-Eighteenth-Century London', in *The Lustrous Trade: Material Culture and the History of Sculpture in England and Italy c. 1700–c. 1860*, ed. C. Sicca and A. Yarrington (2000), 94–131.

with Cheere for 25 vases and the same number of 'Bustoes' of distinguished former fellows; in November his commission was to treat with Cheere's more famous pupil François Louis Roubiliac, 'about a Marble Bust of the Founder, and to bespeak 3 Mahogany Stepladders in London for the New Library'.[16] By that time, the old library in the medieval quadrangle had been emptied of its books and partitioned as rooms for the jurist fellow Robert Vansittart, part of a flurry of minor works carried out over the next three years: reslating the north quadrangle; further fitting out and decorating the Wharton building; painting the library interior, the common room, the woodwork of the new quadrangle and the warden's lodging; making alterations to the bursary; rebuilding the warden's stable, the college woodhouse, and 'necessary house' on a sliver of adjoining land newly purchased from Magdalen College; and erecting a 'Gothick Pavilion' or summer-house in the college garden. Many, if not most, of the entries authorizing these projects are written and signed by Blackstone.[17]

The same cannot be said of the set of regulations for the Codrington Library which formed the opening entry of the newly-instituted 'Library Minute Book', having been first approved for an initial 12 months by the college meeting in November 1751 (and subsequently renewed). But their opening clause, prescribing that books should be 'ranged in Classes according to their several sciences; and that particular Parts of the Library be allotted to each Class' substantiates Clitherow's reference to Blackstone having both 'hastened the Completion' of the library and 'formed a new Arrangement of the Books, under their respective Classes', so that (in the words of Richard Graves, another former All Souls colleague and friend), 'the books [were] arranged according to a systematical method, which, I believe, was Sir W. Blackstone's own'.[18] Besides instituting a subject classification (in stark contrast to the Bodleian, which continued to sort its bookstock by donor and size of volume), subsequent clauses provided for the compilation of subject and alphabetical catalogues, and the daily attendance of a sub-librarian, overseen by a newly-constituted 'Standing Committee for the Library'. In organizing and regulating the institution

---

[16] Codrington, Acta in Capitulis 1707–53, fos. 180v, 184v.

[17] Codrington, Acta in Capitulis 1707–1753, 182 (19 April 1750), 183v (10, 18 August 1750), 185v (1 January 1751), 186v (12, 15 March 1751), 190 (22 July 1751), 195 (17 December 1751), 196 (6 February 1752), 197 (2 April 1752), 201v (28 December 1752), 202v (10 April 1753); Acta in Capitulis 1753–1800 [unfoliated], 22 August 1753. Blackstone may have written out some of these entries *ex officio*, as senior jurist fellow: Burrows, *Worthies of All Souls*, 409.

[18] Codrington, Acta in Capitulis 1707–1753, fos. 192v–194v (8 November 1751), 199v (6 November 1752): successive annual renewals continued until December 1756, when an amended set of library orders was adopted: Acta in Capitulis 1753–1800 [unfoliated]; Library Minute Book [unfoliated]; Clitherow, viii. Graves, *Triflers*, 56.

which he had effectively brought into existence as Oxford's largest scholarly resource after the Bodleian Library, Blackstone displayed the diligence, energy, and clarity of vision which characterized his impact on college life in general.

To quote Richard Graves again, 'in every situation and department of business or office . . . he made useful discoveries or improvements: not from a busy, innovating disposition; but from his penetrating and extensive views of every subject, he discovered what had escaped the attention of less discerning optics'.[19] After his initial probationary year, in other words as soon as he became a full fellow, Blackstone continuously occupied one or other college office over the next eight years: deputy bursar in 1745, dean of laws in 1746, junior bursar in 1747, dean of laws again in 1748, law lecturer in 1749, dean of laws in 1750, senior bursar in 1750, and law lecturer a second time in 1752.[20] This list is derived from a document drawn up by Clitherow after Blackstone's death, headed 'Sir W.B's Acct of profits of All Souls Fellowship annually'. That title underlines an important point: Blackstone's evident eagerness to take on a wide range of administrative tasks cannot be attributed solely to public-spirited altruism, nor even a radical passion for imposing order on inefficient chaos. For Clitherow's summary shows that, in Blackstone's two stints as bursar, his college income was at least three times what he received in other years, when it never rose above double figures.[21] These personal financial benefits must have been particularly important while he was attempting to establish himself at the London bar, and before he had developed significant alternative sources of income, especially since there is no indication that he was drawing any support from lands or property bequeathed by either of his parents.

The elaborate system of internal government originally laid down for his college in Chichele's founding statutes had inevitably suffered various kinds of change over the centuries. The most comprehensive near-contemporary description of its complex workings is part of a late eighteenth-century 'history' of the college compiled in seven volumes by Thomas Wenman, who became a fellow in 1765 and Regius Professor of Civil Law in 1789. Yet gaps and puzzles remain; a mid-twentieth-century fellow attempting to understand the relative responsibilities of steward and bursar in Blackstone's day was forced to conclude that the 'problem

[19] Graves, *Triflers*, 55.
[20] LMA, ACC 1360/586/1. See Appendix II below. Clitherow uses the college term 'Cas. Pos.' [*Casus Positor*, lit. 'case putter'], more formally 'lecturer in law'.
[21] See Appendix II below.

remains teasingly obscure'.[22] Fortunately for our purposes, it is enough to note that the two major middle-management positions of bursar and dean were duplicated, one for each of the two faculties of arts and law, with an eye to minimizing conflict between their members. These posts were supposedly filled annually by election, although by Wenman's time and possibly before, the lucrative senior bursarship was occupied in rotation, 'taking away that contention and ill-will, which a rivalship for the same office so naturally produces'.[23] The two deans were similarly chosen in order of seniority. The narrow statutory electorate for these offices comprised the warden, sub-warden, six senior fellows (three artists, three jurists), plus the deans (for the bursars), and the bursars (for the deans). The bursars' duties were wholly financial; they received the rents of the college estates plus any other income, and managed all college expenditure. The deans were academic officers, charged 'to preserve a strict moral discipline' and to maintain scholarly exercises. In this latter task they were assisted by two lecturers: one in law, the other in natural philosophy, positions not mentioned in the original statutes.

If Blackstone was understandably keen to take on any college post which might augment his income, the tally of offices he held indicates that the warden and fellows of All Souls for their part were not slow to recognize the outstanding administrative abilities of their newest recruit. They subsequently demonstrated high satisfaction with his achievements by electing him to the senior bursarship (the most valuable place at their disposal) only four years after his first stint as bursar. Still earlier evidence of institutional approval was Blackstone's appointment in 1749 to another post, that of 'steward of the manors' or estates steward. Within the warden's gift, although his choice was evidently ratified by the college, this was another non-statutory appointment, which may explain its omission from Clitherow's list.[24] While little trace of Blackstone's activities as dean of law, law lecturer, or deputy bursar survives, his remarkable impact as bursar and steward, the key to his 'ascendancy in college affairs, which lasted for two and twenty years', is still readily visible in the college records.[25]

---

[22] Codrington, Wardens MSS 22–31; G. Faber, *Notes on the History of the All Souls Bursarships and the College Agency* (p.p., n.d. [c. 1950]), 24n; Faber's research appears to have been confined within a narrow compass.

[23] Codrington, Wardens MS 22/2, 146–7, 149, 152, 188, 200, 204–5; 22/3, 214–15.

[24] Codrington, Warden MS 22/3, 221–2; the deed formalizing Blackstone's appointment is now Bodl. MS D.D. All Souls c 266/21. Warden Niblett sought Blackstone's advice on a dispute over college lands in Northamptonshire as early as February 1747: *Letters*, 5–6.

[25] Robertson, *All Souls*, 191.

Among the All Souls archives now deposited in the Bodleian Library is a vellum-bound book, its spine decorated with gold blocking, with a faded and barely distinguishable front-cover title: 'Rental of the Manors of Edgeware and Kingsbury'. This volume was presented to the college in 1952 by a London firm of land agents and surveyors, in whose office it had been, as their covering letter states, 'for a very long time'. The title page, written in Blackstone's clear hand, describes it more fully: 'A Rental of the Manor of Edgeware & Kingsbury with its Members in the County of Middx. Shewing The Names, Abutments, Rents, & Qualities of the several Estates held by Copy of Court Roll. The Owners of those Estates at the Time of the last Court of Survey held A.D. 1631. The present Owners of them, with the date of their Admission, the Fines that have been paid, & the Interest of the respective Tenants. Such Surrenders, Charges, & Incumbrances, as appear in the Court-Rolls. Compiled A.D. 1753 W Blackstone Steward'. A further note in the same hand adds 'NB This Rental was, at the time of its Compiling, diligently compared, with the Court of Survey A.D. 1631, the Court Rolls from thence down to the present Time, and the College Maps; and agrees with them all. WB'. Running to 262 pages, plus a five-page index or 'Table of the Names of the several Lands &c', this manorial terrier lists down the left hand of each page the name(s) and topographical location of each parcel of land, together with its area in acres, rods, and perches: thus for example, the opening entry runs as follows:

oa. 2r. 30p., Broadfield, abutting N. on Millponds, E. on Combes Croft, SW on Pope's Acres. The Grove adjacent . . . Longcroft adjoining to Broadfield, between the two Pope's Acres. Combes Croft abutting N on Milponds, West on Broadfield, E on Millponds (copy), SE on Broke Field.

The names of the tenants follow; both those who held the land in 1631 and currently, while the right-hand margin lists the rent paid. As this information usually takes up at most a few lines on the top half of each page, there was room for Blackstone's successors over the next century and more to update it. In a few instances the original compiler supplied a good deal more explanatory detail, as for example with:

The Lone Field al[ia]s Robbins al[ia]s Lewis Longcroft abutting E on Goodwins Lane, W on Hickharrows, N on Goodwins Lane S on Hallis Croft.
N[ota] The true name of this Field is Robbins; & Lone Field or Long croft is properly that of the Close in Kingsbury (pag. 131) but in 1608 Jonathan Owen, being seised of both, surr[endered] them to Richard Crane, whose son Thomas 1705 surr[endered] his Kingsbury Estate to Edmund Stacey, & Robbins by Mistake, as parcel of that Estate. In 1707 he surr[endere]d his Edgeware Premises to James Marsh, from whom it came to John Franklyn by the name of Lone Field.

Franklyn therefore now holds Robbins under the Name & Rent of Lone Field, & Mary Rawlins holds Lone Field under the Name & Rent of Robbins.[26]

Both in conception and execution, the Edgeware rental typifies Blackstone's hyper-orderly approach to the management of most aspects of everyday life—not least his own—as well as his scholarly interest in getting to the bottom of things. Clitherow specifically refers to the 'constant accurate Knowledge he had of his own Income and Expenses'.[27] One might speculate that such perfectionist zeal for the avoidance and correction of error, especially but not exclusively in regard to financial matters, reflected awareness of the disarray in which the father he had never known left his business affairs, and determination to avoid the same fate. But whether or not an orphan's insecurity underlay or heightened Blackstone's drive to master chaos in whatever form it presented itself, his quest for certainty, method, precision, and regularity undoubtedly achieved results.

A further productive outcome took the form of a treatise on the college accounts compiled as a practical handbook in 1752–3, but not published until the end of the nineteenth century, when it was understandably presented as little more than an antiquarian curiosity.[28] Addressed to his friend Benjamin Buckler, five years older than Blackstone and a fellow of All Souls since 1739, this document purported merely to 'throw together a few Observations with regard to the Method of keeping the Accounts of All Souls College' for the help and benefit of a newly-elected bursar. The medieval charge-and-discharge system of keeping and reconciling accounts, 'rather more minute & tedious in some Instances than could be wished' Blackstone writes, 'in which my good Fortune was pleased to engage me very early, & to continue me for a considerable Time either as an Accomptant, an Assistant, or an Auditor' has recently been described as 'no more than a system of double-entry accounting if in somewhat obscure language'.[29] This may understate its complexity, not to mention the initial difficulty of comprehending what Blackstone termed 'the Variety and Multiplicity of the Books and Articles', how the oddly-named funds and documents under which various forms of income and expenditure were recorded related to each other, and the far-from-transparent conventions under which they operated. If Blackstone's skill in clarifying

---

[26] Bodl. MS D.D. All Souls, c 245 (box marked 'Terriers'), Bundle S, tp, 1, 68, 72, 121.

[27] Clitherow, xxvi.

[28] Codrington, MS 300 (i), p. 44 (dated 1 January 1753; additional holograph annotations at pp. 12v and 47 show Blackstone returning to the text until 1760 at least); *Dissertation on the Accounts of All Souls College, Oxford . . . Presented to the Roxburghe Club by Sir William Anson* (1898).

[29] Ibid., 3–4; Neill, 'Blackstone, Oxford and the Law', 275.

the complexities of terminology and usage does succeed in making it all seem relatively straightforward, part of the reason is the conversational tone and lightness of touch generally maintained throughout what is really a book-keeping manual. There are even some mildly jovial passages, as in the opening paragraph with its reference to:

those venerable Records in the Bursar-house, which had they related to any Branch of Roman Housekeeping, would have made (in the words of that painful Antiquarian Bishop Fleetwood) 'the Salmasius's, the Grœvius's, & the Gronovii almost out of their Wits for very Joy'. That learned Writer seems particularly fond of this Species of Knowledge; he never speaks of old Computus's, College-Rolls, and Bursar's Accounts, without a kind of Rapture & Enthusiasm: though one of his Observations is undoubtedly a serious Truth; that 'if you will now & then relax from Studies of more Attention, to inspect these lighter Matters, they will not make You a less useful Member of your Society'.[30]

Besides carefully conducting readers 'through all the Intricacies of our domestic Oeconomy (a sort of Maze, I confess, yet not without a Plan)', Blackstone cannot altogether resist suggesting some minor technical enhancements. He nevertheless protests that 'in Justice to our Method of Accounts, they seem in general to be admirably constructed for the Purposes they are intended to serve'; indeed, but for two stated exceptions, 'I cannot conceive that any Alteration can possibly be made in them for the better'.[31] The similarity to his later pronouncements on the common law is striking.

The bursars' many duties included renewing tenants' leases of college lands. It appears that one of Blackstone's earlier projects was to compile a 'Book of Renewals', which enabled information about such leases to be 'readily found'.[32] The 'Dissertation' also includes a mildly and some-what atypically boastful recollection that during his first term as bursar he had 'compared all the Leases, then subsisting, with the Rental, and . . . corrected a great many Mistakes; most of them to the disadvantage of the College . . . some of them of near Seventy Years standing'.[33] Such an outcome was doubtless welcomed by his colleagues, even those who might

---

[30] Ibid., 3, 4. W. Fleetwood, *Chronicon Preciosum, or An Account of English Gold and Silver Money* (1745), 7, 92. Fleetwood refers to the humanist classical scholars Claudius Salmasius (1588–1653), J. G. Graevius (1632–1703) and J. F. Gronovius (1611–71); his own pioneering history of prices purports to be addressed to a college fellow.

[31] *Dissertation*, 27–8. An architectural metaphor is also employed in the opening characterization of the accounts as a 'Structure' with 'Foundations' (3).

[32] Codrington, Wardens MS 29, 172: 'Book of Renewals. This was co'posed chiefly by Sir Wm Blackstone'; *Dissertation*, 42.

[33] Ibid. Cf. Graves, *Triflers*, 55: 'When he was of standing in the College to be made Bursar, and he came to inspect the system of accounts, he rectified blunders which had gone on from one generation to another.'

have accepted some responsibility for perpetuating such errors during their own previous terms of office. On the other hand, Blackstone could hardly have endeared himself to his predecessors when he noted against a claim for the sum of 11/6d from the bursars of 1749 that their rightful credit was only 9/4d, 'they having turned over 2s too much in Baker's Rent 1749', while in fact they really owed the college 8d, having omitted to take account of 'Shelwells Cottage 1749 10/– when it appears by their Day Book Dec. 19. that it was paid'. In summarizing the 'Moneys and Bills turned over' to his successors on 23 December 1751, Blackstone noted the sum of four guineas, due from 'The Bursars of 1750 for Mistakes'.[34]

Equally characteristic, if perhaps less likely to cause offence (above stairs, at all events), was his expressed impatience with the defective records of wine stocked in the All Souls cellars, 'very much confused and mistaken, through the Inaccuracy of Servants'. A total reworking was called for, with the accounts 'corrected by the Cash Book which was liable to no Mistakes; & the Quantities being this day examined in person by W. B. Bursar'.[35] Unfortunately even such hands-on intervention did not always produce the desired effect; in 1752, immediately following Blackstone's term of office, the college cellar book records no fewer than 14 dozen bottles of wine as unaccounted for. Yet this is something of an exception, in that Blackstone's administrative initiatives, like his architectural and building projects, seem generally to have yielded positive results, even when the precise nature of their impact may be difficult to trace at this distance, as with his reorganization of the college archives.[36]

Alongside his various activities within the walls of All Souls College, in the late 1740s and early 1750s Blackstone took on an increasingly prominent external role, most notably in resisting the claims on fellowships of candidates who purported to be 'founder's kin', as collateral descendants of Archbishop Chichele.[37] While his own election in 1743 had occurred during a lull in founder's kin applications, the following year Sir Peter Rivers, one of an unusually small field of five candidates, attempted to establish his 'Consanguinity to the Founder', but then evidently decided against appealing to the archbishop of Canterbury as visitor when the college dismissed his claim as 'not sufficiently proved'.[38] In 1745, two of the

[34] Bodl. MS D.D. All Souls c 263, items b, c.
[35] Bodl. MS D.D. All Souls E 331 (unfoliated), 'cellar book', entry dated 23 March 1750/1.
[36] Clitherow, viii: 'finding the Muniments of the College in a confused, irregular State, he undertook and compleated a thorough Search, and a new Arrangement, from whence the Society reaped great Advantage'.
[37] See generally J. Davis, 'Founder's Kin', in *All Souls under the Ancien Régime*, 232–62.
[38] Codrington, Acta in Capitulis 1707–53, fo. 152 (5 November 1744); cf. Simmons List.

ten candidates claimed preference as founder's kin, but further proofs were demanded of both. In the end, one was elected and the other rejected on the grounds that he had failed to produce the requisite genealogical evidence. Next year, his formal appeal against this decision was heard by a panel of three civil lawyers, who found in his favour, despite an 'Objection against his Chastity 4 years before' presumably mounted as a last-ditch defensive gambit by the college. A further consequence of these proceedings was the displacement of three non-kinsman candidates elected as scholar-probationers by the college four months earlier, only two being subsequently reinstated by archiepiscopal mandate.[39] While no founder's kin presented themselves for the next election in November 1746, Blackstone may have begun to turn his attention to the matter before the year was out, since on 23 December 1746 he is recorded as having ordered up in the Bodleian Library two manuscript compilations on the constitution, history, and statutes of All Souls from the collection brought together by the recently-deceased antiquary (and former fellow of All Souls), Bishop Thomas Tanner.[40]

November 1747 saw a bumper crop of 12 candidates, with 5 fellows elected and once again, not a kinsman in sight. But in 1748, Henry Bennet of Balliol College presented his claim of collateral consanguinity well before the election. Although Bennet was the grandson of a fellow admitted as founder's kin earlier in the century and hence himself undeniably related to the founder—if only very remotely, in the thirteenth degree—his case was the subject of a long entry written up by Blackstone in the college register, setting out in detail the various familial relationships the claimant must demonstrate, with all extracts provided from wills and heraldic visitations to be 'properly attested upon Oath by some credible & indifferent witnesses'.[41] Immediately after the formal poll, where Bennet was unsuccessful, a further minute (this time not in Blackstone's hand) noted that he would almost certainly appeal to Thomas Herring, the personable Whig who had been created archbishop of Canterbury a little under a year before. If he did so, a memorandum to the visitor was to be prepared (by persons unspecified, perhaps because Blackstone's principal role was already assumed) stating that 'we do not apprehend that the Preference claimed by Founders Kinsmen is given by the Statutes of the Founder', but even if it were so given, 'Mr Benet has not proved himself a Founders-Kinsman'. On Christmas Eve 1748, following the news that

---

[39] Simmons List; Codrington, Acta in Capitulis 1707–53, fos. 157, 159, 161 (20 September, 4 November 1745, 26 April 1746); LPL, Secker Papers 6, fo. 103v.

[40] Bodl. Lib. Recs. e 555, fo. 11v (23 December 1746); MSS Tanner 153, 340.

[41] Codrington, Acta in Capitulis 1707–53, fo. 173v (7 October 1748).

Bennet had indeed lodged his appeal, Blackstone and Edward Greenly, a civilian proctor, or church court lawyer, were appointed as syndics to represent the college in this case.[42] Meanwhile Blackstone had 'talked over the Matter largely' with the civilian Dr Richard Smalbroke, another former fellow of the college, and reported cheerfully that he 'concurs with us in the Sense we would put on the Statute in question'.[43]

But his optimism about the college's defence against Bennet's appeal proved sadly mistaken. While Blackstone was given access to the Lambeth Palace archives (in order to obtain an attested copy of an injunction by Archbishop John Stafford, Chichele's successor, deemed 'very material' to the college's case), Archbishop Herring showed himself unresponsive to attempts to vary the traditional form of hearing before a panel of ecclesiastical lawyers headed by the dean of the Arches. The problem with this procedure, from Blackstone's and the college's point of view, was that its outcome depended solely upon the assessed validity of pedigrees and other forms of genealogical evidence produced by the appellant. If they were deemed to demonstrate Bennet's kinship to the founder, as they could hardly fail to do, that would be the end of the matter, giving the college no opportunity to introduce any substantive arguments in bar of Bennet's claim. Seeking to avert such an unpalatable outcome, early in February, a formal petition from the college was presented to the archbishop by Blackstone, who almost certainly bore prime responsibility for its drafting. This document asserted that, while the archbishop's commissaries had already assigned a date of hearing to test the validity of Bennet's pedigree, the college had two more pleas 'of much more extensive Consequence'.[44] These were, firstly, that even if the authenticity of Bennet's pedigree were accepted, 'he is too far removed from the Founder to be deemed a kinsman within the meaning of the College Statutes'. And second, that although he might be a founder's kinsman, this fact alone did not make him eligible for a fellowship, since he had not actually been 'previously nominated in the Scrutiny', or in other words, formally proposed for election as a fellow by an existing fellow of the college.[45] Both of these issues should be determined before Bennet was allowed to produce the proofs of his collateral descent from Archbishop Chichele, at a hearing before the current archbishop in person. Further, because one of these points (probably the second) had never before been raised in this context, the college sought leave to have its case, which 'principally depends on the Construction and

---

[42] Ibid., fos 174v (7 November 1748), 175 (24 December 1748); G. D. Squibb, *Founders' Kin: Privilege and Pedigree* (Oxford, 1972), 54, 63–4, 83.

[43] *Letters*, 9.   [44] LPL, Secker 6, fos. 6–7.

[45] Ibid. I am grateful to Paul Brand for clarifying this latter point.

Interpretation of the College Statutes', presented by as many legal counsel, both civilians and common lawyers, as its importance demanded.[46]

In formulating his almost wholly negative response to this petition, as also to Niblett's earlier request for the whole matter to be dealt with in a private hearing, rather than that 'the reasons of our Conduct shall be debated in a publick and solemn manner',[47] Herring was undoubtedly influenced by advice from Dr John Bettesworth, Dean of the Arches, the archbishop's elderly chief judicial officer and one of the two commissaries charged to hear Bennet's appeal. Bettesworth would hardly have shown enthusiasm for proposals tending to marginalize his own role in the proceedings and threatening to expand the role of common lawyers, while also upsetting a well-established line of judicial procedure.[48] Even if outright political partisanship may not have played an overt part in Herring's decision, this ex-Cambridge Whig prelate was unlikely to be predisposed in favour of any proposals emanating from a stronghold of Oxford Toryism.[49] At all events, although Herring did agree to attend the hearing in person, every other request of the college was more or less gracefully declined. So Bennet's appeal inevitably succeeded, with costs awarded against the college, to which he was admitted as a full fellow (since founder's kin did not have to serve the usual probationary year) in June 1749.[50]

Despite the odds stacked against them, Blackstone and a majority of his All Souls colleagues were unwilling to accept that they now faced a wholly intractable situation, or that the force of rational argument might not eventually prevail. At Bennet's appeal, the archbishop had apparently indicated that he would be willing to consider 'such Reasons as could be suggested against the infinite Extension of Consanguinity', if these were presented in a context other than a judicial hearing. Accordingly, in August Blackstone forwarded to Lambeth what he modestly termed 'a rude Essay' on the subject. This sought to show that the college's 'Notions are not so totally void of Foundation as may have been suggested', while

---

[46] Ibid.

[47] Ibid., fos. 1–iv.

[48] Ibid., fos. 3–4v, 5–5v. Bettesworth served as president of Doctors' Commons, the London-based society of civilian advocates, for nearly fifty years: G. D. Squibb, *Doctors' Commons* (Oxford, 1977), 187.

[49] On All Souls and Blackstone's politics, see Chapter 6 below. For Herring's adherence to 'Whig principles' and suspicion of Jacobitism in Tory dress, see *Letters from George III to Lord Bute 1756–1766*, ed. R. Sedgwick (1939), xxiv–xxv.

[50] LPL, Secker 6, fo. 13; Squibb, *Founders' Kin*, 64. A last-ditch petition to the archbishop sought to block Bennet's admission on the grounds that the founder's statutes restricted fellowship elections to early November: Codrington, Appeals etc., Martin no. 589.

if they were mistaken 'they have at least erred upon plausible Grounds', and for 'Reasons, to which they do not apprehend they had ever heard an Answer'.[51] The archbishop apparently acknowledged receipt some three weeks later, in a letter which has not survived, but which may well have encouraged Blackstone and his supporters to draft yet another petition, considerably longer and rather more assertive in substance than its predecessor, if equally deferential in form and tone. In this document, dated 10 October 1749 and delivered to Lambeth by Blackstone and his college colleague Dr Chardin Musgrave, the warden and fellows, 'your grace's humble sons and servants', sought 'Resolution of certain Doubts and Queries of great importance for the future Quiet and Wellfare of our Society'. The first of these questions addressed what Blackstone plainly saw as the fundamental issue: should consanguinity, or kinship, be regarded as 'without end or Boundary', or did it rather cease 'at any certain Period or Degree? If the former, whether it be not necessarily Universal; if the latter, what that certain Period or Degree is?' The remainder dealt with more peripheral but nonetheless highly significant matters, in view of the light they cast both on the college's practices and Blackstone's own concerns. The archbishop was asked to determine whether kinsmen must always be preferred, even 'when inferior to other candidates in Merit'; and again, if kinsmen might be justly excluded on the grounds of lack of 'literary merit', as determined in 'the exercises performed . . . before the Election or by way of subsequent Examination'. Could proofs of kinship be allowed 'other than what would be evidence in a court of law', and whether on appeal, additional evidence of a candidate's pedigree could be admitted 'than what was laid originally before the College'? While none of these questions had received any formal decision in the past, the 'daily Increase of Claimants' (with another claim for election as kinsman already presented and many more believed to be in preparation) necessitated some resolution. For, notwithstanding all the particular cases which had been heard on appeal, 'the College is still in the dark as to the general Rules of Action'. The final paragraph appeared to give the archbishop two choices. Either he could hold, as the college 'most humbly yet ardently' hoped, that consanguinity did not extend indefinitely over all succeeding generations from Chichele's parents and siblings. Or if he did not so decide, 'we shall have the more reason to wish for some positive Determination' on the

---

[51] *Letters*, 10. This document was plainly a draft of the *Essay on Collateral Consanguinity* published anonymously the following year: see below, pp. 90–94. It may have been first compiled as early as the previous year: see the 'Postscript' published by Blackstone in his *Tracts, chiefly relating to the Antiquities and Laws of England* (Oxford, 1771), 193, unless indeed 'Written in 1748' is simply a mistake for '1749'.

other issues, since to admit the claims of collateral consanguinity without such guidance 'in the infinite Latitude required would not only be repugnant to Reason, and the spirit of all laws, but would violate the Letter and frustrate the Intention of their statutes'.[52]

Unfortunately for Blackstone and All Souls, rhetoric and reality were poles apart: the college could only request what the archbishop was under no compulsion to give. Hence Blackstone's strategy, if such it was, did not achieve its immediate objective. Following Dr Bettesworth's written advice that the All Souls petition was 'not only premature, but likewise altogether unreasonable', as well as unprecedented, groundless in terms of the numbers of kinsmen admitted as fellows over the past half-century, and unappreciative of their founder's 'full liberty by the laws of this Land to extend his favour at large to all succeeding generations', the archbishop penned in reply a masterpiece of elegant evasion. He claimed to have 'paid the greatest Regard' to the college's petition, considering it 'as maturely as I can'. But having found 'upon the whole . . . the Matter of the Queries so interesting, so nice, so various, and so full of consequence . . . I think it would be very unbecoming me to proceed to give a general Decision upon any one of them'.[53] Warden Niblett felt obliged to express thanks for some 'very kind Expressions of Affection and Regard', while still wishing, rather lamely, that 'your grace had seen the necessity of giving the college some positive and determinate directions . . . the only means of fixing our future Elections upon a sure and stable foundation'. Dr Bettesworth, on the other hand, characterized the archbishop's answer 'such in all respects and expressed with so much tenderness, as the College ought thankfully to acquiesce in'. If they did not, and rather chose to 'appeal to the Publick, as seems to be intended by the Essays [sic] left with your Grace', as also by 'saying, that they have not hitherto had an answer, I am firmly persuaded a full and satisfactory one will be returned to it'.[54]

Blackstone's *Essay On Collateral Consanguinity, Its Limits, Extent and Duration; More particularly As it is regarded by the Statutes of All Souls College in the University of Oxford* did not appear in print until the following year (and then only anonymously); it attracted little public notice and no immediate refutation. But neither was there a deluge of kinsmen at the November 1749 election. From a smallish field of seven candidates in total, the college elected no fewer than five scholars or probationer-fellows; this unusually large number and proportion may well have reflected a determination to assert their independent electoral prerogative, even in the face

---

[52] LPL, Secker 6, fo. 16.   [53] Ibid., fos. 17–18, 20–21v.
[54] Ibid., fos. 19, 20, 22–22v.

of the potential threat from founder's kin.[55] In 1750, however, two kinsman candidates did come forward; both were rejected, and both appealed
to the visitor, whose powers to intervene in the election of fellows had
already been queried in briefs for counsels' opinions drawn up at mid-year
by Blackstone. He was investigating these cases as early as 15 November
1750, disbursing two guineas for 'Searches, Extracts and Affidavits' at
the College of Arms, where the heralds kept a register of pedigrees of
founders' kin, and a further pound the next day for similar research in the
records at the Tower of London and Rolls Chapel.[56] Formal proceedings
before the archbishop's commissaries sitting at Doctors' Commons began
during the first week of February 1751. Shortly afterwards, All Souls signalled a change of tactics. Yet another petition to the visitor noted that
the college's two syndics (again led by Blackstone) sought to contest the
admissibility of the genealogical evidence presented by the appellants, on
the grounds that this included additional material which had not been
produced to All Souls at the time of the elections. Because determination
of this point would create a significant precedent, the college's 'humble
but earnest Request' was for it to be decided by the archbishop himself,
rather than referred to 'Civilians, however Eminent, however Impartial
they may be Esteemed', since 'the Rules of Evidence in the Roman Law
are in many Points repugnant to the Common Law of the Land'. (That
Dr Blackstone, who had gained his DCL the previous April, was now
as well qualified a civilian as Drs Bettesworth and Paul, who were presiding over the appeals, lends a certain piquancy to this assertion.)[57] The
archbishop returned directly to Blackstone an equivocal response. To the
extent that the issue was merely procedural, he was content to have it
determined by his commissaries. But when the merits of the case came
to be tried, he would 'Endeavour to give the Just weight to every objection that shall be brought to the Pedigrees'. In so far as this answer suggested that the archbishop intended to hear the substance of the college's
objections himself, it was not welcomed by the commissaries.[58] When
Blackstone produced it before them on 25 February they despatched their
actuary or registrar, one Edward Rushworth, to seek from the archbishop

[55] One of these five was Robert Master, a newly-minted BA of Balliol College, who put up a
pedigree in 1749 (see Squibb, *Founders' Kin*, 170) but evidently did not choose to stand for election
as founder's kin: Simmons List; *Al. Oxon.*, ii.926.

[56] Bodl. MS D.D. All Souls, e 266, fo. 9. Codrington, Appeals etc., Martin nos. 572–7.

[57] Ibid: Blackstone paid 'coachhire to Lambeth 5 times & twice to Drs Commons' on 5–6
February 1751. LPL, Secker 6, fo. 26 (18 February 1751); Codrington, Appeals etc., Martin no. 582,
draft copy in Blackstone's hand; *The Catalogue of Graduats &c in the University of Oxford . . . 1747
to . . . 1760* (Oxford, 1760?), 6.

[58] Codrington, Appeals etc., Martin no. 583.

further clarification of his letter to 'Dr Blackiston'(*sic*). More than a fortnight later, Rushworth reported that, having waited on Herring with the
contentious letter to 'Doctor Blakeston'(*sic*), his grace had confirmed that
the intention was for his commissaries to hear 'the previous point'. Rather
than voicing further procedural objections at this stage, the college's other
syndic immediately launched into a lengthy refutation of the evidence
relied on by the appellant Richard Harvey, questioning the authenticity of a purported descent which relied on the testimony of pedigrees in
the 'Heralds' books'.[59] Blackstone then further endeared himself to the
commissaries by forwarding to the archbishop his own petition against
their actuary Rushworth, whom he accused of being the real manager of
Harvey's appeal, although another's lawyer's 'name be made use of to save
Appearances'. Hence Rushworth was clearly disqualified from acting in
Harvey's case, and 'not to be deemed altogether unbiassed' in the other
appeal, it being 'of the very same nature': for 'by the Rules of Law, and
the universal Practice of all Courts, ministerial Officers . . . especially
the Registrars or Actuaries, ought to be entirely free from Connections
with either Party, and superior to all Suspicion of Partiality'.[60] The immediate outcome of these serious allegations is unknown, but Rushworth
was evidently still officiating on behalf of the commissaries in February
1752, when he conveyed their report on the second appellant's case to the
archbishop, who again upheld it and mandated his admission as founder's
kin.[61] Although Harvey's appeal had been upheld much earlier, in May
1751, he did not long enjoy the fruits of his success in what was an arguably
tainted process, being expelled from All Souls for the 'enormous crime' of
'notorious Fornication attended with divers aggravating Circumstances' in
December 1752.[62]

Over the remainder of the decade, Blackstone seemingly took no further active role in repelling founder's kinsmen from All Souls. This was,
in part at least, because no such applications are recorded between 1753
and 1761, even if John Carne, having mounted an unsuccessful candidacy
as a kinsman in 1752, was elected an ordinary fellow the following year.[63]
Nor can it be merely coincidental that Blackstone's departure from All

[59] LPL, Secker 6, fos. 27–8, 31, 32–7 (18, 25 February, 14 March 1751).

[60] Ibid., fo. 42 (undated). Blackstone endorsed his autograph draft of this petition 'No Answer':
Codrington, Appeals etc., Martin no. 586.

[61] Ibid., fos. 42–42v (27 February 1752). The second appellant was, confusingly, another Bennet,
Thomas of Wadham College. Codrington, Appeals etc., Martin nos. 598–600.

[62] Ibid., fos.46–46v (20 May 1751). Codrington, Acta in Capitulis 1707–1753, fos. 201–201v (22–23
December 1753).

[63] Simmons List (but note, information gap from 1756–8 inclusive); Squibb, *Founders' Kin*,
66. It would seem that Blackstone advised Carne to withdraw his appeal against his previous

Souls in 1761 heralded a positive avalanche of kinsman candidates. For despite failing to win the three cases he had defended as the college's syndic, Blackstone's unremitting opposition to the claims of founder's kin must have strengthened the resolve of his colleagues, and at least deterred some potential applicants. On the other hand, his attempt to defend the college's position in print seems to have had much less immediate impact. In October 1750, Chief Justice Sir John Willes, himself a former fellow of All Souls, told Warden Niblett that, having read and reread Blackstone's *Essay on Collateral Consanguinity* over the summer, he was still not persuaded, 'tho' he is a very ingenious and learned man, and has said I believe everything, that can be allegded on that side of the question'. Having recently fallen into discussion with 'a very learned Brother of mine', and discovering that this judge was of the same opinion 'greatly confirmed me in my own'.[64] Such judicial scepticism in the face of Blackstone's formidably learned examination of the limits placed on collateral consanguinity by 'civil law, canon law, common law, Norman law and feudal law in relation to successions, tenure by parage, frank-marriage, writs of right *de rationibus parte*, appeals of death, proofs of villenage, prohibitions of marriage, refusing a judge or juror, exceptions to witnesses, maintenance, distribution of personal estates, and general legacies to kindred'[65] need not be entirely ascribed to an authoritarian anti-intellectual reaction against a young man too clever by half. For the problem with Blackstone's central argument is clear enough. If Archbishop Chichele did intend to limit the preference enjoyed by his kinsmen in elections to fellowships at his college, he failed to say so in his founding statutes. While it might be desirable from the college's viewpoint for the visitor to supply that omission by laying down a limit (in terms of degrees of closeness to or distance of relationship from the founder), there was no obvious way to establish exactly what limit would best conform with the founder's imputed wishes, avoiding the unjust exclusion of kinsmen who happened to fall on the wrong side of the line, wherever that line were drawn. So, especially while the college was not visibly overwhelmed by an excess of kinsman fellows

---

non-election as founder's kin, so as to be eligible to stand in the forthcoming election: Acta in Capitulis 1753–1800, 26 October 1753.

[64] Taussig Collection: Willes to [Stephen Niblett], 23 November 1750. Willes's reference in the second paragraph of this letter to 'my thoughts on the queries left with me, which I am afraid you will like no better than my other opinion' may refer to the Blackstone holograph 'Abstract of so much of the Charter of Foundation of All Souls College as may refer to the Elections of Fellows there, or the Power of the Archb[isho]p of Canterbury as Visitor', with Willes's appended answers to three questions: Warden's MS 17.

[65] Squibb, *Founders' Kin*, 64–5.

(and Blackstone admitted early in 1751 that there were then only four such fellows, even though in the mid-1740s there had been for a short time as many as nine together),[66] the case for radical intervention by the visitor was hardly compelling.

Blackstone did not put his name to the first (1750) impression of the *Essay*, although his responsibility for that work can never have been less than an open secret, and it was explicitly acknowledged in his letter forwarding a presentation copy to Archbishop Herring. Nor can there be any doubt of the strength of his commitment to curbing the role of founder's kin in the life of All Souls College. While certainly owing something to a sense of institutional loyalty and resentment of outside interference, Blackstone's commitment to this issue also reflected the urge to make better use of existing resources which characterized all his contributions to college administration.

One final example relates to his role in the organization of the capacious wine cellars which still lie below the Codrington Library, the first such facility established by any Oxford college. The earliest surviving All Souls 'Wine Book' dates from his first term as bursar in 1747, while its opening entry listing the 'Stock of Bursary Wine' seems to be in Blackstone's handwriting. The first 'Cellar Book' dating from the same time includes Blackstone's detailed lists, memoranda, and notes on the operation and stocking of the cellars, including the names and addresses of the college's wine and spirits merchants and the supplier of bottles ('Mrs Batchelor Glass-Maker at Stourbridge, Worcestershire'). There is also an analysis of 'The Expence of a Pipe of Wine', which at just over £39 for 105 gallons could be sold off in bottles to the fellows at 5/6d a gallon, yielding a profit of just under one pound per pipe: 'But note, they must provide their own bottles. This is the Rule for Port Wine.' His contemporary and friend Richard Graves emphasized the importance of this 'seemingly trifling oeconomical plan, during his Bursarship . . . laying in wine by the pipe, in the college cellar, so that the sober part of the college might drink a pint, or even half a pint, of good wine, and return to their studies, without going to the tavern across the street; where the jovial part went after dinner, to drink bad wine; and where they were often tempted, I fear, to loiter a good part of the afternoon'. Encouraging the fellows of All Souls to drink within the walls of their own society, rather than frequenting neighbouring inns and tippling

---

[66] *Letters*, 19–20. Although Blackstone spoke of four kinsman fellows, his detailed list suggests that only two were still fellows in March 1751.

houses, might thus serve the cause of scholarship, while also helping to augment the bursars' profits.[67]

But if Blackstone as college administrator was the committed adversary of confusion, disorder, lethargy, and waste in general, his campaign to restrict privileged access to fellowships on the grounds of descent from the college's medieval founder went further, explicitly seeking to deny the claims of birth, or family, over those of individual academic attainment. As he carefully explained, there might well be 'Gentlemen as well qualified for a Fellowship in Morals, Disposition and Learning, *with* Pedigrees as *without* them; but the Misfortune is, that according to the Doctrine which has hitherto prevailed, they are not obliged to be very eminent in either. Excellence, it seems, is not required in them, whatever it may be in other Candidates; but the weight of a Pedigree is sufficient to overbalance superior Merit.'[68] A sustained defence of academic merit in the unreformed University of Oxford halfway through the eighteenth century may seem an implausible scenario, given the well-known critiques of Edward Gibbon and Adam Smith, to say nothing of the anonymous contemporary claim that 'interest' and 'favour' now determined fellowship elections, largely excluding 'scholars of low condition, whatever be their merit'.[69] Yet if Blackstone's own family background placed him firmly among the middling sort rather than the common people, patronage or lineal-family connections had not hitherto played any noticeable part in his Oxford career, which does seem to have been driven essentially by his own exertion and talents. Nor is it surprising that such a person sought to implement the broadly enlightened, humanistic, and improving principles he espoused not only within, but beyond the walls of his own college.

---

[67] Bodl. MS D.D. All Souls, e 330, 331; Graves, *Triflers*, 56; cf. Doolittle, 12.

[68] *Collateral Consanguinity*, 11. See also his holograph interpolations to the college's answer to the appeal of Thomas Bennet, 29 July 1751, emphasizing that 'the said Appellant was in no Degree equal in Scholastic Merit to the Gentlemen elected by the College, and particularly that his Compositions were mean, his Translations notoriously faulty [and erroneous: *interlined*] and he appeared in the publick Disputations to be so entirely ignorant of the first Rudiments of Logic and Philosophy that [he could not at all enter into ye parts of either Opponent or Respondent: *interlined*] but after a pause of above a quarter of an hour was obliged to be dismissed from his Seat': Codrington, Appeals etc., no. 595.

[69] Anon., *A Series of Papers on Subjects the most Interesting to the Nation in General, and Oxford in Particular* (1750), 13.

CHAPTER 6

'The General Benefit of the University at Large' (1750–53)

HAVING acquired his bachelor's degree in civil law without first graduating in arts, Blackstone had to wait a further five years before he could take the higher degree of DCL, or the doctorate in laws, in April 1750.[1] The reason he bothered (and paid a fee of more than £30) to do so, even while keeping up at least a cursory presence in Westminster Hall, was not to qualify to practise as a civil lawyer, but rather because the higher degree would admit him to Convocation. As the main deliberative assembly of Oxford's permanent academic members, Convocation elected the two 'burgesses' who represented the university in the House of Commons, together with numerous professors and other university officers, including even the chancellor: its titular, symbolic, and not entirely powerless head. Convocation also provided a forum for the doctors and masters, fellows of colleges and halls, as distinct from the university's ruling oligarchs, the heads of houses, vice chancellor and proctors assembled in the weekly meetings of their Hebdomadal Board.[2] This chapter traces Blackstone's initial ventures into this larger academic world.

---

[1] *HUO*, 486–7, 602; in addition to their required standing, candidates for the DCL supposedly delivered six lectures, and participated in college exercises. There is no evidence as to how, if at all, Blackstone fulfilled these formal requirements.

[2] The 1636 table of fees, still current in 1750, provided that a resident graduate with an annual income of £40 or more paid £31.3/4 to 'supplicate' for the DCL: OUA SW1/1. W. R. Ward, *Georgian Oxford* (Oxford, 1958), 3–6; *HUO*, ch. 8. Clitherow, xi: as DCL his subject 'became a Member of the Convocation, which enabled him to extend his Views beyond the narrow Circle of his own Society, to the general Benefit of the University at large'.

I

Having served as royalist headquarters during the first English civil war, and subsequently the venue for Charles II's last parliament, Oxford almost inevitably emerged from the fierce political and sectarian strife which followed the Glorious Revolution as a Tory-Jacobite stronghold. While the university's traditional Church-and-King identification continued unabated after 1714, for another generation the monarch toasted by dons and undergraduates was as likely to be an exiled Stuart as a crowned Hanoverian. When the first King George came over, similar sentiments had been much in evidence at the sister university, but Cambridge's Whiggish and latitudinarian-Low Church reputation soon reasserted itself.[3] Even so, there is nothing to suggest that Blackstone was sent to Oxford rather than Cambridge for party-political reasons, as distinct from family ties (the Biggs were strongly represented at New College, Oxford) and geographical–logistical considerations (Cambridge traditionally tended to recruit from the north and east of the country, Oxford from the south and west, although both attracted Londoners in large numbers). William's father may well have been a City tradesman Tory, but he had no direct say in the choice of his posthumous son's baptismal name, which echoed that of the Dutch (albeit Stuart) invader of 1688, William of Orange. Other hints that his mother and her family did not wholly share her deceased husband's politics include the mobilization of Sir Robert Walpole's patronage to gain William a valuable place at Charterhouse, the medal depicting the republican poet Milton presented by the Whig MP William Benson, and Thomas Hearne's description of Mary Blackstone's elder brother as 'a great Whig'.[4] So while William certainly absorbed the predominant local Toryism after his arrival in Oxford, the lingering effect of familial influence may at least begin to explain some of the difficulty experienced by both contemporaries and later historians in attempting to characterize his political beliefs and principles.

The blurred nature of party allegiance and identity around the middle years of the eighteenth century adds further complexity to that task. In 1748, an anonymous commentator suggested that Whigs and Tories 'bear so near a Resemblance one with the other, that the Difference between them is not worth the Tossing up for; a Whig, out of Place, making an

---

[3] P. K. Monod, *Jacobitism and the English people, 1688–1788* (Cambridge, 1989), 275–7.
[4] Cf. Doolittle, 15; Chapter 2 above, pp. 21, 25; *Remarks and Collections of Thomas Hearne. Vol. VIII*, 314. See also Ward, *Georgian Oxford*, 111.

exceedingly good tory; and a tory, give him a Place, turning out a staunch Whig'.[5] Perhaps unsurprisingly, the very term 'Tory' was losing favour with those for whose alignments and views it might still seem entirely appropriate. Thus in Oxford, both the local (pro-Tory) newspaper, and its readers, typically referred to the 'Old Interest' to characterize those who might otherwise have identified themselves as 'patriot', 'country', or 'opposition' supporters of the university's threatened independence, in the face of the Whig administration's long-standing efforts to impose its influence on this prime Anglican seminary and élite lay finishing school.[6] Of course, there were alternative perspectives. Their opponents—and Oxford's Tory citadel always contained a substantial minority of ministerial clients and followers—saw, or claimed to see, obstinate disaffection, rank disloyalty, and treasonable Jacobitism underlying such purported professions of academic principle. This view was also widely held outside the university. How far such accusations and suspicions were justified is now impossible to determine. But if the government and its advocates gained some political mileage from denigrating Oxford's public image in this way, the university continued to provide those critics with ample grounds for doubting its fidelity to the Hanoverian regime. We might instance, for example, the fiery and perhaps deliberately ambiguous public speeches of the Jacobite fellow-traveller Dr William King on such grand occasions as the public inauguration of the Radcliffe Library in April 1749.[7]

Blackstone joined Convocation at a crucial stage in the university's political history. Oxford scholars had not flocked to the standard of Prince Charles Edward Stuart on his ill-fated march into England in 1745. Yet the university's failure to lend more than limited and token support to a loyal association promoted by the county's leading Whig magnates in response to this invasion was taken—at least by those predisposed to believe the worst—as confirming that institution's crypto-Jacobite allegiance. William himself may have encountered active Jacobitism in his early years at Pembroke College, although there is no hint of any sympathy for the 'Rebels' in his comment to his uncle early in 1746 that even victories would reduce their numbers, 'while we are continually recruiting'.[8] Two years later he found himself standing surety in the sum of £20 for the good behaviour of Rowney Noel, a junior All Souls colleague, who admitted

[5] [A Gentleman of the Middle Temple], *De Toryismo, Liber: Or, A Treatise on Toryism* (1748), ii.
[6] J. J. Sack, *From Jacobite to Conservative* (Cambridge, 1993), 50–51.
[7] Ward, *Georgian Oxford*, 177–80. B. Harris, *Politics and the Nation: Britain in the Mid-Eighteenth Century* (Oxford, 2002), 67–8.
[8] Ibid. 37; Bodl. Gough 138 (13); J. C. D. Clark, *English Society 1660–1832* (Cambridge, 2000), 242n; *Letters*, 4.

being part of a late-night demonstration (or drunken riot) outside Exeter College, then perhaps Oxford's leading centre of Whiggery, featuring two musicians who played a Jacobite song ('The king shall enjoy his own again') while Noel relieved himself against the college gate.[9] Since Blackstone was serving that year as dean of laws, his role may have been at least partly *ex officio*. At all events, Noel was not expelled from the university, unlike the ringleaders on this occasion, who were repeat offenders and about to go on trial in King's Bench for a similar performance earlier in the year, following an official information filed by the attorney general, overriding the university's own disciplinary processes. Blackstone attended and took brief notes of their trials and notably lenient sentences, which included nominal fines, good behaviour bonds, and imprisonment for two years or until their fines were paid and sureties found.[10] The real target of the ministry's wrath was the incumbent Vice Chancellor Dr John Purnell, who also incurred an information brought by the attorney general for neglect of duty in not sufficiently punishing the Jacobite revellers. This prosecution was dropped as soon as the unhappy and ill Purnell made his appearance in court, but then revived, only to be countermanded again on 17 November, two days before the trial was due to commence. Blackstone 'with great Satisfaction' reported the news of the stay of proceedings, that 'triumphant Event', to his college friend George Bingham: 'after all the big Words and Blusterings of our great Men'—presumably a reference to Henry Pelham, Lord Chancellor Hardwicke, and other ministers— 'the Abuse that has been so plentifully scattered both on the University, and its Magistrate', and worst of all 'a very heavy Expence with which an innocent Man has been saddled', so 'has this mighty Affair ended, in a manner which does as much credit to its abettors, as the manner in which it was begun and continued'.[11] But in fact, the end was still to come, as Blackstone discovered on the last day of Michaelmas term 1748, when Attorney General Ryder moved for a peremptory rule 'directed to the proper officers of the university to permit their books, records and archives to be inspected, in order to furnish evidence against the vice-chancellor'. Fortunately for the university, King's Bench refused that motion and 'only granted a rule to shew cause'. This was debated the following term, when the judges accepted the contention of the university's counsel, that to grant such a rule would effectively force the accused to produce evidence against himself. Blackstone's extensive case notes conclude with the

[9] Bodl. MS. Dep. b 48, fo. 46; *HUO*, 121.
[10] *Reports*, i. 37 (*R v Whitmore and Davies*); *The Yale Edition of Horace Walpole's Correspondence*, ed. W. S. Lewis (New Haven, 1937–83), xx. 6 and n.
[11] *Letters*, 8.

indignant observation that 'this extraordinary motion seemed only to have been intended, as an excuse for dropping a prosecution, which could not be maintained; and it was accordingly dropped immediately after, having cost the defendant to the amount of several hundred pounds'.[12] Fifteen years later, the radical Wilkeite bookseller–publisher John Almon recalled the government's cat-and-mouse treatment of Vice Chancellor Purnell as 'a politico legal game', a 'Star-chamber weapon' resorted to 'because there was no evidence to convict', but 'in order to oppress'.[13]

Tension continued between Oxford and the Pelham administration, which only reluctantly abandoned plans for legislative intervention in the university's affairs when the high political costs of such a venture became apparent. Not all members of the ministry may have taken the Jacobite threat at Oxford equally seriously, but concern on this score could reinforce long-standing unease about the overall state of the university as an educational institution, a subject which was still attracting much attention from journalists and pamphleteers, as well as members of parliament.[14] Blackstone did not directly involve himself in these controversies, except in so far as his All Souls campaign against founder's kin addressed broad issues of academic autonomy and integrity. But towards the end of 1750, the prospect of a by-election resulting from the elevation to the peerage of one of the university's two MPs launched Blackstone into the mainstream of Oxford academic politics.

As with most parliamentary constituencies in eighteenth-century England, such elections rarely resulted in a contested poll, but were rather decided by prior agreement among potential rival candidates, their patrons, and supporters. However when 'Publick Elections' for the university's MPs did occur, they were said to be 'usually entred upon here with a Precipitation and Passion that are perfectly suprizing in Liberal persons', and 'conducted throughout with . . . Eagerness and Acrimony'.[15] In this particular contest, Blackstone was the sole identifiable figure among a shadowy group referred to by a contemporary participant-observer as 'the All Souls people', who had evidently decided that the university's next parliamentary representative should be Sir Roger Newdigate. A cultivated, energetic, independent-minded landed proprietor with estates in Middlesex and Warwickshire, Newdigate, then in his early thirties, was an alumnus of University College. Although both Newdigate's degrees

[12] *Reports*, 38–46; *Walpole's Correspondence*, xx. 6.

[13] [J. Almon], *A Letter Concerning Libels* (1764), 8.

[14] Harris, *Politics and the Nation*, 37; Ward, *Georgian Oxford*, 175–87. Cf. *Correspondence of John, Fourth Duke of Bedford* (1842), i. 594 (Newcastle to Bedford, 31 December 1748).

[15] [Anon.], *A Letter to the Rt. Hon. Henry Lord Viscount Cornbury* (1751), 16: Bodl. G.A. Oxon. 8° 6 (6).

were honorary ones, this classical scholar and virtuoso possessed two further attractions for Blackstone and his friends: impeccable High-Church
Tory credentials, and availability, having lost his previous parliamentary
seat as the member for Middlesex in the anti-Jacobite swing of the 1747
general election. After indirect initial approaches via a Newdigate relative
whom Blackstone may have met in London, and James Clitherow, another
Middlesex landowner whose son (also James) had just been elected to an
All Souls fellowship, Blackstone introduced himself to Sir Roger by letter
in mid-January 1751.[16]

The first problem was to convince Newdigate that, in case of a contested
election, he had sufficient support to avoid any danger of splitting the 'Old
Interest', thereby letting in a candidate less inclined to uphold the university's autonomy in the face of ministerial pressures. Hence it was necessary
to explain in some detail how an original planned 'Compromise' (whereby
the backers of Sir Edward Turner—another former MP who had also lost
his seat in 1747—would have been persuaded to support Newdigate in
order to avoid a contested election which their candidate could not win)
foundered when a younger son of the aristocratic Harley family was 'proposed by the Gentlemen of Christ Church' as a third candidate. In this
situation, while canvassing was 'going on with all imaginable Assiduity',
Blackstone set out for Newdigate's benefit a detailed analysis of likely
voting by college, concluding that he could 'reckon above 200 sure Votes'
from a total of just over 400, 'including above 100 ministerial Men' (in
other words, careerists or Whigs).[17] Newdigate's draft reply indicated that
he was not wholly convinced. In response, Blackstone supplied further
details of the continuing negotiations between the various camps, focus-
ing on the unwillingness of either of the other candidates' supporters to
guarantee that all their votes would go to Newdigate if their own nominee
withdrew. In this situation, he argued, Newdigate's 'standing a contested
Election here' would not 'prejudice the old Interest', but rather ensure its
preservation, since the 'common Enemy is, almost to a Man, listed under
one or other of your Antagonists' Banners'.[18] True, the same could be
said of 'not a few of Our old Friends'; but 'the main Body is still united in
your Support, and we think ourselves absolutely sure of Success' should
all three stand, whereas 'should we think of retreating at present, we give
up the Point to those Persons, who will always be ready to disturb our

---

[16] Doolittle, 15–16; *Tory and Whig: the Parliamentary Papers of Edward Harley . . . and William Hay*, ed. S. Taylor and C. Jones (1998), 266–7; *ODNB*, s.v. Newdigate, Sir Roger.

[17] *Letters*, 14–15.

[18] *The Correspondence of Sir Roger Newdigate of Arbury, Warwickshire*, ed. A. W. A. White (Dugdale Soc., 37, 1995), 45–6; *Letters*, 16–17.

Tranquillity'. Newdigate allowed himself to be persuaded by these martial assurances, together with a following hasty note to the effect that the election date had been set for the end of the month, and concerted efforts were under way to whip in non-resident voters.

On the day of the poll, Newdigate's actual majority proved slightly less comfortable than Blackstone had predicted, possibly (as he claimed), for the 'bad Reason' of 'the whole body of Whigs, a very few excepted, uniting' in Harley's support. It was nevertheless sufficiently convincing for an elated and clearly relieved Newdigate to express his 'greatest satisfaction' at the preservation of the 'General Interest' in the face of Whig 'treachery'.[19] That 18 of the 21 votes cast at All Souls went to Newdigate points to the personal ascendancy Blackstone had now achieved within his own college. Moreover, his central role in orchestrating this intense electoral campaign undoubtedly enhanced his university-wide profile, if perhaps not his popularity among supporters of the defeated candidates, one of whom described the 'All Souls people' as having 'behaved very ungenerously'.[20] Yet while Blackstone's determined and well-calculated efforts on Newdigate's behalf may have aroused local resentment, they had also gained him the friendship of a man who remained one of Oxford's representatives at Westminster throughout the rest of Blackstone's life.

At their first meeting, which seems to have occurred in London only after the election, the young lawyer was still in his late twenties, while his visitor was just four years older.[21] Since Newdigate's diary entries provide only a brief and often cryptic record of events, while most of his letters to Blackstone do not survive, our knowledge of their relationship is far from complete. Yet, besides proximity in age and political outlook, the two were plainly drawn together by mutual aesthetic, antiquarian, intellectual, and literary interests, as well as a shared attachment to the University of Oxford. Newdigate also appears to have possessed a sociable disposition, with a wide range of friends and acquaintances, and a genuine respect for men of learning. An archetypal country-squire backbencher, determined to maintain his independence from party leaders and ministers alike, the very fact that he had no great store of favours or patronage to dispense may indeed have helped bridge the gulf in wealth and status which otherwise separated the two men. At the same time Newdigate could and did introduce Blackstone to a wider sphere, both in London and at home in Warwickshire, where under his direction, Arbury Hall was being transformed into what one authority terms 'the most impressive

[19] Ibid. 16–19; *Newdigate Correspondence*, 47, 50.   [20] *Tory and Whig*, 266.
[21] Newdigate Diary, 16–17, 24 February 1751.

eighteenth-century Gothic house in England'.[22] Their relationship was actively maintained over nearly three decades, even despite some apparent differences of opinion on church–state relations which developed during the 1770s.[23]

Notwithstanding a gap in their surviving correspondence between the Oxford University by-election and July 1753, Newdigate's diary shows that the two men met in London for breakfast on 1 March and 29 November 1751, with another unspecified contact on 7 May. These appear to have been essentially social gatherings, but early in 1752, Newdigate's Chancery suit against his brother-in-law John Ludford brought Blackstone together with Newdigate's other counsel for several consultations, as well as a walk through St James's Park to Westminster Bridge. On 13 March, Newdigate dined with Blackstone, Peregrine Palmer (a former fellow of All Souls, now the university's other parliamentary representative), and Dr Thomas Winchester, fellow of Magdalen College, who was about to acquire the young Edward Gibbon as his (notably unappreciative) tutorial pupil. On 21 March, the day before he left London for Oxford, Blackstone was invited by Palmer to another dinner attended by Newdigate and five other guests. Blackstone appeared as counsel at the hearing of *Newdigate v Ludford* before the Lord Chancellor in Lincoln's Inn Hall on Friday 17 April, speaking 'very short but well enough', according to his client. A consultation on 22 April preceded the final hearing, where despite having 'always mentioned me with honour' and contrary to the expressed expectations of all his counsel, the Chancellor finally dismissed Newdigate's petition, in a speech lasting an hour and a half. Fortunately, Newdigate professed himself 'very easy under this disappointment'.[24]

Early in July, Newdigate visited Oxford for Encaenia, when feasts and speeches marked the culmination of the academic year, calling on Blackstone at All Souls even before paying his respects to the vice chancellor, taking supper with Blackstone and a small party of dons that evening, coming again to Blackstone's rooms for supper the following night, then next morning viewing the Codrington Library and dining in the college hall (although his hosts on this occasion were evidently the bursars and sub-warden). In the next month Newdigate more than repaid this Oxford hospitality by entertaining Blackstone and his junior All Souls

---

[22] G. Tyack, *Warwickshire Country Houses* (Chichester, 1994), 9; A. Lewer, 'Sir Roger Newdigate and Sir William Blackstone: a forgotten friendship' (1995); I am grateful to Andrew Lewer for a copy of this unpublished paper.

[23] Ch. 13 below, pp. 277–8.

[24] Newdigate Diary; *Newdigate Correspondence*, 62–5.

colleague, future brother-in-law, and biographer James Clitherow for nearly a fortnight at Arbury. Besides visits and meals with local notables, attending the Lichfield races, and stopping on the way home to inspect the cathedral and view the Norman keep of Tamworth Castle, Blackstone enjoyed the opportunity for some antiquarian field work. His 'Plan of the Chapel at Nuneaton', part of the nearby ruined abbey, survives among Newdigate's papers, with Sir Roger's admiring annotation: 'Made out by the very extraordinary Genius of Wm Blackstone, Dr of Laws'.[25]

Newdigate may also have admired Blackstone's untitled contribution to the volume of obituary verses published by the university following the death of Frederick, Prince of Wales, in March 1751. We do not know whether he was in on the secret that this poem was the work of Blackstone rather than James Clitherow, to whom it is credited in the collection, but who revealed the true author in his preface to Blackstone's posthumously-published *Reports*. Quite possibly he did not, since well after Blackstone's death, but before the *Reports* appeared in print, Robert Lowth (himself a poet of repute) referred to 'Mr Clitherow's Poem on Frederick Prince of Wales' as 'the best in that, or perhaps in any Collection of the kind'.[26] It was not unusual for such academic anthologies, customarily issued to mark royal births, marriages, and deaths, to include verses composed by someone other than their nominal author, especially in the case of 'the rather high proportion of sons of peers and baronets whose names, with particulars of parentage, appear beneath these Latin odes and elegies'.[27] Blackstone plainly had no such motive for concealing his authorship; apart from anything else, the language of his poem is patriotic English, although most of its companion pieces were in Latin or Greek. It seems more likely to have reflected the same concern to present himself as fully committed to a legal career which had earlier prevented the publication of his architectural treatise, and also ensured that when his first two books did appear in print, neither bore his name on the title page.

Newdigate would certainly have approved of the general sentiments expressed in this tribute to the prince, whose falling-out with George II had made him a major focus of opposition hopes, as well as the designated ally and patron of the University of Oxford during its political difficulties following the Jacobite scandals of the late 1740s. Who, asked the poem, shall now 'prop, like him, *Britannia's* falling State?' Still more

[25] Newdigate Diary; Warwickshire County RO, CR 136/B2587; see Plate 11.
[26] *Epicedia Oxoniensia in Obitum Celsissimi et Desideratissimi Frederici Principis Walliae* (Oxford, 1751), sig. 9 Hr. J. Nichols, *Literary Anecdotes of the Eighteenth Century* (1812–15), i. 644; *ODNB*, s.v. Lowth, Robert.
[27] *HUO*, 519–520.

to the point, who else shall 'Rear from the Dust fair Learning's laurel'd Head', and 'to Arts their pristine Honour bring'? These elegantly turned tributes to the departed Frederick's non-military virtues (the contrast with his royal father's notorious philistinism would hardly have escaped contemporary readers) are followed by a recounted vision of one *'Lorenzo'*, to whom appears a quartet of 'royal Shapes on Iv'ry Thrones'. These are Frederick and three of his predecessors: Edward the Black Prince, Henry VII's son Prince Arthur, and James VI and I's elder son Henry. Having welcomed the newcomer to the 'Mansions of the Good and Great', where 'Crowns immortal wait on virtuous Deeds', the Black Prince expresses on behalf of his colleagues some apprehension that the consequences of Frederick's death may be no less dire than those which followed their own 'untimely Fate', when 'Heav'n's dread Vengeance smote each sinful Age'. However, in this case, Heaven fortunately agrees that Frederick's death has itself already caused more than enough earthly woe. So as daylight breaks the 'unbodied Phantoms' fade, and 'The fond illusion all dissolves in air'.[28] While its waking dream format is reminiscent of *The Pantheon*, this shorter poem seems better controlled and more effectively realized, notwithstanding the absurdly extravagant tributes to 'poor Fred', once allowance is made for the various aesthetic, linguistic, political, and social conventions within which it was written.

II

But Blackstone was by now more concerned with establishing his reputation as a man of business and law than as a man of letters and poetry. Despite his failure to gain more than the occasional brief at the Westminster bar, we have already seen that, by 1750, he was playing an active role in discussions involving the vice chancellor and the university's legal advisers about the university's rights to license traders in the city of Oxford. In the following year, he helped promote a 'Scheme of Amendment' for the road through Berkshire from Wallingford to Faringdon via Sparsholt (a project naturally supported by his uncle Seymour Richmond), giving evidence before a House of Commons committee set up to enquire into the necessary private bill, and manoeuvring successfully to neutralize John Morton, MP for Abingdon, who saw the proposal as potentially threatening the interests of his own constituents, but nevertheless 'owned we had so artfully managed the Matter, that he did not know how or where to

[28] *Epicedia Oxoniensia*, sig. 9Hr.

begin an opposition'.[29] His assiduous efforts at Doctors' Commons and Lambeth Palace to restrict the rights of founder's kin to All Souls college fellowships were outlined in the previous chapter. Early in 1753, the leading Tory barrister Randle Wilbraham called on Blackstone's expert knowledge of academic or university law in relation to a controversial and politicized case arising from efforts by the duke of Newcastle, chancellor of the University of Cambridge, to impose a more rigorous disciplinary regime on that institution. Responding to Wilbraham's request for his views on 'a Question . . . of great Concern I apprehend to the Constitution of both our Universities', Blackstone provided an opinion, running to well over two thousand words in the surviving draft, on the rights of appeal from sentences handed down by Oxford's vice chancellor 'in Matters of Academical Discipline'.[30]

Whereas the Cambridge case originated with a concerted protest against Newcastle's new regulations, particularly one requiring undergraduates to be back inside their colleges by eleven o'clock every night, the Oxford issue concerned a senior member of Christ Church. Dr William Lewis, 'labouring under an Imputation of a very bad Kind' in respect to his indiscreet dealings with a choirboy, had been called before the vice chancellor and censured, but not committed to trial in the university (or chancellor's) court.[31] Despite protests at the apparent leniency of these proceedings, Vice Chancellor Purnell refused to allow the matter to proceed any further. The validity of the vice chancellor's position was subsequently upheld by a vote in Convocation. Blackstone, however, argued against what was indeed the orthodox and generally accepted view, by maintaining that appeals from the vice chancellor lay 'as well in Matters of Discipline as in any other Cause'.[32] He listed five grounds for this opinion, ranging from the most general—as for instance that the university's 'good Order' would be best preserved if appeals were allowed, thereby guarding against the possibility of wrongful decisions in particular cases on the one hand or 'any seditious Clamours' on the other—to the very particular. Indeed the bulk of his opinion depends upon close readings of the relevant university charters and statutes, and the assertion that a right of appeal

[29] Above, Chapter 4, p. 73; *Letters*, 20–21 and references there cited.

[30] *Letters*, 23–8; D. A. Winstanley, *The University of Cambridge in the Eighteenth Century* (Cambridge, 1922), 199–222; P. Searby, *A History of the University of Cambridge Vol. III 1750–1870* (Cambridge, 1997), 354–5.

[31] [G. Wilmot], *A Serious Enquiry into some Late Proceedings in the University of Ox[for]d* (1751); [W. Lewis], *An Answer to the Serious Inquiry* (n.d., [1752?]); [G. Wilmot], *A Letter to ------------ M.D.* (1752).

[32] Cf. T. Chapman, *A Further Inquiry into the Right of Appeal* (Cambridge, 1752), 76: 'even in our sister university of Oxford, no appeal is permitted in matters of discipline'.

'if not given in express words, is yet strongly implied'. Notably greater sympathy for civil law evidentiary procedures appears than in his previous arguments over founder's kin; it now suited his case to point out that, while there were good reasons for the differences between common and civil law in this regard, the latter (which was 'the Rule of the University') permitted appeals on questions of fact because it employed evidence in the form of written depositions assessed by a single judge, rather than the once-and-for-all decisions of a sworn jury on oral testimony. Overall, Blackstone's opinion could be seen as supporting those Cambridge dons who had resisted what they saw as politically motivated interference with the internal affairs of their university, their Oxford counterparts who feared a similar fate, and more generally, the broad body of academics as against the university's chief executive officer. In short, his position was a radical one, in that it rejected established opinion and precedent, while also upholding the immediate interests of the governed rather than the governors.

Concluding with a modest and not necessarily insincere avowal of his willingness to be corrected by Wilbraham's 'better Judgment', Blackstone added a significant postscript: 'What is become of our Prof. of Law, who is . . . a standing Member of the Committee for dubious Appeals, and might therefore give you more authentic Information, Mr Gould upon the Delegacies can give better Account than I'. Exactly what Gould might have been able to tell Wilbraham is unclear. But the gratuitous reference to Oxford's chair of civil law, vacant since the death of Dr Henry Brooke on 24 November 1752, indicates that the subject of Brooke's successor was near the front of Blackstone's mind some six weeks later. Indeed he seems to have been considering his own prospects for this position at least as early as July 1752, when Brooke was still alive but doubtless visibly ailing. This we know from a remarkable letter written to Newdigate a year later, on 3 July 1753. Here Blackstone announced his intentions both 'no longer to attend the Courts at Westminster, but to pursue my Profession in a Way more agreeable to me in all respects, by residing at Oxford', and 'to engraft upon this Resolution a Scheme which I am told may be beneficial to the University as well as to myself', of presenting a course of lectures on the common law. He goes on to refer to 'the Thoughts I was taught to entertain of the Professorship; for which also I found I wanted *some* Qualifications; as you rightly guessed, at this time twelvemonth'.[33] This takes us back to Newdigate's visit to the Oxford Encaenia at the beginning of July 1752, when he must have warned Blackstone not to raise his

---

[33] *Letters*, 29 (underlining in original italicized).

hopes too high about the possibility of succeeding Brooke as professor of civil law. For while most Oxford professorships were elective offices filled by Convocation, appointments to the Regius Chairs (of which law was one) were made by the Crown on the advice of the government of the day. Under the first two Hanoverians, such places, like most other jobs in the gift of ministers, were available only to reward political friends and buy off opponents. Since Blackstone's loyalties were firmly and publicly identified with those of the Old Interest and Newdigate as its representative, he could hardly have expected to be offered the Regius Chair unconditionally. That he did receive an offer with strings attached, which he effectively rejected because he was unwilling to abandon his Tory allegiance and identity, seems highly probable. Some such incident presumably provided the basis of a story first printed many years later by the Lincoln's Inn conveyancer John Holliday, in his biography of another famous contemporary lawyer—Blackstone's senior by nearly 20 years—William Murray, later earl of Mansfield, and chief justice of King's Bench from 1756 to 1788.

According to Holliday's account, which has been widely followed and embroidered by subsequent writers, Blackstone 'was by Mr Murray introduced and warmly commended to the duke of Newcastle' in connection with the vacant Oxford chair. However, when Newcastle decided to press Blackstone on his political principles, the following dialogue ensued:

'Sir, I can rely on your friend Mr Murray's judgment as to your giving law-lectures in good style, so as to benefit the students; and I dare say, that I may safely rely on you, whenever any thing in the political hemisphere is agitated in that university you will, Sir, exert yourself on our behalf'. The Answer was 'Your Grace may be assured that I will discharge my duty in giving law-lectures to the best of my poor abilities'. 'Aye! Aye!' replied his Grace hastily, 'and your duty in the other branch too'. Unfortunately for the new candidate he only bowed assent and a few days afterwards he had the mortification to hear that Dr Jenner had been appointed the civil-law professor.[34]

Sadly, for all its circumstantial detail, Holliday's story is too good to be true as it stands. Apart from the verbatim reporting of what would presumably have been a confidential conversation, this purported interchange supposedly occurred only just before the appointment of Jenner, which was not announced until April 1754—that is, nine months after Blackstone wrote to Newdigate, having by then clearly abandoned his former hopes of the chair (without, so he claimed, either disappointment or resentment). Yet Murray may well have suggested to Newcastle that Blackstone could be worth considering as a possible candidate, despite

[34] J. Holliday, *The Life of William Late Earl of Mansfield* (1797), 88–9.

his known political stance and relative youth (professorial appointments under the age of 30 at mid-eighteenth-century Oxford were highly unusual, despite one recent precedent in the election of the 29-year old William Hawkins as professor of poetry in 1751). Nor in view of his own and the government's concern with the political and disciplinary state of both universities is it unlikely that Newcastle should have sought to find out whether this prominent Oxford Tory might be tempted to come on board in return for the prize of an Oxford chair. Further, on hearing of his refusal to accept such an offer, Murray could well have advised Blackstone (as Holliday's story continues) 'to sit down at Oxford to read law-lectures to such students as were disposed to attend him'.[35]

Quite when Blackstone first decided to offer a lecture course at Oxford is not clear. His former All Souls colleague and friend George Bingham later recalled that, after Brooke's death, a plan had been floated for 'introducing the study of the common law into the university, under the direction of a resident professor, and Dr Blackstone was the person proposed; but for reasons I apprehend merely ministerial, this plan was laid aside, and another appointed. Yet this did not prevent him from reading a course of private lectures under the sanction of the vice chancellor . . .'.[36] No other account of quite such a proposal at this time has come to light, and it may be that Bingham's memory deceived him in one or more particulars. But his recollection is not wholly implausible, especially since Thomas Wood's arguments for introducing common law studies to the academic curriculum had been circulating in print since the first decade of the century.[37] At all events, his version suggests that Blackstone had begun seriously planning his lectures by late 1752, if not as early as the middle of that year. Blackstone's own July 1753 letter to Newdigate states that his 'Scheme for Lectures' began when the prospect of his filling the Regius Chair was first put forward. But of course that chair was in civil law, so any lectures would have needed to include a substantial civilian component, even if they were also intended from the start (along the lines suggested by Wood) to embrace the common law as well.

It was just at this point that a second potential Oxford job appeared on the horizon, providing yet further incentive for Blackstone to quit the London bar. Charles Viner, the eccentric Oxford alumnus who amassed a

---

[35] L. S. Sutherland, 'William Blackstone and the Legal Chairs at Oxford', in *Evidence in Literary Scholarship: Essays in Memory of James Marshall Osborn*, ed. R. Wellek and A. Ribeiro (Oxford, 1979), 230–5.

[36] G. Bingham, *Dissertations, Essays, and Sermons*, ed. P. Bingham. (1804), i. xliii–xliv.

[37] T. Wood, *Some Thoughts Concerning the Study of the Laws of England in the Two Universities* (1708); *HUO*, 600–601.

fortune from sales of his self-published multi-volume reference work, the *General Abridgement of Law and Equity*, had long contemplated endowing a professorial chair in the common law at his old university. But the now elderly and childless Viner, who seemingly felt himself under an obligation to repay Oxford for various unspecified 'indiscretions there in his infancy', only drafted a will giving effect to this intention in July 1752. Although no conclusive evidence has as yet emerged to clinch the point, it is likely that Blackstone became aware of Viner's plans almost immediately (despite his friend Benjamin Buckler's later insistence that he embarked upon his lectures 'some years before Mr Viner's benefaction was forseen or expected').[38] The vital information may have come via William King, whom Viner consulted about the best means of realizing his ambition to establish the common law as an academic subject at Oxford, or from the Tory barrister and deputy high steward of the university, Randle Wilbraham (who, as we have just seen, had elicited Blackstone's professional opinion earlier this same year).[39]

In telling Newdigate of his determination to quit Westminster Hall, Blackstone was at pains to emphasize that he had reached no hasty decision. On the contrary: 'It has been growing upon me for some Years. My Temper, Constitution, Inclinations, and a Thing called Principle, have long quarreled with active Life, at least the active Life of Westminster Hall.'[40] (The moral scruples alluded to here recall the ethical concerns rehearsed in 'The Lawyer's Farewell to his Muse'.) Besides these various aversions, inhibitions, or reservations, Blackstone cited the crucial vocational deficiency to which Clitherow partly attributed his sluggish initial progress at the bar, that is 'certain Qualifications for being a public speaker, in which I am very sensible of my own Deficiency, and happy that I am sensible so early'. Thus it now seemed altogether prudent to withdraw 'from that Branch of the Profession, in which I can promise myself no considerable Success, the bustling practical Part; in order to be the more at Leisure to cultivate another, in which I have better Prospects, the thinking theoretical Part'.[41] This is where the planned lectures came in. Having begun to think about what might be done with a chair in civil law, which he evidently planned to treat as anything but a sinecure, 'it was not easy to leave it off, especially as I found a Pleasure in it; and have the Satisfaction to find my Design meets with the Approbation of Persons of the greatest

[38] BL MS Additional 35587, fo. 202–203v; [B. Buckler?], *Elisha's Visit to Gilgal* (1760), 29.
[39] D. J. Ibbetson, 'Charles Viner and his Chair: Legal Education in Eighteenth-Century Oxford', in *Learning the Law*, ed. J. A. Bush and A. Wijffels (1999), 315–28; above, pp. 106–7.
[40] Ibid.   [41] *Letters*, 29.

Eminence and Learning, as well in the Inns of Court, as at Oxford' (a reference perhaps to Murray, among others). He closed by mentioning that, although he 'desired to take the civil law into my Scheme', it seemed best to leave that field for whoever might be appointed to the still vacant chair, especially since he himself had been 'so much talked about for the Professorship'.[42]

For all its copious circumstantial detail, this July 1753 letter is silent on one crucial point. Blackstone makes no reference whatever to the additional lure of a prospective endowed chair in the common law at Oxford. Even granting that there are some matters about which it is difficult to speak, as well as some best left unsaid, this was surely a remarkable omission, as Sutherland pointed out some time ago:

> The fact that in 1752 Charles Viner, a benefactor already in his seventy-fifth year, had completed plans to foster the study of common law at Oxford, where it had been completely neglected; that the core of his scheme was the endowment of a well-paid Professorship to be held, on attractive conditions, by a qualified civilian who was also a barrister-at-law, and that within a year William Blackstone, an able and ambitious young DCL and barrister . . . should present himself to lecture on his own initiative on precisely this neglected topic, is on the face of it a somewhat surprising series of coincidences.[43]

By the same token, his brother-in-law's bland statement that 'finding the Profits of his Profession very inadequate to the Expence' Blackstone decided in the summer of 1753 'to retire to his Fellowship, and an academical Life' can be no more than half the truth, at best.[44] Negative economic pressures—bluntly, inadequate fee income from his London practice—doubtless played a part in that decision. But Clitherow disregards the various positive attractions which Oxford held for Blackstone, the extent to which his life remained centred on All Souls College and the university even while he was supposedly devoted to building a legal career at the Middle Temple, and his continued distaste for 'wrangling courts and stubborn Law', as first expressed in 'The Lawyer's Farewell to his Muse'.[45]

On the other hand, even disregarding the career inducements offered by a vacant Regius Chair in civil law and a prospective Vinerian Chair in common law, Blackstone's planned offering of a full year's course of

---

[42] Ibid. 30.

[43] Sutherland, 'Blackstone and the Legal Chairs', 237.

[44] Clitherow, x.

[45] Clitherow, xxix, does however note that after Michaelmas term 1750, Blackstone 'resided chiefly in Oxford, and had much of his time taken up in composing his lectures'.

lectures on 'the laws of England'[46] promised significant financial gains in its own right. Whereas medieval Oxford and Cambridge had pioneered the lecture as an effective pedagogical instrument, that whole scholastic system of education was now moribund. Apart from occasional teaching in anatomy, Arabic, Hebrew, and the physical sciences, public or university lectures for undergraduate students were virtually extinct, while college tutors' lectures were 'generally very insignificant, only read to their Pupils, who pay but little attention'.[47] Most lecture courses offered in the university were private, fee-paying, and open to students only with their tutor's permission. But at six guineas a head, the relatively large sum Blackstone charged for his lecture course, an enrolment of 20 students would bring him £130 in fees. According to his own accounts, summarized by Clitherow as his executor, Blackstone's actual gains from students' fees in 1753 amounted to £116 and nearly twice that amount (£226.16/o) the following year, although takings dropped back to just over £111 in 1755. By comparison, the cash 'profits' of his All Souls fellowship amounted to only just over seventy pounds during each of those three years. In fact, the payments he received from the college were considerably less than that, although the in-kind benefits of the fellowship admittedly included free lodging and heavily subsidized board or commons.[48]

From fashionable undertakings like the endowed Boyle lectures, which sought to demonstrate the congruence of natural philosophy with revealed religion, to the more commercial and entertaining lecture-demonstrations of astronomy, chemistry, and physics given by Benjamin Martin and Joseph Priestley, among many others, the lecture was a popular form of entertainment and instruction in eighteenth-century England.[49] But most lectures were presented in metropolitan London and provincial urban centres, not at the two unreformed English universities. Far from being part of the standard academic routine, mounting a lecture course at Oxford in the middle years of the eighteenth century demanded exceptional energy and initiative. Blackstone undoubtedly possessed both qualities in abundance; nor was he at all reluctant to challenge, at least implicitly, existing curricula and teaching arrangements.

[46] [W. Blackstone], *In Michaelmas Term next will begin A Course of Lectures on the Laws of England* (Oxford, 1753).

[47] Folger MS M.a. 11, fo. 27; *HUO*, 472–3 and n.

[48] LMA, ACC 1360/586/1,5 (reproduced Appendix II below). Bodl. MS D.D. All Souls e 30–33 ('Song books' 1753–5, summarizing each fellow's accounts with the college, including receipts for annual payments made by the bursars).

[49] Cf. my *Albion Ascendant: English History 1660–1815* (Oxford, 1998), 228–9.

His scheme may have gained some added impetus from the fact that an introductory lecture course for students under the bar had begun at Gray's Inn in London from January 1753. Unfortunately, virtually nothing is known about Danby Pickering, the lecturer, or the content of his lectures, other than that they were a total innovation so far as the Inns of Court were concerned. The bench minutes of Gray's Inn reveal Pickering's venture as being strongly supported and possibly initiated by the society's rulers, who paid Pickering an annual honorarium of £60 for his 40 lectures, plus an additional £20 bonus at the end of the first year 'as a mark of their esteem'. While expressing concern 'at the many difficultys that young gentlemen who are unassisted meet with in the course of their studys of the Law', the benchers doubtless hoped that their initiative 'to promote a regular method of study for the students of this Society' would help boost its flagging enrolments.[50]

Blackstone possibly drew more inspiration for his planned lecture series from a source closer to home. As a jurist fellow of All Souls, he was twice appointed, in 1749 and 1752, to the college office of lecturer in law, a post whose duties were later outlined by Thomas Wenman: 'he presides over the law disputations on Wednesday, and is to read a lecture on every Saturday in full term. He is to see the *Casus positio* properly observed, i.e. that a law question is duly put, opposed and answered according to the orders made on the eighth of January 1587. Hence he is vulgarly called Cas. Pos.'[51] All Souls' law lecturers would have been formally concerned with the civil law alone. But it is tempting to speculate that Blackstone, ever alert to opportunities for improvement, and fully recognizing how far Oxford's undergraduate curriculum and teaching arrangements stood in need of reform, was emboldened by serving as 'Cas. Pos.' to embark on the more ambitious pedagogical venture for which he first issued a printed advertisement or prospectus on 23 June 1753. This broadsheet emphasized that the course was intended not solely for would-be common lawyers, but for others 'desirous to be in some Degree acquainted with the Constitution and Polity of their own Country'. Hence it was proposed to 'lay down a general and comprehensive Plan of the Laws of England; to deduce their History; to enforce and illustrate their leading Rules and fundamental Principles; and to compare them with the Law

---

[50] Lemmings, *Professors*, 126–7; *The Pension Book of Gray's Inn*, ed. R. J. Fletcher (1901–10), ii.274; *ODNB*, s.v. Pickering, Danby. No copies or student notes from Pickering's lectures appear to have survived. In 1759 Pickering edited a reissue of Henry Finch's *Law or a Discourse* (1627), a work Blackstone particularly admired; cf. my 'The Dialectical Origins of Finch's *Law*', *Cambridge Law Journal*, 36 (1977), 326–48.

[51] Codrington, Wardens MS 22/3, p. 213.

of Nature and other Nations'. All this would be done, moreover, 'without entering into practical Niceties, or the minute Distinctions of particular Cases'. Divided into four parts, one for each academic term, the series would commence on Tuesday 6 November; those wishing to attend were asked give their names to 'Dr Blackstone, of All-Souls College', some time in the preceding month.[52]

Even in modern universities, where student choice is limited by various formal curricular requirements, putting on a new course is always something of a gamble. Given that his lectures were an untried optional extra, offered outside the existing (albeit much decayed) framework of university and college teaching, Blackstone risked at very least loss of face if he failed to attract and retain an audience of respectable composition and size. In the event, his venture paid off handsomely, even if Clitherow's claim that he attracted from the start 'a very crowded Class of young Men of the first Families, Characters and Hopes' must be qualified by the indications that, whatever their quality, his initial enrolment comprised fewer than twenty students. Yet notwithstanding his self-confessed shortcomings as an orator at the bar, and despite a mode of delivery which the hostile Jeremy Bentham later characterized as 'formal, precise, and affected', Blackstone proved highly effective when speaking from a prepared text, presenting his carefully-arranged material in an accessible and polished fashion, with even the occasional joke.[53] He was also careful from the first to provide comprehensive teaching aids in the form of printed handouts, including diagrammatic analyses or plans of each of the parts into which the course was divided and lists of suggested reading to accompany and supplement his oral presentations.[54]

In July 1754, with the first lecture round completed, Blackstone issued a second and fuller prospectus. This begins by referring to 'the favourable Reception' given to his 'present Design, for cultivating the study of the Municipal Law in OXFORD'—the first public announcement of what had now evidently become a far more ambitious academic programme than a single lecture series—'and the particular Indulgence which has been shown to this Course of Lectures, in their first and imperfect Draught'. For both 'THE READER' offered his 'sincerest Acknowledgements', while expressing his intention 'again to submit his Endeavors to the Candour of the University, with such corrections

[52] *In Michaelmas Term next will begin* . . . I am grateful to the late Professor G. Curtis for providing me with a photocopy of this document.

[53] Clitherow, x; *The Works of Jeremy Bentham*, ed. J. Bowring (Edinburgh, 1843), i.45. J. H. Baker, 'A Sixth Copy of Blackstone's Lectures', *Law Quarterly Review*, 84 (1968), 466.

[54] See Plate 15.

and Improvements as his future Leisure and Experience may supply'. Expanding the assurance of his 1753 advertisement, that the lectures were not primarily aimed at budding barristers, Blackstone restated his ambition to:

lay down a general and comprehensive Plan of the Laws of England; to deduce their History and Antiquities; to select and illustrate their Leading Rules and fundamental Principles; to explain their Reason and Utility; and to compare them frequently, with the Laws of Nature and of other Nations; without dwelling too minutely on the Niceties of Practice, or the more refined Distinctions of particular Cases.

In short, the aim was to present a broadly humane, liberal, and 'scientific' overview, far removed from the arid, inchoate technicalities, the 'mystic, dark, discordant lore' of traditional common law learning.[55] This was to be embodied in a course of seventy lectures (five more than in the first series), commencing at 10 a.m. on Tuesday 12 November and continuing on Tuesdays, Thursdays and Saturdays over the four terms of the academic year, 'being, for the greater Convenience, divided into four distinct Parts', as outlined in an accompanying 'Syllabus', or 'Scheme of the Course', together with a list of 'Books recommended'.[56]

No holograph copy of Blackstone's lecture scripts seems to have survived. But we are fortunate to possess comprehensive notes taken at the first year's lectures by Thomas Bever and Alexander Popham, two junior jurist fellows of All Souls, who doubtless considered themselves duty bound to support their senior colleague's venture. Both men went on to become practising lawyers: the civilian Bever later staged his own lecture series on jurisprudence and the civil law after joining Doctors' Commons as an advocate, while the barrister Popham took over Blackstone's Inner Temple chambers in 1761, and was among the four 'worthy friends' singled out in his former teacher's will.[57] Bever's notes are fair copies written up in large folio volumes, and subsequently re-copied; no fewer than three sets now survive, two at the Law Society and another (covering only the second half of the course) in the British Library. All three are heavily annotated by successive owners and readers of the manuscripts. By contrast, Popham's notes seem to have been through fewer hands and owners before

---

[55] Cf. D. Lemmings, 'Blackstone and Law Reform by Education: Preparation for the Bar and Lawyerly Culture in Eighteenth-Century England', *Law and History Review*, 16 (1998), 211–255.

[56] Bodl. G. A. Oxon. b. III (50), (55b–c).

[57] *ODNB*, s.v. Bever, Thomas and Popham, Alexander. Squibb, *Doctors Commons*, 193; Doolittle, 97–8; *Calendar of the Inner Temple Records 1750–1800*, ed. A. R. Roberts (1936), 108; Inner Temple Archives, CHA/2/1, fo. 96; below, p. 277.

they reached their present home in the Somerset Archives and Record Office. Three larger volumes (each measuring approx. 11.5 x 21 cm) comprise parts 1, 3, and 4 of the lectures written out at length, albeit with numerous crossings-out and corrections; the volume devoted to part 2 is missing. The inclusion of indexes and the foliation of these manuscripts suggest that they were working copies, compiled, in part at least, from the two smaller note-books (11.5 x 20 cm) which form part of the same deposit, and seemingly contain Popham's own rough notes as taken down at each of the lectures he attended.[58] All lectures from parts one and four of Blackstone's course as given in November–December 1753 and June–July 1754 are included, but only the first six lectures of part two (February–March 1754) and the last three lectures of part three (May 1754), seemingly because Popham missed the intervening classes. (Such absences for whatever reason—perhaps illness—may help to explain why Blackstone introduced a concessional fee for repeat attendance at his second round of lectures by previously enrolled students.) Blackstone, Bever, and Popham must have been in reasonably constant contact at All Souls, where the lectures were presented in the college's dining hall.[59] Some query on Popham's part may account for the inclusion in the second volume of his written-up notes for Easter term 1754 of a sixteen-page fair copy reproducing the text of the last two lectures from a subsequent series on that same third part ('Of the Redress of Civil Injuries'). While the handwriting is neither Blackstone's nor Popham's, this text uses the first person to address its audience directly in a style which casts some further light on Blackstone's success as a lecturer. The following passage comes at the end of the final lecture, on Chancery and other equity courts:

I have thus gone through what I proposed in this Lecture, *viz.* to touch generally upon the Nature & Method of Proceedings in the very extensive Practice of the Courts of Equity; & shall now, Gentlemen, take a short leave of you [till this day fortnight when we shall enter: *interlined*] In the 4th & last part of our Course we shall enter on the Nature & Punishment of Crimes & Misdemeanours which perhaps you'll find more interesting & less embarrassed with technical & Barbarous Phrases, than many of the Lectures of this & the preceding Term.[60]

---

[58] Law Society, BLA/V61A (2 vols.); BL, MS Additional 38838; Somerset [Archives and] RO, DD/WY/183.

[59] Codrington, Acta In Capitulis 1753–1800, 4 November 1754: 'It was agreed by the Warden and Fellows that Dr Blackstone may have the use of the Hall to read his lectures in'. Since no previous grant of permission is recorded, it seems likely that this order merely regularized the status quo.

[60] Somerset RO, DD/WY/183, 'A Course of Lectures | on the Laws of England by Dr Blackstone |Of All Souls College Oxon | Part III. | Of the Redress of Civil Injuries | Read in Easter Term 1754', inserted fair copy of lectures 15 and 16, at p. 10.

The disarming ease of this admission that some among his audience may have been not totally absorbed by an exposition of property law and civil remedies seems far distant from the 'affected' manner which Bentham would later attribute to Blackstone as a lecturer. Formality and precision, the other elements of Bentham's charge, are manifest in the characteristic reiteration of the subject just concluded, and the signalling of what is next to come. But many of Bentham's fellow students would surely have welcomed these regular signposts at the beginning and end of each lecture. They contribute to the overall clarity of structure which is a particularly striking general characteristic of the lectures as we now have them. The plan of the whole series, with the more difficult and extensive legal material of the middle two parts preceded by a general discussion of law and government in part one, and followed by an accessible account of crime and punishment in part four, was also well calculated to maintain his hearers' interest.

Could Blackstone really have compiled his initial course of 65 lectures in some 15 months, from early July 1752 (when he seemingly discussed his chances for the chair in civil law with Newdigate) to early November 1753 (when the first lecture was delivered)? Clitherow later hypothesized that from November 1750 Blackstone 'most probably . . . resided chiefly in Oxford, and had much of his time taken up in composing his Lectures, which he began to read in 1753, and in preparing for which he been for some Years before principally employed'.[61] Yet this scenario of lecture writing extended over a period of some three years possibly takes too little account of Blackstone's exceptional appetite for work, as well as his demonstrated taste for synthesizing and expounding complex bodies of knowledge, both most recently demonstrated by his treatise on the All Souls accounts, completed on New Year's Day 1753. We also know that within two years after beginning serious study of the common law in 1746, he boasted of having 'reduced it to a system', the system from which Richard Graves supposed 'he formed his Syllabus'.[62] Despite minor changes on specific points of detail over the 13 years between his first and last course of lectures, the main elements, especially the basic division of subject matter into four main parts beginning and ending with matters of public law, continued largely unaltered, until transformed into the four volumes of the *Commentaries on the Laws of England*. So we may doubt whether Blackstone's attention and energies had been 'principally' preoccupied with the task of

---

[61] Clitherow, xxix; cf. Doolittle, 48.
[62] Graves, *The Triflers*, 54.

preparing his course of lectures during the three years from late 1750 onwards, especially as it only became clear after the second half of 1752 that he would not succeed to the Regius Chair in Civil Law. By the same token, even while delivering those lectures from November 1753 onwards, he showed no signs of diminished capacity or enthusiasm for involvement in other aspects of Oxford life.

CHAPTER 7

'An Active, Enterprising Genius'[1]
(1753–58)

D URING the five years between his first lectures on the laws of England and his election as the world's first professor of the common law, William Blackstone's life remained centred on Oxford. While his legal practice continued and diversified, he became an increasingly prominent university figure, arousing considerable enmity along the way.

I

Blackstone's expertise in matters of university law had early on led to his drafting cases for the opinions of more senior practitioners, and in turn (as we have seen) the soliciting of his own views on complex juris-dictional questions.[2] His reputation in this specialized field was further boosted in 1753 when he was appointed assessor, or chief legal officer, of the chancellor's court. As he explained to his lecture class early next year, the university courts of Oxford and Cambridge enjoyed 'privileges of a very peculiar nature', since jurisdiction over academics and students was exercised according either to the common law, or to their own cus-toms, which in effect, meant that they mainly followed 'the Rules of the Civil Law, that being the most known in the Universities'. He also noted, with perhaps pardonable pride, that while the chancellor acted as a judge through the person of his deputy, the vice chancellor, the latter 'has an assessor to assist him in points of law, and which Assessor is likewise Judge

---

[1] Northamptonshire RO, Dolben papers, D (F) 88: Theophilus Leigh to Sir William Dolben, 21 May 1756.

[2] Codrington, Wardens MS 22/3, 'Clitherow's Case, abstract of 1752. Original in the archives. This case was drawn up by Sir W. Blackstone'; above, Chapter 6, pp. 106–7; *Letters*, 12–13, 23–8.

by Deputation'.[3] In point of fact, the fragmentary surviving records of Oxford's chancellor's (or vice chancellor's) court during Blackstone's tenure of office suggest that the vice chancellor himself generally attended only once a year, for the formal appointment and swearing-in of his assessor. Otherwise the 'Worshipful Wm Blackstone Dr of Laws' presided, sitting some eight to ten times every year between late 1753 and 1759, while also dealing with such business as the swearing-out of warrants in his college rooms.[4] The court functioned primarily as a small claims tribunal, handling three or four debt cases per session, mostly for amounts of less than £10 which Oxford artisans, shopkeepers, and tradesmen sought from undergraduates, from each other, and occasionally from college fellows to whom they had extended credit. By far the largest sum claimed in any of the surviving documentation from Blackstone's term of office was £650, which a London druggist attempted to recover from David Hopkins, a fellow of Jesus College, in 1758; Hopkins had already been sued by three plaintiffs in two separate actions, seeking just under £100 from 'the fruits and profits of his fellowship'. Besides these 'instance' cases, the court also had a public or 'office' jurisdiction, under which a gentleman commoner of Wadham College was cited for the 'carrying of arms' within the university's precincts, while Blackstone's colleague and pupil Alexander Popham, in his role as the university's 'warden of the streets', prosecuted a number of citizens and academics, including the principals of St Edmund Hall and Hertford College, for failing to illuminate the streets outside their premises.[5] The chancellor's court generally followed civil law procedures, with most parties represented by a proctor, although Blackstone occasionally resorted to viva voce evidence rather than relying on written depositions. We have the typescript copy of a manual outlining the court's processes, interspersed with proposals for improvements to save 'Much Time and Expence'. The original was possibly Blackstone's work, as was more certainly the appended set of rules of court, dating from January 1755 and signed by Blackstone and Vice Chancellor Huddesford. A preamble noted that 'divers unnecessary Delays have in Process of Time arisen in the Practice of this Court; occasioned by a gradual Departure from the plain

[3] BL MS Additional 38838, fos. 36–7. This reference to the assessor as judge does not appear in the corresponding section of the *Commentaries*, iii.84.

[4] OUA, Hyp/A/72, fo. 324; Chancellor's Court papers 1758, p. 23. Although the vice chancellor's accounts show Thomas Bever succeeding Blackstone as assessor in 1758–9 (OUA, WPβ), the latter was still acting in that capacity in April and June 1759: Chancellor's Court papers 1759, 1:5, 5:2.

[5] OUA, Hyp/A/60, fos. 9v–10v, 13v–14. Chancellor's Court papers, 1758/16:1; 1759, p. 16. The 'masters of the streets nominated annually by the proctors in congregation from among its regent masters ... were to oversee lighting and sanitation': *HUO*, 208.

summary Method prescribed by the University-Statutes, and adopting in its Stead the Rules and Proceedings of other Courts, which however wisely instituted are by no means suitable to that Ease and Expedition which are requisite in all limited Jurisdictions'. The document then reiterated the existing statutory provisions for dealing with both cases not over 20 shillings and those 'of greater Moment', emphasizing that from the first day of the next Hilary term these would be observed 'as the standing Orders and general Practice of the Court'.[6]

Apart from a small annual salary and the fees attached to the assessor's office, the main benefits of this preferment were prestige, visibility, and perhaps opportunities for influence which might arise from occasional association with the university's chief executive officer. When seeking to explain Blackstone's slow initial progress at the bar, Clitherow (it will be recalled) cited his lack of 'powerful Friends or Connexions'. At the outset of their careers, most young barristers depended largely on kinship and neighbourhood networks to bring them business. For all the best efforts of his Bigg and Richmond uncles, Blackstone was disadvantaged in that respect as an orphan, and possibly also as a Londoner (bearing in mind the demographic mobility and sheer scale of the metropolis). But the better he became known in Oxford, the greater his chances of attracting fees from local—albeit gown rather than town—sources. Having long provided legal advice to the warden and fellows of his own college, just after beginning his first lecture course in November 1753, Blackstone was called in to assist their neighbours from The Queen's College, in the High Street next door to All Souls, in disputes arising from the well-intentioned bequest of John Michel. This wealthy Queen's alumnus had left most of his large estate to his old college, envisaging the establishment within it of a semi-autonomous foundation, comprising eight fellows and four students, to be housed in an extension to the front quadrangle. Unfortunately, if not surprisingly, when Michel died in 1739 the college's existing fellows took alarm, concerned that these supernumeraries might dilute the value of their own benefits; they accordingly proposed to charge the foundation rent for any accommodation erected to house its members, while raising various other cavils to the whole scheme. The visitors or trustees set up to administer the foundation reacted with a Chancery suit against the college, raising the real prospect that Michel's estate would be largely consumed in legal fees, or alternatively, revert to the Crown if the

[6] Doolittle, 33–4, and references there cited; OUA, WPα/23/6; WPα/57/12. Bodl. Don. b 12 (64). M. Underwood, 'The Structure and Operation of the Oxford Chancellor's Court', *Journal of the Society of Archivists*, 6 (1978), 18–27.

121

terms of the will could not be carried out. Fear of these outcomes eventually resulted in agreement to seek a private bill to resolve the conflict, whereby the visitors and the college were empowered 'to do all such Acts as shall be necessary for the better effecting the Purposes of Mr Michel's Will'. That vague provision proving inadequate to the task, Blackstone was commissioned by the college to draft a detailed set of articles to be agreed between the contending parties 'as a foundation for a more solemn Deed'. This was the beginning of a long but eventually productive involvement with the contentious Michel Foundation, first as an occasional legal adviser to Queen's College, then from 1757, as one of the three Michel visitors, in which capacity he continued to work towards a 'Plan, calculated to improve Mr Michel's original Donation, without departing from his Intentions'.[7]

Clitherow, probably echoing Blackstone himself, regarded his role in securing the eventual implementation of the Michel bequest as sufficiently noteworthy to merit no less than two paragraphs of his biographical sketch, which can be corroborated and enlarged from the extensive surviving records still kept at Queen's College. But because Blackstone's fee book and personal accounts have not survived, our understanding of other aspects of his private legal practice is inevitably incomplete. We do know that he was once again called upon for advice about the administration of a deceased estate in the month after his first intervention in the affairs of the Michel Foundation, but it seems likely that this was by way of a lucky fluke rather than indicative of a general trend. William Jones, another wealthy landed gentleman with extensive properties in Berkshire and Wiltshire, had named among the four trustees to whom he left the administration of his estate Dr Edward Ernle, a senior jurist fellow of All Souls, and Blackstone's uncle, Thomas Bigg. In return for drafting his marriage settlement two years before, Bigg bestowed on his nephew a fee amounting, as the latter put it, to 'a cool Hundred', so he may well now have been the key figure in requisitioning Blackstone's advice on seven points regarding the obligations and rights of his fellow trustees and himself with regard to the widow and her surviving children.[8] In response, his nephew clarified and confirmed the deceased testator's right to bequeath specific items of his wife's jewellery (since she could own no separate personal property during the marriage unless it had been held for her use by trustees, any gift made by her husband 'is in reality only a permission to

---

[7] C. Mallet, *A History of the University of Oxford* (1927) iii. 88–9; Queen's College Archives, 5 M, items 4–21, 22 (1), 60; Doolittle, 34–5; 'Blackstone and Oxford', 39–40, 41–2; Clitherow, xii.

[8] Northamptonshire RO, Langham (Cottesbroke) Collection, L (C), 447/1–18; *Letters*, 21.

use the thing presented during the husband's pleasure, the property still remaining in him', while her undoubted right to her 'paraphernalia' only included 'Necessary Apparel', not 'those Ornaments which he permitted her to Use in his Lifetime'). More generally, he suggested that it would be prudent for Bigg and his fellow trustees to 'act under the Direction and Indemnification' of the court of Chancery, lodging their accounts regularly as a precaution against eventual suits from the beneficiaries of the estate, since 'A Court of Equity in Case of Accident or Oversight is not very Liberal in making Allowances to Guardians of Large Estates who have Chosen to Act without Directions'.[9] Clear, succinct, and to the point, Blackstone's advice on this occasion once again provided the basis of a professional association which continued well into the following decade, since as late as 1767 he helped prepare the marriage settlement of Elizabeth Jones, one of the 'Young Ladies' whose interests had been the subject of his opinion thirteen years before.[10]

How much more general counselling Blackstone managed to attract during his hiatus from the London bar is very difficult to tell. Bits and pieces undoubtedly came his way on occasion. In October 1755 he prepared another written opinion, this time for the university itself, which having distrained on the goods of a tenant named Bateman for a year and a half's back rent, discovered that he had been declared bankrupt before the distress was taken. Blackstone confirmed that in such cases the appointed commissioners in bankruptcy were entitled to reclaim any monies raised from the sale of the defaulting tenant's goods, while the university enjoyed no priority as against other claimants or creditors. But, on the other hand, his second paragraph went on to point out that the relevant statute 'enacts That no Farmer, Drover, or Grazier, shall (as such) be entitled to be deemed a Bankrupt'. Hence the university should make 'diligent Enquiry', so that if Bateman 'appears not to have been bona fide a Trader within the Intent of the Statutes, proper Methods may [be] taken to supersede the Commission of Bankruptcy'.[11] Nor were Blackstone's professional services called upon only by kinsmen and fellow academics. Next year Dr James Luck, the vicar of Charlbury, a parish in North Oxfordshire, who was suing one of his parishioners in a dispute over tithes, found that his adversary's 'Answer (. . . now in the Exchequer)' had been drawn by 'Mr Blackston of All Souls'.[12] Further indication of Blackstone's

---

[9] Northamptonshire RO, L (C) 447/16–17.
[10] *Letters*, 128n [for Mary, read Elizabeth]; *VCH Wiltshire*, xii. 19 20.
[11] OUA, NW/4/7; cf. *Commentaries*, ii. 475.
[12] *The Correspondence of Thomas Secker, Bishop of Oxford 1737–58*, ed. A. P. Jenkins (Oxfordshire Rec. Soc., 57, 1991), 262–3.

growing local prominence is provided by a newspaper announcement in May 1756 of his nomination as standing counsel to a projected prosecution association or 'Scheme for Punishing Murder, Theft and Robbery in the County of Oxford'.[13]

That the promoter of this initiative was at pains to deny any suggestion of acting with 'a View to Party-Interest' raises the possibility that Blackstone's appointment had something to do with his strong Tory connections. This public-political identity had been reinforced the previous year, when he appeared as the junior of three counsel for the prosecution in a murder trial at Oxford assizes, resulting from a riotous High Street counter-demonstration against a 'New Interest' or Whig procession following the famously contentious, corrupt, and expensive county election of April 1754.[14] Yet Blackstone took no other public role in that celebrated contest. While there could be little doubt as to either his overall political sympathies or specific support for Newdigate's re-endorsement as one of the university's parliamentary representatives in the same general election, he played no visible part in the protracted Oxfordshire campaign. Some contemporaries believed they had detected his hand at work behind the scenes in polemical journalism and pseudonymous pamphleteering for the 'Blue', Old Interest, or Tory cause. But these claims were seemingly based on little more than Blackstone's known alignment and personal standing within the university.[15] After the bitterly contested but inconclusive poll he was engaged, together with Vice Chancellor Huddesford and the city's mayor, in taking depositions arising from the 'Rag Plot'. This supposed discovery of a 'false, malicious, infamous and treasonable libel'—a versified Jacobite call to arms, no less—in a bundle of rags left outside a city grocer's shop appears to have been organized by a group of county and university Whigs seeking further to compromise and discredit their opponents, since the sheriff's return had left the House of Commons itself to decide whether the Tory or the Whig candidates had been duly elected. Early in 1755, before that unusually long-drawn-out parliamentary process concluded, Blackstone may have been responsible—the evidence is merely circumstantial—for publishing copies of statements taken down before the mayor and vice chancellor, together with the presentation of

---

[13] *Jackson's Oxford Journal*, 22 May 1756; renewal subscriptions to the association were called for in ibid., 2 April 1757.

[14] Ibid., 5 June 1756; ibid, 8 June 1754, 19 July 1755; *The Tryal of William Turton, Esq: for the Murder of John Holloway at the Assizes Held at Oxford, on Thursday, the Seventeenth of July, 1755* (1755), 1. R. J. Robson, *The Oxfordshire Election of 1754* (1949).

[15] Robson, *Oxfordshire Election*, 37, 79; Ward, *Georgian Oxford*, 197; *HUO*, 135n, 139–40, 140n; Doolittle, 18.

the Whig-dominated grand jury which had touched off the 'Rag Plot', seeking to demonstrate its flimsy nature and the partisan motives of its promoters.[16] A further set of printed 'informations' from some of those already examined, this time presented before a more receptive group of Whig justices, depict him cross-examining the principal informant, Mrs Mary Carnall, 'in a very sneering Manner', and making light of the supposed treasonable material in a 'ludicrous' fashion.[17] Here, as previously, Blackstone's public identification with the Tory camp was firmly coupled with his legal persona.

It remains possible that he was engaged, either in person or through the agency of like-minded friends and colleagues such as Dr Buckler of All Souls, in waging paper warfare against supporters of the ministry in the university and county before, during, and after the April 1754 election. What cannot be doubted is his close involvement in the ensuing struggle to prevent the Whig candidates, who had received significantly fewer votes than their Tory opponents, from securing the two county seats as the result of a House of Commons vote. Even before he began gathering the 'informations' which exposed the dubious basis of the so-called plot, Blackstone had met more than once with Newdigate, up in Oxford for the installation of Lord Westmorland as the university's new high steward, 'upon the County Election'.[18] As it happened, the House did not begin formal consideration of the Oxfordshire returns until November, when the fractious and ambitious William Pitt, seeking to bolster his parliamentary standing with the Whig majority, recounted as recent experience his recollections of Jacobite drinking songs echoing through the streets on a visit to Oxford more than five years before.[19] Blackstone was quick to congratulate Newdigate on his 'able and hearty' defence of 'our much injured Body' against this depiction of the university as a hotbed of sedition by 'the Orator'. For indeed 'the noble Independence, which has ever been the Principle of the University, however it may unjustly be branded with the Name of Disaffection, is thoroughly consistent with Loyalty,

---

[16] *Informations and Other Papers Relating to the Treasonable Verses Found at Oxford, July 17 1754* (Oxford, 1755). Sutherland states that this work 'was obviously written by Blackstone, who had interrogated the witnesses' (*HUO*, 135n); for Doolittle the pamphlet 'bears every sign of Blackstone's authorship' (Doolittle, 18n), while Robson refers to Blackstone as its publisher (*Oxfordshire Election*, 131). However plausible, these claims seemingly lack independent corroboration.

[17] Bodl., Gough 39 (16b), 31–3.

[18] Newdigate Diary, 5 July 1754.

[19] The university's other parliamentary representative forwarded a graphic report of this speech, with a request for material to counter its anticipated damage to Oxford's public image: Bodl. MS Top. Oxon. c 209, fos. 25–26.

and inseparable from a Zeal for constitutional Liberty'. In Blackstone's eyes such liberty was most immediately endangered by 'the Torrent that threatens to overbear us all', a reference to the administration's tactics during the House's prolonged investigation of the Oxfordshire result, which had already attracted national attention, thanks to the expense and ferocity of what turned out to be the sole disputed county poll in that general election.[20]

Newdigate's diary entries suggest that the 'Oxfordshire Elect.' remained his major parliamentary preoccupation well into the new year. In the last week of January 1755, he recorded no fewer than five London meetings with Blackstone, sometimes in company with other Oxford dons, including Thomas Winchester and Richard Bagot. The election outcome must have been discussed on these occasions; indeed Clitherow later recalled that Blackstone had been 'engaged as Counsel in the great Contest'. Precisely what such engagement amounted to is unclear; there is no positive evidence of his arguing the case for the two Tory candidates at the bar of the house, as distinct from assisting to marshal their arguments.[21] Part of that latter task involved coming to terms with the general issue of voter qualifications, especially the claim that a certain class of copyholders by inheritance, who enjoyed greater security of tenure than those holding their lands merely at the will of a manorial lord, should be regarded as freeholders, and hence entitled to vote for the parliamentary representatives of the county, the knights of the shire. Many of these so-called 'customary freeholders' had in fact been allowed by the sheriff to cast their votes at the Oxfordshire poll, mostly as Whigs. But if individual returning officers, annually appointed by the government of the day, were to determine the eligibility of voters in county elections, the ministry would effectively control the composition of a large and influential component of all future parliaments. Or so argued Sir Francis Dashwood, another Oxfordshire Tory MP (albeit sitting for a Kentish borough), who on 23 January proposed a motion designed to settle the question of copyholder eligibility in principle. The ministry circumvented this ploy by postponing the vote, and the matter remained unresolved even after the Oxfordshire election result was decided (against the Old Interest) three months later.[22]

---

[20] *Letters*, 31–2; Ward, *Georgian Oxford*, 199.

[21] Newdigate Diary, 22, 25, 27, 28, 31 January 1755; Clitherow, xii. *CJ*, xxvii. 41–2, 45, 106 refers to (unnamed) counsel for the two Old Interest candidates; but they are named as 'Whitaker' and 'Parrot' in the Exeter College Blacow transcripts, p. 7.

[22] B. Kemp, *Sir Francis Dashwood* (1967), 38–9. For the prolonged proceedings as reported from the Whig side, see *An Eighteenth-Century Correspondence*, ed. L. Dickens and M. Stanton (1910), 241–52. *HUO*, 139–40. Clitherow, xii.

Next year a bill to settle the right of election was introduced, and on this occasion Blackstone prepared a detailed statement of the case against allowing any kind of copyholder a vote in county elections, 'for the private use of some members of parliament, who wished to entertain a clearer idea of the matter in question'.[23] That bill foundered; but on its reintroduction in 1758 by the Tory stalwart Sir John Philipps, Blackstone's draft was published anonymously, under the cumbersome title *Considerations on the Question, Whether Tenants by Copy of Court Roll According to the Custom of the Manor, Though not at the Will of the Lord, Are Freeholders Qualified to Vote in Elections for Knights of the Shire.*[24] Generally cited as *Considerations on Copyholders*, this takes the form of an extended legal opinion, complete with an opening statement of 'The Case', reciting that 'A. B. has an estate of above forty shillings *per annum*, within the manor of C. which is holden by copy of court roll (but not said to be "at the will of the lord" . . . '. The 'Question' follows: 'Whether A. B. is a freeholder, within the meaning of the laws now in being, so as to entitle him to vote in the election of knights of the shire?'

Blackstone's conclusion in the negative was developed over 50 pages of legal-historical argument and exposition, the whole prefaced by a brief 'Advertisement' to the reader, explaining the need to 'obviate the doubts that have recently arisen' by clearly distinguishing 'between those who do and do not possess the right to vote'. Since this line was indeed 'already drawn by the masterly hands of our ancestors', no new law was required, only a revival of the old.[25] Having summarized the fifteenth-century statutes which laid down the provisions whereby knights of the shire were to be elected by 'the county at large', that is to say, by its (understood male) freeholders, Blackstone proceeds to describe the defining characteristics of four main species of feudal lay tenure, concluding that those particularly in question formed a class somewhere between freeholders and 'common copyholders' (whom it was universally agreed had no legal entitlement to vote in county elections), but closer to the latter than the former. Having determined the nature of the tenure, it only remained to be shown that such estates could not come within the compass of the relevant statutes as 'freehold' or 'free lands'.

---

[23] W. Blackstone, *Tracts, Chiefly Relating to the Antiquities and Laws of England* (Oxford, 1771), 237.

[24] *CJ*, xxviii. 120, 181; P. Langford, *Public Life and the Propertied Englishman 1689–1798* (Oxford, 1991), 279. Blackstone's authorship was confirmed four years later in his collected *Law Tracts* (Oxford, 1762), i. 99–166. Although Philipps introduced the bill, Clitherow claims his subject was 'prevailed upon' to publish by Sir Charles Mordaunt, the long-serving member for Warwickshire: *H of P 1754–90*, iii. 162–3; Clitherow, xii.

[25] *Considerations on Copyholders*, i–ii, 1–2.

The issue was complicated by a semantic ambiguity, since 'freehold' might refer either to lands (more strictly the estate or interest held in lands), or else to the form of tenure by which that estate was held. Thus, while a tenant for life had an undoubted freehold *interest*, only those laymen holding lands 'in free socage' (that is, under the condition of certain and honourable service rendered to the manorial lord) could be said also to enjoy freehold *tenure*. There follows a systematic demonstration that lands not so held can hardly enfranchise their tenants, despite some admitted confusion arising from legal references 'especially of late years' to 'customary freeholds'. These were indeed, according to Blackstone, 'of such an amphibious nature, that, when compared with mere copyholds, they may with sufficient propriety be called freeholds; and, when compared with absolute freeholds, they may with equal, or greater propriety, be denominated copyholds'.[26]

Prefiguring the discussion of 'the ancient English tenures' in Book Two of the *Commentaries*,[27] this pamphlet provides another example of Blackstone's remarkable talent for clear, concise, fluent, and methodical analysis of complex subject-matter. The *Considerations* is also of interest for its opening account of the 'true theory and genuine principles of liberty', whereby 'in every free state' each member of 'the community, however mean his situation' has a voice in choosing 'those delegates, to whose charge is committed the disposal of his property, his liberty, and his life'. True, 'persons of indigent fortunes, or such as are under the immediate dominion of others' cannot be allowed a vote, given the probability that it would not be freely exercised. Excluding them from the suffrage, as having 'no will of their own', does however enable those 'whose wills may be supposed independent' to be 'more thoroughly upon a level with each other'. While this classical defence of a propertied franchise paid no regard to the very different realities of current electoral practice, Blackstone nevertheless insisted that his purpose was not to determine 'what *would be* the best and most equitable constitution for this purpose, according to the modern state of property in this country; but what really *is*, and long has been, our legal constitution'. There might well be good reasons, 'were we now to frame a new polity with respect to the qualifications of voters', for enfranchising copyholders, tenants at will, and leaseholders, while 'greatly' raising the value of eligible freeholds, presumably to reduce the potential for electoral corruption. But—in characteristic architectural terms—'this would be removing foundations; or at least pulling down the superstructure, and erecting another in its stead'. So, until 'the constitution is remodelled',

26 Ibid., 38–9, *et passim.*   27 *Commentaries*, ii, chs. 5, 9.

the existing laws must be attended to as 'the only criteria to decide the present question'.[28] The ideological position represented here fits neatly with a recent characterization of the political outlook of the Country or Old Interest opposition to the Whig regimes of the later 1740s and 1750s: a central emphasis on English liberties and the need to preserve or restore them, a conservative cast of mind ('change being conceived of as restoration'), but also a 'strong populist, even republican edge'.[29]

Blackstone's public identification with the Tory cause had been reinforced by his role during and after the 1754 general election. It received a further boost, in academic circles at least, even while the Commons continued to debate the Oxfordshire election returns. For on 13 February 1755, Sir Roger Newdigate wrote separately to Vice Chancellor Huddesford and to Blackstone, advising them of the Countess of Pomfret's decision to present Oxford with a valuable collection of classical busts, statues, and other marbles—the largest surviving portion of the first major British collection of Greek and Roman antiquities. Put together in the early seventeenth century by Thomas Howard, Earl of Arundel, a few of whose pieces had already come to the university, this collection had survived various hazards and misfortunes, most recently, the financial crisis which obliged the second earl of Pomfret to dispose of the statuary gracing his Nicholas Hawksmoor house at Easton Neston, near Towcester, in Northamptonshire. While his mother, the Dowager Countess, had come to their rescue, her evident determination that the university receive her gift 'with due honor and regard' was fully echoed by Newdigate, who also sought Blackstone's assistance in finding a suitable place to house and display the works.[30] In swift response, Blackstone forwarded on 16 February a sketch plan of the Old Schools or Bodleian Library quadrangle to illustrate his proposal of reuniting what would henceforth be known as the Pomfret marbles with existing items from the Arundel collection, by taking over two rooms at the south-east corner of the building. (There is no indication that he had sounded out the views of current occupants and users of the schools of Logic, Moral Philosophy, and Music, perhaps because they were relatively few and infrequent.) Picking up a hint from Newdigate, Blackstone was at pains to emphasize the 'great Gratitude, and thorough Sense, which I, and all I have conversed with, entertain of the distinguished Regard and honourable Preference intended by her Ladyship to this Seat of the Muses'.[31]

[28] *Considerations on Copyholders*, 3–5.
[29] Harris, *Politics and the Nation*, 71.
[30] *Newdigate Correspondence*, 76–7.
[31] Ibid; *Letters*, 32–4.

Sir Roger took Blackstone's letter with him when he visited Lady Pomfret in London two days later, and replied to it the day after that, following a second meeting with Lady Pomfret, at which he had been accompanied by a very high-level delegation, comprising the university's chancellor, high steward, and vice chancellor, as well as his fellow burgess Peregrine Palmer.[32] While thankful for 'the curious and entertaining Catalogue You was pleased to send me of Lady Pomfret's noble Benefaction', as also the news that she had appreciated the 'Demonstrations of Respect shewn to her Ladyship by the University', Blackstone had to confess 'entre nous' some disappointment at the reaction of his more senior academic colleagues:

I think our great Men here, from a Coldness of Constitution natural to those advanced in Years, did not receive the Notice of this inestimable Donation with that Rapidity of Gratitude which it demanded, nor seem to have Virtù enough to set a proper Value upon it, having heard it insinuated more than once from that Quarter, that several of the Statues are maimed. You will laugh at this, as I do.[33]

Fortunately 'the insensibility of our Chiefs is amply compensated by the Zeal, almost amounting to Rapture, which is expressed by the whole *Body* of the University'. Yet if decisions about housing the marbles were to rest with 'Persons better qualified perhaps for adorning the University with their Learning, than their Taste in the politer Arts', there was some danger that considerations of 'Frugality' might prevail. Already there had been talk of placing 'these fine Remains, in the Room under the Museum, a common Thoroughfare, and of no size; in the Anatomy School, up one pair of Stairs, and a Lumber Room for dry Bones and stuft Alligators; with other Places equally unsuitable'. So wholly inappropriate an outcome might be avoided were Lady Pomfret to 'recommend' that the disposition of her collection be decided with the advice of Newdigate himself, as her relative by marriage. Speaking 'as a Lawyer', he also thought that 'some more formal Donation of so great a Treasure, than barely delivering the keys' would help prevent any future 'Controversies with Executors'.[34]

Newdigate again responded by return on Saturday 1 March, commissioning Blackstone himself to draft a document. Forwarding this to Newdigate on Monday for Lady Pomfret's approval, Blackstone explained that 'I have endeavoured to unite, as well as I could, the magnificent

---

[32] Newdigate Diary, 19–20 February 1755.

[33] *Letters*, 34–5. The catalogue was presumably a copy of the two-page document now in the Newdigate papers at the Warwickshire RO, CR136/B2977.

[34] Ibid. 35–6.

Stile of a Donation, and the legal Precision of a Deed of Gift'.[35] He also repeated his determination to do 'all in my Power, poor Commoner as I am, to keep up a proper Spirit in our House of Lords', so far as the 'Elegant and Ornamental Disposition of the Benefaction' was concerned. On that last front, Newdigate was advised to let the vice chancellor (Dr George Huddesford) know that Lady Pomfret had seen and approved his plan for the housing of her gift: 'a small incidental Mention of my Name may give a better Grace to my interfering in these Arcana of State'.[36]

Notwithstanding the slightly awkward compound of condescension, frustration, and mock-humility in these comments on his academic superiors, Blackstone continued to act as Newdigate's Oxford agent while delicate negotiations with Lady Pomfret proceeded over the next couple of months. His significance in this role is indicated by the postponement of a planned gathering at Easton Neston on 1 May because of a clash with his court-keeping duties at the All Souls College manor of Edgeware, Middlesex. Nearly three weeks later, Blackstone, Vice Chancellor Huddesford, and Sir Roger Newdigate dined with the countess and 'Saw the Statues', presumably for the first time. By then the university had formally accepted Lady Pomfret's benefaction, and preparations were under way to transport the marbles to Oxford, where they would be placed in the former Logic School, in accordance with part at least of Blackstone's initial proposal.[37] He nevertheless continued to hope and lobby for a purpose-built museum to house them 'and such other Curiosities of the same Kind' as would doubtless accrue to the university 'when once we had opened a Treasury, with so rich a Stock to begin with'. Huddesford was sufficiently convinced to devote a portion of his annual vice chancellorial oration in October 1755 to urging 'very earnestly' the provision of 'a proper Mansion for these illustrious Wanderers'. A week or so later, that scheme was decisively countermanded by Lord Westmorland, the university's high steward, perhaps primarily on economic grounds. Yet quite apart from the apathetic, boorish, or ignorant philistinism which he detected among some senior academics, Blackstone may have overestimated the extent to which his own enthusiasm for Lady Pomfret's splendid gift was shared

---

[35] The vellum deed of gift, dated 10 March 1755, transferring 'All those her Statues Bustoes Sarcophagi Columns Relievoes Inscriptions and other Marbles Antiquities and Curiosities whatsoever' is now OUA, SP/C/11; see also Convocation Register, 11 April 1755: OUA, NEP/ Subtus/Reg Bg, 165–6.

[36] Warwickshire RO, CR136/A 586, 1–4 March 1755; *Letters*, 36–7.

[37] *Letters*, 38–9; Newdigate Diary, 19 May 1755; Craster, *Bodleian Library*, 4–5. The Arundel marbles evidently remained in the former Moral Philosophy school: *The New Oxford Guide* (Oxford, 1759), 7–8, 135.

among his colleagues. Given the charged political atmosphere which persisted in Oxford long after the divisive election of 1754, members of the substantial Whig minority had reason to regard the Pomfret benefaction with considerable reserve at best, tainted as it was by association with its prominent Old Interest sponsors. In a satirical pamphlet of March 1755, Blackstone's All Souls friend Benjamin Buckler has the embattled Whigs of Exeter College complaining that the university, under their adversary, Vice Chancellor Huddesford, 'had the Assurance to accept the Pomfret Collection of Antique Statues . . . and to talk most unacademically, of laying out several thousands of pounds in a Room to receive them'.[38]

II

If (for reasons perhaps as much personal as political) Blackstone's role in securing the Pomfret marbles did not enhance his popularity throughout the university, neither was his professed sense of insignificance in the management of its affairs widely shared. When Joseph Warton encouraged his brother Thomas in July 1755 to stand for election as Oxford's professor of poetry, he asked, among other pertinent questions, 'is Blackstone *absolutely* steady to you?'[39] Earlier that month John Tracy, Blackstone's slightly younger colleague at All Souls, had taken advantage of his position as senior proctor to propose his friend for a vacancy among the body of 'Delegates' appointed by Convocation to oversee the university's printing operations. This was a controversial step, less because of Blackstone's involvement than that the proctors thereby challenged the long-standing practice of successive vice chancellors, who had assumed the right to confer all such appointments on their own peers, the heads of houses. One problem with this arrangement was that those so appointed usually had much bigger fish to fry in terms of university administration and politics. Hence the proctors claimed in a defence of their actions, published according to custom as a printed pamphlet for circulation around the college common rooms, the 'many abuses, which had crept into the University Press (through the numerous avocations of those to whose charge it was committed)' could only be remedied if henceforth individuals 'who might be induced to attend' to their responsibilities were appointed as delegates.

---

[38] *Letters*, 37–9; B. Buckler, *A Proper Explanation of the Oxford Almanack for this present Year MDCCLV* (1755), 25. Buckler also represents Vice Chancellor Huddesford 'and his Assessor' (Blackstone) as jointly responsible for commissioning the allegorical engraving which this tract supposedly elucidates: ibid., 13.

[39] *The Correspondence of Thomas Warton*, ed. D. Fairer (1995), 54.

Blackstone was plainly one such person, and Vice Chancellor Huddesford made no attempt to block his assessor's election, despite maintaining in principle his own right, *ex officio*, to appoint all Press delegates.[40]

Huddesford's compromise brought temporary peace, although a further nomination by the proctors to the Press delegacy would shortly reveal the full divisive potential of this issue. Meanwhile, Blackstone set about familiarizing himself with the operations of the university's press, and the printing trade generally. Little is known of his activities during the second half of 1755, other than that he spent most of September with the Newdigates at Arbury, accompanied for at least part of the time by two younger All Souls friends and colleagues, James Clitherow and Richard Bagot. They were entertained on the bowling green, went shooting, and took long walks with Sir Roger. They played at cards ('Pope Joan'), dined with neighbours and other visitors (including the Tory MP Heneage Finch, Lord Guernsey), and were invited to Richard Geast's Blyth Hall, and to Blithfield, home of Sir Walter Bagot, Richard's father and yet another Tory parliamentarian stalwart, where they stayed for several nights.[41] Given the nature of the company, national politics was doubtless a major topic of conversation, as it was in the letters exchanged between Blackstone and Newdigate before and after this excursion. Blackstone's expressed political sympathies were unmistakably but not exclusively Tory, at least to the extent that he was prepared to quote with approval the Whig Joseph Addison and to ask Samuel Richardson (who identified the New Interest in the Oxfordshire election as synonymous with the national interest) to review his draft analysis of the problems facing the Oxford University Press.[42] Indeed, his broadly anti-ministerial outlook, fearful of the threat to 'Freedom of Elections' posed by an over-powerful executive, 'armed as they are with military Power, and the Nation weak and defenceless', had more than an tincture of Old Whig about it, notwithstanding his dislike of 'Continent[al] Measures', and faith or hope that the independent 'Country Gentlemen' MPs would eventually manage to implement such 'proper Measures' as repeal of the Septennial Act, more effective legislation against placemen, and reduction of the army's size and influence.[43]

---

[40] I. G. Philip, *William Blackstone and the Reform of the Oxford University Press in the Eighteenth Century* (Oxford, 1955), 1–3; B. Buckler, *A Reply to Dr Huddesford's Observations Relating to the Delegates of the Press* (Oxford, 1756), 3–4.

[41] Newdigate Diary, 2, 3, 5, 6, 8, 14, 19, 22 September 1755.

[42] *Letters*, 38, referring to Addison's *Cato* (1713), ii. 43; Philip, 39–42; *The Correspondence of Samuel Richardson*, ed. A. L. Barbauld (1804), iii. 113; no further contacts between Blackstone and Richardson have been traced.

[43] *Letters*, 38, 40–1, 46.

Even the remarkable rise to power of William Pitt—a politician whom Blackstone had regarded with deep mistrust ever since his 1754 parliamentary attack on Oxford Jacobitism—and the simultaneous outbreak of hostilities with France in 1756 did not entirely dispel these aspirations. But while he might censure or commend from a distance the parliamentary performance of Newdigate and his colleagues in their 'great World', Blackstone's involvement in the hothouse microcosm of Oxford politics was direct and personal.

There he presented himself as an upright, independent representative, serving his constituents (the university's academic community assembled in Convocation) by the diligent investigation and uprooting of abuses and corruption. Unfortunately, from the autumn of 1755 onwards, his surviving letters to Newdigate become far less forthcoming than those which enable us to reconstruct in some detail his role in relation to the Pomfret bequest. They contain little by way of insights or reports on the Oxford scene, but rather respond to Newdigate's reports of Westminster politics. Doubtless arising from mixed motives of circumspection, modesty, and propriety (a sense that the university's dirty linen should not be aired before the university's parliamentary representative), this reticence, especially about his own part in often turbulent events, helps explain why progressive improvement is typically taken to be the hallmark of Blackstone's next few years at Oxford. Yet for our understanding of his life, at least as much importance attaches to the weight of antagonism and opposition aroused among his academic colleagues by his efforts to rehabilitate Oxford's printing and publishing operations (1755–8), to inaugurate the Vinerian Chair in English Law (1757–8), and to emancipate the university from the dead hand of its seventeenth-century constitution (1758–9).

The splendid classical facade of Hawksmoor's Clarendon Building on Broad Street, Oxford's purpose-built printing house since 1713, belied the 'very deplorable condition' to which the Press itself had sunk by the mid-eighteenth century: 'languishing in a lazy obscurity, and barely reminding us of its existence, by now and then slowly bringing forth a programma, a sermon printed by request, or at best a Bodleian catalogue'.[44] This mordant characterization comes from the open letter *To the Reverend Doctor Randolph Vice-Chancellor of the University of Oxford* which Blackstone published in May 1757, nearly two years after first becoming a delegate for the Press. During that period he had sought to acquire a detailed knowledge of the printing and book trades in general, so as better to tackle the particular problems afflicting Oxford's University Press. The first result of

[44] Philip, 45–6.

these investigations was a memorandum prepared for circulation in manuscript to his fellow delegates on 25 March 1756, under the unassuming
title 'Some Thoughts on the Oxford Press'.[45] This document is unusual
among Blackstone's writings in its narrowness of focus and unrelievedly
technical content, much of the latter derived from Daniel Prince, the
Oxford bookseller with whom he may have dealt over the publication of
the 'Rag Plot' papers in 1755, as well as the London author and printer
Samuel Richardson. Solely concerned with the 'present excessive Prices'
charged by the university's printers, which are bluntly and doubtless sim-
plistically attributed to 'the Exactions of the Workmen, left as they are to
their own Discretion, through the Weakness and Age of [their] Overseer',
Blackstone lays out a complex array of figures and tables in order to show
how London printers' prices are set, and the level at which they should
henceforth be fixed in Oxford.[46]

Having explained the traditional trade practice of costing compositors' work in types of different sizes by using the lower-case letter 'n' as
a basic unit of measurement, he proposed a complex new method of his
own devising, based on the principle of measuring the area of each printed
page and determining how much type of a given font is required to fill that
space. This process evidently involved measuring 'a vast variety of Books
in all Sizes and Letters', as well as 'Mr Caslon's metal Types', in order to
produce a table showing the number of 'n's per square inch in six different
standard fonts, which Blackstone believed would be more immediately
understood by authors and other laymen (doubtless including his fellow
delegates) than the normal trade method. Unfortunately that is only the
first step in an involved series of calculations 'To propose a Scheme of
Tables, for fixing the Prices at the Oxford Press', with an accompanying
'Set of explanatory Orders', and a lengthy analysis of the distribution of
payment received as between compositors, pressmen, overseer, and the
university itself. The document concludes with a disclaimer submitting
his scheme 'to maturer Judgments', and an afterthought to the effect that
members of the university under the degree of MA or BCL should be
debarred from the Press, 'unless on Business'. (This last was apparently
inspired by Prince's observation that the Press had become another Oxford
tourist attraction; casual visitors taking a 'cursory View of what is doing'
were acceptable, but problems could and did arise when 'Gentlemen of the
University', looking over work in progress, found themselves 'tempted to
advert on some mistaken or controverted Passage'.)[47]

[45] Ibid., 23–42.   [46] Ibid., 23–38.
[47] D. Prince, 'Some Account of the University Printing-House' in Philip, 22.

Blackstone later claimed that his memorandum was never formally considered by the delegates. Such lack of response doubtless reflected the desultory and disorganized fashion in which Press business had been customarily conducted up to this point, as well as the resentment of many delegates, especially the more senior and elderly, at the intrusion of this young activist, whose proposals they accordingly met with 'gloomy and contemptuous silence'. Perhaps (as he later suggested) these same heads of houses, including the President of St John's College, Dr William Derham (c. 1703–1757), the Provost of Oriel College, Dr Walter Hodges (1696–1757), and the Master of Balliol, Dr Theophilus Leigh (1693–1785),[48] did indeed imagine 'that any steps towards reformation would be an acknowledgement of former negligence'.[49] On the other hand, neither in form nor content were Blackstone's 'Thoughts' well calculated to command the attention, let alone the assent of busy, distracted (and in some cases, no doubt, apathetic or lazy) men, who almost certainly failed to share its author's fascination with the commercial and 'mechanical' matters which he canvassed. Whatever the abstract merits of his overall case, its reception may also have been adversely affected by his role in two further issues agitating Oxford's academic community at this time, both of which involved significant challenges to the prerogatives of the university's chief administrative officer, and arguably, the entire structure of academic government.

Blackstone's own collection of 'Controversial Papers relating to the Delegacy of the Press and the Reform there Made A.D. 1756, 7, 8' includes a series of printed pamphlets generated by the dispute between Vice Chancellor Huddesford and the two proctors, John Tracy and Charles Mortimer, who after nominating Blackstone, subsequently attempted to add the university's librarian to the Press delegacy. The first two of these documents, dating respectively from March and May 1756, are detailed defences of the proctors' constitutional rights to nominate delegates in Convocation irrespective of the vice chancellor's consent, with reference both to the university's statutes and previous practice dating back over several centuries.[50] While issued under the proctors' names, it was widely and doubtless correctly assumed that Blackstone played a major role in compiling one or both pamphlets; indeed, the master of Balliol attributed the whole 'troublesome dispute' to Blackstone, together with 'two or three others, Fishers in troubled waters'.[51] The second pamphlet,

---

[48] Ibid., 55.   [49] Ibid.

[50] [G. Huddesford], *Observations Relating to the Delegates of the Press* (Oxford, 1756), reprints these two tracts at pp. 1–3 and 5–16: Bodl. MS Top. Oxon. d 387.

[51] Northamptonshire RO, D (F), 88, Theophilus Leigh to Sir William Dolben, 21 May 1756.

which was evidently 'sent about the Common Rooms', seems particularly to have upset Huddesford, who clashed openly with Blackstone on 21 May at a stormy meeting of Congregation (the other, slightly smaller and less powerful academic assembly). According to Leigh, writing that same day, Blackstone 'attempted a Combustion at this morning's Congregation; nothing was effected; probably this may be brought before a Meeting, and then into Convocation'. Some background to that 'Combustion' appears in a letter Blackstone promptly dispatched to Huddesford, formally demanding ('Notwithstanding the very great Distance of our Stations, in the University') that he either substantiate or retract the 'very dark Expression which you was pleased to make use of in Yesterday's Congregation . . . that it was my Custom, in reciting of the Statutes, to omit such words as did not suit my Purpose'.[52]

Huddesford's response was restrained and conciliatory, expressing regret that a 'hasty spark' had led him to reflect unfavourably upon 'a Gentleman, my Friend, and my Assistant' (presumably referring to Blackstone's role in the Chancellor's court), while insisting nonetheless that various passages from the university registers in both pamphlets were indeed misleadingly quoted. In his reply, Blackstone made no corresponding gesture of good will, choosing rather to stand on his dignity and deploy an extended series of defensive assertions and distinctions relating to his role vis-à-vis the pamphlets 'of which I am supposed to be the Compiler'.[53] Huddesford again responded in a placatory fashion, admitting 'my Expression was hasty, and grounded on a wrong Presumption, and I ask your Pardon for my Mistake', although reiterating his determination not to give way on the substantive constitutional issue. There matters as between the vice chancellor and his 'Assistant' rested uneasily for the moment. But the proctors' challenge to the vice chancellor's powers had clearly aroused passions and tempers on both sides of the dispute. Dr Leigh lamented that John Tracy 'was made a Cats-foot, while in Office last year, by the Genius above mentioned', asserting 'if that Genius be not suppressed, there's an End to Government here!' But when that 'Genius' (used here in the classical sense of guiding 'spirit' or influence) informed Tracy a few days later of the vice chancellor's accusations, the reply to 'Dear Blackstone' from his 'most faithful Friend' expressed

---

[52] *Letters*, 42. Proceedings, as in Convocation, were conducted in Latin; the phrase to which Blackstone objected was 'tuum est aliquando omittere Verba, ut mox demonstrabo'.

[53] Bodl. MS Top. Oxon. d 387, fos. 16–16v; *Letters*, 42–44: Blackstone claimed that once the materials for the pamphlets had been collected, 'I was consulted thereupon, and had no inconsiderable Share in digesting these Materials into Form'.

pointed surprise at the conduct of 'our supreme Magistrate', and no good opinion of either Huddesford's candour or veracity.[54]

III

Fears of 'faction and rebellion' were further inflamed following the death of Charles Viner on 5 June. Huddesford's initial reaction was to appoint Thomas Walker, a prominent local attorney and town clerk of Oxford as the university's representative to prove the will and administer the estate, under the supervision of the Hebdomadal Board (comprising heads of houses and the vice chancellor). However, in the course of several stormy public meetings, Blackstone took a prominent part in urging Convocation's ultimate right to determine these arrangements, thereby blocking the vice chancellor's plan. Huddesford's subsequent artful offer that he himself might undertake that role was (so Blackstone subsequently claimed) 'rejected with a suitable indignation'.[55] This was a prudent as well as a virtuous refusal. Now that Viner's death had brought the prospect of a handsomely endowed Chair in English law into sharp focus, Blackstone's chances of gaining that prize might be severely compromised were he not to distance himself from arrangements to implement a benefaction in which he had such an obvious personal interest. Fortunately for Blackstone, that interest was unlikely to be overlooked, since the group of five delegates eventually appointed by Convocation to administer the will and determine how the proceeds of Viner's estate might best be mobilized to fulfil the testator's intentions included his close collaborator and friend Benjamin Buckler.[56]

How could Huddesford have thought that Blackstone might be lured by the offer of such a relatively low-level job? Possibly because there was a view around Oxford at this time that he was hungry for preferment of any kind.[57] A fortnight before Viner's death, Dr Leigh claimed that Blackstone's eyes had long been set on the Camden Professorship of Ancient History, a position held since 1727 by the now elderly physician Richard Frewin. Indeed, the master of Balliol voiced his uncharitable hope that Blackstone would 'wait . . . much longer for Dr Frewin's Professorship,

---

[54] Northamptonshire RO, D (F) 88; Bodl. MS Top. Oxon. d 387, fos. 22–22v.

[55] Philip, 70.

[56] Ibbetson, 'Charles Viner and his Chair', 323–4; Doolittle, 49–50.

[57] In 1759 it was claimed that Blackstone had actively canvassed 'Votes and Interest' for 'the Registership of the County', referring to the anticipated establishment of a county register of deeds in 1758: see below, p. 158.

than he hath hitherto done'.[58] A sliver of indirect support for Leigh's claim is provided by a letter Blackstone wrote on 2 June (three days before Viner's death) to Sir John Eardley Wilmot, the reclusive lawyer with antiquarian interests who had been made a justice of King's Bench the previous year, enclosing a copy of the 1216 reissue of Magna Carta recently acquired by the Bodleian Library.[59] Besides explaining the conventions adopted in his transcription of the original document, Blackstone was at pains to demonstrate his historiographical acumen, pointing out that the date attributed to the manuscript by the medieval chronicler Walter de Hemmingford must be incorrect, given the text's reference to a papal legate known to have left England in the early years of Henry III's reign. This transcription, together with related documents also sent to Wilmot, formed the basis of the edition of Magna Carta which Blackstone eventually published three years later. This delay very possibly reflected a major shift in his priorities following the news of Viner's death. It is also notable in this context that 1756–7 appears to be the only academic year between 1753–4 and 1765–6 in which Blackstone did not deliver a course of lectures. We have seen that his takings for the third series commencing in Michaelmas term 1755 fell below the amount received for the first, which may well have suggested that his potential student audience had by now been largely exhausted. At all events, he evidently decided against delivering a lecture course in 1756, since the posthumous summary of income from his 'Law Lectures' is blank for that year, and no other evidence contradicts James Clitherow's accompanying annotation, 'I presume he did not read'.[60]

If it was only from June 1756 that securing the still-to-be-created Vinerian 'Professorship of the Common Law' became a significant goal for Blackstone, his last known poetic composition was most probably written at some point during the preceding five months. 'Friendship: An Ode' survives as a manuscript, not in Blackstone's handwriting, annotated 'Verses by Judge Blackstone', together with the date '1756'.[61] But there seems no reason to doubt the authenticity of this gracious exploration and celebration of Blackstone's close personal relationship with his junior colleague Richard Bagot, who had been elected to a fellowship at All Souls in 1753. Both the classical form of the ode, and the subject of male–male friendship, were entirely characteristic of the mid-eighteenth

---

[58] Northamptonshire RO, D (F) 88. Leigh's hostility evidently went back to the university election of 1751, when his son-in-law (Sir Edward Turner) was defeated by Newdigate: ibid., 87a (6 March 1752).

[59] *Letters*, 45; Craster, *Annals of the Bodleian*, 252.

[60] See Appendix II below.

[61] I am grateful to Anthony Taussig for a copy of this document.

century.[62] We have already seen that Bagot accompanied Blackstone on visits to Sir Roger Newdigate in Warwickshire the previous autumn, and in London before that. Yet at first sight (as Blackstone's poem begins) the two were hardly well matched, either by 'equal Birth', or indeed by 'rival Youth', since 'My rugged brows had felt the Cares, Of ten more Springs than Thine'. So while the well-born and much younger Bagot might reasonably expect to 'Glide Down Life's Resplendent Stream', attaining 'Riches, Glory, Power' as a lawyer (albeit spurning with 'brave Disdain | The low-born Arts of sordid Gain') and legislator, his older friend was destined for a humbler lot: with 'Cloyster'd Clerks to dwell, | And Court in calm Oblivion's Cell, | That Liberty I loved'. Nor were they similarly sociable spirits, delighting in 'mutual Mirth'; for 'How much unlike my turbid Noon, Is thy unclouded rising Sun!' What they did have in common, it seems, was some quality of beneficent emotional sympathy, or empathy:

> The Heart's well-meaning glow,
> The Soul that scorns a private end
> That feels the transport of a friend
> And melts at human woe.

This disposition, wholly virtuous in itself ('For Vice had never Friend'), might nevertheless be perverted to some unspecified 'wicked end'. But Blackstone indicated that he would seek to avoid any such undesirable outcome:

> Amid Temptation's slippery ways
> Be Virtue still my [Bagot's] praise
> I'll copy where I can:
> Bid ev'ry wayward Passion cease
> And from the fair well finish'd piece
> New Modell all the Man.

Exactly what kinds of slippery temptation Blackstone may have had in mind is not further specified; nor is it entirely clear whether the poet's persona, or Bagot, or both, were thought to be under threat. But the reference is more likely to irrational or self-seeking thoughts or feelings in general, rather than the physical expression of homoerotic attachment. Blackstone seems essentially to be saying that henceforth he will try to reconstruct his own character along the virtuous lines so well exemplified

---

[62] R. Cohen, 'The return to the ode', in *The Cambridge Companion to Eighteenth-Century Poetry*, ed. J. Sitter (Cambridge, 2001), 203–224; G. Hagerty, 'Horace Walpole's Epistolary Friendships', *British Journal for Eighteenth-Century Studies*, 29 (2006), 201–218.

by Bagot's. Be that as it may, the poem turns to depict 'with eager Joy' the 'shining Track' which Bagot is destined to follow, both at the bar and before 'the attentive Senate', where he will not only 'guard Britannia's laws', but 'With equal Zeal support the throne'. Finally, of course, all must end; the poem contrasts its author's eventual fate ('Forgotten I shall fail') with the likely survival of his friend's 'Fame', comparable to that of such earlier legal eminences as 'Talbot, Holt, or Hale'. Yet the 'Pleasing hope' remains that 'Friendship's holy Love' will not be wanting in the afterlife—for otherwise, 'T'were hard to guess at Heaven'.

While apparently speaking more directly of the poet's affections and emotions, his social status, and interactions, than Blackstone's earlier verse writings, it is hard to know how far 'Friendship: An Ode' can be read as something other than an accomplished exercise in the period's conventional poetic rhetoric. Blackstone may have deliberately chosen to depict himself in markedly self-deprecatory fashion, both to conform to an orthodox literary *topos* of authorial modesty, and better to enhance or flatter the merits of his friend. Yet such a strategy is also consistent with that 'natural Reserve and Diffidence which' (according to Clitherow) 'accompanied him from his earliest Youth, and which he could never shake off'.[63] So the strong sense of personal inadequacy running through the poem probably should not be attributed merely to literary artifice or convention, just as the same character trait helps to explain the prickly sensitivity with which Blackstone reacted to perceived slights. More speculatively, the lack of any hint that its author entertained thoughts of life beyond his monastic 'Cell', and the silence about the nature of his pursuits within that restricted compass, do nothing to detract from Leigh's suggestion that Blackstone was seriously interested in the possibility of succeeding to Richard Frewin's history chair. But in the event, of course, it was the 78-year-old Charles Viner, rather than the 75-year-old Frewin, who died in the summer of 1756.

IV

From this point forward, no more is heard of Blackstone as a prospective professor of history. Early in July 1756, his attendance with other red-robed doctors at the 'grand Convocation' and solemn Commemoration of Benefactors in the Sheldonian Theatre, followed by dinner with Newdigate

[63] Clitherow, xxvii. Cf. Malone's reference to Blackstone as 'extremely diffident of his opinion': J. Prior, *Life of Edmond Malone* (1860), 431.

and Lady Pomfret, may have provided some welcome distraction from the struggle against Vice Chancellor Huddesford's attempts to maintain control of both the Viner bequest and the University Press.[64] (Blackstone would later recount his summoning on 13 July 'at ten o'clock at night' by a university beadle to a meeting of the Press delegacy next day, but only if he came as a 'stated' delegate, thereby recognizing the vice chancellor's disputed authority to control such appointments: 'if not, his Attendance is not required'.)[65] Otherwise he kept a low profile for the remainder of this year, making no direct answer in kind to Huddesford's September attack on the proctors and their allies, despite various slighting references in that pamphlet to the 'Skill in the Law' and citation of university statutes 'more *craftily*, than *fairly*' of an unnamed 'Mr Paper Writer', almost certainly aimed at Blackstone. Yet it is hard to believe that he did not play some part in assisting his colleague John Tracy with drafting the extensive *Reply* to Huddesford which appeared before the year's end, and not least its reference to principles of statutory interpretation favoured by civilians, and the reduction of the former vice chancellor's arguments to 'a regular series and method, the want of which is frequently no small support to a lame and feeble cause'.[66]

During the autumn of 1756, Blackstone's characteristic reticence was almost certainly reinforced by preoccupation with reworking and greatly expanding the original four diagrammatic plans of his lecture course, provided as printed broadsheets for the benefit of student audiences from 1753 onwards. The result was a compact but substantial text and teaching aid, *An Analysis of the Laws of England*, running to just under 200 pages in its first octavo edition of 1,000 copies, which were printed for Blackstone at the University's Clarendon Press.[67] The author's preface, dated from All Souls College on 2 November 1756, recalled that his lectures aimed to provide a 'Plan of the Laws of England' which was both comprehensive ('as that every Title might be reduced under some or other of it's general

[64] Newdigate Diary, 6 July 1756; *Jackson's Oxford Journal*, 10 July 1756. Besides speeches and verses declaimed on the day, separate commemorative publications included W. Thompson, *Gratitude* (Oxford, 1756); [Anon.], *A Poem on the Countess of Pomfret's Benefaction* (Oxford, 1756), and [Anon.], *A Poem on the Pomfret Statues* (Oxford, 1758).

[65] Philip, 48–9; the original summons is now Bodl. MS Top. Oxon. d 387, fos. 66–66v.

[66] [G. Huddesford], *To the Reverend and Worshipful the Heads of Colleges and Halls* (Oxford, 1756), II, XI; [C. Mortimer and J. Tracy], *A Reply to Dr Huddesford's Observations Relating to the Delegates of the Press with a Narrative of the Proceedings of the Proctors* (Oxford, 1756), 8, 15, 31: both bound up in Bodl. MS Top. Oxon. d 387, the latter (dated 12 November 1756) with annotations and corrections in Blackstone's handwriting. Huddesford's term as vice chancellor expired in October 1756: *HUO*, 889; OUA, Hyp/A/60, fo. 13; cf. H. Carter, *A History of the Oxford University Press: Volume I. To the Year 1780* (Oxford, 1975), 328.

[67] Carter, *History*, 553.

Heads') but yet 'so contracted, that the Gentleman might with tolerable Application contemplate and understand the Whole'. To achieve that end 'he found himself obliged to adopt a Method, in many respects totally new', notwithstanding previous efforts by those 'who have laboured in reducing our Laws to a System'. Sir Matthew Hale's was 'the most natural and scientifical of any, as well as the most comprehensive', but even Hale's plan was only 'principally followed', since Blackstone had 'rather chosen, by compounding their several Schemes, to extract a new Method of his own, than implicitly to copy after any'.[68]

This decision produced 'one Inconvenience', in that when his hearers missed or misunderstood a point in his oral presentation, they lacked any 'written Compendium to which they might resort'. Hence the *Analysis*, which 'exhibits the Order, and principal Divisions, of his Course', and should be regarded as 'a larger *Syllabus*, interspersed with a few Definitions and general Rules, to assist the Recollection as such Gentlemen as have formerly honoured him with their Attendance; or such as may hereafter become his Auditors, till this Task shall fall into abler Hands, and the Province, which he originally undertook in a private Capacity, shall be put upon a public Establishment'.[69] Despite the conventionally modest reference to 'abler Hands', Blackstone must surely have expected this, the first book published under his own name, to bolster his claims on that anticipated 'public Establishment', in the shape of the Vinerian Chair.

As well it might, for the *Analysis* represented a marked advance on any previous introduction to English law. Its coverage was truly comprehensive, including constitutional, civil and criminal law, public and private law, substantive law and procedure, as well as some introductory jurisprudential content in the first two chapters 'Of the Nature of Laws in General' and 'The Grounds and Foundation of the Laws of England'. Succinctly expressed, in coherent sentences rather than note form, Blackstone's material is clearly organized and presented, each chapter consisting of a sequence of consecutively numbered paragraphs. Key words are printed in small capital letters, but there are no potentially confusing or distracting marginal references to legal authorities, while the whole is preceded by diagrammatic analytical tables summarizing the contents of the four books, much like the printed broadsheet outlines of the lecture course. The attractive typography and uncluttered

---

[68] W. Blackstone, *An Analysis of the Laws of England* (Oxford, 1756), iv, v, vii.

[69] Ibid., viii. Relatively little scholarly attention has been paid to this work; see however J. Cairns, 'Blackstone, An English Institutist: Legal Literature and the Rise of the Nation State', *Oxford Journal of Legal Studies*, 4 (1984), 340–1; J. M. Finnis, 'Blackstone's Theoretical Intentions', *Natural Law Forum*, 12 (1967), 163–83.

layout of each page doubtless owed something to Blackstone's recent crash-course in the technical aspects of the printer's craft, and are in marked contrast to the cramped appearance of Hale's posthumously published *Analysis of the Law*. Following the 131 pages of main text is a 47-page appendix, with sample documents illustrating common modes of land transfer and other legal transactions (e.g. 'Proceedings on an Action of Debt, in the Court of common Pleas, removed into the King's Bench, by Writ of Error'); these are preceded by tables of descents and of consanguinity (the latter borrowed from his own 1751 *Essay on Collateral Consanguinity),* all 'explaining certain Principle, and Matters of daily Practice; of which it was however impracticable to convey an adequate Idea by verbal description only'.[70]

Hailed by the *Monthly Review* as 'an elegant performance', and one 'calculated to facilitate this branch of knowledge', the *Analysis* was a runaway publishing success.[71] Three more editions, each of 1,000 copies, appeared over the next three years, a fifth in 1762 and a sixth and final edition in 1771, by which time the availability of the *Commentaries* had made the *Analysis* largely redundant, even as an 'Outline or Abstract' of that work.[72] While the basic contents and organization remained largely unchanged, Blackstone did make minor corrections and additions to each successive printing, as he would later with his magnum opus. A note appended to the preface of the third (1758) edition explains these authorial revisions as prompted by the book 'having, by some means or other, met with a more general Reception out of the University than he ever apprehended it could have done'. That edition also included the author's recent inaugural lecture as Vinerian Professor, placed there (as he claimed) 'to relieve the Attention of the Reader by some inquiries more interesting and amusing, than the dry Method of analytical Distribution, or the dull Forms of Conveyancing and Entries'.[73]

In the period of nearly two years between the first publication of *An Analysis of the Laws of England* and his election to the Vinerian Chair, Blackstone ended his self-imposed exile from Westminster Hall, attending and noting cases in Michaelmas and Hilary terms, largely those argued before Mansfield in King's Bench, without seeking briefs for himself.[74] He also provided occasional legal advice and formal written opinions to Queen's College and its Michel Foundation, and to the fellows

[70] Ibid., ix, 133–80.
[71] *Monthly Review,* 16 (March 1757), 224–5.
[72] Carter, *History,* 329, 406; W. Blackstone, *An Analysis of the Laws of England* (Oxford, 1771), xi.
[73] W. Blackstone, *An Analysis of the Laws of England* (Oxford, 1758), x–xi.
[74] Clitherow, xxiv; Blackstone, *Reports,* i. 65–123.

of Oriel College. Otherwise, surprisingly little trace of his activities in Oxford during this period has survived. We know that he was present at meetings of the delegates to the University Press in July, October, and November 1756, when arrangements for the long-delayed printing of a second edition of Bishop Edmund Gibson's manual of ecclesiastical law were eventually finalized.[75] But of delegates' meetings for the following year there is no record whatever, some indication in itself of the deplorable state into which the university's printing affairs had now sunk. Blackstone seems to have hoped that the new vice chancellor, Dr Thomas Randolph, would prove more receptive than his predecessor to the case for a radical overhaul of the Press's management, administration, and finances. But his extensive open letter to Randolph, outlining in detail the main problems and solutions as he saw them, which was published in May 1757 with additional copies circulated to members of Convocation, seems to have had anything but the desired effect.[76] While Randolph possibly shared fewer political sympathies with Blackstone and his All Souls friends than George Huddesford had done, one main reason for his resistance to Blackstone's wide-ranging proposals for reform was the simmering dispute about the respective rights of proctors and the vice chancellor to nominate delegates to the Press. Far from having been exhausted in the various printed exchanges of 1756, this remained a sufficiently sensitive issue for Blackstone to lament that such a 'difference of opinion, in a matter comparatively of little consequence, should unfortunately obstruct the reformation of the press itself'.[77] Yet apart from Randolph's understandable reluctance to give up any vice chancellorial prerogatives, Blackstone's opponents represented his reform programme as 'a rebellion of factious spirits against the legal authority of the heads of houses' (who had previously monopolized the Press delegacy), or 'as the effect of private resentment against one gentleman' (presumably Vice Chancellor Huddesford), 'or (at best) of private attachment and bigotted friendship to another' (presumably Blackstone himself).[78]

---

[75] *First Minute Book of the Delegates of the Oxford University Press 1668–1756* (Oxford, 1943), 58–9; see also W. Gibson, 'Bishop Gibson's Codex and the reform of the Oxford University Press in the Eighteenth Century', *Notes and Queries*, 42 (1995), 47–52.

[76] W. Blackstone, *To the Reverend Dr Randolph, Vicechancellor of the University of Oxford* (Oxford, 1757), in Philip, 45–76. Although Blackstone speaks of Randolph 'not having been yet called to the burthen of either the delegacy of the press, or of accounts' (46), he chaired meetings of the delegates in late 1756: *First Minute Book*, 58–9.

[77] Philip, 68–9. *An Accommodation of the Matters in Dispute, concerning the Delegates of the Press* (Oxford, 1757), drawn up by the junior proctor John Vowell on 31 March 1757, is probably the unsuccessful compromise proposal referred to by Blackstone.

[78] Philip, 69.

During the course of 1757 some progress occurred towards an acceptable compromise position, eventually embodied in a new statute passed by Convocation on 12 December 1757. Besides providing that Press delegates should henceforth be jointly nominated by the two proctors and the vice chancellor, it also stipulated regular quarterly meetings of the delegacy, and that no more than three delegates of accounts might serve at any one time as Press delegates.[79] But these measures did not go far enough for Blackstone, who had drafted another statute which would have replaced the existing delegacy with a wholly new board of eight 'Curators of the Press' nominated by the proctors alone.[80] He now prepared a further scheme embodying the main financial and administrative proposals from his published open letter, and forwarded them to Vice Chancellor Randolph, as the basis of a motion intended for the next delegates' meeting on 24 January 1758. Unfortunately Randolph neither acknowledged receipt of Blackstone's proposals, nor even drew them to the attention of the meeting. This apparent slight provoked an angry and bitter response. After expressing dismay that he had been denied the 'Civility . . . due from one Gentleman to another, your Equal in the Care of the Press, notwithstanding my acknowledged Inferiority in other respects, within the Limits of this University', Blackstone announced that if 'every Proposal which comes from me, in regard to the Press, shall be treated with the same Hauteur and Neglect that I have experienced for these two Years past', it was now plainly time to 'use other Arguments than those of Persuasion, in order to procure to the Cause of the University, and of Learning, a *full* and *extensive* Justice'. He proceeded to inform Randolph that the university's transactions were being closely watched 'by Persons of the highest Rank both in Church and State', including 'the first Commoner in the Kingdom'—seemingly a reference to William Pitt, now secretary of state and de facto prime minister—who had very recently sought from him 'an Account of the University Press'. So, while remaining 'ready to concur in any healing Measures that shall be consistent with the Duty I owe to the University', as long as his 'Endeavours to serve the Public are to be received with a silent supercilious Contempt', and 'the Justice due to our Constituents (the University) . . . refused or eluded at home', it could hardly be surprising 'should we be called upon to justify our Conduct before another, less indulgent, Tribunal'.[81]

---

[79] Carter, *History*, 329; Philip, 75–6.

[80] 'Heads of a Statute to direct the Appointment, & to declare the Qualifications, Power, Office & Duration of Curators of the Press 1757': Bodl. MS Top. Oxon. d 387, fos. 7–8v.

[81] *Letters*, 48–9; Blackstone's draft of this letter initially included references to justice being obtained, or answers demanded, in 'another Place'.

Faced with this blunt threat of ministerial and parliamentary intervention, the vice chancellor protested that he 'designed no Incivility and can't help saying that you take Fire with very little Provocation'. The delegates' meeting had been wholly taken up with other business, but 'you may remember that I thanked you for your Papers'. While 'ready to give your Proposals a due Consideration', Dr Randolph also noted that 'this Place has many Enemies, who are very ready to lay hold on any Cause of Complaint whether real, or groundless'; but in doing his duty 'I shall fear no Enemies either within, or without the University'.[82] Blackstone's impassioned reply reiterated the long history of 'gloomy Reserve and Neglect'[83] with which his 'proposals for regulating the Press' had been treated over 'more than two years past', expressed concern that central issues were still being avoided, and reminded Randolph that his proposals were 'in Nature of a Compromise ... *on condition* that we go on regularly in the manner pointed out in the future'. Should this condition not be met, 'I shall then be at Liberty to call for an Account of the Application of the Press Revenues for 20 years past. If that also be refused me, I know where I both may, and in Duty must seek for Redress.' As for 'your unkind Insinuation', such 'words so vague and unmeaning ... shall never frighten me from ... the Duty which I owe to my Constituents', who would have no difficulty in determining the 'genuine Characteristics of an Enemy to this University'.[84]

Blackstone's first letter of protest might appear an overreaction, since the very meeting which precipitated it had actually endorsed one of his central demands, for copies of charters and statutes relating to the Press to be 'fairly transcribed in order of time in a Book to be kept by the Registrar of the University' for the information of delegates.[85] Yet it still took three more meetings over the next month before his other major proposals, measures relating to the keeping of comprehensive accounts, the crediting to the Press of misappropriated university revenues, and the appointment of 'a Person properly versed in both Branches of the printing Business, as well Casework as Presswork, to be their Warehousekeeper and Overseer', won acceptance.[86] Two more meetings in early March were required to gain approval for Blackstone's elaborate set of regulations and tables governing prices to be charged for printing at the University Press; at the next gathering of the delegates the vice chancellor himself, perhaps emboldened

---

[82] Bodl. MS Top. Oxon. d 387, fos. 36–36v.

[83] His draft has 'Contempt &c': *Letters*, 50.

[84] Ibid., 50–1. [85] Philip, 90; Carter, *History*, 330.

[86] Ibid., 91–3; the successful candidate 'unanimously chosen' was Blackstone's associate Daniel Prince.

by the absence of Drs Leigh and Jenner, moved from the chair a vote of thanks to Blackstone 'for his Care and Trouble'.[87]

William Blackstone's successful campaign to regulate the Press has been described as 'the most ruthless single-handed reform in eighteenth-century Oxford'.[88] While competition for that title was scarcely intense, the historian of Oxford University Press suggests that it 'would be hard to find in English history another such victory of reform with no significant compromise'. It 'may have saved the Press from extinction' and 'almost certainly saved learned publishing by corporately-owned university presses', besides profoundly shaking the university itself: 'for what could be done in the Press could be done in other departments . . . '.[89] Nor was it only privileged heads of house like Dr Leigh who recognized the radical thrust of Blackstone's activities. In 1762 John Wilkes's opposition journal acclaimed Blackstone as 'lawyer Keene', the 'honest lawyer', who found a deficiency of £20,000 in the Oxford University Press accounts, 'not a farthing of which sum could be produced or accounted for, it having (as is generally imagined) been spent in feasting &c., which work of iniquity he published to the whole University'.[90] But if Blackstone won plaudits outside as well as within Oxford for his courageous and relentless efforts to revive scholarly publishing at the Clarendon Press, that same stance and actions inevitably aroused much academic antipathy and ill-will. So, while it may indeed have been 'peace at last' so far as the printing house was concerned, in the university at large, conflict and discord continued to swirl around the formidable figure of Dr Blackstone.[91]

For on 8 March 1758 the syndics appointed to prove and execute Viner's will reported to Convocation.[92] Printed copies of the resolutions they intended to recommend in their other capacity, as delegates for administering Viner's benefaction, touched off brief but furious paper warfare. Nearly 30 flysheets and pamphlets survive, all anonymous, many undated, produced by opponents and supporters of the delegates' proposals before and after the crucial meetings of Convocation on 13 June and 3 July 1758. The break-neck pace at which charge and counter-charge were exchanged sorely tested the capacity of Oxford's printing presses,

[87] Philip, 94–5. Randolph may also have been responding to a markedly more conciliatory attitude on Blackstone's part: *Letters*, 51–2.

[88] Philip, 1.

[89] Carter, *History*, 330–1.

[90] *The North Briton* (1763), ii. 60 (No. 29, 18 December 1762).

[91] Carter, *History*, 331.

[92] OUA, Reg. 1757–66, NEP/Subtus/Reg. Bh, fos. 11–12; see fuller accounts in Doolittle, 50–54, and Ibbetson, 'Charles Viner and his Chair', 323–8.

to such an extent that several contributions may have circulated only in manuscript.[93] Although attribution can be based on little more than stylistic grounds, Blackstone himself may well have supplied at least four separate items, besides possibly intercepting and adding his own dismissive answers to a set of questions raised by some of his opponents even before it reached the press.[94] If the fact of his authorship cannot now be conclusively established, there is little doubt that his friend Buckler had ready access to his advice and suggestions in drafting what can more confidently be identified as defences of the scheme put forward by his fellow delegates and himself.[95]

In the whole controversy it is difficult to distinguish issues of principle from what one pamphlet delicately termed 'prejudice arising either from friendship or pique to any particular person'.[96] Critics of the delegates' proposals focused on what they represented as the excessively generous provision envisaged for the Vinerian Chair, especially the annual salary of £200, which would absorb most of the available endowment income. They argued that Viner had seen his professor as a person 'actually engaged in the Practice of the Law', who would deliver a few public lectures each year for a fairly nominal fee, while the remaining revenue from his benefaction went to support various fellows, tutors, and scholars of the common law—a potential law school, in other words. Since Viner had drafted and cancelled several wills, the last of which left most details to be determined by Convocation, there was room for debate as to what his real intentions had been and how they might best be fulfilled. Because Blackstone was the obvious local candidate for Viner's professorship, suspicions that the whole scheme was drawn up with him in mind provoked a predictably hostile reaction. Yet those opposing the delegates' resolutions felt bound to deny that they were merely 'acting from base Motives of Envy, Malice, and Spleen against this truly learned and ingenious Man'.[97] Such disavowals may not have been wholly insincere, since the scheme proposed

---

[93] See Bodl. Gough Oxon. 96 (28), (28a), both headed *Advertisement*, and directed respectively to the Magdalen and Brasenose College common rooms; also (32a), *Articles submitted....*

[94] Doolittle, 50, 52n. Blackstone's own anonymous contributions to the Vinerian chair controversy almost certainly include the following: (i) *Some Doubts having arisen with regard to Mr VINER's Intentions...*, Bodl. Gough Oxford 96 (14, 15); (ii) *Short Remarks on a Paper dated June 30, 1758*, Bodl. Gough Oxon. 96 (29); (iii) *That it may be the more readily apprehended...*, Bodl. Gough. Oxon. 96 (33); (iv) *A Question having been started, with regard to the Power of Congregation*, Bodl. Gough Oxon. 96 (51); and (v) *The Members of Convocation are desired seriously to consider the following...*: Bodl. Gough 96 (52).

[95] Another copy of Bodl. Gough 96 (22), *An Examination of the Objections to the Resolutions...*, in Bodl. G. A. Oxon. b 19 (779) is annotated 'By Mr Buckler of All Souls'.

[96] *June 3rd, 1758. The Resolutions of Mr Viner's Delegacy*, Bodl. Gough Oxon. 96 (20), 3.

[97] Bodl. Gough Oxon. 96 (23), *A Reply to the Examiner*, 4.

was open to objection on various grounds, above all the lack of institutional structure to ensure the long-term viability of legal education in Oxford. Yet personal animosity to Blackstone was clearly present, voiced in Convocation by 'some who were too honest to disguise their Zeal with the semblance of Candour', as well as in broadsheets and pamphlets. We have no way of discerning how widely such enmity was expressed in less formal settings around Oxford.[98]

In the end the delegates prevailed, and their plan, or the greater part of it, was subsequently embodied in statutes establishing the Vinerian Chair. However this initial acceptance was only achieved by the very narrow margin of two votes, which immediately raised constitutional questions about the voting rights of the proctors and the vice chancellor, without whose support the entire scheme would have foundered. Further, Blackstone's hopes of establishing an Oxford society for common lawyers on the lines of Cambridge's Trinity Hall for civilians were dashed when Convocation jibbed at the prospect of removing the Vinerian fellows and scholars from their existing colleges or halls. Nor could it be safely assumed that Blackstone's accession to the Vinerian Chair itself was a mere formality. A week before the election date, one don heard that because Blackstone's 'opponents are sullen and won't speak, it is thought adviseable by his friends, to guard against a surprise' by summoning in well-disposed voters from the nearby shires. Not until the day before the poll could the publisher of Oxford's newspaper confidently report 'there is not any Opposition talked of, so that Dr Blackstone will have it quietly'.[99] His prediction was entirely accurate, for on 20 October 1758 Dr William Blackstone was elected unopposed by Convocation as the Foundation Professor of English Law in the University of Oxford.

---

[98] Bodl. Gough Oxon. 96 (25), [B. Buckler], *A View of the Misrepresentations*, 1 July 1758, 2.

[99] Clitherow, xvii–xviii; *Letters of Richard Radcliffe and John James*, ed. M. Evans (Oxford Historical Society, ix, 1888), xxx; Royal Institution of Cornwall, BLP/1/49, William Jackson to William Borlase, 19 October 1758.

CHAPTER 8

'A More Public Scene' (1758–61)

O N Saturday 21 October 1758, the day after he was 'duly and legitimately elected' to the Vinerian Chair, a printed broadsheet announced that 'by the Appointment and with the Approbation of the Vice-Chancellor . . . Mr Viner's Professor' would 'read a general introductory Lecture in the History School' the following Wednesday, 'at the Hour of Eleven'.[1] This 'first Solemn Lecture on the Common Law' was duly delivered to what the local newspaper reported as 'a crowded Audience'. Hastened into print less than a fortnight later as *A Discourse on the Study of the Law*, by late December a London correspondent claimed to hear Blackstone's lecture 'commended wherever I go'.[2] What one reviewer termed 'this sensible, spirited, and manly exhortation to the study of the law' was reprinted in a further thousand copies next year; it also prefaced subsequent editions of the *Analysis of the Laws*, and eventually the first volume of the *Commentaries*. Reflecting 'honour upon its author and the learned convocation by whom he is appointed public professor' according to the *Critical Review*, the *London Magazine* agreed that it was 'an excellent and learned discourse' which 'plainly shews how well the university have been directed in their choice', while the *Annual Register* praised 'a solid, judicious and elegant oration, containing at once, a history of our law, a just panegyric on it, arguments for putting the study of it under proper regulations, and a spirited persuasive to make that study so regulated, a considerable part of academical education . . .'.[3] Large slabs appeared in an anthology of improving 'Thoughts, Moral and

[1] OUA, Convocation Register 1757–66, NEP/Subtus/Reg Bh, 48–9. Bodl. Gough 96 (36), 'Oxford, 21 October, 1758. Notice is hereby given . . .'.
[2] *Jackson's Oxford Journal*, 28 October 1758. OUA, WPα 22/1, fos. 18–18v.
[3] *Critical Review*, 6 (November 1758), 438; *London Magazine*, 27 (1758), 619; *The Annual Register . . . 1758* (7th edn., 1783), 452; see also *Monthly Review*, 19 (November 1758), 486–88; *London Chronicle*, 4 (16–18 November 1758), 484–6.

Divine', while the short-lived *Lawyer's Magazine, or Attorney and Solicitor's Universal Library* claimed that 'the extremely happy . . . Sentiments' of the 'judicious Dr Blackstone' on the current deficiencies of common-law education were what 'first gave rise to this Magazine', which had as its 'real Design' the propagation of 'plain and easy Rules for pursuing a Course of Law Study'.[4]

I

Within the University of Oxford however, Professor Blackstone's whole performance, including his consciously enlightened appeal for 'a more open and generous way of thinking' about the academic curriculum in the face of 'monastic prejudice',[5] predictably met with less than universal approval. Paper warfare recommenced on 20 November, the same day that his now very well-subscribed private lecture series opened, with an anonymous three-page flysheet defending Convocation's recent decision not to dispense the two Vinerian scholars from their statutory obligation to attend the professor's lectures, even though they had already sat through two complete lecture courses before the Vinerian Chair was established. The same publication also charged that Blackstone had '*violated the Statutes of the University, by arbitrarily changing the Day appointed for reading his solemn Lectures*'.[6] This italicized quotation comes from an icy two-paragraph response of 22 November, which called on his 'nameless Accusers to stand forth, and maintain their Accusation', while affirming in the face of 'so injurious a Treatment' that his lecture had not been one of those prescribed by statute for particular dates on the university calendar, but rather 'with the Leave of the Vice-Chancellor a supernumerary public Lecture, by way of general Introduction to the Course'.[7]

Blackstone would have been better advised to ignore the sniping of his critics as no more than 'the impotent Resentment of a *disappointed Party*' (to quote again from the anonymous flysheet, whose authors naturally claimed a very different motivation). But at this point he may not

[4] C. Wellins, *A Collection of Thoughts, Moral and Divine, upon Various Subjects* (Manchester, 1761), 145–52; ibid. (Exeter, 1764), 137–43. *The Lawyer's Magazine, or Attorney's and Solicitor's Universal Library* (1761), 17–18.

[5] *Commentaries*, i. 4, 16–27.

[6] *A Petition having been propos'd* [Oxford, 1758], 1–3; the dispensation was refused notwithstanding letters of recommendation from the Chancellor: OUA, NEP/subtus/Reg Bh, Register of Convocation 1757–66, 52–3.

[7] *Dr Blackstone finding himself personally charged*: Bodl. Gough Oxon. 96 (38).

have fully recovered from the 'late Hurries', which (as he told Sir Roger
Newdigate on 12 November), together with 'too great a Quantity perhaps
of dyed Tea, have lately put my nervous System a little out of order'. While
hoping 'to be quite stout in a Week more', his condition had evidently
seemed sufficiently serious to require him to point out that 'the Report of
my Death was groundless'. He nevertheless insisted that he was making
an excellent recovery, aided by 'Spa-Water . . . a Sabbath as to mental
Employment, and a regular Use of gentle (very gentle!) Exercise', even if
'much Writing does not yet agree with me'.[8]

Nothing more is known about the nature or extent of what must have
been a nervous or psychological collapse in the immediate aftermath of
his inaugural lecture. But it is difficult to believe that the next act in this
extraordinary drama would have occurred if he had been fully himself. For
on Friday 24 November 1758, 'William Blackstone, Dr of Laws, Assessor
of the Revd. Dr Randolph, Vice Chancellor of the University of Oxford,
Vinerian Professor of Common Law, Fellow of All Souls College in the
said University and also a Matriculated Person of the same', launched a
suit before Dr George Huddesford, sitting as pro-Vice Chancellor in the
same university court where Blackstone himself was accustomed to pre-
side as assessor, against 'William Jackson of the City of Oxford Printer in
a Cause of Injury and Damage to the Value of £500 occasioned by printing
and publishing a scandalous Libell notoriously reflecting on the Character
of him the said William Blackstone'.[9]

Besides publishing Oxford's weekly newspaper, Jackson's general printing business attracted the custom of those who for whatever reason did
not wish to use the university's Clarendon Press. Given Blackstone's high
profile as a Press delegate, any members of the university who sought
to attack him in print without disclosing their own identity might well
find it prudent to employ Jackson, especially if printing in London were
inconvenient. Jackson was a skilled craftsman, with whom the Cornish
antiquary Dr William Borlase FRS maintained a cordial correspondence
long after first experiencing Jackson's 'great good nature' during the protracted Oxford production of his *Antiquities of Cornwall* and its successor,
the *Natural History of Cornwall*. In one of these letters, written somewhat
after the event, Jackson's own account of the affair refers to 'the violent
Attack my old Friend Dr Blackstone launched on me'.[10] While the precise
nature of their previous relationship is unclear, Blackstone had certainly

---

[8] *A Petition having been propos'd . . .* , 2; *Letters*, 37.
[9] OUA, Hyp/A/72, fos. 328–328v.
[10] P. A. Pool, *William Borlase* (Truro, 1986), 103, 144, 176; Royal Institution of Cornwall, BLP/1/50:
Jackson to Borlase, 15 August 1759.

used Jackson's newspaper earlier in the year to advertise one of his own publications, and may also have employed him to print anonymous pamphlets and other controversial material. Indeed, in reply to Blackstone's demand of 22 November that they should identify themselves, his anonymous adversaries now offered to reveal not only their own names, but so far as possible the identity of '*all* the Persons who were concerned in writing any Paper against the Resolutions of the Delegacy' on Viner's bequest, on condition that '*he himself* will . . . own *upon Honour* all the Papers which he wrote, overlook'd, or procur'd to be printed, during the late Contest'.[11] While Blackstone showed no intention of rising to this bait (understandably enough, given the scale of his own anonymous output), Jackson for his part evidently refused to identify the authors of the 20 November pamphlet to which his former friend had taken such exception, despite considerable pressure to do so: 'neither fair promises nor unchristian menaces could persuade me to be the sneaking Creature he hoped to find me'.[12] It was apparently this recalcitrance which provoked Blackstone to sue Jackson in his own court.

Both plaintiff and defendant lodged bonds to guarantee their appearance at the next sitting day (Blackstone's 'stipulation' in the sum of £20—half that required of Jackson—was made by his All Souls friend and colleague John Tracy), but no record of any further proceedings in the case has been found. In August 1759 Jackson told Borlase that the whole affair, which he was 'very innocently drawn in to be an Instrument', had 'unhappily produced a Division in the University', although the rift had since 'subsided'.[13] Another, notably more hostile source claims that Blackstone had threatened to prosecute the printer 'in a superior Court', and indeed 'actually gave orders for carrying on this Prosecution in the Court of King's-Bench . . . and was very angry with his Friends, for prudently disobeying such imprudent Orders'.[14] Whatever the truth of this last (uncorroborated) claim, Jackson's suggestion that his personal

[11] *Jackson's Oxford Journal*, 25 March 1758, iii (Bodl. copy, annotated with names of those lodging advertisements). *Dr Blackstone having desired the Authors of a Paper dated November 20, 'to maintain their Accusations'*: Bodl. Gough Oxon. 96 (39), 3; this undated piece bears a strong typographical resemblance to its predecessor, Bodl. Gough Oxon. 96 (37).

[12] Royal Institution of Cornwall, BLP/1/50: Jackson to Borlase, 15 August 1759.

[13] Ibid. OUA, Hyp/A/72, fo. 328. Blackstone may not have been present in court during these proceedings, although he acted as assessor on the same day in at least one case, that of *Elizabeth and Mary Barnes v Edmund Faunce*: OUA, Chancellor's Court Papers 1758, p. 29.

[14] F. Bassett, *The Case of a Gentleman, Unjustly deprived of his Vote at the Election of a Chancellor of the University of Oxford* (1759), 23; Jackson is not mentioned by name, but there seems little doubt that he (rather than Bassett himself) was Blackstone's 'Antagonist' in this 'Transaction': cf. Ward, *Georgian Oxford*, 210. See further below, p. 158.

confrontation with Blackstone had been responsible for splitting the university was plainly exaggerated, since Blackstone's divisive role in Oxford academic politics went back at least as far as the 1751 election campaign. Yet apart from what his heavy-handed reaction to Jackson might reveal about Blackstone's judgement and self-control (even taking into account the possible after-effects of his recent illness), the apparent lack of surviving contemporary comment on this clash possibly indicates that it was seen as of less interest or significance than other interrelated academic controversies around this time.

The first of these was prompted by the death of Oxford's veteran Chancellor, Charles Butler, Earl of Arran, in mid-December 1759. The chancellorship was an elective office which, to quote an early nineteenth-century commentator, 'has always been an object of ambition to the highest nobility in the kingdom'.[15] In Oxford's politicized academic environment, the contest for such a prize was inevitably decided along party-political lines: as one of Blackstone's junior All Souls colleagues put it, 'I need give you no further account than that it was a Tory & Whigg cause.'[16] Given the overwhelming Tory power in the university at large, the only hope the sizeable Whig, administration, or government minority had lay in splitting the 'Old Interest' vote. This seemed a real possibility when two Tory peers allowed their names to go forward as candidates. Blackstone and a majority in most colleges predictably favoured John Fane, Earl of Westmorland, who had held the largely honorific post of high steward of the University since 1754, over his younger and generally more lightweight rival George Lee, Earl of Lichfield. But because Westmorland did not enjoy an absolute majority, his Whig opponent Richard Trevor, Bishop of Durham, might have carried the day if both peers had actually gone to the poll. Such an outcome was totally unacceptable to their respective supporters, since 'the main object was the rejecting the Bishop'; yet 'fears and great animosities amongst the Torys' meant neither camp would willingly switch votes to the rival candidate.[17]

The impasse could only be broken by persuading one or other candidate to withdraw. This Blackstone undertook to do, once a person or persons unknown had raised the issue of Lichfield's eligibility for the chancellorship and sought counsels' opinion on that question. The resulting legal advice seemed to be that, although Lichfield's name had remained on the books of St John's College after he left the university, the fact of his having

---

[15] N. Whittock, *A Topographical and Historical Description of the University and City of Oxford* (1829), 34.

[16] Morrab Library, MOR/Bor/2E: George to William Borlase, 15 February 1759.

[17] Ibid. See also *HUO*, 144–6; Doolittle, 22–3.

subsequently accepted the freedom of the city of Oxford (from which he hastily resigned the day after Arran's death) did not necessarily put him in breach of a seventeenth-century university statute declaring the absolute incompatibility of academic and citizen status.[18] Blackstone took an entirely different view. As he reminded the university's counsel Randle Wilbraham in a long letter drafted on Boxing Day 1758, he and others opposing Sir Edward Turner's candidacy for the university's vacant parliamentary seat in 1750–1 had canvassed a similar argument. The rest of this letter outlines the main points and some of the actual phraseology incorporated in what would be his own decisive intervention in the chancellorship election. Explicitly disavowing the form of a legal opinion, 'being too much interested in the present Election, as a Voter, to set up for an indifferent Arbiter', Blackstone's four-page flysheet was unsigned, although readers were assured that the identity of its author could be ascertained by enquiry from the printer (presumably not William Jackson).[19] After trenchantly criticizing the actual case which had been stated for counsels' opinion, because it 'laid down as indisputable Points . . . the very Matters in Question', Blackstone proceeded to cite a range of authorities—'Charter, Act of Parliament, and Statute'—to support his central contention, that matriculation alone was what made a 'Member of the great Body corporate of the University', irrespective of whether the matriculated person subsequently maintained any form of connection with an Oxford hall or college. Further, the incompatible nature of civic freedom and university membership meant that those who accepted the former must automatically forfeit the latter; this was achieved 'not by *depriving* the Party of those privileges which he has already surrendered, but by perpetually *excluding*, or preventing him from resuming for the future, that Membership of the University, which he has previously thought proper to exchange for the Freedom of the City'.[20] The tract concludes with a brief paragraph endorsing the 'wise and affectionate Caution' given by 'two Gentlemen, who are confessedly the foremost in their Profession' with 'regard to the Dangers that may accrue to the University from electing an unqualified Chancellor'. Using black-letter type for emphasis, Blackstone warned Lichfield's supporters that such an election might **'entangle them in a tedious legal Controversy (the Event of which may be very precarious) and may possibly terminate**

---

[18] OUA, WPα/22/2 (2).

[19] *Letters*, 59–62; OUA, WPα/22/2 (3): *Oxford 30 Dec. 1758| Copies of the Opinions of three very eminent and learned Gentlemen . . .*, 1. Clitherow, xiii, acknowledges Blackstone's authorship, under the title *Reflections on the Opinions of Messrs Pratt, Morton and Wilbraham relating to Lord Litchfield's Disqualification*. See also Bodl. G. A. Oxon. b 19 (97), fo. 98v.

[20] Ibid., 4.

in the Appointment of a Person disagreeable to the Inclinations of a great Majority of the Body of Electors'.

Having drafted his own text soon after sighting the legal opinions,[21] Blackstone evidently provided a copy to the Vice Chancellor, Thomas Randolph, who was busily negotiating a 'Treaty of Coalition' with the Lichfield camp. In three successive notes sent on 29 and 30 December Randolph urged him to delay publication, presumably fearing that the appearance of his 'Observations' might make the caucuses of Lichfield supporters at the King's Arms and New Inn Hall less rather than more amenable to switching their votes. Even the mere mention of his name could be damaging, according to Randolph.[22] While complying with this request, Blackstone had his flysheet printed that same day. After hearing from his friend Chardin Musgrave, provost of Oriel College, that negotiations had progressed no further, Blackstone forwarded a copy to Lord Lichfield's house at Ditchley Park, 12 miles north of Oxford. His blatantly equivocal covering letter assured the recipient that 'were it not for this fatal Objection which I know not how to overcome I think there is no Nobleman in England excepting Lord Westmorland that is at present so justly entitled to every Honour the University can bestow . . . '.[23] Three days later, on the eve of the poll, Lichfield formally withdrew, even as one of his supporters attempted to counter Blackstone's case by arguing that Lichfield's eligibility was a 'Question rather of *Fact* than of *Law*, and of which Members of the University are the most proper Judges'.[24]

While Blackstone may have recovered from the worst effects of whatever psychological disorder laid him low just after his inaugural lecture, the hard-fought chancellorship election can hardly have reduced his stress level. Even before his pamphlet appeared, a friend was suggesting that he should not take too seriously 'the dirt that may have been thrown, it is but too common in all elections . . . '. But this well-meaning reassurance was no better fulfilled than the accompanying prediction that 'as people grow cool they will see clearer, and change their reproaches into thanks'.[25] On the contrary, disgruntled Lichfield partisans continued to voice resentment at the 'subtle men' who had artfully engineered the defeat of their

---

[21] Some version of his argument was supplied to Thomas Lisle before 27 December: see OUA, WPα /22/1, fos. 18–18v.

[22] OUA WPα/22/1, fos. 20–22v; fo. 21. Morrab Library, MOR/Bor/2E: George to William Borlase, 15 February 1759.

[23] OUA, WPα/22/1, fos. 27–27v: Chardin Musgrave to William Blackstone, 30 December 1758; *Letters*, 62–3.

[24] OUA, WPα/22/2 (1): *Some Considerations Submitted to the Members of the Convocation*, endorsed by Blackstone 'Printed Considerations circ. 3 January 1759'.

[25] OUA, WPα/22/1, fo. 18v.

candidate.[26] Blackstone was also singled out for public abuse by an infuriated alumnus who had been barred from voting in the chancellorship election on the grounds of his previous acceptance of freedom of the city of Oxford. Besides charging that his threat to prosecute William Jackson in King's Bench breached his matriculation oath to uphold the university's jurisdiction, the independent-minded Francis Bassett also accused him of having violated at least the spirit of the very university statute that, according to Blackstone, Lichfield had infringed. For, according to Bassett, Blackstone had applied to several prominent Oxfordshire Tory landholders who were also freemen of the city for their support towards his obtaining 'an Employment of great Value . . . viz. the Registership of the County'.[27] This claim cannot now be verified. All we know is that in March of the previous year, when the outcome of the Vinerian bequest remained uncertain, Blackstone had placed an advertisement in Jackson's newspaper urging readers not to commit themselves to any particular candidate for the proposed office of county registrar of deeds, until it became clear whether parliament would indeed establish a national system of land titles registration.[28] Yet however embarrassing he may have found any revelation of his previous interest in preferment which had failed to materialize, even more potentially galling was Bassett's sneer that 'a Man of *small Fortune*, under *such* Obligations, is more exposed to Temptation, than a Man of large independent Fortune'.[29]

As the Cambridge philosopher David Hartley noted, presumably on the basis of personal experience, 'nothing can easily exceed the vain-glory, self-conceit, arrogance, emulation, and envy, that are found in the eminent professors of the sciences, mathematics, natural philosophy, and even divinity itself'.[30] Only a small fraction of the total outpouring of gossip, rumour, slander, and speculation generated by the fractious dons of mid-eighteenth-century Oxford still survives, but Blackstone's popularity and standing within the university had plainly suffered since the

[26] Morrab Library, MOR/Bor/2E, George to William Borlase, 15 February 1759.

[27] Bassett, *Case of a Gentleman*, 20–24. Borlase dates the publication of this pamphlet to 14 February 1759; a copy survives among Blackstone's papers (OUA, WPα/22/4). Ward, *Georgian Oxford*, 211; *H of P 1754–90*, i.62. Bassett seems to have been living in Northamptonshire rather than on his Cornish estates: Royal Institution of Cornwall, MEN 37, 48, 118.

[28] *Jackson's Oxford Journal*, 25 March 1758, iii (annotated copy, Bodleian Library); this information may have come from Jackson via Bassett's friend Borlase: Pool, *William Borlase*, 38; Morrab Library, MOR/Bor/2E ('Original Letters Vol 5'): Peter Sherwin to William Borlase, 3 June 1759. For the failed land registry bill of 1758, see *CJ*, xxviii. 325, and Langford, *Public Life and the Propertied Englishman*, 50–51.

[29] *Case of a Gentleman*, 21, 23.

[30] D. Hartley, *Observations on Man* (1791; first published 1749), i. 458.

Vinerian Chair controversy. Nor was he indifferent to the hostility now directed towards him. By early March 1759 Thomas Winchester was reporting to their mutual friend Roger Newdigate that 'Dr Blackstone has put me & the rest of his Friends into very low Spirits by a resolution he has taken of having Chambers again in the Temple', so as to spend the four legal terms in London, coming to Oxford only for his lectures. In a few years he would doubtless desert Oxford altogether, with disastrous consequences for the Vinerian Foundation, while 'the flourishing State of the Press will fall back into its former torpid Condition'. Winchester could only 'tremble' for the whole university 'as a Learned Body' and virtually the sole institution in the kingdom 'that has kept its Independency'. The reasons were clear enough: 'the many ill returns he has received here for all his good actions, and the little redress he has had for the injuries he has received from those whose station required them to have given it'. Winchester believed that 'the treatment he has received in the late affair' (presumably a reference to the chancellorship election rather than the Vinerian Chair controversy), consisting of 'dark misgivings and cold treatment', had 'returned back upon his mind'. For 'instead of finding that repose he expected . . . he has met with nothing but a perverse and evil spirit of opposition to all his well meant designs'. But perhaps there was still a chance of changing Blackstone's mind, if 'all his friends would join to make him alter his resolution, and to help dispel that Cloud that at present hangs over him, and which I can't but think would in a little time vanish of itself, If we could but persuade him to think so'.[31]

These hopes were not to be fulfilled, perhaps in part because hostility towards Blackstone was more widely diffused throughout the academic community than Winchester indicated or realized. Blackstone could not even count on majority support within his own college, as became apparent when he stood unsuccessfully for election to the office of vice warden in April 1759. One of his senior colleagues, the theologian Dr John White, his colleague as bursar in 1751, then employed against him the same electoral technique he himself had used to such effect in the recent chancellorship contest, challenging his eligibility on the grounds that tenure of the Vinerian Chair with its handsome salary was incompatible with an All Souls fellowship. Responding to this ingenious initiative, and Blackstone's counter-claim that White's curacy disqualified him, a formal meeting of the warden and college officers declared that the college statute which debarred from fellowships those possessing other substantial sources of income, or posts incompatible with serious study, had not been

---

[31] Warwickshire RO, CR136/B4099.

infringed.[32] Whether such an outcome offered much consolation for what in Blackstone's darker moments might easily seem like a vote of no-confidence from his nearest peers and associates is another question. By early June, faint echoes of this affair had reached a remote Cornish parish, as one Oxford-bred clergyman reported to another on recent doings at their alma mater:

Dissension has at length crept into, what was once deem'd the most unanimous House—All Souls; The two Parties are headed by Dr. Blackistone & White and are from thence distinguished by the names of Blacks & Whites. The First of these will convey no very good Idea to you; nor indeed ought you to conceive a very good one of the Leader, since he has made himself from the Darling, the most disliked of the University, by his so greedily assuming to himself (as Professor) almost the whole Income of Viner's Foundation, leaving but a very small Pittance to the Scholers.[33]

II

This depiction of Blackstone as leader of an eponymous collegiate faction is a story almost too good to be true. Yet notwithstanding his embarrassing defeat in the election for vice warden, Blackstone was still a significant figure at All Souls, where a cohort of fellows, both junior and senior, including a future warden in John Tracy, remained his friends and supporters. One of these partisans, most probably Benjamin Buckler, preached in the college chapel next All Souls' Day (2nd November) a sermon which ostensibly commemorated the founder while expounding an obscure Old Testament story as an elaborate allegory of college life. But it also sought to vindicate Blackstone, 'the present worthy Professor, who still continues a fellow, and the ornament of that society' against the 'malice and envy, love of strife and dissension' of his college enemies.[34] Next year two pamphlets by Richard Scrope of Magdalen College attacked this 'most licentious performance', deploring the 'uncharitable Insinuations obliquely aimed at *one Part* of his Fellow-Collegians, in order at any Rate to compliment another'.[35] We cannot now identify

---

[32] Codrington, MS 36, Warden Niblett's Notebook, 20, 27 April 1759; Acta in Capitulis 1753–70, 27 April 1759. Bodl. MS D.D. All Souls b 15; White was elected to a fellowship in 1740 (not 1753 as stated by *HUO*, 194n): Simmons List; *Al. Oxon.*, iv. 1539. Robertson, *All Souls College*, 27.

[33] Morrab Library, MOR/Bor/2E: Sherwin to Borlase, 3 June 1759.

[34] [B. Buckler?], *Elisha's Visit to Gilgal* (1760), 19, 28–9.

[35] [R. Scrope], *Elisha's Pottage at Gilgal, spoiled by Symbolical Cookery at Oxford* (n.p., n.d.), iii; [R. Scrope and T. Nowell], *A Dissertation upon That Species of Writing called Humour, when applied to*

the individual members of these groups, although besides Buckler and Tracy the pro-Blackstone party must have included Alexander Popham and Richard Bagot, perhaps also the jurist fellows Thomas Bever and Robert Vansittart whom Blackstone named in 1761 as deputies to read his lectures in his absence.[36] Even fewer opponents are visible, although the few surviving fellows originally admitted as founder's kin, including Henry Bennet and John Carne, would scarcely have regarded Blackstone as a natural ally or friend. The unfortunate Charles Grainger, who on being sued by creditors in the chancellor's court in April 1759 had the proceeds of his fellowship sequestered to pay his debts under an order signed by Blackstone, was perhaps no better disposed.[37] Outside All Souls, Blackstone's standing is even more difficult to assess. While Sherwin's account may accurately reflect the extent of his fall from academic grace in the aftermath of the Vinerian Chair controversy, Blackstone always seems to have socialized mainly within his own college. We shall see that he nevertheless still retained sufficient influence to pilot a significant body of legislation through the university's deliberative assemblies over the next two years, while also continuing to play a very active role in the affairs of the Press.

As for the sources of anti-Blackstone feeling, jealousy or more principled resentment of the favourable terms under which he now occupied the Vinerian Chair cannot be discounted. Even when not the sole motive cause, such feelings may often have added an edge to ill-will derived from other sources. Party-political antagonism towards the leading Old Interest operative within the university over the past decade was also a powerful force. Some of the anti-Blackstone sentiment ventilated outside All Souls may have reflected a lack of sympathy for members of that uniquely constituted, aloof, and privileged society. Nor should we underestimate resistance to Blackstone's reform agenda from those ensconced in comfortably undemanding positions of academic authority.

Yet his personal style also aroused antagonism and did little to assuage or mollify opposition. Combined with a certain reserve, Blackstone's lack of physical grace and fluency in speech conveyed an unbending if not arrogant public persona. His determination, focus, and indefatigable energy in pursuit of causes to which he committed himself could irritate as well as intimidate those of a more relaxed disposition. While quick

---

Sacred Subjects. Occasion'd by the Publication of a Sermon preached at All-Souls College in Oxford on the Second Day of November last (1760), 17–22 (both pamphlets bound up in Bodl. Gough Oxf. 131).

[36] OUA, V/3/5/14.

[37] Bennet was admitted in 1750, Carne and Grainger in 1753: Simmons List; OUA, Chancellor's Court Papers 1759, 4:1, 4:3, 5:6.

to take offence at perceived slights on his own character and motives, he could also show surprising indifference to the effect his words and actions might have on others. One glaring example from June 1758: he published as a flysheet the text of a heated formal protest signed by 16 named dissident Masters of Arts (including an All Souls colleague, the above-mentioned John Carne) against the vice chancellor's denial of their right to debate the Vinerian statutes, under a sarcastic headline inviting members of Convocation 'seriously to consider the following most *decent, liberal, academical* and *gentlemanlike* Performance'. This intervention not only invited a retort in similar terms, but could very plausibly be represented as tending 'to *inflame* Matters still more, and to encrease and perpetuate those unhappy Animosities, which every real Friend to the University wishes heartily to see at an End'.[38] In short, Blackstone too often allowed himself to become exasperated by what he perceived as self-interest, or stupidity, or both, on the part of those who stood in the way of his numerous plans and projects. Whether he would have been a more successful academic administrator and politician had he exhibited more caution, circumspection, and restraint in such circumstances is another question. Given the various cultural and institutional obstacles facing any aspiring reformer in mid-eighteenth century Oxford, we may be doubtful. But in any event, Blackstone's future career would not be confined to the groves of academe, even though his final departure from Oxford was still some six years away.

III

The year 1759 saw only the beginnings of this protracted parting. His acclaimed introductory lecture helped spread Blackstone's reputation well beyond the University of Oxford. But an invitation to read his lectures before Prince George, the future King of England, seemingly stemmed from the recommendation of a former undergraduate pupil and future prime minister, young William, Viscount Fitzmaurice, later the second earl of Shelburne, who had himself 'attended Blackstone's lectures with great care, and profited considerably by them'[39] during his brief Oxford sojourn in 1755–6. However gratifying to receive such a proposal from the earl of Bute, official tutor to the Prince of Wales, it was

[38] Bodl. Gough Oxon. 96 (52), (57), italics in original; Doolittle, 51–2. Another of those so ridiculed was Richard Scrope, for whom see above, p. 160. See also *A Reply to the Examiner*: Bodl. Gough Oxon. 96 (23).

[39] E. Fitzmaurice, *Life of William, Earl of Shelburne* (1875), i. 19.

plainly impractical, given Blackstone's various Oxford commitments, not least those to his present student audience. He nevertheless undertook to provide the Prince with loaned copies of a number of lectures from his first and more general course, and possibly others as well. George had already developed a keen interest in the theory and practice of government, not least the crucial topic of public finance, which was the subject of 'two lectures on the King's Revenue' Blackstone forwarded to Bute on 15 March 1759. His covering letter strikes an assertively independent stance, assuring Bute that the topic was handled 'with a Freedom which I hope is decent as well as constitutional', and in no way self-censored to spare royal susceptibilities: 'for I should scorn to suggest anything to my Audience in the University, which was improper to be seen in another place'.[40] Any underlying concerns about the reaction of Bute or his pupil were presumably removed later that year with the arrival of the huge sum of £200—the amount of his annual Vinerian salary—as a 'present from the Prince of Wales'.[41] While Blackstone's future relationship with Bute would be short-lived and ultimately unhappy, in George he had secured an appreciative, loyal, and soon to be incomparably influential patron, whose beneficial interventions marked several key turning points during the rest of his life. The reciprocal influence exercised by Blackstone's lectures on the future King's political beliefs and conception of his own role as monarch is more difficult to determine, partly because Blackstone's views were closely in accord with the Country and Patriot ideology George had already absorbed from his mentors. When Charles Garth MP, London agent for South Carolina, claimed that George 'believed himself to be a lawyer because he had read Blackstone before publication', he presumably had in mind this early exposure to the lectures, rather than any monarchical scanning of the *Commentaries* in page proof.[42] Yet Blackstone must surely have strengthened the Prince's sense of the high responsibility he would soon bear to govern his people 'according to Law . . . for the preservation of their Religion and Liberties'. More speculatively, Blackstone's emphasis, following Montesquieu among others, on the necessity of separating the judicial from the executive branch of government may have

---

[40] *Letters*, 50; the two lectures were evidently nos. 9 and 10, on the King's ordinary and extraordinary revenues; see *Analysis*, 16–18 and UCL, MS Add. 120, fos. 24v–31v (lecture notes of John Wilkinson, 1757–8.) Blackstone anticipated the return of 'a Book of Lectures' via Fitzmaurice, while promising 'the others . . . as soon as the Slowness of my Amanuensis will permit'. The one surviving set of lecture notes from the 1758–9 series is incomplete, including just three lectures from the first part of the course: Oxfordshire RO, JXXVI/a/1.

[41] See Appendix II below.

[42] R. Barry, *Mr Rutledge of South Carolina* (New York, 1942), 117.

helped inspire legislation shortly to be 'enacted at the earnest recommendation of the King himself from the throne', whereby judges henceforth kept their offices notwithstanding the death of a sovereign, and payment of their salaries was guaranteed from the civil list.[43] George's 'Thoughts on the British Constitution', compiled early in 1760, also contains possible echoes of Blackstone's lectures, with its emphasis on the benefits of a militia over a standing army and the importance of maintaining trial by one's peers, 'a most wise institution'.[44]

While Blackstone had resumed noting cases in the court of King's Bench several years before, he evidently attended Westminster Hall only in Michaelmas and Hilary terms, and not always even then. Thus, although his published reports include a lengthy account of judgments delivered in Chancery on 24 January 1759, this was evidently compiled by the veteran Tory lawyer Nicholas Fazakerly, and provided by Bamber Gascoigne, another Lincoln's Inn barrister.[45] At midyear, however, Blackstone took the indispensable next step to resume practice at the London bar, by purchasing a set of first-floor chambers on King's Bench Walk at the Inner Temple, rooms vacated by their previous occupant only because he had moved on to an even more desirable set of bench chambers. Having been formally admitted to membership of the Inner Temple, as required by the house rules in order to hold a set of chambers, he subsequently sought to finalize the transfer by reclaiming the penal bond he had signed on first coming into commons at the Middle Temple next door. These transactions might suggest an entirely pragmatic approach, lacking any sense of personal loyalty to either Temple society. Yet a fortnight after he had seemingly severed all ties with the Middle house, its governing body formally ordered that 'the Thanks of this Parliament be given to William Blackstone Esquire late a Barrister of this Society . . . for his correct Edition of "The Great Charter and Charter of the Forest &c" which he hath presented to this Society'.[46]

[43] UCL, MS Add 120, fos. 24, 26; D. Duman, *The Judicial Bench in England 1727–1875* (1982), 97n. Cf. the strikingly eulogistic passage in the *Commentaries*, i.258, on the statute 1 Geo. III, c. 23, quoting George's speech (which Blackstone possibly heard in person) to his first parliament, 3 March 1761: *CJ*, xxviii.1094. Samuel Johnson thought Bute had persuaded George to push this measure: *Life of Johnson*, 619–20; but cf. F. Thackeray, *A History of the Life of the Rt. Hon. William Pitt* (1827), i. 497.

[44] P. D. G. Thomas, '"Thoughts on the British Constitution" by George III in 1760', *Bulletin of the Institute of Historical Research*, lx (1987), 361–3. S. Skinner, 'Blackstone's Support for the Militia', *AJLH*, 44 (2000), 1–18.

[45] *Reports*, i. 123–8; *The Records of the Honourable Society of Lincoln's Inn: the Black Books*, ed. W. P. Baildon (1898), iii. 346.

[46] IT Archives, CHA/5/2, fo. 40; CHA/2/1, fo. 96; MT Archives, Parliament Book, K10, 241–2, 244.

Three years before, when Blackstone transcribed a version of Magna Carta recently bequeathed to the Bodleian Library, he also questioned the accepted date of this manuscript.[47] The Vinerian Chair campaign proved a major distraction from such antiquarian pursuits, let alone the associated prospect of succession to the Camden Professorship of Ancient History. But in the summer of 1757 Blackstone was reading a selection of early thirteenth-century monastic chronicles in the Bodleian and Codrington libraries. After calling up some relevant manuscripts held by the Bodleian in April 1758, he seemingly put the task aside for nearly 12 months. Another major bout of work in March and April 1759 saw the text of what would become *The Great Charter and the Charter of the Forest, with other authentic Instruments* ready for the press by July, although an unusually protracted production process then delayed publication until November.[48]

Elegantly printed on heavy paper, with wide margins, illustrated initials, and engraved tailpieces, Blackstone's *Great Charter* remains an outstanding aesthetic and technical achievement: as his brother-in-law biographer justly noted, 'the external beauties in the printing, the Types, &c. reflected no small Honour on him, as the principal Reformer of the *Clarendon Press* . . .'.[49] In fact *The Great Charter* was privately printed and not an official Press publication (Blackstone having been given special permission by his fellow delegates to produce 'an Edition of Magna Carta at the University Press'), so credit for the volume's handsome appearance must go largely to its author's own design skills and typographical expertise. But this edition of 14 charters from the reigns of John, Henry III, and Edward I was also a major piece of pioneering scholarship, as the first critical, systematic attempt to sort out the sequence and distinguish clearly between the different texts of the great charter itself, the 1224 charter of the forest, and numerous royal confirmations and reissues down to the end of the thirteenth century.

In an editorial introduction of nearly 80 pages, Blackstone began by explaining the origins of 'the original articles or heads of agreement at the congress in Runingmede in the fifteenth year of King John, whereupon his great charter was founded', going on 'to trace them, with their several variations and amendments during the infancy of King Henry

---

[47] *Letters*, 31; above, p. 139.

[48] Bodl. MS Library Records, e 559, fo. 119, 18 August 1757, fo. 123v, 8 April 1758; e 560, fo. 2v, 14 April 1759; Codrington, Library Borrower's Book, 24 July, 20 December 1757, 5, 10 March, 5,6, 11 May 1759. Clitherow, xiv.

[49] Ibid. Cf. J. Watson, *Memoirs of the Ancient Earls of Warren and Surrey* (Warrington, 1785), i.184.

the third, to the dangers which they underwent and the timely supports which they received during his riper age; and at length to their peaceful establishment in the twenty ninth year of King Edward the first'.[50] His prime concern was with the manuscripts themselves, rather than their substantive content, except in so far as the latter illuminated the chronology and origins of the former. This documentary focus involved collating variants of charters held in public libraries and private hands across the country. Relying on others to copy or examine texts in Cambridge and Durham, Blackstone himself took responsibility for those in the Bodleian Library and Oriel College, Oxford, in the Tower of London, the British Museum, the Guildhall, the College of Arms, and Westminster Abbey. He also acknowledged the 'utmost politeness' of one private owner who had 'permitted the editor to correct the following edition, as it came from the press, by this original' of the first document printed, the articles to which King John attached his great seal at Runnymede on 19 June 1215.[51]

The Great Charter embodies a tradition of legal antiquarian scholarship dating back to the early seventeenth century and before.[52] Yet it also reflects more contemporary cultural and intellectual influences, most notably in its clarification of hitherto prevailing confusion, explicit and rigorous editorial methodology, and conscious appeal (via elegance of form as well as clarity of content) to the educated general reader, not just dry-as-dust antiquaries. Despite styling himself 'Barrister at Law' on the title page, Blackstone's exposition made little use of technical legal expertise. Finally, his somewhat unexpected methodological conclusion—that 'the compiling and digesting of a general complete history of England is a burthen too heavy to be undertaken by any single man, however supereminently qualified'—has a remarkably modern ring. So does his consequential recognition that if some such 'great and extensive work' were eventually to be compiled, it might well lack 'that critical attention to dates, and names, and other minuter circumstances, which would be requisite in those who would act out the subordinate departments'. However certain that for these purposes his own role fell firmly into the latter category, Blackstone might nevertheless have been gratified to know that his scholarly work remains a standard reference to the

---

[50] *Great Charter*, ii.

[51] Ibid., xvi.

[52] Cf. R. J. Smith, *The Gothic Bequest: Medieval Institutions in British Thought, 1688–1863* (Cambridge, 1987), 93; R. Sweet, *Antiquaries: The Discovery of the Past in Eighteenth–Century Britain* (2004), 235.

present day, thereby continuing 'to illustrate this important part of our English juridical history'.[53]

Somewhat more immediately, this edition helped make Blackstone 'well known to the learned World' as 'particularly skillful in the legal and historical Antiquities of our Country', hence 'a useful and worthy Member' of the London-based Society of Antiquaries, to which he was elected in February 1761.[54] This genteel body, which aspired to a role and status in antiquarian and historical scholarship comparable to that of the Royal Society in natural philosophy, might have been more immediately forthcoming had not Blackstone expressly excluded from his *Great Charter* a manuscript roll belonging to the aristocratic clergyman Charles Lord Lyttelton, an active member and future president of the society. After Blackstone was proposed for membership, but before his election, Lyttelton delivered a 'memoir' to a meeting of the society which sought to defend the authenticity of the roll Blackstone had omitted (on the grounds that it was a contemporary copy rather than an original issue of Magna Carta). In his response, read to the society on 10 June, at only the second meeting he attended, Blackstone presented a civil yet altogether devastating rebuttal of these claims, explaining precisely why he came to regard Lyttleton's roll with 'less reverence . . . than he finds was expected of him'. Despite being exposed as credulous, ignorant, superficial, and unobservant, on this subject at least, Lyttelton made no attempt to defend himself. Blackstone for his part appears to have been present at only two more meetings before the society's minutes cease recording attendees in 1769, although he did deliver another paper on a less controversial topic in 1775. William Bray, the Surrey solicitor and by then a stalwart of the society, may well have been reflecting a consensus among its members when he compiled a highly unflattering character sketch of Blackstone among other 'candid biographies' of contemporaries.[55]

Blackstone's second 1759 publication was of a wholly different character. Whereas *The Great Charter* retailed for 15 shillings, copies of *A Treatise on the Law of Descents in Fee Simple* cost a mere 18 pence. The difference was

---

[53] *Great Charter*, lxxv–lxxvi. W. S. McKechnie, *Magna Carta: A Commentary on the Great Charter of King John*, 2nd. edn. (Glasgow, 1914), 168, 176–7. *The British Museum Catalogue of Additions to the Manuscripts 1936–1945*, 2 vols. (1970), i. 320–1; J. C. Holt, *Magna Carta*, 2nd. edn. (Cambridge, 1992), 2, 253n, 429; *idem, Magna Carta and Medieval Government* (1985), 217, 265–6.

[54] Society of Antiquaries, Minute Book 7, 1757–62, 267 (18 December 1760); nomination by Lord Willoughby and seven other members, including the law reporter James Burrow and the attorney Philip Carteret Webb.

[55] Ibid. 292, 322; Minute Book 9, 1762–5, 1–7, 9, 146; Minute Book 11, 1769–70, 94. *Great Charter*, xlviii; Surrey History Centre, Bray Family Papers, G52/8/10/1 (see further below, p. 272); Sweet, *Antiquaries*, 45–6.

functional as well as financial. A brief prefatory 'Advertisement' explained that the *Treatise* was essentially a learning aid, written for the benefit of his students:

The author, having found by repeated experience how difficult it is to give an adequate idea of the matters discussed in the ensuing treatise by any oral instruction, however assisted by tables, has therefore been induced to commit to the press the hints which he had collected for the use of his academical pupils. Being calculated for their information merely, the learned reader must not expect any thing new, nor the curious any thing entertaining, on so dry a topic. Perspicuity and precision are the only things endeavoured at: the subject is incapable of ornament.

The technical subject matter covered by this brief survey was however 'of the highest importance . . . indeed the principal civil object of the laws of England', in so far as it laid down the rules by which landed property was transferred, whether by direct inheritance or at one remove by purchase, 'as a *datum* or first principle universally known, and upon which their subsequent limitations are to work'.[56]

The success of *An Analysis of the Laws of England* may have encouraged Blackstone to explore the potential market for more specialized guides to specific branches of law, while the need to provide versions of his lectures for the Prince of Wales possibly provided an incentive to experiment with more expansive treatments of particular topics than the normal one-hour lecture format permitted. But whatever spurred its composition, Blackstone's *Treatise* is of particular interest because of its relationship to the *Commentaries*. The text first published in 1759 is reproduced, virtually word for word, as chapters 14 and 15 of the second book of *Commentaries*, which would not appear in print for another seven years. The whole subject of lineal and collateral kin relations was of course one in which Blackstone had a long-standing interest, so much so that he was able to recycle yet again the 'Table of Descents' initially drawn-up for his 1750 *Essay on Collateral Consanguinity*. But to the extent that we can rely on surviving student notes of his lectures as an accurate reflection of their contents, it would seem that before 1759 Blackstone's treatment of this topic comprised not much more than an enumeration of eight specific rules of descent (or 'Canons of Inheritance', as they were termed by the *Analysis*).[57] However the *Treatise*—and similarly the *Commentaries*, in due course—not only illustrates these rules with hypothetical examples of their operation in particular circumstances, but discusses at some length the historical origins, moral justification, and social rationale for provisions such as that

---

[56] *Treatise*, 6.
[57] E.g. UCL MS Add. 120, pp. 64–6 (John Wilkinson's notes, 1757–8).

excluding half-brothers 'not of the whole blood' from succeeding as collateral heirs.[58]

Its unpretentious format and subject-matter, and the fact that it went
through only one authorized edition (besides being included with other
reprints in Blackstone's 1762 *Law Tracts*), help explain why the significance
of the *Treatise* as a prototype of the *Commentaries* has been overlooked. Yet
despite an initial run of 1,000 copies, and the appearance of a presumably
cheaper pirated Dublin edition in 1760 (the first such dubious compliment paid to any of his published works), the *Treatise* was evidently out
of print within three years of its first appearance.[59] If an exposition of a
single branch of law could attract demand on that scale, the commercial
prospects of a general survey of the whole body of English law might
well prove very attractive indeed. This is not to suggest that in writing
and publishing the *Commentaries* Blackstone was motivated solely by the
prospect of financial gain. But such considerations, as likewise the generally positive press reception of the *Treatise*, cannot have been entirely
absent from his thinking. Favourably noticed in its first month of publication by the *London Magazine* as the work of an 'ingenious and learned
author', the *Treatise* was next discussed and excerpted over four pages in
the *Monthly Review*, which maintained that 'the learned Reader will not
find himself uninformed, or the curious unentertained, by the perusal of
this little tract'. In October 1760 the rival *Critical Review* hailed 'the hand
of a master', whose 'sensible epitome' had relieved law students 'of the
necessity of consulting whole piles of learned lumber'. That Blackstone
was not indifferent to the opinions of his reviewers is suggested by the fact
that a paragraph singled out for criticism by the *Monthly Review*, where he
had somewhat speciously attempted to justify the rule against inheritances
ascending from child to parent as stemming from 'magnanimity, honour
and parental affection' rather than the imperatives of feudal policy, is one
of very few passages not later incorporated in the *Commentaries*.[60]

IV

As before he became Vinerian Professor, Blackstone's literary labours at
Oxford were not confined to his own publications. He remained an active

---

[58] *Treatise*, 13–21, 21–2.

[59] Because the *Treatise* was not part of the 1771 edition of Blackstone's tracts Holdsworth relied
on for his account of 'Blackstone and his Commentaries', he omits any mention of this work: *HEL*,
xii. 709–11. Oxford University Press Archives, OUP/PR/1/18/4, 143; Eller, 98, 101.

[60] *London Magazine*, 28 (1759), 673; *Monthly Review*, 22 (1760), 35–8; *Critical Review*, 10 (1760),
326. *Treatise*, 17–19.

delegate for the Press, spending much time and effort in the autumn and winter of 1758–9 on the difficult project of a continuation of the *History of the Great Rebellion* by Edward Hyde, Earl of Clarendon. Profits from the first three volumes having financed the construction of a new home for the university press some 40 years before, the news that Clarendon's heirs had commissioned the university to publish the remaining portion of his manuscript autobiography, covering the first seven years of Charles II's reign, must have been very welcome. Unfortunately it soon became clear that the family, in the person of Charles Douglas, duke of Queensberry, who had married one of Hyde's descendants, was only prepared to allow a partial transcript of the original manuscript to be published under the immediate direction of a favoured agent, Dr Paul Forester of Christ Church. Blackstone was unable to persuade a majority of his colleagues to take a more assertive line with Queensberry, or the duke himself to modify his position. Something of his resultant frustration is revealed by the acerbic corrections and queries with which he peppered the proof sheets of a preface to the work which had been prepared to appear under the name of Vice Chancellor Randolph.[61]

Although it is not always possible to distinguish Blackstone's personal role in the affairs of Oxford's Press following the far-reaching reforms of 1757–8, he seems to have been actively involved in most major publishing projects undertaken in the late 1750s and early 1760s. These included the snail's-pace production of a revised edition of Bishop Gibson's treatise on ecclesiastical law, various mooted catalogues of Oxford's manuscript collections, and Richard Chandler's updated inventory of sculpture and other 'marbles', the *Marmora Oxoniensia* (Oxford, 1763). Blackstone was also present at a delegates' meeting in January 1760 which agreed to subsidize the research of Humphrey Kennicott on manuscripts of the Hebrew bible 'for three years next immediately ensuing (renewable as occasion may require)', and may well have drafted the terms of this de facto research fellowship. He was certainly responsible for what he later recalled as 'a great Plan for publishing an entire edition of all the Classics in an elegant manner and at a very cheap Rate for the benefit of Students, and also to provide constant Stock Work for the Employment of our Compositors and Pressmen'.[62] But after his fellow delegates had agreed to begin with an edition of Cicero's works, the scholars chosen to undertake this task, 'feeling the Strength of their own abilities and ambitious

---

[61] Philip, 101–4; *Letters*, 57–9, 63–6; Bodl. MS Top. Oxon. d 387, fos. 41–42v, 55–56v: Queensberry to Blackstone, 18 December 1758, 16 January 1759; Bodl. MS Eng. misc. a 23, fos. 26–31.

[62] *Letters*, 155.

of doing something more than discharging the dull duty of Correctors', determined to expand the project to include a collation of all the 'valuable MSS. that can be procured, particularly those in Oxford, Cambridge, and the British Museum'. Blackstone claimed to have gone along with this amended proposal very reluctantly, 'forseeing, what soon after happened, that the extensiveness of such a Search, in respect to an Author so voluminous as Cicero, would soon abate the ardour of the most able and persevering Editors'.[63] While the project did indeed falter, and collapsed altogether after a few years, in the early 1760s Blackstone was sufficiently identified with it for Charles Morton, librarian of the British Museum, to send him several consignments of collations from manuscript collections in Paris for transmission to the Oxford editors. Of further if indirect relevance to our present concerns, the first use made of the type specially acquired for this scheme was to print Blackstone's own *Commentaries*.[64] A more straightforward and unambiguously successful initiative enabled the Press to resume routine claims for a statutory refund or 'drawback' of excise duty paid on the paper used for printing any book in a 'learned language', such as Latin or Greek.[65]

Blackstone also seemed in no hurry to liquidate or reduce his other academic-administrative commitments. While resigning as assessor of the chancellor's court in favour of his former student and All Souls colleague Thomas Bever in June 1759, he kept his position as estates steward of All Souls College until October 1760, when he was succeeded by Alexander Popham, another former pupil and fellow barrister.[66] In February of that year Blackstone very probably drafted the college's lengthy and unanimous response to their archiepiscopal visitor's questioning of Popham's right to hold an artist fellowship while professing the common law, rather than taking holy orders. Archbishop Secker was informed that their founder's 'Plan of Education is much more comprehensive and enlarged' than those of his contemporaries. True, Archbishop Chichele's statutes made no mention of the common law, for that subject was 'entirely neglected' in fifteenth-century Oxford. But since the Reformation, 'the greater Utility of the Law of the Land for public Government beyond that of the canon & civil, is universally felt & acknowledged; and as the University itself has lately been enabled . . . to adopt it as an academical Study and to put it on a public Establishment; we think there is reason to suppose, that had

[63] Ibid., 156.
[64] Ibid. Bodl. MS Auct. V. 4.31, fos. 332–3; Philip, 115–6.
[65] Philip, 13–14, 49, 114.
[66] Clitherow, xiii; OUA, WPβ , Vice Chancellor's Compotus 1758–9; OUA, Chancellor's Court Papers, 1759, 1:5, 30 June 1759. Codrington, Acta in Capitulis 1753–70, 17 December 1760.

the Study of the Common Law been then under the same Circumstances as at present, the Founder would also have made an express Provision in favour of this academical Science.' However hypothetical this chain of reasoning, the archbishop appears to have given Popham the necessary dispensation.[67]

In the spring of this same year Blackstone undertook, to use his own words, 'some share of the College Business' by negotiating the final repayment of a long-standing loan from a former fellow towards completion of the Wharton building some 15 years before. Other college matters in which he was at least peripherally involved included a new arrangement for Childs, their London bankers, to hold stock and receive dividends on the college's behalf, and a resolution permitting double fees or fines to be charged to tenants who delayed more than three months in paying whatever was due for renewal of their leases.[68] Notwithstanding his new London chambers, and resumed attendance at Westminster Hall from Michaelmas term 1759, Blackstone was still more often than not on hand to engage with All Souls' business, since he spent by far the greater part of that and the following year in Oxford. Indeed the surviving records suggest that in 1759 he was only out of commons at All Souls for a month from late January (overlapping with the Hilary law term), a fortnight in November (covering part of Michaelmas term), and possibly the two weeks before and after Christmas. In 1760 his absences nearly doubled, but still only to 14 whole weeks, thus barely extending beyond the duration of the four law terms, which amounted to some 12 ½ weeks in all. Not all his time away from Oxford was spent at the courts in London, for we know that in September 1760 he stayed over at least a weekend in Warwickshire with the Tory landowner MP Sir Charles Mordaunt, who two years before had been instrumental in encouraging publication of his *Considerations on Copyholders*.[69]

We have little idea of how Blackstone spent his time from day to day when he was in Oxford. But besides his lectures, his reading, writing, and attention to college and Press delegacy matters, he evidently found it difficult to give up all involvement with general university business. Here

[67] Codrington, Acta in Capitulis 1753–70, 26 February 1760; MS 36, Warden Niblett's Notebook, 13 February 1760.

[68] Codrington, Acta in Capitulis 1753–70, 4 March, 10 April, 18 October, 17 December 1760. *Letters*, 67–8, 69, 71.

[69] Clitherow, xiv; Codrington, Steward's Book, 1754–60. Since only absences of a full week or more are noted in the stewards' books, Blackstone may have been out of Oxford more often than this source appears to indicate, although its record is largely corroborated by other evidence of his location and movements. Newdigate Diary, 19, 21 September 1760. See above, p. 127, n. 24.

indeed his last major initiative was of such fundamental importance as to form the centrepiece of a separate chapter in the volume of the university's modern official history devoted to eighteenth-century Oxford.[70] Admittedly the volume editor, who also wrote that chapter, had a particular interest in Blackstone, but his prominence is not merely by editorial *fiat*. For in 1759–60 Blackstone established that the University of Oxford need not rest in perpetuity under an immutable body of statute law drawn up by Archbishop William Laud more than a century earlier, although this 'Laudian Code' had been confirmed by King Charles I's letters-patent and acknowledged by the university at the time as its 'eternal laws'. Had his undertaking not succeeded, academic conservatives would have had a much stronger constitutional and political case for resisting the reforms which in the later years of the eighteenth century began to create the foundations of Oxford's modern system of undergraduate education.

The main issue Blackstone addressed concerned the disputed membership of Convocation, which of course entailed the right to vote in elections of the chancellor, various other university officials, and the university's parliamentary burgesses. But while the extent of the franchise and the related question of whether university membership was wholly inconsistent with freedom of the city of Oxford were particular points of contention during and after the chancellorship election campaign of 1758–9, this was not the first time that Blackstone had contemplated the general issue. A rough outline of his later manuscript 'Considerations on the power of the University to make, alter, or repeal Statutes, without royal License' refers specifically to provisions concerning delegates to the University Press, and so presumably antedates the new Press statute enacted in December 1757.[71] But the central tenet of both documents (foreshadowing the emphasis on parliamentary sovereignty in the first book of the *Commentaries*) is the inherent right of all corporations to govern their domestic affairs, and hence their inability to make fundamental laws restricting the legislative powers of their successors, just as no parliament can effectively prevent its legislation being repealed by a future parliament.

Besides the unique manuscript 'Considerations', which has never been printed (although several written copies are known to have been in existence as late as the 1830s), Blackstone appears to have been responsible for a two-page printed flysheet containing (in the words of his own annotated copy) 'Amendments proposed to the first Draught of Statutes, Mar. 1759'.[72]

---

[70] L. S. Sutherland, 'The Laudian Statutes in the Eighteenth Century': *HUO*, 191–203.

[71] Bodl. MS. Top. Oxon. c 209, fos. 27–8, 28c. These papers were formerly owned by Philip Bliss (d. 1857), who bought them from a descendant of John White, Blackstone's All Souls antagonist.

[72] OUA, WPα/22/2(5). *HUO*, 200 and n.

Designed with characteristic typographic ingenuity and fitness for purpose, both pages are divided into two vertical columns. The draft text of
two statutes, one seeking to define precisely Convocation's membership,
the other to remove the perpetual ban on university members accepting
Oxford citizenship or freedom of the city, is printed down the left-hand
column, while the 'Proposed Amendments' appear in their respective
places on the other side of the page. Each of these suggested changes is
supported by a cryptic footnoted explanation or justification. The small
collection of Blackstone's papers which includes this item also has the
first, second, and final printed drafts of the statutes themselves, the last
(dated 21 June 1759, according to Blackstone's annotation) incorporating
virtually all the amendments he had proposed some two months before.[73]
Two other anonymous printed documents in the same collection seem
also to have come from Blackstone's pen. The four-page 'Case' prepared
for counsel's opinion, annotated 'Case and Opinion of Counsel 2 June
1759' contains an outline history of the university's constitutional status
with special reference to the Laudian Code and preparatory to three questions concerning the extent of its legislative autonomy, followed by the
responses—highly satisfactory, so far as Blackstone was concerned—of
the barristers John Morton and Randle Wilbraham.[74] But as was almost
inevitable, especially given Blackstone's prominent role, the issue had by
now become highly contentious, with opposition to the proposed statutes
from a minority bloc of New Interest heads of houses accompanied by a
veto on their passage through Convocation by the two proctors for the
year, who both happened to be New Interest supporters. The success of
this blocking tactic could be only temporary, however, for when a new
set of proctors succeeded to office the statutes passed without difficulty,
despite a desultory last-minute attempt to rally opposition on more or
less technical legal grounds. This provoked what would be Blackstone's
final published contribution to the debate, a single page dated 2 July 1760,
written in response to a longer anonymous document circulated two
days before, the work (according to Blackstone's annotation) of one 'Mr
Sk-nn-r CCC'.[75] Professing, in the opening words of his own broadsheet,
'to obviate the Mistakes of an Explanatory Paper sent to the Common
Rooms on Monday last', Blackstone asserted that while the royal charter
which confirmed the Laudian statutes did not repeal all former university
statutes, neither did it distinguish 'Royal statutes' unchangeable without
royal—or governmental—consent, from the remainder, which might be

[73] OUA, WPα/22/2 (6, 7).   [74] OUA, WPα/22/2 (10).
[75] i.e. Richard Skinner of Corpus Christi College: *Al. Oxon.*, iv. 1303.

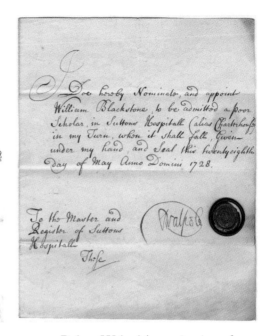

1. Mary Blackstone's business card
(see pages 13, 19)

3. Robert Walpole's nomination of
Blackstone as a 'gown-boy' (see page 21)

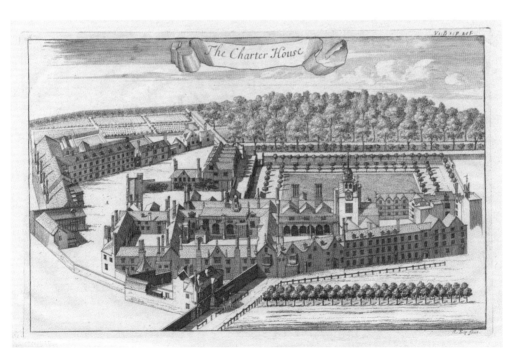

2. Charterhouse buildings and gardens, *c.* 1720

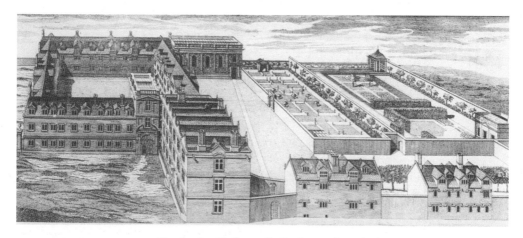

4. Pembroke College, Oxford, 1744 (see ch 3)

5. Blackstone's undergraduate
contemporary Thomas Tyers
in academic dress (*left*)
(see pages 42–3)

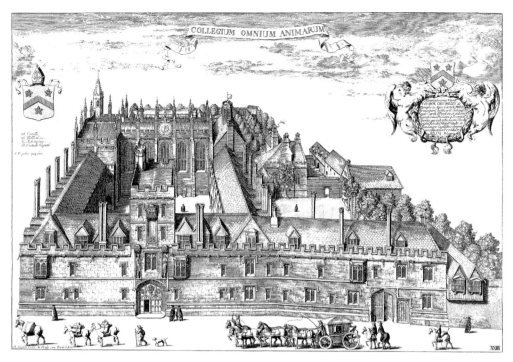

6. All Souls College, Oxford, before Hawksmoor's North Quadrangle

7. The North Quadrangle: Codrington Library, Wharton Building, Gothic Towers

8. The Codrington Library, interior (see pages 75–80)

intind of them, & not to be wholly escaped. Others think they might better be retained both together in y same buildings, & added one and here by, as if y Composite was never to be employed, &c.

Perhaps we may go on & be surer upon this subject when we consider that some of y most virtuous Masters in this Art have employed it in their most elegant Structures, say, y rate of Corinthian adorned to it. One it is not unlikely, inspects an uniform &c ... to have remained unregarded ... itself, which this ... at the subject ... kept one or more of these Pillars, & to have liberty, ... in the right ... stuff, under y places ... part of uniformity & subjects ... One is not, ... may, we have the respect to ... the ... & other kinds, nor ... may ... of name preferable, as many of y old Architects have ... & amounted to it. to ... as nearly of use &c, likely upon it as the Canons of all Religions & ... and & ... & ... Religion & which ... has been ordained with this noble Science.

Hereby that considered of ... & contained parts of an Order, aforesaid of the ... of y Orders, & ... from this ... Superstition will respect to one another, we shall in y ... Chapter proceed to consider y particular Properties of y ... Orders, & their private Proportions, whereof y ... Master is another. And first of y ... Order.

Chapter 9. ~
Of the Tuscan Order.

The Tuscan Order has its Name from an ... Rank of y Nation, its ... and of Asia people ... & built after this Order. It is also called y Gothic Order from its Coarseness, & y Gigantic from its Massiveness & Strength. The Proportions are said to be those of a Strong, well-built Man. ... whereas its slenderness used

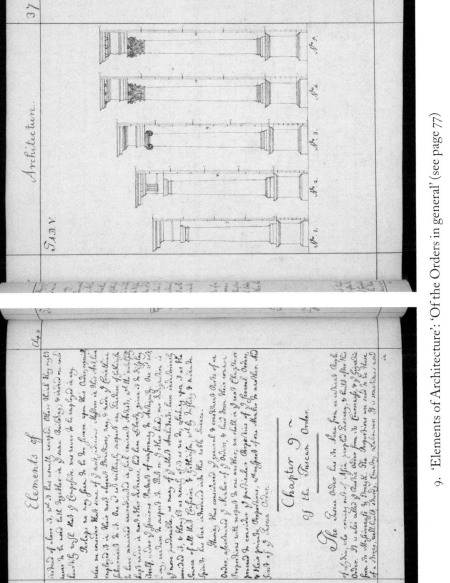

No 1.   No 2.   No 3.   No 4.   No 5.

9. 'Elements of Architecture': 'Of the Orders in general' (see page 77)

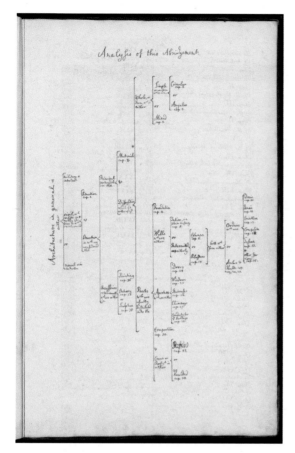

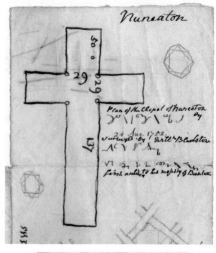

10. *Above left*: 'Abridgement of Architecture':
tabular 'Analysis' (see pages 44–5)

11. *Above right*: 'Plan of the Chapel at
Nuneaton', admiringly annotated by
Newdigate (see page 104)

12. *Right*: Spire of St Peter's Church,
Wallingford, by Robert Taylor (see page 282)

13. Priory Place, Blackstone's Wallingford 'Cabin' (see pages 189–90)

14. No. 55 Lincoln's Inn Fields, Blackstone's last London house (see page 235)

A

COURSE of LECTURES

ON THE

LAWS of ENGLAND.

Commencing *November* 6. 1753.

Introduction, { Utility of the Study of the Laws of ENGLAND. } *Lect I*
{ Causes of the Neglect of this Study.
{ Propriety of it's Revival in the University.

The Nature of Laws in general. ———————— *Lect II*
The Grounds and Foundation of the Laws of ENGLAND. ——— *Lect III*
The Countries subject to those Laws. ————————— *Lect IV*
The Objects of the Laws of ENGLAND, *viz.*

I. The Duties and Rights of Persons, with the Means of acquiring and losing them,
  1. Natural Persons, their Duties and Rights
    1. Absolute, *viz.*
      { 1. Life.
      { 2. Liberty. } *Lect V*
      { 3. Safety.
    2. As they stand in Relations
      1. Publick, either as
        1. Magistrates, who are
          1. Supreme,
            { 1. Legislative; *viz.* The Parliament. ——— *Lect VI*
            { 2. Executive; *viz.* The King; wherein of his
              { 1. Title.
              { 2. Dignity } *Lect VII*
              { 3. Duties.
              { 4. Councils.
              { 5. Prerogative, in relation to his } *Lect VIII*
                { 1. Power.
                { 2. Revenue, ————
                  { 1. Temporal. } *Lect IX & X*
                  { 2. Ecclesiastical,
              { 6. Royal Family. } *Lect XI*
          2. Subordinate. *Magistrates* } *Lect XI*
        2. People, who are
          { 1. Aliens. ——— } *Lect XII*
          { 2. Natives, who are }
            { 1. Clergy.
            { 2. Laity, who are either in a State
              { 1. Civil.
              { 2. Military. } *Lect XIII*
              { 3. Maritime.
      2. Private, *viz.*
        { 1. Husband and Wife. } *XIV*
        { 2. Master and Servant. }
        { 3. Parent and Child.   Therein of Bastardy. } *XV*
        { 4. Guardian and Ward.   Therein of Infancy. }
  2. Bodies-politic, or Corporations. ———————— *Lect XVI*

The preceding Articles compose   Part I. }   { *Michaelmas* Term.
II. The Rights of Things, with the Means of acquiring and losing them.   Part II. } to be read in { *Lent* Term.
III. Civil Injuries, with the Means of Prevention and Redress.   Part III. }   { *Easter* Term.
IV. Crimes and Misdemeanors, with the Means of Prevention and Punishment. Part IV. }   { *Act* Term.

15. Printed syllabus of Blackstone's first law lectures (see page 114)

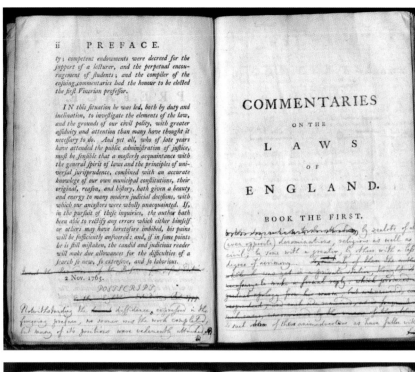

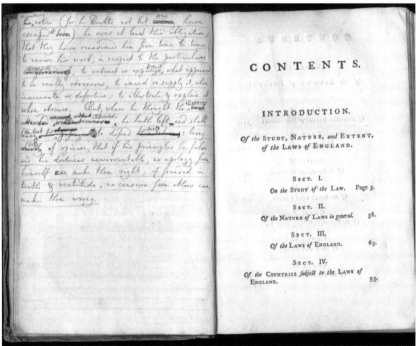

16. In response to Bentham and other critics: Blackstone's holograph postscript for the 1778 edition of the *Commentaries* (see page 296)

17. *Top left*: William Blackstone, by Charles Dixon (see page 278)

18. *Top right*: Sir William Blackstone, by Thomas Gainsborough, 1774 (see page 277)

19. *Above*: Sir William Blackstone, by John Bacon, 1782 (see page 304)

20. *Right*: Sir William Blackstone, stained-glass window by James Powell & Sons, 1891; removed from the Hall of All Souls College, Oxford, for safe-keeping in 1939; presented in 1979 to the Marshall-Wythe Law School, College of William and Mary

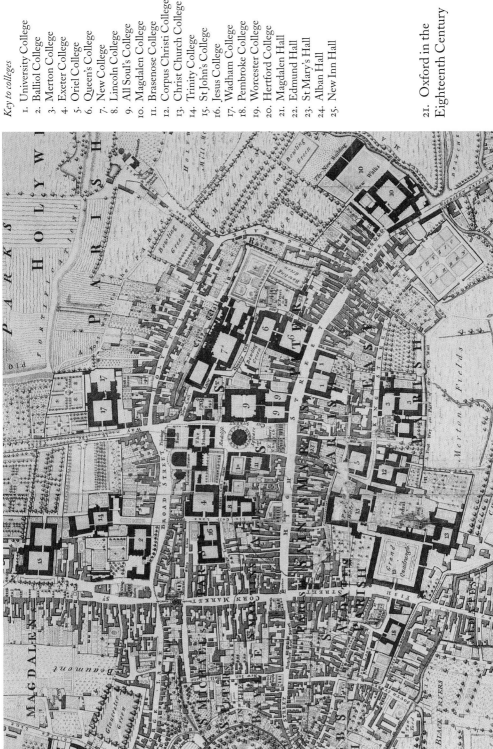

21. Oxford in the Eighteenth Century

freely altered at the university's pleasure. Yet however compelling his close reading of the Latin texts in question, the brusque and dismissive manner in which it was presented can have done little to mollify his academic critics and opponents.[76]

V

In February 1760 the poet William Shenstone pronounced that 'Dr Blackstone has raised himself to a very eminent figure indeed in the world of letters'.[77] Whether or not Shenstone was, as he claimed, 'without one particle of envy', Blackstone's growing reputation beyond Oxford's more or less cloistered walls could hardly be denied. Self-consciousness of his heightened literary stature could well have contributed to the slightly disdainful tone of the tract just discussed. So too might his sense of making real progress as a common lawyer, in what had plainly become his chosen vocation.

During the year of his election to the Vinerian Chair Blackstone apparently had been 'pressed' by Sir John Willes, chief justice of Common Pleas, and his judicial colleague Henry Bathurst, to accept the now sadly diminished 'Honour of the Coif', as a serjeant at law.[78] While Willes (himself a former fellow of All Souls) might have hoped to raise the general standing of the monopoly practisers in his court by recruiting Blackstone to their number, from the latter's perspective such a move would have made little sense in what was seemingly an era of stagnation for the business as well as the jurisprudence of the court of common pleas. But by choosing to decline the now much devalued promotion as serjeant, Blackstone also signalled that his sights were set on higher things. His hopes of gaining better professional preferment must have been significantly boosted by his dealings with Bute and the Prince of Wales from 1759 onwards, as also by signs of growing demand for his services, both in court and in chambers. The first case included in Blackstone's posthumously-published reports where the reporter himself figures among the named counsel was *Robinson v Bland*, heard before Mansfield in King's Bench during Trinity term 1760. Here Blackstone maintained at length, and very learnedly (albeit at last unsuccessfully) that a gaming debt incurred in France was not recoverable in England

---

[76] OUA, WPα/22/2 (12). This is the only flysheet among the thirteen collected by Blackstone not annotated by him; the case for his authorship is otherwise dependent on style and content.

[77] W. Shenstone, *Works in Verse and Prose . . . Volume III* (1769), 315.

[78] Clitherow, xiv.

by action of assumpsit. But this was almost certainly not the first time he had appeared or moved during his second venture into Westminster Hall, since his *Reports* (or at least the first volume, extending to 1769) 'do not contain a regular series of Reports of the Determinations of any one Court . . . [but] only such, as he had selected out of many from his rough Notes'.[79] Inspecting the vast bulk of surviving central court records in order to identify cases in which Blackstone was retained between mid-1759, when he again took chambers as a practitioner, and early 1770, when he became a judge, would be a daunting and not wholly rewarding task. For the surviving rule books and other records do not always list the names of counsel who moved or pleaded in their respective jurisdictions, especially in suits where more than one barrister was retained by either party; indeed for King's Bench, the busiest common-law court, only the names of a single barrister, not his supporting colleagues, are consistently supplied.[80] So a detailed reconstruction of Blackstone's Westminster Hall practice is beyond our reach. What can be said with confidence is that, while he was not among the few 'great counsel' who dominated King's Bench during the 1760s, Blackstone apparently managed to obtain a relatively steady flow of different kinds of litigious work as a barrister, somewhat more than the occasional brief here and there. Yet since he was never one of the leaders at the bar of either King's Bench or Exchequer, the two courts in which he mainly appeared, out of court counselling or chambers' work—general advising, drafting legal instruments, and writing opinions—was always a vital part of his legal practice.

These services were increasingly in demand from the late 1750s onwards. As before, Blackstone continued to respond to occasional requests for assistance from Oxford colleagues and institutions. In 1757 he first received a nominal annual retainer from Magdalen College as one of two 'standing counsel'; the college accounts suggest that this arrangement (which continued until 1770, having doubtless been initiated by his friend Thomas Winchester) did not bring in much work, although he is known to have provided advice in 1759 about a fire insurance claim, and to have received a guinea fee the following year for helping in a dispute with tenants on a

[79] Ibid., xxviii.
[80] On the sources and their limitations, see Lemmings, *Professors*, 71, 165–6. A survey of King's Bench pleas side rule books for successive Michaelmas terms between 1759 and 1769 turned up only three cases where Blackstone is named as counsel which do not appear in his *Reports*, viz. *Goodlittle on the demise of Gerrard* (TNA, KB125/156, 1760), *Tyler v Johnson* (TNA, KB125/157, 1765), and *Hay v Barrett* (TNA, KB125/160, 1768).

college estate.[81] His role as visitor to the Michel Foundation was a good deal more demanding, generating complex and protracted negotiations with the fellows of Queen's College, and in the first few years, with one of his more senior fellow trustees. When a new building designed to be occupied by fellows and scholars on Michel's Foundation was finished in June 1760, the visitors promptly vetoed the college's intention of electing the first beneficiaries, pending promulgation of a set of statutes to regulate such elections. In November the college responded with a series of formal objections to the proposed statutes (the latter we may safely presume to have been largely or wholly drafted by Blackstone), rejecting among others a provision that in case of appeals the visitors might 'judge of the literary Merits of the Candidates by their written Exercises'. Following further exchanges, coordinated on the visitors' side by Blackstone, a Chancery suit ensued to prevent the college holding an election in the absence of any agreed statutes. When he first became a Michel visitor, Blackstone had vigorously resisted the urgings of a fellow trustee to impose their will on the college by such action, but after further experience had presumably concluded that resort to litigation might be a regrettable necessity.[82]

Efforts to reach a viable settlement between the Michel visitors and Queen's College continued until the end of the decade. Meanwhile Blackstone had already begun to find legal employment further afield. His most lucrative and durable professional association was with the aristocratic but financially embarrassed Bertie family. On the death of the debt-laden third earl of Abingdon, Willoughby Bertie, in June 1760, Blackstone was chosen by the earl's executors and trustees, the wealthy middle-aged Oxfordshire Tory Sir James Dashwood, and the much younger Henry Howard, earl of Suffolk, recently graduated from Oxford where he had almost certainly attended Blackstone's lectures, as their man of business. The fourth earl, who had been Howard's contemporary as a gentleman-commoner at Magdalen College and was only 20 years old at his father's death, spent much of the 1760s travelling on the Continent. Blackstone meanwhile busied himself in attempting to rehabilitate the family fortunes. But even as he oversaw a massive series of land sales to pay off debts and meet other obligations under the third earl's will and marriage

---

[81] Magdalen College Archives, Liber Compotus, 1757–69; MS 476, item 2, Thomas Winchester to [President of Magdalen College], 10 January 1759. W. D. Macray, *A Register of the Members of St Mary Magdalen College, Oxford*, n. s. vol. 5 (Oxford, 1906), 19.

[82] Queen's College Archives, 5M60, 'Extracts from original and authentic Papers, touching the Foundation of John Michel'; 5M87: 128, Blackstone to Robert Leybourne, 17 August 1757; 130, James Dawes to Blackstone, 13 June 1760; 133, Blackstone to William Walker, 10 November 1760; same to same, 27 December 1760; same to same, 17 January 1761.

settlement, he also found himself doling out large sums of money from the trustees 'for Lord Abingdon's Use'.[83] From that point of view a more satisfactory professional relationship had been first established as early as 1753 with the executors and heirs of William Jones, a large landowner in Berkshire and Wiltshire. In April 1760 Blackstone provided a written counsel's opinion on the wills of two more family members, cast in briefer and more conventional form than his earlier advice. The nature of the ongoing association between the Jones's, their trustees, and Blackstone as legal adviser is only hinted at by these two documents, and it would hardly be surprising if his expertise were called upon more frequently than the surviving evidence may suggest.[84]

It was around this time, Clitherow tells us, that '[f]inding himself not deceived in his Expectations in respect to an Increase of Business in his Profession, [Blackstone] now determined to settle in Life'—in other words, to marry, and hence abandon his All Souls fellowship.[85] Two other circumstances, unmentioned by Clitherow, almost certainly prompted that momentous decision. The first was an event of national significance: the sudden and unexpected death of the old King on 25 October 1760, and the consequent succession of his 22-year-old grandson as George III. This meant, not only the end of 45 years in the political wilderness for the Tories, but the immediate elevation of Bute, the former Prince's tutor, to pre-eminence at the new royal court. Understandably hastening to take advantage of their recent association, Blackstone called upon Bute in London less than three weeks later 'to pay his humble Respects to his Lordship & to Request the Favour that his Lordship would be pleased to present to his Majesty the address (herewith left) from a Borough of which Mr Blackstone is the Recorder'. While no reply from Bute survives, this approach can have done Blackstone no harm.[86]

A month earlier, Thomas Bigg, the maternal uncle who had loomed so large in Blackstone's early life, died at his house in Chilton Foliat, Wiltshire. By his will, made six years before, Bigg bequeathed legacies of £1,000 to each of his two elder Blackstone nephews, and £700 to their younger brother William, 'having lately given to him three hundred pounds'—a large gift of which we know nothing else. Although expressing his intention to disburse these funds 'within a few Months (if it shall please God I

[83] Doolittle, 76–80; Bodl. MS Top. Oxon. d 378, 'Thomas Walker's Account with the Earl of Abingdon's Trustees', 29 July 1761.
[84] See above, Chapter 7, pp. 122–3 and below Chapter 9, pp. 185–9; Northamptonshire RO, L (C) 453.
[85] Clitherow, xv.
[86] *Letters*, 74–5; *H of P 1754–90*, i. 96. See further below, pp. 180–182.

so long live)' to those 'three Worthy Young Men, thinking the Money may be of more Service to them . . . to Advance them in the World than hereafter', in William's case, Bigg does not seem to have gone through with his plan. Or so it would appear from the fact that William's marriage settlement made on 30 April 1761 lists among his assets a bond for £700 due on 17 July 1758 from Thomas Bigg. Paid over 18 months later by Bigg's executors, this sum represented nearly half the capital assets Blackstone brought to the marriage—the balance being South Sea annuities, calculated to be worth some £796. If for whatever reason—perhaps a falling-out between the two—the youngest Blackstone brother had been unable to obtain the remainder of his legacy during his uncle's lifetime, Thomas Bigg's demise early in 1761 may not have appeared an entirely unredeemed tragedy.[87]

We have it on good authority that 'Fellows of All Souls seeking a wife tended to look around at the sisters of colleagues'.[88] Blackstone's choice was Sarah Clitherow, the eldest surviving sister of James Clitherow, elected a fellow of All Souls in 1750 at the age of 19, who abandoned his fellowship three years later on inheriting his father's estate at Boston House, Brentford, Middlesex.[89] The Clitherows, originally a London merchant family, had acquired this compact Jacobean mansion with its attached acreage of farm lands less than a century before. In Arthur Devis's 1759 portrait, James Clitherow stands formally posed in a plum-coloured suit, his house partly visible though a break in the background trees, looking alertly towards the viewer. While rural, the setting is neither wholly bucolic nor pastoral; no animals appear, and Mrs Clitherow (born Ann Kemeys) holds a lute. The Clitherows were lesser or parochial gentry rather than great landed proprietors; James indeed found on entering into his inheritance that 'after my mother's joynture paid, the interest of the sums charged on it for younger children, and Repairs and Taxes, would scarce afford me a tolerable Maintenance . . .'.[90]

When she married by special license 'William Blackstone of the Inner Temple London Esq' in the parish church of St Mary's, Ealing, on 5 May 1761, Sarah Clitherow was 26 years old (just 3 years younger than her brother James, but 12 years her husband's junior).[91] According to James, William spent with Sarah 'near nineteen Years in the Enjoyment of the

---

[87] TNA, PROB 11/864/118. LMA, ACC 1360/580/1.

[88] J. McManners, *All Souls and the Shipley Case (1808–1810)* (Oxford, 2002), 3.

[89] Codrington, Acta in Capitulis, 1707–53, 200; Bodl. MS D.D. All Souls e 30.

[90] J. McNamara, *Boston Manor Brentford* (Hounslow, 1998), 15–19; LMA, ACC/1360/169/11.

[91] A. J. Howard, 'Boston Manor and the Clitherow Family: a preliminary survey' t.s., Guildhall Library, 1969, 122; LMA, MS DRO37/A1/16; Brentford was part of the parish of Ealing until 1863; I am grateful to Dr Jonathan Oates for assistance on this point.

purest domestic and conjugal Felicity, (for which no Man was better calculated) and which, he used often to declare, was the happiest part of his
Life'.[92] Something of their mutual bliss in the immediate aftermath of the
wedding is captured in his letter of 14 May, which returns to Newdigate
'Mrs Blackstone's & my own sincerest Thanks for Your very early and very
polite Congratulations upon an Event the most interesting to Ourselves,
in every Light both of present & future Happiness. If we can but in any
Degree copy that Example of conjugal Felicity which has been set us by
our Friends at Arbury, I have no manner of Doubt but that our Satisfaction
will, at the distance of many many Years, be altogether as complete as I
assure You it is at present'.[93]

VI

The high spirits which underlie Blackstone's cheerfully facetious account of
military manoeuvres by 'Chelsea Cuirassiers and Hammersmith Brigades'
which he witnessed while on honeymoon were doubtless bolstered by his
new-won status, professional and public as well as marital. The initiative in
proposing Blackstone as a prospective member of parliament came from
Lord Fitzmaurice, the youthful former pupil, now appointed aide-de-camp
to the new King, who had clearly cast himself to fill a role hitherto conspicuously lacking in Blackstone's life, that of aristocratic patron. In February
1761 Fitzmaurice mentioned Blackstone to Bute as 'a man much devoted
to you', in the context of the need to find an acceptable candidate for the
Wiltshire borough of Hindon, a thoroughly corrupt 'potwalloper' constituency which had been placed at Bute's disposal by his parliamentary manager
Henry Fox.[94] Early next month Fitzmaurice renewed his representations,
recommending Blackstone as 'a man of business, and may be more so, and
perhaps more useful', not least through his links with the earls of Suffolk
and Abingdon, and hence perhaps the Tory gentry of Oxfordshire and
the West Midlands. Bute apparently accepted this proposition, agreeing
to come up with the money required to pay off the Hindon electors from
his own resources. Blackstone himself initially found the whole prospect
too daunting, both on account of his 'present Avocations . . . being just
upon the Eve of settling in a domestic Way', and also because he lacked
the technical landed qualification for a borough member, 'the Whole of my
Property being at present personal'. But two days' reflection, and no doubt

---

[92] Clitherow, xvi.   [93] *Letters*, 81.
[94] Hindon had about 200 head-of-household voters: *H of P, 1754–90*, i. 415.

consultation with friends, changed his mind sufficiently to evoke a guarded acquiescence in 'the great and unmerited Honour, which your Lordship, with the Approbation of his Majesty, and the Concurrent good Opinion of Lord Bute, is so good as to leave at my Option'. This was written in hurried response to a further letter from Fitzmaurice, now offering his good offices in relation to the vacant chief justiceship of Ireland, a suggestion Blackstone firmly quashed: 'I have so much of a provincial Narrowness in my Constitution, that I could rather wish to exert the little Share of Abilities I am Master of, and which your Lordship greatly overrates, in my own native Country'. But that the King himself approved of his proposed election to parliament was not a fact to be lightly ignored.[95]

Hence Blackstone's willingness to overlook 'the little private domestic Inconveniences, that I thought I foresaw', so long as it were possible to find 'any Way, in which I can with Honour and Conscience satisfy the Law and my Oath in regard to a parliamentary Qualification'. A solution to that problem ('by purchasing an Annuity for my life on landed Security, and settling an equivalent Annuity out of my personal Estate') came to him the following day, 12 March, when he saw 'only one Difficulty remaining . . . that the Expense of obtaining the Seat you propose shall not be such as may injure my private Fortune; which is confined within moderate Bounds, though sufficient to supply all that a prudent Man should desire'. This residual obstacle was also removed four days later, when Fox handed Blackstone's name to one of the two effective proprietors of Hindon borough, together with the sum of £2,000.[96]

A false alarm about the election result on 29 March produced a hasty letter in which Blackstone declared 'how little I expected or sought for a seat in Parliament'.[97] But news of his return as member for Hindon was confirmed the following day. This brought a further problem, 'in regard to the Silk-Gown, with which your Lordship [Fitzmaurice] informed me the King intended to honour me'.[98] If George III had indeed stated an intention to promote Blackstone to the rank of king's counsel, his election had complicated the situation, since an MP who took silk must resign and stand again. However, that requirement might be avoided were he to receive a royal patent of precedence (or pre-audience) at the bar, rather than the office of king's counsel. Both before and just after the Hindon poll Blackstone raised this issue with Fitzmaurice, although it was not until

---

[95] H of P, 1754–90, ii.96; Doolittle, 58–9; Letters, 75–7. The Bath physician Dr Rice Charlton claimed that Blackstone's election occurred because 'the King insisted upon it, as he was a man of learning and ingenuity': M. Williams (ed.), The Letters of William Shenstone (Oxford, 1939), 580.
[96] Letters, 76–7; H of P 1754–90, ii. 96.
[97] Letters, 79.   [98] Ibid., 80.

the day after his marriage that the patent of precedence was enrolled, just possibly as a royal wedding present.[99]

Blackstone's other main concern was to establish the exact nature of his new patrons' expectations, and hence his own political obligations. This was a matter of sufficient importance for him to remind Fitzmaurice of the latter's verbal undertaking to 'make Enquiry what was expected from me with regard to Hindon'.[100] Although Fitzmaurice's response has not survived, in the letter to Newdigate discussed above Blackstone claimed that 'the Honours I have received'—that is, presumably, both his parliamentary seat and the patent of precedence—'were conferred unsought, and accepted unconditionally'. Moreover 'this Independence of your Friend' was no mere negative liberty, for he had been 'positively desired to follow his own Sentiments in such Matters as shall come before Him . . .'.[101] As an Oxford academic politician, Blackstone had made much of his own and the university's 'independence', a theme 'central to English conceptions of manliness, political virtue and constitutional legitimacy by the mid-eighteenth century'.[102] So he was doubtless well pleased to take these comforting assurances at face value—and at this early stage in the new reign they may even have been sincerely meant. Yet it would not be long before the pressure of political realities cast matters in a rather different light.

[99] J. C. Sainty, *A List of English Law Officers, King's Counsel and Holders of Patents of Precedence* (1986), 227.

[100] *Letters*, 78.   [101] Ibid., 81.

[102] *Letters*, 32 ('noble Independence, which has ever been the principle of the University'); 50 ('any Man of Sense and Independence in the Place'). M. McCormack, *The Independent Man Citizenship and Gender Politics in Georgian England* (Manchester, 2005), 80.

CHAPTER 9

'Hopes of Advancement' (1761–66)

WHETHER or not bestowed as a personal mark of royal favour, envious fellow barristers might have been pardoned for regarding Blackstone's patent of precedence as premature. The last five lawyers to be appointed king's counsel had ranged in age from 39 to 47 years, while the recipients of the two most recent patents of precedence, granted in 1758 and 1760 after a 16-year hiatus, were then aged 45 and 53 respectively. At 37, Blackstone was not merely the most junior of these eight men in terms of length of standing at the bar, as well as age, but he had resumed practice in Westminster Hall less than two years before, after a six-year break.[1] Further, if Dr Blackstone's broad legal learning could hardly be questioned, his standing as a common law advocate was plainly less impressive. In these circumstances, he could be considered very lucky to have already risen so far and so fast.

I

Having gained his silk gown, Blackstone's practice continued to burgeon. In June 1761, already working on his plaintiffs' brief in the important copyright test case of *Tonson v Collins* before Lord Mansfield in King's Bench, he successfully sought the erudite Solicitor General Charles Yorke's assistance to obtain copies of relevant Chancery injunctions, as directed by Mansfield at the adjourned Trinity term hearing of the case. Blackstone possibly chose to approach Yorke because the latter enjoyed privileged access to the papers of his father, the former Lord Chancellor Hardwicke.

---

[1] KCs: Charles Ambler (1761), Eliab Harvey (1758), William de Grey (1758), Richard Aston (1758), George Perrott (1753). Patents of precedence: Richard Hussey (1760); John Morton (1758): Sainty, *Law Officers*, 94, 277.

While the willingness of this notable Whig scion to fulfil the professional request of an Oxford Tory colleague may have had something to
do with the invocation of Mansfield's name, it also speaks volumes for the
transformation of the party-political climate following George III's accession. His extensive report of his own argument next Michaelmas term
shows Blackstone making good use of Yorke's notes from the voluminous
Chancery registers, together with other fruits of his personal researches
'among Mr Bagford's manuscripts in the British Museum' and 'Serjeant
Hussey's MSS'. Following Alexander Wedderburn (a future lord chancellor), and responding to Edward Thurlow (another future chancellor) and
Joseph Yates (who himself would shortly join Mansfield's court) for the
defendant, Blackstone deployed a remarkable range of historical, legal, and
literary reference to support the assertion that authors enjoy 'sole exclusive
right of multiplying the copies' of their mental labours, since copyright was
a form of property fully recognized by the laws of England.[2] This was a case
ideally suited to Blackstone's interests and talents, given his now considerable familiarity with the book trade, and because a lack of common law
precedents left the way open to construct arguments *ab initio* drawn from
painstaking historical research and jurisprudential first principles. While
in itself inconclusive, because held over for hearing before all 12 judges
in Exchequer Chamber and then abandoned, *Tonson v Collins* rehearsed
the basic parameters of the debate over the existence and ownership of
literary property which would be conducted in the better-known case of
Millar v Taylor before Mansfield's court from Trinity term 1767, when
Blackstone again appeared for the plaintiff.[3] More immediately *Baskett v
Cunningham*, another book-trade case, saw Blackstone make one of his few
recorded appearances in Chancery, where in Trinity term 1762 he argued
unsuccessfully, albeit in the distinguished company of George Perrott KC,
the veteran Chancery leader Randle Wilbraham, and young Wedderburn,
against an attempt to suppress a version of the statutes printed in weekly
instalments with extensive explanatory notes, on the grounds that this
work did not infringe the King's printer's monopoly rights.[4]

Some other self-reported cases in which Blackstone appeared as counsel
also reflect his personal background and interests, most obviously the suit

---

[2] *Letters*, 82–3; *Reports*, i. 321–45; M. Rose, *Authors and Owners: The Invention of Copyright*
(1993), 74–8; Langford, *Public Life and the Propertied Englishman*, 27.

[3] Rose, *Authors and Owners*, 78–82; *Millar v Taylor* is reported by Burrow (98 *ER* 201) but for
some reason not by Blackstone himself, perhaps because his successful arguments there were little
different from those he had previously advanced in *Tonson v Collins*.

[4] *Reports*, i. 371; *ODNB*, s.v. Perrott, George; for Wilbraham, see Lemmings, *Professors*, 178, 350,
353; *H of P 1754–90*, iii. 637–8; *Letters*, 23–8.

launched on behalf of the earl of Lichfield as chancellor of the University of Oxford in Hilary term 1764, claiming 'conusance' or jurisdiction in an action for assault brought against a fellow of Brasenose College.[5] His general expertise in matters of academic law was also called upon in a complex case involving the election of a high steward—another Hardwicke—at the University of Cambridge. Following the 1760 case of *Robinson v Bland* already mentioned, he argued on several further occasions in King's Bench matters involving conflicts of law, international law, or jurisdiction over aliens, including *Thiquet v Bath* (1764), where the English defendant successfully claimed protection against arrest for debt arising from his employment as secretary to the Bavarian ambassador, notwithstanding the best efforts of Blackstone and Edward Thurlow KC, yet another future chancellor. Later that year he was retained for the prosecution in *R v d'Éon*, arising from the feud mounted by the colourful cross-dressing Chevalier d'Éon against Louis XV's newly-appointed ambassador to the court of St James. He then successfully defended the latter in Easter term 1765 on the grounds of ambassadorial immunity against a malicious prosecution launched by d'Éon, sufficiently impressing the court with quotations from Livy, Cicero, Grotius, Montesquieu, the civilian Cornelius Bynkershoek, and the historians Camden, Robertson, Hume, and Smollett to have the indictment quashed.[6] In this matter Blackstone was opposed by Serjeant Glynn and John Dunning, two well-known legal adherents of the celebrated radical John Wilkes. The year before these two had also argued against Blackstone and his colleagues for the defence in the case of *R v Webb*, which Wilkes brought as a private prosecution against the treasury solicitor (and antiquary) who had testified as a defence witness in Wilkes's action for trespass, following the seizure of his papers after publication of *North Briton* No 45.[7]

While largely conducted before the court of King's Bench and—to a much lesser extent—the Exchequer (he would later describe himself as having 'attended but little' on Chancery and other equity jurisdictions),[8] Blackstone's Westminster Hall practice was evidently very general in nature. In addition to the cases mentioned above, during the first five

---

[5] *Reports*, i. 454–5 (*Kendrick v Kynaston*).

[6] *Reports*, i. 471–5, 510–17, 545–7, 548–53. In a maritime ransom case (*Ricord v Bettenham*, 1765), Blackstone obtained written opinions from two distinguished Continental lawyers, Élie de Beaumont and Gerard Meerman, as to how such an action would fare in their respective jurisdictions: ibid., 328; Museum Meermano–Westreenianum, MS 257/61, 63.

[7] *Reports*, i. 460–1; P. D. G. Thomas, *John Wilkes A Friend to Liberty* (Oxford, 1996), 46; Langford, *Polite and Commercial People*, 571.

[8] *Commentaries*, iii. 429.

years of George III's reign he was retained in suits concerning debt, wills, tithes, wharfage in London, the powers of an ecclesiastical judge, pauper settlements, distraint of livery carriages, advowsons, and the validity of a bond for cohabitation (where he appeared on behalf of a kept woman who sought to recover in debt from her deceased lover's estate).[9] When occasion demanded he was entirely prepared to engage in narrowly technical argument on fine points of procedural or substantive law, as for example in *Bishop of Lincoln and Whitehead v Wolferstan* (1764), a dispute over a church living where much turned on the precise time and sequence of each clergyman's induction or institution, as stated in the pleadings to the case.[10] Blackstone's notes of actions in which he was retained may well understate the number of times he actually addressed a court over several terms; thus in the 1765–6 *London Wharfs* case the Exchequer records suggest that he appeared on at least four separate occasions, whereas his own report refers only to a single motion before that court.[11] In short, Blackstone's performance on his second attempt at the London bar was of a very different order to his previous, rather half-hearted, efforts.

Nor is it difficult to understand why this should have been so. Now older, more single-minded, and determined, the experience of preparing and delivering his lectures over the previous decade, and advising clients both within and beyond the university, plainly enabled him to draw on vastly broader and deeper stores of legal knowledge than he had possessed on his first attempt at the bar. The prestige and reputation of the Vinerian Chair and his various publications, especially the *Analysis of the Laws*, also undoubtedly helped attract clients, even before the first volume of *Commentaries* appeared in November 1765. Although such connections were not a necessary guarantee of success at the bar, he now had various well-placed acquaintants, friends, patrons, and supporters, both within and beyond the legal world, including influential young aristocrats like Shelburne who had been impressed by his Oxford lectures. And besides its prestige and symbolic significance, his patent of precedence conferred the valuable right of being heard in all courts after king's counsel but before all other barristers, while still enabling him to act for defendants in Crown cases. The patent also earned him admission to the governing body of the Middle Temple. Although call to the bench of their Inn of Court was no longer an important career milestone for most Georgian barristers, in Blackstone's case it could be seen as a form of recognition by

---

[9] *Reports*, i. 365–7, 420–21, 423–6, 430–32, 433–6, 446–51, 483–4, 499–6, 517–18, 519–21.
[10] Ibid., 490–6.
[11] *Reports*, i. 581–90; TNA, E161/97, 26 April, 3 May, 7, 12, 15 June, 9 December 1765.

his non-academic peers, and a means of better integrating himself into the professional community of the bar. He was henceforth usually present at two or three Middle Temple bench meetings (or parliaments) every year until he became a judge.[12]

In concert with the growing demand for his services as an advocate in Westminster Hall, Blackstone's out-of-court or chambers practice was also looking up. As before, much of this work was generated by family and friends, often in connection with the responsibilities of executors and trustees for winding-up deceased estates. Thus in March 1762 his uncle Walter Bigg mentioned that another uncle, Seymour Richmond, was 'forwarding the affair' of a conveyance 'with the Advice of Counsellor Blackstone', while on Christmas Eve of that year, Blackstone added a postscript of 'further Explication' to the opinion he had already provided Bigg on a bequest to Winchester College. Although Bigg was concerned that 'I have troubled Mr Blackstone already so much for 2 Guineas', over the next few years he furnished the fellows of Winchester College (among them his own brother Charles) with written advice on at least three separate matters, including the 'many Doubts and Difficulties' arising from the disputed will of Dr Thomas Cheyney. Following the death of William Shenstone in 1763, his will was sent to Blackstone for advice by the poet's executors, Richard Graves, and Blackstone's former publisher Robert Dodsley.[13] Oxford colleges also continued to seek assistance with the interpretation of their statutes and other legal problems; in February 1762 Blackstone appeared for 'the Gentlemen of All Souls College' in a founder's kin appeal case heard before Archbishop Secker, once again failing to convince the visitor and his assessors of the need to limit the bounds of collateral consanguinity.[14]

But there were also new clients from further afield, among them the Cornish landowner, merchant and Tory MP Jonathan Rashleigh, and his son Philip, who succeeded to his father's estate in 1764, and to his parliamentary seat for the borough of Fowey the following year. Another wealthy country squire, William Freke of Hannington, Wiltshire, obtained Blackstone's advice first on a draft of his will in January 1765, and then in October of that year on his powers to grant leases under the terms of his grandfather's marriage settlement.[15] Closer to home, in 1762

---

[12] Lemmings, *Professors*, 258; MT Archives, K10, 270 (22 May 1761). Clitherow, xvi.

[13] BL MS Additional 28670, fo. 160; *Correspondence of Dodsley*, 482, 484; Winchester College Muniments, 330a, 8542c, 13360, 20361, 23205a–b.

[14] *Letters*, 90–2; Squibb, *Founder's Kin*, 66–7, 77n (Pembroke College, Oxford, 1761); Jesus College Archives, RE 6, Bursar's Register 1711–1851, fos. 381–381 v (1764).

[15] Cornwall RO, R/15444, 15447; BL MS Additional 21507, fos. 225, 226v–228.

the Oxford city parish of St Ebbe's received Blackstone's formal opinion warning against any attempt to remove one James Meers, his wife, and children from the house they occupied in the parish, despite doubts about the validity of Meers's title to the premises and the possibility that he and his family might become a liability under the poor law. This and other matters from Oxford and vicinity may well have been referred by the attorney James Morrell, or his business partner Thomas Walker, town clerk of Oxford, both of whom worked closely with Blackstone during the 1760s, especially in connection with the Abingdon family estate.[16]

All such occasional calls on his professional services were doubtless welcome, if only for the fees they brought in. But the affairs of the Berties and their titular head, the fourth earl of Abingdon, provided Blackstone's most constant and profitable source of out-of-court employment throughout the decade before he became a judge. Not all this work was specifically legal in nature. His financial acumen made him a natural choice to audit, negotiate, and settle accounts, while checking through the details of new and renewed leases would have been a routine task for a former steward of All Souls College. Hard proof is lacking, but it seems likely that Blackstone also played a major part in formulating the overall strategy of consolidation and debt reduction pursued by the trustees of the debt-burdened Abingdon estates, which involved the sale over seven years of some 18 manors and farms in Lincolnshire, Oxfordshire, and Wiltshire to raise the huge amount of £181,126.[17] Blackstone went about this complex and prolonged task with characteristic diligence and drive. Thus in August 1761, accompanied by Thomas Walker and two of Abingdon's estate managers travelling in two post chaises with a spare horse, he set off to conduct the sale by auction of Abingdon's Knaith estate in northeast Lincolnshire, justifying his intention of following a very indirect route, from Wallingford to Lincoln via London, by 'Consideration of Northampton Races, and the Dangers of bad Weather, and Accidents upon a cross Road upon so long a Journey'.[18] For that expedition he received a fee of £52.10/0, in addition to the £105 he had already been paid in February for auditing trust accounts and what was obscurely referred to as 'o[the]r Business'; next year a trip to view the lie of the land at the family's parliamentary borough of Westbury in Wiltshire earned him £36.15/- in addition to expenses, while in 1763 his

[16] Oxfordshire RO, MS D.D. Par. Oxford St Ebbe's c 12 e; CH/L. II/1; B. Allen, *Morrells of Oxford: the Family and their Brewery 1742–1993* (Oxford, 1994), 10–11; Doolittle, 76–7.

[17] J. Habakkuk, *Marriage, Debt and the Estates System: English Landownership, 1650–1950* (Oxford, 1994), 372–3; Bodl. MS Top. Oxon. b 177, fos. 41–2.

[18] Bodl. MS Top. Oxon. b 177, fos. 35–40, 41–2; MS Top. Oxon. d 378 (Thomas Walker's Accounts with Earl of Abingdon's Trustees, 1761–8); MS D.D. Bertie c2/43; *Letters*, 85.

fees for auditing accounts, perusing leases, negotiating with the former Countess of Abingdon's executors and 'extra trouble in going through the sale of the Lincolnshire Estate' amounted to just over £191. The Abingdon trustees and the new earl (for whom Blackstone later became a trustee himself) continued to pay out substantial fees over the rest of the decade, as Blackstone's role extended to the drafting and passage of acts of parliament designed to provide jointures and portions for wives and younger children, and to enhance the estate's profitability by means of ambitious construction projects on Oxford's western outskirts and approaches.[19]

II

Despite losing his All Souls fellowship six months after his marriage (since in pre-reformed Oxford, only heads of colleges and halls escaped the formal requirement of celibacy) and leasing a London house (or part thereof) in Carey Street off Chancery Lane, a short stroll from the Temple, Blackstone was in no hurry to sever all his remaining academic ties. Thomas Winchester had predicted that he would desert the university within three or four years of resuming practice at the bar, 'for by that time I doubt not he will find himself so well establish'd in business, as to make what he has here incompatable with it'.[20] Yet not until April 1765 did Blackstone finally announce his intention to retire from the Vinerian Chair on completing his last course of lectures in the following spring, when he also resigned as principal of New Inn Hall, a post he had held since 1761. That appointment, made by Lord Westmorland as chancellor of the University, was probably a quid pro quo for Blackstone's key role in the former's election two years earlier, not to mention his flattering dedication of *The Great Charter* to Westmorland as 'The Assertor of those Liberties of Which his Ancestors Witnessed the Confirmation'. It was certainly a sinecure, since New Inn Hall had few if any students or other members, while nevertheless providing 'an agreeable Residence during the Time his Lectures required him to be in Oxford'.[21]

Before taking up the headship at New Inn Hall, Blackstone had brought his bride back to Wallingford, almost certainly to the spacious three-storeyed villa by the River Thames which was to be the family home for the rest of their married life. Priory Place, leased and possibly owned by his uncle Thomas Bigg throughout the 1750s, may have been occupied

---

[19] Doolittle, 78–9.   [20] Warwickshire RO, CR 136/B4099.
[21] Clitherow, xvi.

by Blackstone on his occasional visits to Wallingford as recorder during that decade (Clitherow refers to his 'more or less frequent Residences there from about the year 1750'). At Thomas's death in February 1761 the property passed to his clergyman brother Walter, but on 8 August a vestry meeting of the parish church of St Peter's (to the rebuilding of which Blackstone had recently subscribed £50) noted that 'William Blackstone Esq should be put in the Next Rate in the Roome of the Revnd Mr Bigg'. Blackstone as tenant thereby assumed responsibility for local church and poor rates assessed on the basis of an annual value of £28, plus a further £2 for an adjacent garden or orchard. This was by far the highest valuation in the parish, where 72 householders paid the churchwarden's rate for the past year at Easter 1762. While Blackstone did not actually purchase the premises previously leased from his uncle Walter and nephew Lovelace Bigg until October 1763, what he would later characterize in jocular fashion as 'my Cabin in Thames Street, Wallingford' saw a good deal of entertaining as soon as Sally and he had set up house there.[22] One early overnight guest was William Petty, the former pupil now succeeded to the peerage as second earl of Shelburne, accompanied by a military colleague, and their respective servants, although an unfortunate attack of gout, and 'the accidental Visit of Country Relations'—perhaps the Richmonds from Sparsholt—apparently took the edge off this occasion so far as Blackstone himself was concerned. A more successful aristocratic visitation occurred a few months later, when Shelburne's younger brother Thomas, recently returned to England from an educational sojourn with Professor Adam Smith at Glasgow, was invited by Blackstone 'to spend a couple of Evenings with me at Wallingford'.[23]

Wallingford's location, only 12 miles, or several hours journey by horse-drawn chaise or buggy from Oxford, made it relatively easy to stay in touch with university affairs, as Blackstone would to some extent continue to do even after he had formally resigned all his academic positions. In the months immediately following his marriage in April, he made little effort to tear himself away from familiar haunts. He was back in Oxford less than a fortnight after his wedding, attempting to arrange for

---

[22] Clitherow, xx; Doolittle, 101–2; Berkshire RO, D/P 139/11/1; D/P 139/5/2. The deed of bargain and sale, in private hands locally, shows the total purchase price as £4,000, including various additional parcels of land and houses in Wallingford, and across the river in Crowmarsh Gifford: David Pedgley kindly provided this information. *Letters*, 133.

[23] *Letters*, 84–5, 86–7; *The Correspondence of Adam Smith*, ed. E. C. Mossner and I. S. Ross (Oxford, 1977), 81–3. Blackstone maintained contact with Fitzmaurice, who attended his lectures, assuring Shelburne in October 1762 that 'your Brother is well, studies hard, and desires to be affectionately remembered to Your Lordship': *Letters*, 100.

Convocation's approval of the appointment of deputies to deliver his lectures, in case he 'should meet with any Accident which might render him incapable of reading'.[24] (The very task of establishing his new household in Wallingford possibly brought home the greater practical difficulties he now faced in being obliged to lecture in Oxford on given dates.) Then after apparently spending most of June in London, Blackstone returned to Oxford at the beginning of July. He remained in commons at All Souls over the next two months, and again for a further six weeks after 25 September. Surviving letters dated from Wallingford on 16 and 19 July and 4 August indicate that these mid-summer absences from the marital home were not unbroken. But he was certainly back reading in the Bodleian Library on 1 October; his lecture course began two weeks later, while a day after that he wrote out and signed a page of lease renewals in the official college register of All Souls business.[25] He may even have attended and voted at the election of new fellows next month, since his own fellowship was not actually voided until 6 November, while the election had to be held on or within three days of All Souls' Day (2 November).

However attached he was to All Souls, Blackstone now clearly entertained very mixed feelings towards the University of Oxford. In the summer of 1761, lingering resentment at his treatment during and after the Vinerian election was exacerbated by what he characteristically took to be a calculated series of personal rebuffs and slights from the vice chancellor, Dr Joseph Browne of Queen's College, and at least some of his fellow heads of houses. The statutes under which Blackstone held his Chair distinguished between the four annual 'solemn' or public lectures he was required to offer as Viner's professor and his private course of lectures to fee-paying students. While both could be discharged by deputy under certain stated conditions, in the case of the quarterly public lectures, any deputy had to be endorsed by Convocation, and all Convocation meetings on Vinerian business required at least ten day's prior notice. As this would hardly be practicable 'in case of any sudden Indisposition or other unforseen Impediment', Blackstone decided to nominate in advance a pool of potential deputies, including four All Souls colleagues, friends and pupils, plus Robert Chambers of University College, who would eventually succeed him as Vinerian Professor. Vice Chancellor Browne apparently approved of this plan as outlined in a draft which Blackstone had printed

---

[24] [W. Blackstone], *The Vinerian Professor is extremely concerned . . .* : OUA, V/3/5/16. See further below.

[25] Ibid.; MT Archives, K10, 270, 5 June 1761; Soc. of Antiquaries, Minute Book 7, pp. 1–7, 9 (10, 24 June 1761); *Letters*, 83–5; Bodl. MS Library Records e 560, fo. 31; BL MS Additional 36093, fo. 1; Codrington, Acta in Capitulis, 1753–1770, 15 October 1761.

and distributed on 21 May, but then announced—without further consultation, and in Blackstone's absence—that Convocation would be asked to
give its approval of the nominated deputies for one year only.[26] Blackstone
predictably took this 'very material Alteration' as 'a personal Indignity
offered to the Characters of his Friends, and in consequence to his own
Nomination'. So Browne was requested by letter to put to Convocation
either his original proposal (without time limit) or none at all.

On his return to Oxford in early July, Blackstone called on the vice
chancellor, and after 'some Expostulation on the Politeness of the Usage he
had received', presented him with another paper explaining the rationale
of his original motion, which he again sought to have put to Convocation.
Browne agreed to do so, on condition that the document was first seen
and approved by the heads of houses, something Blackstone believed both
'unnecessary and unconstitutional'. But when Browne insisted 'that it
was customary', Blackstone left the paper with him, understanding that
it would be presented to the heads the same day, then returned to him
for printing and circulation around the colleges. While this happened
as planned, Browne unfortunately failed to mention that the heads had
insisted, presumably with his acquiescence, on retaining the one-year
limit in the motion proposed to Convocation.

Blackstone responded by appealing to the university in a four-page flysheet, which after a detailed account of his dealings with Dr Browne,
attacked the heads' actions as an unprecedented and unconstitutional
infringement on Convocation's rights, recalling his stance in the dispute
over nominations to the Press delegacy some years before. As for himself, the author (writing in the third person) denied having given 'just
Cause (or any Cause that dares to be avowed) for the Series of peevish
Opposition and personal Insult, which he has met with in the Execution
of his present Employment'. He had tried to 'discharge his Duty as labori-
ously and as punctually as any other Professor in the University'—hardly a
ringing endorsement of his professorial colleagues (Browne among them,
as the undistinguished holder of a Chair in natural philosophy)—having
himself made no previous use of deputies, 'except once or twice for a single Day in the midst of his private Lectures'. But because 'neither the
Persons contending, nor the Thing contended for, are worth the Trouble
of a Contest', he would take matters no further, lest he 'occasion an unsea-
sonable Ferment, and give rise to new Tumult and Faction'; having besides
'too much Regard for the Gentlemen named, to expose *them* to the mean

[26] *The Vinerian Professor is extremely concerned . . .* , 1; OUA, V/3/5/14; T. M. Curley, *Sir Robert
Chambers: Law, Literature and Empire in the Age of Johnson* (1998), 34–8.

Resentment of low and little Minds'. Hence he had determined to revoke his nominations altogether, as 'an effectual Stop to the present extraordinary Proceeding'.[27]

Despite the measured tone of much of this pamphlet, its several outbursts of contemptuous indignation at Oxford's academic rulers, together with a pointed reference to 'the Remainder of the Time that he proposes to continue in his present Capacity', might suggest that the normally cautious Blackstone had finally decided to burn his boats so far as the university was concerned. Yet just over a fortnight later, he accepted the New Inn Hall position, which gave him a seat alongside other heads of house on the Hebdomadal Board, if he chose to take it, besides a convenient Oxford *pied à terre*.[28] He also occasionally attended meetings of the delegates of the Press,[29] and remained actively involved in efforts to settle the Michel bequest at Queen's College; this latter role may incidentally account for some of the difficulties he experienced in dealing with Dr Browne, who had served as head of that college since 1757. While these undertakings required no more than an occasional personal presence in Oxford, his lectures were more demanding in that respect. They also continued to attract a growing audience of fee-paying undergraduates, with receipts rising from £258 in 1760 and £266 in 1761 to reach a peak of £340 for the following year.[30] Together with his annual professorial salary, these earnings constituted a large part of his annual income, even if their relative importance doubtless declined as his legal practice slowly expanded.

However much he may have resented ill-treatment received from men whom he despised, Blackstone found leaving Oxford more easily threatened than accomplished. Indeed, when he wrote to his youthful patron-protégé Shelburne just after Christmas 1761 to seek his assistance in applying for further preferment, he was careful to point out that the post of chief justice of Chester which he was now pursuing was 'the best suited of any in the Law to my Situation and Wishes; as the Duty of it will not interfere with the Duty of my Oxford Professorship, which with me is still a very favourite Point'.[31] He was indeed prepared 'willingly to engage' to continue in Oxford as Vinerian Professor '(which otherwise my Avocations in Town will in a Year or two induce me to resign) and to

---

[27] *The Vinerian Professor is extremely concerned*..., 1–4. Clitherow however states that publication of Blackstone's pamphlet ended the opposition to his proposals: Clitherow, xvi.
[28] Clitherow, xvi, dates the appointment to 28 July 1761. No Hebdomadal Board minutes survive from the 1760s: *HUO*, 216.
[29] From 1761 until his resignation in October 1765, Blackstone attended at least one but no more than three delegates' meetings each year: OUP Archives, Orders of the Delegates of the Press.
[30] See Appendix II below. [31] *Letters*, 71–2.

apply my whole Vigour and Talents to cultivate and improve my original Plan in that Place'. This was presumably a reference to the scheme for establishing in Oxford a college or hall dedicated to legal studies, analogous to Trinity Hall in Cambridge, despite his earlier failure to persuade Convocation that all those supported by Viner's endowment should be brought together in a single institution. With the Chester post secured, he would even 'willingly renounce my Attendance at the Bar', something 'imprudent, and unjust to my Family, to do at present'. And that would create the opportunity:

to open another Plan which I have long meditated, and which my present Situation in the University (as Principal of a Hall) would give me Opportunity to put in Practice. I mean some Improvements in the Methods of academical Education; by retaining the useful Parts of it, stripped of monastic Pedantry; by supplying its Defects, and adapting it more peculiarly to Gentlemen of Rank and Fortune: Whereas the Basis of the present Forms is principally calculated for the Priesthood; while the Instruction of Laymen (whatever be their Quality or Profession) is only a collateral Object.[32]

This is the first recorded occasion on which Blackstone seized the initiative as client to patron in seeking a specific judicial promotion; characteristically, he took a paragraph to spell out the detailed justification and substance of his claims for 'some farther Advancement'. But it would be unduly cynical to suppose that his discussion of the rationale for modernizing and secularizing undergraduate education at Oxford amounted to no more than fanciful trimming on a narrowly self-interested plea for preferment. For this was not the sole occasion on which Blackstone took up that same theme. Nor is it difficult to see his own introduction of studies in English law and government to Oxford as potentially leading the way to a general substitution of modern subjects (history, languages, and science) for part, or all, of the obsolete scholastic curriculum.[33] Whether even Blackstone could have overcome the entrenched forces inevitably resisting any such development is another question, however, especially given the personal animosity he had generated across the university over the past few years.

What made it entirely clear that he was not destined to preempt the royal commission and parliamentary legislation which eventually reformed nineteenth-century Oxford was another contested chancellorship election, following Lord Westmorland's death in August 1762. Blackstone's hopes of the chief justiceship of Chester had remained unfulfilled in the meantime. So likewise, a further appeal to Shelburne at the end of

---

[32] Ibid.   [33] Doolittle, 27–8; see also *Letters*, 99.

July 1762, 'that you may prevail upon Lord Bute to recommend me to his Majesty's Notice',[34] in the event of an anticipated vacancy on the court of Common Pleas. At the same time Blackstone was becoming more demanding and forthright, emphasizing that '[m]y Ambition now rises to the Post of an English Judge, for which I hope that my Studies have in some degree qualified me . . . though I fear that my natural Diffidence will never permit me to make any great Progress at the Bar; for which talents very different are required from those which will qualify for the Bench'.[35] This was nevertheless an exceedingly ambitious goal for a man in his 30s, given that the average age of puisne judges appointed over the previous reign was nearly 44, while all but two of the last five appointees were aged over 50 at the time.[36] A further letter of 7 September apologized for the previous 'false Alarm', expressing concern lest he appear 'an importunate Petitioner', since '[i]t is one thing to present oneself to View in the Circle, and another to press insolently forward before those who have better Pretensions to their Prince's Notice'. While here as generally elsewhere only Blackstone's side of this exchange has survived, it may be that Shelburne had attempted to deflect or divert his older client with talk of the importance of his Oxford work. If so, Blackstone was having none of it. Notwithstanding a mollifying assurance that his 'first Wishes concur with yours', to stay and 'do that little Service in my Power to that Place and its Plan of Education', Blackstone informed Shelburne that he could not 'answer it to my Friends and my growing Family (for so I may call it, being lately increased by the Birth of a Son) to confine my Prospects to that narrow Spot; unless I could be assured of some Equivalent for those Advantages, which I may reasonably expect, in the common Track of my Profession'. Yet having made that personal point, Blackstone turned to what was obviously Oxford's question of the moment—'whom we are to have for our Chancellor'.[37]

This was no merely academic issue. Both the prestige attached to the office itself, and the university's distinctive national role during the past two reigns as Tory citadel and seminary made the choice of Oxford's next chancellor a matter of political and public interest. Jockeying and speculation on the likely field of candidates began well before the announcement

---

[34] *Letters*, 93.   [35] Ibid.

[36] Duman, *Judicial Bench*, 72, 81; the youngest of the last five was Henry Bathurst, appointed judge in Common Pleas at the age of 40 in 1754 entirely on account of the influence of his courtier-peer father: L. Colley, *In Defiance of Oligarchy: The Tory Party 1714–1760* (Cambridge, 1982), 239. The other four were William Noel, Henry Gould, John Eardley Wilmot and Richard Lloyd, whose ages at appointment ranged from 46 to 62.

[37] *Letters*, 94.

of Westmorland's death on 26 August. His obvious successor was Lord Lichfield, whose last-minute withdrawal from the previous poll, thanks largely to Blackstone's machinations, had handed victory to Westmorland and his Old Interest supporters. But some of them, including Blackstone, remained adamantly opposed to Lichfield on essentially personal grounds, despite the latter's Tory credentials, court connections, and office as high steward of the university. Another possibility was Bute, whose election might be taken as symbolizing the end of Oxford's self-imposed isolation from court and government, besides providing a mirror image of the Whig magnate Newcastle's chancellorship at Cambridge. One perceptive observer nevertheless believed Bute could only succeed if Lichfield withdrew, 'and that Blackston[e] must concur and cooperate'.[38] He might well have been amenable, since he owed his parliamentary seat to Bute, and had expressed support for Bute's political leadership on various occasions. However, much to Blackstone's discomfiture, while Bute proved unwilling to stand himself, he was prepared to mobilize his considerable ministerial influence behind Lichfield's candidacy.

This placed Blackstone in an extremely awkward position. He saw Lichfield—accurately enough—as an ineffective nonentity, 'one from whose Nothingness nothing good or bad is to expected, but only to let us dream on in the same dull Track; ashamed of the scholastic Fopperies in the Learning of the last Age, but substituting nothing better in its stead'.[39] In sharing this judgement with Shelburne, who was also Bute's follower and protégé, he obviously intended it to reach the first minister, together with his concern that Bute might choose to 'disoblige two or three noble Families in order to direct the Weight of Government in favour of any one Candidate'. Nor did he attempt to disguise his own commitment to Henry Howard, Earl of Suffolk, one of the Bertie family trustees, and almost certainly among the 'noble and ingenuous youth' who had paid their fees to sit at Blackstone's feet.[40] But as a potential chancellor, Suffolk had two large disabilities; 'youth, and his connection with Blackstone', according to the Oxford correspondent of another Bute ally, writing on the same day. Yet another Oxford report noted that Vice Chancellor Browne had endorsed Lichfield, while dismissing Suffolk as 'a good candidate 20 years hence'; Browne further remarked that 'he did not like the persons he [Suffolk] was set up by, which was understood to mean Dr Winchester and Dr Blackston, though perhaps he might be

[38] *The Jenkinson Papers 1760–1766*, ed. N. S. Jucker (1949), 51; *HUO*, 151–3; Doolittle, 60–61.
[39] *Letters*, 94.
[40] 'A Discourse on the Study of the Law', in *Analysis* (1762), lxxi; Howard had matriculated from Magdalen College in 1757 and graduated DCL (as a peer) in 1761: *Al. Oxon.*, ii. 699.

mistaken with regard to Dr Blackston'.[41] Whatever the precise import of that final clause, Blackstone was plainly identified as supporting Suffolk against Lichfield, although his partisanship may have been more apparent on paper and perhaps in Oxford than face to face in London, where he was said to declare his 'neutrality', speaking in 'a language . . . which does not correspond with his activity here [in Oxford] by his emissaries; for his personal appearance would be detrimental to the cause he wishes well'.[42]

Unlike most of his side of their correspondence, Shelburne's draft response to Blackstone's appeal of 7 September does survive. Written four days later from London, it emphasizes Bute's firm intention to support Lichfield, but also to respect Blackstone's wish to remain 'unembroiled', as conveyed both by Shelburne's younger brother and the sight of Blackstone's own letter. Shelburne also assured Blackstone that while Bute would indeed 'employ the Weight of the Crown' behind Lichfield, who had shown his 'personal Attachment to the King and his Government', he intended to act 'with as much Moderation and Judgement as you could wish and therefore to shock no private Friendship whatever'.[43] This would have seemed to leave Blackstone free to support Suffolk, if perhaps not overtly, although in any case, open partisanship on his part could well be counter-productive, given his decidedly mixed reputation and standing in Oxford. Blackstone certainly undertook some discreet canvassing within his own circle, writing to the Vinerian Fellow Robert Chambers in Newcastle to solicit 'your Company on Thursday in support of Lord Suffolk'.[44] But this may have been a last despairing fling. For the very next day, Suffolk himself received a letter from Blackstone, together with an enclosure from the latter's All Souls friend Benjamin Buckler, who probably conveyed news of impending electoral disaster. The upshot was that Suffolk prepared a formal letter of withdrawal, for production 'when my affairs are desperate', in order to 'authorise my friends to serve a more eligible person'.[45] Yet even this last-minute attempt to build a viable anti-Lichfield vote ended in ignominy, with the election of Lichfield as chancellor on 23 September by a majority of almost two to one.

The 1762 chancellorship election was plainly not Blackstone's finest hour, and his attempt to justify his actions in a long letter written to Shelburne a month after the event reveals his own uneasy recognition of that fact.

[41] *Letters*, 94–5; *Jenkinson Papers*, 53, 54–5.
[42] Ibid., 56.
[43] Taussig Collection (formerly Shelburne MS 35, fos. 157–157v), Shelburne to Blackstone, 11 September 1762.
[44] *Letters*, 96.
[45] Magdalen College Archives, MS 655b, fos. 175, 177.

His claim of having had 'no Share of Management throughout the whole Election' was barely plausible, even if technically correct—which seems unlikely in view of the evidence just cited for his dealings with Suffolk on the eve of the poll. More convincing and interesting is the extended account of his political principles, not least his vehement rejection of 'those ridiculous and slavish Tenets', which he had evidently been accused of abetting, by virtue of his opposition to Lichfield, as the endorsed government candidate. Quite the contrary; he had 'laboured for ten Years together in this University' (that is, since his first course of lectures in 1753), 'explaining, defending and propagating the Principles of Loyalty, and Liberty', as exemplified in the Glorious Revolution, 'at a time when it was thought to require some Degree of Firmness to avow them'. This stance indeed earned him 'a Series of personal Affronts and peevish Obstructions from those very Men (high in Rank and Authority here) who were esteemed for above 30 Years past the Supporters of contrary Doctrines', but now 'so swift is the Transition from one Extreme to another, would wish to be thought the most obsequious Servants of Power'.[46]

Apart from attempting to clarify his personal politics, and expose the hypocrisy of his academic enemies, Blackstone sought to justify his opposition to Lichfield on the same principled grounds that he had outlined before the election: Lichfield as chancellor would offer no encouragement to reforming or 'regulating those Errors in our Theory and Practice of Education, which your Lordship and I have often lamented together'. Hence he could only be judged 'an improper Candidate', whatever other 'Marks of Distinction' he might possess; and 'in a Matter of this Importance, I must think it essential to the Spirit of Liberty to follow my own Convictions'. Both the King and Bute were assured of his personal loyalty, and Bute of his parliamentary support. 'But my principal Ground of Regard for his Lordship's Character, is a firm Persuasion and Belief, that he has ever accompanied (perhaps educated) his royal Master in Sentiments of Moderation and Benevolence; and is never better pleased than by leaving the Actions of such wellmeaning Men as desire to think for themselves (some I know, always wish to be directed) entirely free and independent.'[47]

Blackstone closed this remarkably frank apologia with the rueful comment that he had displayed to Shelburne 'the Rectitude of my Intentions, even rather than the Prudence of my Actions'. He plainly realized that his recorded vote for Lord Foley, the compromise candidate decisively defeated by Lichfield, would not have endeared him

[46] *Letters*, 97–100.   [47] Ibid., 98–9.

to his aristocratic patrons. His retrospective insistence upon the moral right and duty to determine his own course of action, a secular version of the traditional Protestant appeal to the primacy of individual conscience, was certainly more than self-seeking rhetoric. But even the best of good intentions combined with the shibboleth of 'independence' could hardly erase what must have appeared as at least ambivalent, at worst downright disloyal behaviour on Blackstone's part, especially at a time of heightened political tension and mounting attacks on Bute's increasingly embattled administration. Moreover, as luck would have it, John Wilkes's fiercely anti-Bute *North Briton*, which the government had already attempted to suppress as a 'seditious and scandalous weekly paper', took up the Oxford chancellorship election as the theme of its issue no. 29 for 18 December 1762. In Wilkes's elaborately facetious tale of the search of 'Lady *Wiseacre*' for a new husband, Blackstone under the guise of 'lawyer *Keene*' is denounced by 'Mrs *Browne*, the housekeeper' as the promoter of 'lord *Sapling*':

'Look ye, gentlemen, says she, I will have nothing to do with that lord *Sapling*;—I will not be governed by a boy; and, what is still worse, I will not be governed by lawyer *Keene*. You know very well . . . what a noise that fellow made some years ago, upon looking into one part of the accounts, and finding the paltry sum of *twenty thousand pounds* placed on the wrong side of the book' . . . Immediately the cry of *no lawyers* ran through the company; and thus concluded the fate of poor lord *Sapling*, who . . . lost all hopes of success from the untoward circumstance of his being intimately acquainted with an honest lawyer.[48]

For their wayward client to appear as the sole hero in this irreverent lampoon of the university's corruption by 'the Scotsman, to whom she hath been prostituted' can only have added insult to injury so far as Bute and Shelburne were concerned. A fortnight before it appeared, Blackstone himself had professed complete indifference as to 'what is going forward at Oxford' with respect to a casual vacancy in the university's parliamentary representation: regardless of 'whether the Spirit of Independence is quite stunned by the late Blow it received . . . I hope not to be at all concerned in it . . .'.[49] But he cannot have been wholly surprised at his failure to succeed to a judicial vacancy created on the court of Exchequer that month, although remaining sufficiently optimistic to raise with Shelburne yet another possibility, which would 'put me in that Situation in which many of my noble and

[48] P. D. G. Thomas, *John Wilkes* (Oxford, 1996), 23; *The North Briton*, no. 29 (18 December 1762), in *The North Briton* (1763), ii. 60.
[49] *Letters*, 100.

other Friends have wished to see me placed'.[50] His proposal was to bring about the retirement of Sir Michael Foster, an aged puisne justice of King's Bench whose 'Life, poor Man, is hardly worth half a Year's Purchase', by offering him a pension as inducement (judicial pensions being still entirely at the Crown's discretion). If then appointed to take Foster's place, it would be 'a great Satisfaction to some of mine and Your Lordship's Friends, who are inclinable to surmise that (notwithstanding all Appearances to the contrary) my Attachment to a Friend, whom I honour and esteem most highly, in the late Election at Oxford, is taken amiss where (for my own Part) I am thoroughly convinced it is not, nor never has been'.[51]

These last assurances may seem suspiciously overstated. But whether genuine or not, Blackstone's hopes were once again doomed to disappointment. Nor did his fortunes improve, in this respect at least, for a further 12 months, until in mid-December 1763 he was appointed to succeed the Norfolk KC William de Grey as solicitor general to Queen Charlotte. Significantly, Blackstone owed this post neither to Stanhope nor Bute, but to the good offices of Lord Suffolk, who however recognized that it was no more than a sop to his judicial ambitions: 'Since the principal object of his wishes seems at present unattainable . . . and tho' of little emolument, [it] will be taking notice of Mr Blackstone (if conferr'd upon him) in such a manner as will reflect great honour upon him . . .'.[52] Apart from adding a yearly salary of £180 to his income, and further embellishment to the title page of the first volume of his *Commentaries*, for Blackstone the main value of this relatively insignificant office may well have been psychological, in so far as it represented a further personal link with George III and his family. Certainly it carried neither the political responsibilities nor the prospects for promotion to the highest judicial rank associated with the positions of attorney general or solicitor general proper.[53]

III

If Blackstone's role in the Oxford chancellorship election did nothing to advance his legal career, his performance as a member of parliament was no more likely to hasten his progress to the judicial bench. Then as now, loyal parliamentary-political service was a desirable if never absolutely essential qualification for would-be English judges. But even as

[50] Ibid., 101–2.
[51] Lemmings, *Professors*, 273; *Letters*, 101–2.
[52] Free Library of Philadelphia, Suffolk to [George Grenville?], 3 December 1763.
[53] BL MS Additional 17870, fos. 15v, 22v, 62v; Lemmings, *Professors*, 276–7.

the rapid turnover of ministries during the first decade of George III's reign increased the difficulty of choosing the right political horse to back, Blackstone apparently found it harder to overcome his natural reticence and verbal inarticulacy when addressing the House of Commons in St Stephen's Chapel than next door at the bar in Westminster Hall. Hence Sir Lewis Namier's magisterial verdict, quoting Horace Walpole: 'In the House Blackstone was an infrequent and "an indifferent speaker"; during the seven years 1761–8 only 14 speeches by him are recorded, mostly on subjects of secondary importance'.[54]

Yet not all those who heard him address the Commons were quite as dismissive as the waspish (and Whiggish) Walpole; another seasoned parliamentary observer thought Blackstone 'spoke excellently well' on repeal of the Stamp Act in 1766, albeit 'in a manner much like that of reading a lecture in college'.[55] Hanoverian parliaments were also not just political assemblies where leading figures jousted for factional and oratorical supremacy on major issues of public concern. Their more humdrum and down-to-earth institutional business generated 'a vast quantity of small-scale legislation', serving a wide range of interests and needs.[56] Blackstone's own political experience and interests certainly stretched across the full spectrum from parochial to national; prior to becoming a member of parliament he himself had testified before a parliamentary committee on a Berkshire roads improvement bill, subsequently joining the members for the two universities in a delegation to lobby the speaker of the House of Commons about a bill for weighing corn.[57] As a lawyer MP, he belonged to an important occupational sub-group, numbering around 40 in all. While not wholly beloved of their colleagues—Henry Fox 'frequently attacked the lawyers', and William Pitt proclaimed that 'he would live under laws, but never under the government of lawyers'—the 'gentlemen of the long robe' provided the House with much technical expertise in drafting and debating legislation.[58] So they were often added to the membership of select committees charged with the detailed work of considering petitions

---

[54] H of P 1754–90, ii. 96.

[55] Rev W. Palmer, chaplain to the speaker of the House, Sir John Cust, quoted P. D. G. Thomas, *British Politics and the Stamp Act Crisis* (Oxford, 1975), 197.

[56] Langford, *Public Life and the Propertied Englishman*, 139 and ch. 3 *passim*; R. Connors, '"The Grand Inquest of the Nation": Parliamentary Committees and Social Policy in Mid-Eighteenth–Century England', *Parliamentary History*, 14 (1995), 285–313; P. Jupp, *The Governing of Britain 1688–1848* (2006), 69–77.

[57] See above, Chapter 6, p. 105; Newdigate Diary, 25–26 February 1757.

[58] H of P 1754–90, i. 126; L. Namier, *The Structure of Politics at the Accession of George III* (2nd. edn., 1957), 42–4; H. Walpole, *Memoirs of King George II*, ed. J. Brooke (1985), i. 99; Lemmings, *Professors*, 322–3. These were traditional attitudes: cf. my *The Rise of the Barristers* (Oxford, 1991), 252–6.

for statutes, preparing bills, and revising them following debate. It was in this capacity that Blackstone made his first of many appearances in the main official record of the proceedings of the House of Commons during the 1760s, the printed *Journal.*

Blackstone was named on 17 November 1761 to a large committee charged with considering a petition from a body of Oxfordshire turnpike commissioners for an extension of their powers, then appointed three days later with his fellow lawyer John Morton and two other members to prepare a bill accordingly.[59] Over the remainder of the month he was named to three more committees, dealing respectively with a proposed enclosure of common lands near Pershore, Worcestershire, a road in Derbyshire, and the activities of the charitable Gresham Trust in London. Then, on 1 December, the Oxfordshire road bill was given its second reading, and again committed, with Blackstone once more a committee member, while a week later he was the first named among a large committee of over 30 MPs to consider a request from both the City and University of Oxford for transferring to the turnpike commissioners additional responsibilities for various other roads within and adjacent to the city.[60] This was a complex matter, involving significant administrative and fiscal rationalization, hence a variety of conflicting interests, and it was not until late January that Blackstone reported back to the House. As a result of his report it was agreed to instruct the original committee appointed on 20 November (of which he was still a member) to add to the bill they were drafting provision 'for putting the Repairs of the several Mileways, leading from the City of Oxford towards Woodstock and Wheatley, in the County of Oxford, under the Care and Management of the Trustees for the said Turnpike Roads'. In the meantime he had also been joined to several more committees dealing respectively with roads in Devon, Lancashire, and Wiltshire, the naturalization of an alien, a petition from Dumfries, and (with all the other lawyers of the house) laws expiring or about to expire in that session. During February he accepted appointment to four naturalization committees, and others on Liverpool churches, the sale of Sir William Wyndham's estate, a Warwickshire enclosure, and testimony from London freemen in suits concerning the city, plus no fewer than ten committees concerned with roads in different parts of the country.[61]

While members were not usually appointed to committees in their absence, attendance at committee meetings was no more compulsory than

[59] *CJ*, xxix. 16, 25. [60] Ibid., 32, 49, 55, 66.
[61] Ibid., 66–7, 81, 115–116, 121–2, 127, 136, 140, 144, 148, 148–9, 149, 152, 152–3, 159, 171, 176, 176–7, 178, 191, 196, 197, 198.

for sittings of the House itself. So it is likely that Blackstone took no part in some committees of which he was a nominal member. Nor were all committees equally conscientious or hard-working.[62] The diarists on whom we now largely rely for even sketchy details of debates—because verbatim reporting was still subject to prosecution as a breach of parliamentary privilege, and the official *Commons Journals* record only the results of divisions on motions—pay virtually no attention to this routine aspect of the House's proceedings. Indeed the first mention of Blackstone by the 'learned and aimiable' James Harris MP, who was busily compiling the best surviving unofficial account of George III's first parliament while his son attended Blackstone's lectures at Oxford, only occurs in his entry for 24 November 1761.[63] The *Commons Journal* for that day contains no reference to Blackstone, but Harris noted in relation to a proposed amendment of a bill indemnifying sheriffs and gaolers for litigation commenced against them by released debtors that 'several of the Law, Messrs Harvey, Blackiston, Hussey and others spoke to it, most of them for the addition'.[64] Harris's subsequent references to Blackstone are equally scanty, as when he notes engagingly that in a 'long Debate' on the disputed Tamworth election return early in February 1762 'all the Lawyers . . . Morton, Blackistone, de Grey, Gascoyn, Banks, Wedderburn had a share and (like Terence's Lawyers) were some of one mind, some of another'. Blackstone is also recorded as having joined the diarist to oppose an enclosure bill backed by the rich Oxfordshire MP Sir Edward Turner (Dr Leigh's son-in-law), and to have been present among the many lawyers in the house on 28 April 1762, 'it being the first day of Term'.[65] No further mention of his name occurs in Harris's text until 6 February 1764, when he is noted as voting with 'all the Lawyers' for the majority against an opposition attack on general warrants, arising from the Grenville ministry's prosecution of John Wilkes, a position he seemingly reinforced in the long debate on 17 February.[66]

The contrast between Blackstone's frequent mentions in the printed *Journal* and his minimal appearances in Harris's parliamentary diary reflects the different priorities of their compilers. The clerks responsible for the *Journal* were primarily concerned with maintaining an accurate record of the passage of legislation and other business through the House of Commons, whereas the diarist was mainly interested in high political

[62] P. D. G. Thomas, *The House of Commons in the Eighteenth Century* (Oxford, 1971), 266.
[63] *H of P 1754–90*, ii. 588.
[64] Hampshire RO, 9M73/G708, 11.
[65] Hampshire RO, 9M73/G709, 10, 12, 47.
[66] Hampshire RO, 9M73/G713, 33, 68.

issues and personalities. One reason why Blackstone had been able to take a prominent role in Oxford academic politics during the 1750s and early 60s was that Convocation's proceedings were conducted in Latin with a minimum of oral debate, contentious issues being thrashed out rather by means of written flysheets and informal discussion throughout the university at large. It must have been obvious from the start of the 1761 session, if not before, that he lacked the articulacy and presence of a first-rate parliamentary performer, whatever the fond hopes of Shelburne, and perhaps Bute. While intervening more often in debate from 1765 onwards, after he had gained greater first-hand experience in the ways of the House, Blackstone seems never to have been very comfortable in that demanding forum. It cannot have added to his political appeal or effectiveness that this unclubbable man was so sensitive to apparent slights, while painfully anxious to preserve 'independence' by steadfastly following his own convictions, whatever the views and interests of friends and patrons. On the other hand, Shelburne had been quite right to characterize him as a 'man of business'.[67] If many of his fellow MPs found day-to-day committee work tedious, Blackstone evidently revelled in the opportunity it offered to spread order and 'improvement' across the land, even if such activities, however worthy, were in themselves unlikely to further his chances of becoming a judge.

Following his failed bid for a puisne justice's place on King's Bench in December 1762, there is no further record of Blackstone actively seeking preferment via Shelburne until October 1766. William Gerard Hamilton, a talented albeit disappointed back-bencher, claimed in April 1765 to have inside knowledge that 'Dr Blackstone will be made a Judge upon the first vacancy', provided 'he should endeavour to obtain the Vinerian professorship' for his protégé Robert Chambers, who did indeed succeed Blackstone in that post a year later.[68] But Hamilton was not a particularly reliable source, and while Blackstone's desire for a judgeship can have been no secret, it is hard to see how, why, or by whom his commitment to procuring the Vinerian Chair for Chambers could have been made a condition for his own promotion to the bench. In any case, achieving that happy outcome necessarily depended upon there being a vacancy to which Blackstone could be appointed. This was not always a matter of waiting to fill a dead man's shoes, for judges did sometimes retire or move to another court. But there were only nine puisne judgeships in the three superior courts of Westminster Hall (Blackstone could hardly have aspired to be a chief justice or chief baron—plum positions which generally went to

[67] See above, Chapter 8, p. 180.
[68] J. Wooll, *Biographical Memoirs of the Late Revd Joseph Warton DD* (1806), 303.

lawyers 'distinguished by their performance in the House of Commons, as well as Westminster Hall').[69]

Seven puisne judges' places became vacant during the decade after Blackstone took silk and before he himself was appointed a justice of King's Bench in January 1770. He evidently did not put himself forward for the first vacancy, which occurred in the court of Exchequer in November 1761 and was filled by Sir Henry Gould, 'being conscious of my own Inferiority, and of the much better Title which other Gentlemen had . . .'.[70] But when Sir Henry's transfer from Exchequer to Common Pleas in December 1762 created another opening, Blackstone attempted to mobilize Shelburne and through him Henry Fox on behalf of his own claims. Not surprisingly, these failed to carry the day against the candidacy of George Perrott, a man 13 years Blackstone's senior and a leading practitioner in that notoriously idiosyncratic, or at all events specialized jurisdiction. Sir Michael Foster's death next November (11 months after Blackstone had vainly sought to procure his retirement) then inaugurated the first of a series of four successive vacancies in the court of King's Bench. A month after Blackstone became Queen's solicitor general, Foster's place went to Sir Joseph Yates, a very young but outstandingly talented barrister who had recently demonstrated his political soundness by appearing for the Crown in the initial prosecution of Wilkes. The next slot, following a judicial resignation in February 1765, was taken by Sir Richard Aston, now translated from the chief justiceship of Ireland which Blackstone had spurned a few years before. There is no indication that Blackstone put his hand up for either of these positions. We should not discount his claim that 'I always deemed it an indecent thing to be overforward in soliciting for a judicial Office'.[71] Moreover Shelburne, his sole effective politician-patron, had resigned from Grenville's administration in the autumn of 1763 and also lost his post as aide-de-camp to George III for opposing Wilkes's expulsion from the House of Commons.

Shelburne returned to office as secretary of state in July 1766 (an event on which Blackstone duly forwarded his 'warmest and sincerest' congratulations),[72] but Robert Henley, Lord Northington, a former fellow of All Souls, who as lord chancellor had evidently encouraged Blackstone to pursue his judicial ambitions, simultaneously became a casualty of the political instability which marked George III's first decade as king. To his replacement, Charles Pratt, Lord Camden, Blackstone was, as he explained

[69] Lemmings, Professors, 279.   [70] Letters, 88.

[71] Ibid., 116.

[72] Ibid., 114; because 'engaged on a Visit' to his brother Charles at Winchester, Blackstone only learnt of this 'great Revolution in Affairs' five days after Shelburne's appointment: cf. Doolittle, 67.

to Shelburne in October of that year, 'less known . . . than to any other of the judges'.[73] Previously chief justice of Common Pleas, where only serjeants pleaded, and before that a leading Chancery practitioner, Camden was an intimate friend and long-standing ally of Blackstone's political *bête noire*, William Pitt, now earl of Chatham and the latest of George III's prime ministers. He had also more recently distinguished himself as a judicial 'friend of liberty' by a series of decisions against general warrants and in favour of Wilkes. Such a person was unlikely to look favourably on Blackstone's claims to judicial office; yet the chancellor's recommendation was essential to making a judge. So 'believing it would be impertinent in me to propose myself to his Lordship as a Candidate; and yet...sensible of the Respect indispensably due to the great Seal upon these occasions', Blackstone hoped that Shelburne's 'former good Opinion of me so far continues, as to mention me to Lord Chancellor as One that would receive such a Promotion with becoming Humility and Thankfulness...'.[74] Shelburne might have been well-placed to put in a favourable word on Blackstone's behalf. But in the unlikely event that he did so, despite the gulf which now separated their political positions, the solicited promotion failed to materialize. The King's Bench vacancy on which Blackstone's eyes had been fixed went instead to James Hewitt, 51-year-old serjeant at law and MP, who having opposed both the Stamp Act and subsequent Declaratory Act was said to owe his judgeship to his parliamentary support of Chatham's American policies.[75] Hewitt lasted only one year in Mansfield's court, being made lord chancellor of Ireland in November 1767. His successor was Edward Willes, younger son of a long-lived chief justice of Common Pleas originally appointed by Sir Robert Walpole in 1737, and an even less impressive judicial figure than Hewitt. After serving briefly as solicitor general under Chatham, Willes was effectively kicked upstairs to King's Bench in January 1768, so as to free the solicitorship for John Dunning, Camden's close friend and also Shelburne's client. This latter status Blackstone himself had by now certainly lost, given the apparent lack of contact between the two men following his fruitless appeal for Shelburne's intercession in October 1766.[76] Yet if Blackstone's prospects of becoming a judge took a turn for the worse in the summer of that year, his standing as a lawyer had never been higher.

[73] *Letters*, 116.   [74] Ibid.
[75] *Letters*, 114–115; *H of P 1754–90*, ii. 620–1.
[76] Ibid., ii. 367, iii. 642; J. Oldham, *The Mansfield Manuscripts and the Growth of English Law in the Eighteenth Century* (1992), i. 51–3; Bentham was aware of 'a *breach*' between Shelburne and Blackstone, 'but neither time nor particulars ever known to me': *Works*, ed. Bowring, i. 249.

CHAPTER 10

'A Great and Able Lawyer' (1761–69)

PATRONAGE was the accepted means of filling posts great and small in eighteenth-century England. Yet soliciting the assistance of an ex-pupil 14 years his junior in pursuit of a place on the judicial bench cannot have come easily to a man who set such store by personal independence and the 'Spirit of Liberty'.[1] Perhaps this was one reason why Blackstone showed few signs of distress at his failure to gain judicial office during the 1760s. From 1766 onwards he must have realized that his chances were unlikely to improve significantly so long as Camden remained on the woolsack. Yet he probably also retained some confidence that in the long run, whatever the vagaries of politics, he could continue to count upon the good will of the greatest patron of them all, in the person of George III, 'the most amiable Prince that ever yet filled the British throne'.[2] Meanwhile the demands and rewards of private as well as public life provided this very busy man with ample distraction, and fulfilment.

I

William and Sarah's first child, a boy, born on 21 August 1762, was baptized at St Mary's Church, Wallingford, on 15 September. In a somewhat unusual departure from conventional practice of this period, he received two Christian names: the first undoubtedly after his father, the second the family name of his father's best clients, whose titular head, the fourth earl, may well have stood godfather. Unfortunately William Bertie Blackstone

---

[1] E. G. Andrew, *Patrons of Enlightenment* (Toronto, 2006); Lemmings, *Professors*, 162, 259–71; *Letters*, 99.
[2] Ibid., 103.

did not survive to adulthood, although we do not know how old he was when he died. Over the next nine years, Sarah Blackstone gave birth to eight more children, five boys and three girls, of whom all but the last born reached maturity. Their baptismal names reflect a stable and close-knit family tradition. Thus the eldest surviving son was christened Henry after his father's older brother, and the next boy became James, after his mother's brother. Then the first daughter (born in 1765) took her mother's name, while the second (whom William had proudly hailed with a post-script announcing the arrival of 'a jolly Girl') was named after her father's mother Mary, the paternal grandmother whom she would never know. Philippa Blackstone, born in 1768, recalled her mother's younger sister; her brother William, who arrived the following year, again bore his father's name, while in 1770 Charles Blackstone took that of his elder uncle, fellow of Winchester College. Besides Bertie, the one other non-family Christian name used by the Blackstones was George, given in 1771, doubtless from mixed motives of patriotism and gratitude, to the last-born Blackstone baby, who sadly survived only just over six months.[3]

William Blackstone clearly did not take his wife and children for granted. When his wife's younger sister Rachel died in the summer of 1765, Blackstone wrote in a letter of condolence to her husband and his cousin Lovelace Bigg (whom he had proposed for call to the bar at the Middle Temple a few months before) that 'I feel for you as a Friend, and a relation, and the more especially as a Husband . . . '. In mid-January 1766 he brought the whole family with him to live in Carey Street, London, where they seem to have remained over the next couple of months, judging by entries in Sir Roger Newdigate's diary which show him paying calls on Mrs Blackstone in early February and again in March.[4] There had been a similar family visit to London the year before, encompassing the Hilary law term and then continuing through February into March, although on Saturday 9 March, when Newdigate, his wife, and sister dined at Mrs Blackstone's with Sir Charles Mordaunt, Dr and Mrs Winchester, and Richard Bagot, the head of household may well have been absent, since he was scheduled to lecture that morning in Oxford.[5] Letters to relatives and friends often include snippets of family news, and pass on compliments and good wishes from Mrs Blackstone; thus in January 1767 his uncle Seymour Richmond was informed that 'my Wife,

[3] Berkshire RO, D/P 138/1/2 (5 September 1762, 23 September 1763, 8 August 1764, 10 July 1765, 23 January 1767, 5 April 1768); D/P 139/1/1 (28 October 1769, 29 October 1760, 18 October 1771, 7 May 1772); McNamara, *Boston Manor*, 32–3; *Letters*, 121.
[4] MT Archives, K10, 335; *Letters*, 108, 111; Newdigate Diary, 8 February. and 8 March 1766.
[5] Newdigate Diary, 18, 20 January, 7 February, 9 March 1765; Bodl. G.A. Oxon b 111, fo. 55b.

and the future Christian'—their newborn baby Mary, due to be baptized three days later—'are well; and so are the rest of the family. All of us, that can, join in best Wishes and Respects to yourself and Miss Richmond.' On learning later in the year that his former All Souls colleague and friend Alexander Popham was on the way to recovery from a serious illness, Blackstone noted that 'my Wife desires me to express her sincere Joy on the late happy Accounts we have received, and joins in best Compliments and good wishes'.[6]

We know next to nothing about the domestic life of Dr and Mrs Blackstone, whether in Wallingford or London. A family recipe book 'of parchment and bound in vellum' which survived into the last quarter of the twentieth century shows, according to its last recorded owner, that the 'Blackstones seem to have consumed a staggering amount of fish, meat, eggs, cream, sugar, wine and brandy, and to have ignored green vegetables altogether'. Such a recipe collection may more accurately reflect the family diet on high days and holidays than their everyday fare. Blackstone's All Souls friend Richard Graves, who advocated a rigorously restricted intake of food and drink as an aid to longevity (he himself died in 1804 at the age of 89) evidently regarded Blackstone's relatively early demise as the result of 'too studious and too sedentary a turn . . . indolence and want of due exercise' rather than, as with some other former friends, 'convivial parties and the pleasures of the table'.[7] The 'unhappy Aversion he always had to Exercise' remarked upon by his brother-in-law biographer was also acknowledged by Blackstone himself, despite his defensive claim that travelling 'fifty Miles in a Postchaise' was equivalent to the sort of physical 'Activity' urged upon him by well-meaning lady friends. But however singular in that respect, Blackstone's martyrdom to the gout was entirely typical of his era, gender, and status. According to Clitherow 'he was frequently, though not very severely, visited' with gouty attacks from 1759 onwards; gout presumably caused the 'Infirmity of my Foot' which afflicted him in August 1761 and certainly prevented him from arguing a King's Bench case in February 1765, while that September he went to Bath on medical advice to drink the waters, neither his first nor last visit.[8] Two years later, he wrote to his associate

---

[6] *Letters*, 122, 125.

[7] S. Chrzanowski, 'Lady Blackstone's Cookery Book', *American Bar Association Journal*, 64 (1978), 371–3; R. Graves, *The Reveries of Solitude* (1793), 54 and idem, *The Invalid* (1804), v–vi, quoted in C. J. Hill, *The Literary Career of Richard Graves* (Northampton, MA, 1934–5), 14.

[8] *Letters*, 33, 57, 85, 109–110; Clitherow, xxiii; Beinecke Library, Osborn MS Files X–Z, 16549, Charles Yorke to Thomas Rutherforth, 5 February 1765. Museum Meermano–Westreenianum, 257/67, Blackstone to Meerman, 17 September 1765.

Thomas Walker 'from Bed, to which I am at present confined with the Gout in both my Feet and one of my Knees'; a letter of the same date to his uncle Seymour Richmond discloses that the current attack had begun four days earlier, and was likely to prevent him travelling to London for a week or more; it actually kept him from Westminster Hall for the full three weeks of Hilary term. A further visit to Bath in the autumn of 1768 was presumably spurred by hopes of relief from future visitations. Yet in keeping with contemporary notions of gout as a hereditary 'constitutionalist' disorder, Blackstone affected a philosophical stance: 'My Gout has come on very regularly, and if it goes off as well, I hope it will do me Service'. Doses of 'Gout cordial' prepared by his wife from spices, rhubarb, senna, licorice, raisins, and a gallon and a half of brandy doubtless helped maintain that air of jocular detachment.[9]

As to the role of alcohol, beneficial or otherwise, in Blackstone's life, his family showed understandable sensitivity on this subject, taking 'great offence' at a passage in the first edition of Boswell's *Life of Johnson* (1791) which related (on the authority of William Scott, Lord Stowell), that Blackstone had composed his *Commentaries* 'with a bottle of port before him'. Scott himself protested against the implication of a '*sottish* Character . . . which [Blackstone] by no means deserved' in this passage. Boswell's second edition accordingly toned it down, with the addition of 'a sober man', to 'represent him only as a Person who felt his faculties invigorated by a temperate Use of Wine'.[10] Blackstone's role in organizing the All Souls college cellars has already been mentioned, but the records do not permit us to monitor his personal consumption; thus while it appears that in September and October 1751 he paid for a total of nine and a half dozen bottles, plus another six gallons 'of Dr Musgrave's wine', it is not clear over what period these were consumed, and few other purchases are recorded. On the other hand, the impressive collection of largely fortified wines which his widow left in the cellar at Wallingford was presumably not all of her own gathering; it included over 36 dozen bottles of port, some 21 dozen Madeira, and 19 dozen Mountain (Malaga or muscat) wine, together with 2 dozen of claret, 14 of cider, 4 of sherry and nine bottles of brandy.[11]

Blackstone remained recorder of Wallingford throughout the 1760s. Little direct evidence of his activities in that role survives; he seems

[9] *Letters*, 121–2, 136; *Reports*, i. 623; R. Porter and G. S. Rousseau, *Gout The Patrician Malady* (1998), 86–8; Chrzanowski, 'Lady Blackstone's Cookery Book', 372.

[10] *The Correspondence and other Papers of James Boswell relating to the Making of the Life of Johnson*, ed. M. Waingrow (1969), 599–600.

[11] Bodl. MS D.D. All Souls e 331; LMA, ACC 1360/587.

generally to have overseen the swearing-in of the new mayor and corporation officers at the start of the civic year each September, although on occasion his deputy officiated. But the recorder inevitably carried 'a good deal of weight in Wallingford', as Prime Minister George Grenville put it in 1764 when seeking Blackstone's political advice about 'the state of that borough' following the death of one of its two MPs. In August 1762 an extensive order addressing the corporation's need for an increase in revenue and 'proper Improvement of the Estates' by better managing the leases of town lands may well have been a Blackstone initiative, as likewise the appointment of a committee in 1769 'to Inspect the papers and other Contents . . . in two Old Chests in the Town Hall'.[12]

The surviving borough records give glimpses of a growing property portfolio in and around Wallingford, amounting in 1764 to at least 120 acres of arable land and pasture on both sides of, as well as islands in, the River Thames, together with the George Inn on the High Street.[13] Blackstone also owned the advowson or right of presentation to the parish church of St Peter's next to Priory Place. No pastoral duties had been required of the clergyman who held this rectory since the church building itself was largely demolished in the siege of Wallingford during the civil wars of the previous century. But increasing population placed sufficient pressure on the town's main church of St Mary's to initiate a rebuilding campaign in May 1759, shortly before Blackstone moved to Priory Place. Funds were raised over a number of years from townsfolk and local notables, including the earl of Abingdon as lord steward, the borough's parliamentary representatives, and Blackstone himself. His subscription of £50 was half that paid by the MPs and Abingdon, but still comfortably above most other donations recorded in the list which he forwarded to the bishop of Salisbury in May 1768, requesting 'some additional Assistance' towards completing 'so pious and public spirited a Work'.[14] Blackstone took on this task after being elected as one of the parish's two church-wardens the month before, having previously obtained the vestry's agreement to fit out the church interior according to a plan drawn up by the architect Robert Taylor, with whom he was already working on a much larger construction project at Oxford's western approaches.[15] An equally

---

[12] *Additional Grenville Papers 1763–1765*, ed. J. R. G. Tomlinson (Manchester, 1962), 177–8; Berkshire RO, Wallingford Borough Minutes, W/AC/1/1/2, fo. 371; W/AC/1/2/3, fo. 10.

[13] Berkshire RO, D/EH/T1; D/ESt/ L2/3; W/AC/1/1/2, fo. 376; W/FA C1, fo. 150; Doolittle, 101–2.

[14] *Letters*, 134–5; Berkshire RO, D/P 139/5/1; J. K. Hedges, *The History of Wallingford* (1881), ii. 400–402.

[15] See below, pp. 223–5.

characteristic 'Plan which I have in Agitation' for uniting the living of St Peter's with the town's other two main parishes, so as to produce sufficient income 'to establish a *resident* Clergyman in Wallingford' was the other but evidently unfulfilled purpose of this approach to Bishop Hume.[16]

While relative proximity to Oxford doubtless remained one of Wallingford's attractions, Blackstone spent less time in the university city after the chancellorship election of 1762. There was now little to bring or keep him there apart from his lecture course, which he delivered in four parts, each extending over three weeks or so. A surviving printed time-table or 'Scheme of the Course' for the academic year 1764–5 shows the first of 16 lectures comprising part I, the 'Rights of Persons', scheduled for Wednesday 10 October, with three more following over the next three days.[17] Hence he was able to meet the celebrated visiting Parisian *avocat* Jean-Baptiste-Jacques Élie de Beaumont who arrived in Oxford on Friday 12 October, providing some very helpful explanations ('éclaircissements très satisfiants'), as well as a most civil and friendly welcome ('l'acceuil le plus honnête et le plus amical').[18] Sunday and Monday were free, and presumably spent in Wallingford (hence Blackstone's inability to present de Beaumont for his honorary DCL that Monday); then another block of four consecutive lectures was followed by a long weekend. The course resumed on Tuesday 23rd, but with a free day on Thursday, and then a further six lectures (except on Sunday 28th), concluding on Thursday 1 November. The second group of 17 lectures on 'Rights of Property' began three weeks later on Wednesday 21 November, thus clashing with the last week of the full Michaelmas law term (which ran from 6–28 November). However Blackstone records himself as appearing for the defendant in a King's Bench case (*Forbes v Wale*) heard on Monday 26 November, despite having lectures scheduled in Oxford on Saturday 24 November and Tuesday 27 November. The same general pattern of up to four consecutive lectures over a six-day week (Monday to Saturday) enabled him to finish this part of his course by Monday 17 December. The third and fourth parts, 'Private Wrongs', and 'Public Wrongs', each of 14 lectures, were delivered between the two law terms of Hilary (which in 1765 ran from 26 January to 12 February) and Easter (from 24 April to 20 May). Blackstone was certainly in London for Hilary term, when parliament was also in session, resuming on 10 January after an eight-month interval and sitting until

[16] Berkshire RO, D/P 139/5/2, 12 February 1767, 2 November 1767, 5 April 1768; *Letters*, 134–6; see also below, Chapter 13, pp. 281–3. J. Ecton, *Thesaurus Ecclesiasticus* (1788), 323.

[17] Bodl. G. A. Oxon. b. 111, fo. 55b.

[18] [J–B–J. É. de Beaumont], 'Voyages Anciens, Moeurs Pittoresques. Un Voyageur Français en Angleterre en 1764', ed. V. de Gruchy, *Revue Britannique*, September 1895, 362.

25 May. Like other barrister MPs, he doubtless became adept at shuttling between the House of Commons in St Stephen's Chapel and the nearby law courts in Westminster Hall. On 13 February, the day after Hilary term ended, he delivered a lengthy report from the Commons' committee on the Wallingford-to-Wantage turnpike, then presumably travelled back to Oxford, perhaps staying overnight at Wallingford, in order to give the first of his third bloc of lectures the following day.[19] Such a tight schedule demanded considerable powers of organization, and a personality verging on the driven, particularly as manifested in the concern for punctuality which his brother-in-law thought sufficiently remarkable to merit an entire paragraph of his biographical memoir. According to Clitherow, 'during the Years in which he read his Lectures at Oxford, it could not be remembered, that he had ever kept his Audience waiting for him, even for a few Minutes . . . Punctuality was in his Opinion so much a Virtue, that he could not bring himself to think perfectly well of any, who were notoriously defective in it.' We can only speculate as to the fate of students who disregarded the warning sentence printed as tailpiece to the 1764 lecture timetable: 'The Lectures will begin exactly at Eleven in the Morning'.[20]

Continued involvement with the long-drawn-out saga of the Michel Foundation at Queen's College necessitated only occasional visits to Oxford, although much correspondence with his brother visitors, the fellows of Queen's, and other interested parties. In August 1764 Blackstone and his friend Benjamin Buckler (whom he had recently co-opted to join Chardin Musgrave, another friend and former All Souls colleague, as one of the three visitors charged with implementing Michel's bequest) had two separate Oxford meetings, revising and correcting yet another draft of proposed statutes, prior to solemnly sealing and authenticating the engrossed originals, then 'publishing and declaring them to the College'. But the resultant objections of 'the Gentlemen of Queens' were delivered by post to Wallingford on 3 September, and discussed there with Buckler when he 'came over to dine with me the same Day'.[21]

Blackstone was a sporadic presence at Press delegacy meetings in Oxford until October 1765, when he presented as a farewell gift his manuscript copy of 'Extracts from Charters, Statutes and other Records relating

---

[19] Ibid. October 1895, 77. *Reports*, i. 532, 533–42; *CJ*, xxx. 127–8; Newdigate Diary, 11, 13, 18 January, 7 February, 9, 18 March 1765; on Monday 18 March Blackstone unsuccessfully defended his bill on ecclesiastical exchanges at its third reading in the House of Commons, before delivering a scheduled lecture in Oxford next day: Hampshire RO, 9M73, G714, 75.

[20] Clitherow, xxvi; Bodl. G. A. Oxon. b III, fo. 55b.

[21] Queen's College Archives, 5M87, correspondence 1751–69; Blackstone to Chardin Musgrave, 5 August 1764; same to same, 12 August 1764; same to same, 4 September 1764.

to the University-Press Oxon. AD 1758'.[22] But he undertook no new scholarly enterprises. His last recorded visit to the Bodleian was in June 1762, and he presumably returned his key to the Codrington Library on giving up his All Souls fellowship the previous November. At the same time he handed over to Benjamin Buckler the genealogies he had begun collecting in the early 1750s, which subsequently formed the basis of Buckler's own publication. The college's failure in 1762 to persuade Archbishop Secker that the appeals of three founder's kinsmen for election to fellowships should be dismissed (notwithstanding Blackstone's advocacy as counsel, and his private approach to one of the archbishops' assessors, the Oxford civil lawyer George Hay) unleashed a torrent of successful founder's kin applicants. Buckler accordingly sought to 'lay open the Pedigrees of Consanguinity to the Chichele Family, in order to enlarge the Number of Candidates at all future Elections'.[23]

During the five years between his edition of Magna Carta and the first volume of his *Commentaries*, Blackstone published nothing new. In 1762, a two-volume compilation of four previously published works appeared under the title *Law Tracts*, doubtless chosen to affirm their author's professional identity. A studiously offhand prefatory note explained that, as they had been unavailable for some time, the author 'at length consented to his bookseller's request of collecting them together, and publishing them (with a few corrections and additions)'. So while the introduction to the *Great Charter* took note of some additional material supplied since the 1759 quarto edition by the librarian of the British Museum, Charles Morton, and 'the reverend and learned' Dr Richard Burn, the main text is reproduced virtually unaltered from the first edition.[24] A fifth edition of the *Analysis of the Laws of England* was also published in 1762; in what seems a deliberate marketing ploy, the table of descents included in all previous editions does not appear, and a footnote refers to 'the supplemental Volume of *Law Tracts*, where these Matters are discussed more at large'.[25] These self-published reprints were almost certainly intended as money-making ventures.

[22] Oxford University Press Archives, 5/1/1.

[23] Bodl. MS Library Records, e 560, fo. 37v; Squibb, *Founders' Kin*, 44, 66–8; *Letters*, 90–92; B. Buckler, *Stemmata Chicheleana* (Oxford, 1765), iii–iv. Codrington, MS 36, Warden Niblett's Notebook, 14 December 1758: agreed 'that Dr Blackstone be at liberty to publish some Collections made from the Pedigrees in the Coll: & other books and Papers'.

[24] W. Blackstone, *Law Tracts* (Oxford, 1762), II.xxviii, notes however that 'material various readings' derived from Morton's collation of a Cottonian manuscript in the British Museum 'are inserted in the present edition'. The other three texts reprinted in vol. i are the *Essay on Collateral Consanguinity* (1750), *Considerations* (1758), and *Treatise on the Law of Descents* (1759).

[25] W. Blackstone, *An Analysis of the Laws of England* (Oxford, 1762), ix.

Blackstone's few recorded book subscriptions during the 1760s were to legal works, including Danby Pickering's compilation of the *Statutes at Large* (1762) and the first (1763) volume of Richard Burn's manual of *Ecclesiastical Law*, or scholarship of local provenance, such as Benjamin Kennicott's reports on *The State of the Collation of the Hebrew Manuscripts of the Old Testament* (Oxford, 1763 and 1768) and William Lewis's annotated translation of *The Thebaid of Statius* (Oxford, 1767).[26] But if no longer active himself in non-legal fields, Blackstone continued to be regarded as a learned man and friend to scholarship, sometimes to his own embarrassment. So, while welcoming James Merrick's scheme for a comprehensive index of Greek authors, and 'well pleased to contribute my Mite to so useful a Design' by recommending it to his fellow Press delegates, when Merrick proposed to publicize this endorsement Blackstone feared that 'it would appear like Presumption in me to offer any Sentiments on a Language, in which I was never skilled, and have almost lost the little Skill I had, by Many Years Attention to Studies of a different kind'.[27] Yet Thomas Warton's preface to his edition of Theocritus ascribed the origins of that work primarily to the friendly encouragement he had received from Blackstone, 'the best of men, most learned not only in English law but in all humane letters' ('vir summus, non modo juris Anglici sed et omnium humaniorum literarum peritissimus').[28]

II

Now in their second decade, Blackstone's lectures were an established Oxford institution with a national, indeed international, reputation. They attracted not only young undergraduates but elderly dons like Charles Godwyn of Balliol College, who opined that the lecture he attended on Saturday morning 18 April 1763 dealing with the right of succession to the Crown 'was drawn up with great accuracy, and is, I think, the best dissertation upon the subject I have met with . . . I find, it is universally approved of'.[29] John Parnell, a graduate of Trinity College Dublin, came

---

[26] Data from Avero Publications, *Biography Database, 1680–1830*, CD 1 and 2 (Newcastle-upon-Tyne, 1998), and *Eighteenth Century Collections Online*.

[27] Blackstone to James Merrick, Wallingford, 28 October 1764; same to same, Carey Street, London, 15 November 1764 (I am most grateful to Francis Markham for copies of transcripts made by his mother, Sarah Markham).

[28] T. Warton, *Theocrite Syracusii quae supersunt* (Oxford, 1770), i.

[29] Nichols, *Literary Anecdotes of the Eighteenth Century*, viii. 234; *The Diary of a Country Parson*, ed. J. B. Beresford (1924–31), i.13; *Letter Book of John Watts: Merchant and Councillor of New York, January 1, 1762—December 22, 1765*, ed. D. C. Barck (New York, 1928), 13.

to Oxford in November 1762 specifically to sit at Blackstone's feet, only to discover when he arrived that part one of the course was already in progress, and that he needed to be attached to a college as a matriculated undergraduate if he wished to attend. So he gained admission to Christ Church and began with part two, 'determined to hear the first [part] the year following'. Parnell thought Blackstone's lectures 'extremely well calculated to give gentlemen at a University, a general Knowledge of the Laws and constitution of their Country, he touches on every Branch, but is not to be expected to treat as fully on each Particular as is requisite for a Practitioner'. The first block of lectures, which Parnell eventually heard in October–November 1763, had 'a much Easier stile' and were 'more Entertaining than the Later Parts, as they did not descend to the Less Interesting Particulars'.[30]

It was this first part that Jeremy Bentham heard the following year. Then a 16-year-old undergraduate of Queen's College, much later he recalled Blackstone as 'cold, reserved, and wary—exhibiting a frigid pride'. Yet Bentham also remembered Blackstone's lectures as 'popular', even though he claimed to have himself heard 'no small part of them with rebel ears', and 'immediately detected his fallacy respecting natural rights'. It must be said that no such critical doubts or insights appear in Bentham's brief surviving notes from the first ten lectures. How many more he attended is unclear, although he recollected abandoning any attempt at note-taking, since 'my thoughts were occupied in reflecting on what I heard'.[31] The young man who would become Blackstone's most famous critic sent his father in April 1765 an equally bland account of the latest Oxford news about the future of both lecturer and lectures:

Dr Blackstone has deliver'd a paper about the University, in which after many Compliments and reasons for his taking this step, he declares his Resolution of reading 1 course more only, and that then he will resign his professorship, it is said (but whether it is contain'd in this paper, I don't know, as I have not seen it,) that he will publish soon the 1st part of his lectures (of which there are 4) in one Vol. the price of which will be a guinea and a half: thus much is certain that it is almost all printed off: I mean the 1st part only.[32]

No copy of the 'paper' mentioned by Bentham is known to survive, nor any other reference to its existence or circulation. But this testimony makes it clear that Blackstone's decision to discontinue his lectures and abandon

[30] Folger Library, M.a. 11: J. Parnell, 'An Account . . . made during my residence in England, 1763', 23, 32, 245.
[31] *Works of Bentham*, ed. Bowring, ii. 45; I. Doolittle, 'Jeremy Bentham and Blackstone's Lectures', *Bentham Newsletter*, 6 (1982), 23–5.
[32] *Correspondence of Jeremy Bentham*, ed. T. L. Sprigge (1968–2006), i. 86.

his Oxford Chair was prior to and in no way conditional upon the publication of the first volume of the *Commentaries* in 1765.[33] The crucial considerations must rather have been the increased demands, and rewards, of his legal practice, and the reduced profitability of the lectures themselves. While the former cannot be quantified, we do have figures for the latter. They show that, after peaking at £340 in 1762, student fees paid to Blackstone shrank by almost a third during the following year, to £239; remaining at just under that level for the course commencing in 1764, they slumped again to £203 for the final (1765–6) round of lectures.[34] So apart from the demands of those 'researches' into 'the elements of the law, and the grounds of our civil polity', and the 'regular attentions to his duty' as lecturer, which Blackstone mentions in the preface to his first volume as 'inconsistent with his health, as well as his other avocations', the financial benefits of the Vinerian Professorship were evidently shrinking. One reason for that may well have been the circulation of copies of notes taken at his lectures, some (his preface tells us) 'fallen into mercenary hands, and become the object of clandestine sale'. There were also rumours of a pirate edition, 'published or preparing for Publication in Ireland'.[35] All these circumstances, together with Blackstone's detailed and extensive personal knowledge of the book trade, his privileged access to Oxford's university printing facilities, and the success—not merely financial—of his previous publications, clearly combined to make an irresistible case for bringing out his lectures in printed form.[36]

Once that decision was taken, possibly not before the autumn of 1764 when it became clear that student fee income was likely to fall below the previous year's takings, printer's copy had to be prepared. No author's manuscript of the *Commentaries* has survived, but the book's basic structure and content were largely carried over from Blackstone's lectures and successive editions of his *Analysis*. Volume I, which in April 1765 Bentham

---

[33] Cf. R. A. Posner, 'Blackstone and Bentham', *Journal of Law and Economics*, 19 (1976), 569. The news that 'I shall have it in my power to read Dr Blackstone's lectures' reached Richard Chandler in Turkey among other 'literary and academical Intelligence' by mid–May 1765, suggesting that it was current in Oxford some eight to ten weeks earlier: Richard Chandler to John Loveday, 'Sedjacus', 31 May 1765: my thanks to Francis Markham for a transcription of this document.

[34] See Appendix I below.

[35] *Commentaries*, i. ii–iii; Clitherow, xvii. On 18 November 1762 Lord Edward Bentinck wrote to his elder brother William from Oxford requesting his 'Notes and as Blackston begins readin[g] his Second Course of Lectures on Saturday the 20th shall be glad to have them as soon as you can conveniently send them': Nottingham University Library, Portland MS PwF 515.

[36] By printing at Oxford, Blackstone benefited from the university's privilege to issue law books, notwithstanding the monopoly otherwise exercised by the bookseller-printers who held the law patent: T. A. Baloch, 'Law Booksellers and Printers of Agents of Unchange', *Cambridge Law Journal*, 66 (2007), 408.

reported as already largely printed off, was prefaced by Blackstone's now much reproduced introductory lecture as Vinerian Professor. This comprises the first part of the 'Introduction', together with three subsequent sections on the nature of law in general, the laws of England, and the countries subject to those laws, amounting to 115 pages, or just under a quarter of the whole volume. Beginning with an attempt to define 'law', and to distinguish 'municipal' law from divine and natural law, Blackstone went on to discuss the nature of government, the sources of English law, and its geographical reach. The remainder of the first volume, 'Of the Rights of Persons', is an exposition of constitutional law, detailing the respective powers and rights of king and parliament, and of those whom they governed, the people of England, the latter considered in both public and private capacities. Expanding the 16 chapters of the first book of the *Analysis* into the 18 chapters (plus four introductory 'sections') of Book I of the *Commentaries* involved various minor adjustments; for example, chapter 14 of the *Analysis* ('Of the private relations of Master and Servant and of Husband and Wife') is split in half as two separate chapters for the *Commentaries*. On the other hand, the long eighth chapter of the first volume of the *Commentaries* ('Of the King's Revenue') incorporates two separate chapters from the *Analysis*.

The *Commentaries* reproduce much of the actual phraseology of the lectures, in so far as the latter can be ascertained from surviving student notes. However, just as the detailed text of the lectures changed over time, so Blackstone changed, cut, and added additional material to the *Commentaries*. As might be expected, the text of the lectures given in the autumn of 1761 was generally more concise, informal, and outspoken than the corresponding passages printed in the *Commentaries*. For example, Blackstone as lecturer referred to the first Hanoverian parliament as having 'voted itself in for 7 years, an Instance of that uncontroulable Power which before was observed to be lodged in them'. The corresponding passage of the *Commentaries* adds a brief rationale for the Septennial Act ('professedly, to prevent the great and continued expenses of frequent elections, and for the peace and security of the government then just recovering from the late rebellion'), before going on to characterize as 'an instance of the vast authority of parliament', the fact that 'the very same house, that was chosen for three years, enacted it's own continuance for seven'. Again, whereas a lecture on the King's revenue briefly mentioned the 'Immense Accession of Power' and means of 'prodigious Influence' accruing to the Crown since the Glorious Revolution, the *Commentaries* carefully distinguished between the Crown itself and 'corrupt and servile influence from those who are intrusted with its authority', going on to express confidence

in George III as a 'sovereign, who, in all those public acts that have personally proceeded from himself, hath manifested the highest veneration
for the free constitution of Britain'.[37]

Despite Bentham's belief that most of Volume I was already printed
by late April 1765, Blackstone seems to have delayed putting the final
touches to his text for nearly another six months.[38] When it did at last
appear, in mid-November, the response from both readers and reviewers
was overwhelmingly favourable, despite a hefty retail price of 18 shillings
per copy, unbound. At least one-third of the large 1,500 initial print run
had sold before year's end. By mid-February 1766, Blackstone's London
bookseller John Worrall was 'urgent with me for a second impression'.[39]
Sales receipts over that same calendar year totalled just under £1,600.
This was a massive return for any author, even if it amounted to less than
half the professional earnings for that year of William de Grey, the barrister near-contemporary under whom Blackstone would later serve on
the bench of the court of Common Pleas.[40] Those receipts included proceeds from the initial sales of the second volume, published in October
1766, which at just over 540 pages of text and appendices ran to some 60
pages more than its predecessor, and was accordingly priced at a guinea
(21 shillings) a copy. Over the next six years, sales of the *Commentaries*
continued to bring in four-figure sums, except in 1767, when only the first
two books had appeared, and the first pirated Dublin edition may have
cut into Blackstone's earnings.[41]

The psychological rewards can hardly have been less gratifying. As early
as December 1765 the *Critical Review* eulogized 'so learned and ingenious a Commentary . . . elaborate, spirited, and judicious', in the first of
two extended notices running over no fewer than 27 pages, much (as was
customary) taken up by direct quotation or paraphrase. This anonymous
reviewer was not absolutely uncritical, noting 'nothing new' in Blackstone's

---

[37] Codrington MS 300 (ii), Bk. 1, Lect. 6, §10; (iii) Bk. 1, Lect. 10, §9; *Commentaries*, i. 182;
i. 323–6.

[38] The preface to the first edition of Volume 1 is undated; when reprinted in the second (1766)
edition the date 2 November 1765 was added: Eller, 2–3; see also Clitherow, xvii. It was first advertised as published 'This Day' by the *Gazetteer and New Public Advertiser* for 18 November 1765.

[39] *Letters*, 112.

[40] Appendix II below. Oxford University Press Archives, OUP/PR/1/18/4, 187. Clitherow put
sales revenue for 1765 at £380.18/2; booksellers normally received a one-third discount on the retail
price, although Blackstone may have given less: Raven, *Business of Books*, 323; *Monthly Review*,
34, February 1766, 107; below, p. 305. Lemmings, *Professors*, 199.

[41] Appendix II; Blackstone sold his copyright in 1772 to the bookseller-publishers Daniel Prince,
William Strahan, and Thomas Cadell for the huge sum of £2,000: R. D. Harlan, 'Sales and Profits
on Some Early Editions of Sir William Blackstone's "Commentaries"', *Papers of the Bibliographical
Society of America*, 58 (1964), 156–9. Eller, 2–3.

introductory account of the general nature of laws, questioning his rejection of Locke's belief in the people's ultimate authority over the legislature, and even venturing two minor stylistic quibbles, with the apologetic
justification that 'Gold cannot be too much refined'. The barrister Owen
Ruffhead, who had previously reviewed Blackstone's inaugural lecture
and other publications for the *Monthly Review* (a journal which favoured
'pulling down all establishments', according to Samuel Johnson) expressed
some similar reservations, stylistic and substantial, but was more emphatic
and precise about the nature of Blackstone's achievement: 'Our masterly
Commentator takes a wider range, and unites the qualities of the historian
and politician, with those of the lawyer . . . Mr Blackstone is perhaps the
first who has treated the body of the law in a liberal, elegant, and constitutional manner. A vein of good sense and moderation runs through every
page.'[42] The immediate relevance of Blackstone's work to current political
debate was emphasized as early as January 1766 on the front page of the
London Magazine, which after noting that parliament's right to tax 'the
British plantations in America' was 'now much agitated', reproduced his
account of the status of English law in British colonies, from the section of
the Introduction dealing with 'Countries subject to the Laws of England'.
Such free publicity, together with paid newspaper advertising, saw the
first printing sell out well before mid-year, when a firm of Holborn booksellers regretfully reported their inability to supply even so important a
customer as the duke of Bedford: 'We have again made strict enquiry
after Blackstone's first volume, but to no purpose . . . The first copy that
can possibly be procured shall be sent to you.' Thomas Robinson, another
Whig grandee, employed appropriately architectural language when
reporting from Cambridge that December his having 'read the first vol. of
Dr Blackstone with the greatest satisfaction; he proves the foundation of
our constitution to be a rock, he builds the most beautiful superstructure
upon it, shews means of stopping up some few cracks in the masonry'.[43]

The enormous success of the first book of the *Commentaries* owed something to its subject matter: jurisprudence and public law in relation to
government and politics, rather than the drier, more technical private law

[42] *Critical Review*, 20 (December 1765), 424–36; ibid., 21 (January 1766), 1–13; *Monthly Review*, 34 (February 1766), 107–110; ibid., 34 (May 1766), 378–92; *Life of Johnson*, 740; B. C. Nangle, *The Monthly Review First Series 1749–1789* (Oxford, 1934), 39, 64.

[43] *London Magazine*, 35 (January 1766), 3; *Gazetteer and New Daily Advertiser*, 18, 20 November 1765; *St James Chronicle*, 23, 26, 28 November 1765; Bedfordshire and Luton Archives and Records Service: R 3/266, Davis and Reymers, Holborn, to Percival Beaumont, 16 June 1766; L30/14/333/32, Thomas Robinson to Frederick Robinson, 7 December 1766. The *Monthly Review* notice was incorporated without acknowledgement by Edmund Burke in his review of Books I and II for the *Annual Register for the Year 1767* (1768), 286–307.

topics covered by the second and third volumes. But these later books, published in October 1766 and June 1768, received a no less enthusiastic reception: indeed Ruffhead began his notice of Book II for the *Monthly Review* by declaring that 'in our judgment, the farther the learned Author of these commentaries proceeds in his subject, to the greater advantage his extraordinary merits appear'. While now dealing with 'the most nice and difficult part of the law, he has explained the various parts of this complicated subject with an accuracy and perspicuity not to be met with in any other writer on this subject'—even if 'in some points we cannot wholly acquiesce with the conclusions he establishes'.[44] Besides such inevitable assertions of their own expertise and independence, reviewers mindful of their readers' likely interests naturally tended to concentrate on the more general, historical, or theoretical aspects of Blackstone's work. But while noting that the 'scientifical part' (as the *Critical Review* put it) of Book III was 'adapted to the theory and practice of the profession', the same reviewer praised Blackstone's treatment of 'all the wrongs and inconveniences which can arise to the subjects of England from the abuse or disregard of the law'. He went on to assert that to dub Blackstone 'the English Cujas, or the modern Coke' would be too poor a compliment, since neither of those earlier jurists could rival his 'perspicuity and order, which has been so much wanting in the study of the law'. Blackstone had indeed 'cleared it from technical terms', so that 'every gentleman of tolerable good sense, though he is no scholar, by carefully perusing this work, may become no contemptible lawyer'.[45]

III

Such publicity brought collateral benefits for Blackstone's own professional practice. It can hardly be by mere coincidence that for the five years 1765–69 no fewer than 24 surviving counsel's opinions bearing his signature have been identified, as against only eight from the previous five years. On the other hand, there is no evidence that demand for his services as a Westminster Hall advocate was significantly greater during this same period than it was over the first half of the decade. In Michaelmas term 1769, and Hilary term 1770, immediately before becoming a judge, Blackstone's own reports note that 'I attended the Court of Exchequer'. Yet the records of both the common law and equity sides of that court for those two terms include only three cases—all entered on the same

---

[44] *Monthly Review*, 35 (November 1766), 356.   [45] *Critical Review*, 26 (July 1768), 36.

day, 3 February 1770—in which Blackstone is mentioned by name as a pleader; by comparison Alexander Popham, his own former pupil and now fellow MP, was named as moving in at least eight separate suits.[46] If Blackstone thought for whatever reason his chances of picking up briefs might be better in the more specialized Exchequer jurisdiction than in Mansfield's King's Bench, he was evidently mistaken.

But while he may have stood no better chance after than before 1765 of becoming a leader at the bar, the pace of Blackstone's working life scarcely slackened. His Oxford lecturing commitments came to an end in May 1766, but by then he was already hard at work revising the first book of the *Commentaries*, assisted with comments and corrections from Lord Mansfield and his judicial colleague, Sir John Eardley Wilmot. The latter was also sent for 'private inspection his Lectures on Real Property', with a promise that those on personal property would follow shortly. Notwithstanding press advertisements for Book I which claimed in November 1765 that its sequel was 'in the Press and will be published with all convenient Expedition', Blackstone found it hard to stop tinkering with his text. In January 1766 he had asked Attorney General Charles Yorke to review a passage in ch. 15 of Book II where 'I have expressed myself not thoroughly convinced of the Reasonableness and Propriety of Corruption of Blood in Treason and Felony'.[47] Although (as Ruffhead would point out in January 1767), 'this chapter is nearly, if not exactly, the same' as the *Treatise on the Law of Descents in Fee Simple* published eight years before,[48] Blackstone seems once again to have spent many months picking over his proofs before the entire volume went to press. At least the subject-matter of Book II had little obvious political significance, whereas its predecessor included material bearing directly on several major current controversies, including parliament's right to tax the American colonies, and the privileges of MPs (as in the case of John Wilkes). Indeed, the post-publication changes Blackstone found necessary 'upon a careful revisal . . . to supply some omissions and correct many errors, partly from his own observations, and partly pointed out to him by the candor of his learned friends' were sufficient to generate an eight-page 'Supplement'. When 'published

[46] *Reports*, ii. 681. Blackstone's cases: TNA E161/100 (*King v Powel, Price v Elvy, Bree v Chaplin*, 3 Feb. 1770); Popham's cases: TNA, E12/46 (*Courtman v Eastwood*, 3 Feb. 1770); E161/100 (*Hicks v Treise*, 10 Nov., 21 Dec. 1769; *Sawley v Scott, Freebone v Hamilton*, 12 Feb. 1770; *Bennett v Pascoe, Manley v Dawson*, 21 Feb. 1770; *Freebone v Freebone, Lucas v Sorrell*, 28 Feb. 1770).

[47] *Letters*, 111–113. See BL MS Additional 35636, fo. 339, for Yorke's cordial response. In 1783 the *Commentaries* was said to have been 'inspected in manuscript by most of the judges then on the bench': *The Letters of Sir William Jones*, ed. G. Cannon (Oxford, 1970), ii.609.

[48] *Monthly Review*, 36 (January 1767), 35; see above, Chapter 8, 167–9.

separate and given gratis to the Purchasers of the former Edition', this largely replicated the 'corrected and enlarged' second edition of Book I issued in mid-November 1766.[49]

Besides regular term-time attendance in Westminster Hall—although there is no evidence that he subjected himself to the rigours of an assize circuit—and his literary labours with successive volumes of the *Commentaries*, Blackstone continued to devote much time and energy to the affairs of the Bertie family, and its titular head, the fourth earl of Abingdon. In the second half of the 1760s, his emphasis turned from debt reduction to revenue enhancement. The centrepiece was an ambitious construction scheme, designed to exploit the growing volume of vehicular traffic between London, Gloucester, and Wales by constructing a new toll road and bridge across the Thames west of Oxford, where the earl held large landed estates. The details of this complex and expensive 'improvement' project, involving multiple acts of parliament (naturally managed and promoted by Blackstone himself), public subscriptions and private loans, media manipulation, and property deals need not be repeated here.[50] The main point is Blackstone's central role in directing a large and varied cast of players, including the young earl himself, the earl's trustees, other members of the Bertie family, the City of Oxford, the university and colleges, the duke of Marlborough and other county magnates, the lawyers James Morrell, Cornelius Norton, and Thomas Walker (town clerk of Oxford), and the architect-surveyor Robert Taylor. While the outcome did not solve the earl's financial problems, its physical traces remain to this day as the first departure from Oxford's medieval street plan, and one of the few privately-owned toll bridges operating anywhere in Britain. This latter survival may be attributed to the unusual terms of the enabling act, undoubtedly drafted by Blackstone himself, which not only gave the earl and his heirs the right to levy tolls on wheeled traffic in perpetuity, but also prescribed that they were to pay 'no other or greater Assessment, Tax, Rent, Duty, or payment whatsoever' on that income than had been previously borne by the ferry which the Swinford toll bridge replaced.[51]

To build the toll bridge, Blackstone oversaw the expenditure of some £4,850, for which he was reimbursed from the Abingdon estates, while at the Oxford end, he personally invested £2,200—presumably profits from sales of the *Commentaries*—in the trust established as the administrative entity to repair and widen Botley Causeway on the city's western

[49] Eller, 2; *London Evening Post*, 27 November 1766.
[50] See E. de Villiers, *Swinford Bridge 1769–1969* (Eynsham, 1969); Doolittle, 77–9; J. L. Munby and H. Walton, 'The Building of New Road', *Oxoniensia* (1990), 123–30.
[51] de Villiers, *Swinford Bridge*, 13, quoting 7 Geo. III, c. 63; Allen, *Morrells of Oxford*, 10–11.

223

outskirts.[52] In both cases, his private gains from fees and dividends were accompanied by tangible public benefits. But his other major undertaking for the Bertie clan had no altruistic ends in view, being solely concerned to secure the earl of Abingdon's control over the parliamentary borough of Westbury, where the franchise was confined to the tenants of 61 town properties designated as 'burgage tenements'. Although the earl owned most of these, in the past they had been leased out for up to 99 years; and since 'most of the Tenants were poor, it afforded great Scope for any Adventurer to fight his Lordship with his own Weapons by buying off his Tenants'.[53]

This analysis comes from the 'Case of the Borough of Westbury', a document drafted by Blackstone in the form of a brief for counsel's opinion, preparatory to a consultation in June 1767 on 'the proper Methods of supporting Lord Abingdon's Interest' with the bluntly outspoken Yorkshire lawyer Sir Fletcher Norton MP.[54] From this brief, and associated papers, we learn that since the general election of 1761, 'by Attention to a different Plan'—one plainly designed as well as painstakingly implemented by Blackstone—7 of the remaining 11 burgage tenements had been acquired by the earl, along with 38 of the respective leases, which were no longer left in the hands of tenants. Norton evidently endorsed these proceedings, and suggested some additional measures to ensure that only Abingdon's 'trusty Friends' would possess the necessary paper qualification to vote, in the form of leases distributed to them at the time of each election, and returned immediately after the poll.[55] These so-called 'faggot-votes' and 'snatch-papers' gave the earl 'undisputed control of the borough' in time for the next general election in March 1768, when his brother Peregrine Bertie took one seat, and his man of business William Blackstone the other.[56] The first book of the *Commentaries* had deprecated the possibility of 'a great man' enjoying 'a larger share in elections than is consistent with general liberty', while also advocating the desirability of 'a more complete representation of the people'.[57] But there is no hint that Blackstone felt

[52] de Villiers, *Swinford Bridge*, 15, 17. *Letters*, 124.

[53] Bodl. MS Ch. Wilts. c 2(359), fo. 3.

[54] Ibid., fos. 2–3v; *Letters*, 126.

[55] Ibid., fo. 3v (this crossed-out passage reads in full: 'It is proposed that (when Occasion requires) Lord A. should grant proper Leases to a [sic] trusty Friends of a competent Number of Burgage Tenements, which Lessee may assign the same').

[56] Bodl. MS. Top. Wilts. c 5, 'Papers Relating to Westbury, Wilts', fos. 1–22; J. A. Cannon, 'The Parliamentary Representation of the Boroughs of Chippenham, Cricklade, Downton, Hindon, Westbury, and Wootton Bassett, in Wiltshire, from 1754 until 1790', University of Bristol PhD thesis, 1958, i. 270–77; *H of P 1754–90*, i. 420.

[57] *Commentaries*, i.165–6, 167–9.

any unease at the part he had played in, or the personal benefit he derived from, thus completing the corruption of electoral process in the borough of Westbury, even if he did warn Thomas Walker that the draft brief for Norton 'must be engrossed with Secrecy'.[58]

Now a veteran of seven parliamentary sessions, Blackstone was also better placed to participate in the business of the House, no longer having to absent himself to deliver lectures in Oxford.[59] His interventions in debates accordingly become both weightier and more frequent. Thus on 9 May 1765 he was among those who embarrassed Prime Minister George Grenville by urging, albeit 'very temperately' according to Grenville, the inclusion of the Princess Royal (George III's mother) as one of the regents who might be appointed in the event of the King's incapacity, an initiative which her son may have secretly welcomed.[60] Next day, however, he assisted the ministry by interventions on two separate procedural points which helped the bill pass its third reading.[61] Under the succeeding Rockingham administration he spoke out at length against the proposed repeal of the Stamp Act, another government measure for which the King notoriously showed little enthusiasm. Horace Walpole's account has Blackstone '*Tory* as he was', declaring 'that Parliament had no right to impose internal taxes'; what he actually said, according to a fuller and less partial source, was that the right of imposing taxes had nothing to do with the parliamentary representation of those taxed, 'as if it did the House of Commons ought to have the whole right of imposing and not merely that of beginning them'.[62] He subsequently urged that any repeal should uphold the Crown's authority, by applying only to those North American colonies whose assemblies formally expunged any previous resolutions rejecting the Westminster Parliament's fiscal jurisdiction; this motion was lost without division, despite Lord North's speech in its favour. (Reporting

---

[58] *Letters*, 126.

[59] For example, the second half of his penultimate 1764–5 lecture course, delivered between 14 February and 30 March, had clashed directly with the fourth session of the 1761–8 parliament sitting from 10 January to 25 May 1765: Bodl. G. A. Oxon. b. III, fo. 55b. So, after lecturing in Oxford on Friday 15 March, Blackstone evidently travelled to London, participated in Commons' debates on Monday, then returned to Oxford for his next lecture at 11 a.m. on Tuesday: Hants. RO, 9M73/G714, 74–5.

[60] J. Nicholls, *Recollections and Reflections, Personal and Political* (1822), i. 16–19; *The Grenville Papers*, ed. W. J. Smith (1853), iii. 30, 33; J. Black, *George III: America's Last King* (2006), 78; G. M. Ditchfield, *George III: An Essay in Monarchy* (2002), 66; P. D. G. Thomas, *George III: King and Politicians 1760–1770* (Manchester, 2002), 116.

[61] *Grenville Papers*, iii. 36; *The Correspondence of King George III from 1760 to December 1783*, ed. J. Fortescue (1927–8), i. 87–9.

[62] H. Walpole, *Memoirs of the Reign of George III*, ed. D. Jarrett (2000), iii. 17; P. D. G. Thomas, 'Parliamentary Diaries of Nathaniel Ryder, 1764–7', *Camden Miscellany* xxiii (1969), 267–9.

the episode to an American correspondent, Benjamin Franklin described Blackstone as 'one of the late Ministry', a mistake which suggests a somewhat higher parliamentary profile than that of the average unattached back-bencher.) In further debate a passage from the recently-published first volume of *Commentaries* (probably in Section IV of the Introduction, 'Of the Countries subject to the Laws of England') was quoted against him (or possibly his friend the civilian George Hay) by the prominent City politician and pro-American William Beckford. Blackstone evidently responded that he should have 'quoted the whole and not a Part', which sounds as though it should have been an effective riposte.[63]

Possibly a more characteristic intervention occurred next month, when Blackstone joined Lord North in opposing the new window-tax schedule proposed by William Dowdeswell as chancellor of the exchequer. According to Harris, he 'shew['d] the Futility of the Tax, and how easy to be avoided'; a week later Blackstone was listed first among five speakers, again including North, who tried unsuccessfully to prevent the bill being referred to a committee. A detailed analysis of likely revenue from the old and new rates survives in the form of a multi-column spreadsheet, entitled 'Calculations of Window Tax 1766 by Mr Blackstone'. Appended notes suggest that current rates applying to the cottages of the 'inferior Classes' should not be increased, with any resultant revenue shortfall made up by raising the levy on houses containing 18 to 24 windows—in other words, by taxing the middling sort, not the poor.[64] At the end of the year Blackstone again spoke against the Rockingham ministry, when he supported George Grenville on the issue of compensation to those who had suffered from the recent corn export embargo. Dr Johnson was confused by this stance, and may not have been alone, but Blackstone was still described as a government supporter in lists drawn up early in 1767, perhaps largely on the basis of his office under the crown.[65]

Blackstone's attitude towards parliamentary politics was undoubtedly coloured by his Oxford experiences in the 1740s and 50s, particularly his long-standing friendship with Sir Roger Newdigate. The latter's manuscript 'essays on party' dating from early in George III's reign not only embody architectural metaphor and historical perspective in ways strikingly reminiscent of Blackstone's own writings, but strongly endorse the

---

[63] *Papers of Benjamin Franklin*, ed. L. W. Labaree (New Haven, 1959–2006), xiii.173. Thomas, 'Parliamentary Diaries', 314; Hampshire RO, 9M73/G716, 30, 32. *Commentaries*, i. 105; see also the *Supplement*, iii.

[64] Hants. RO, 9M73/G716, 56, 68 (21, 28 April 1766); TNA, T1/434/124.

[65] *Correspondence of George III*, ed. Fortescue, i. 422–3; *The Letters of Samuel Johnson Volume I 1731–1772*, ed. B. Redford (Princeton, 1992), 275–6; *H of P 1754–90*, ii. 97.

principled independence and moderation of the 'Country party as opposed to administration'.[66] Newdigate's rejection of 'party violence . . . at this day when our British King declares he will be King of all his people' was later echoed in Blackstone's own reported 'Aversion' to 'the Rage of contending Parties', doubtless coloured by his uncomfortable experiences in the deeply fractured political world of the late 1760s.[67] Heavily burdened with historical and legal citation, Blackstone's speech of 3 February 1766 against repeal of the Stamp Act might seem ample justification for Namier's dismissal of him as 'over-subtle and ingenious', while lacking 'political common-sense'—a typical lawyer-politician, in short. Doolittle, on the other hand, sees Blackstone as canny and cynical, 'using politics to make his way in the law'. Perhaps the truth lies somewhere in between. While never more than a minor political figure, Blackstone was not a wholly ineffective parliamentary orator and operative. At the same time, an MP who generally appeared as a 'King's Friend' and follower of Bute in 1765–6, but was also quite capable of supporting Grenville against the Rockingham administration on issues other than repeal of the Stamp Act, was hardly a mere careerist.

Away from combative high politics, parliament's mundane legislative function also continued to occupy Blackstone in ways which scarcely contributed to his promotion prospects. Between 10 January 1765, when the fourth session of George III's first parliament began, and the beginning of March, he was named to nearly 50 separate Commons' committees.[68] Most had local if not literally parochial briefs, endorsing petitions for private acts of parliament to enclose specific tracts of common lands, naturalize named foreign-born aliens, or improve particular roads and bridges by establishing turnpike trusts. There were several in whose business Blackstone had direct personal interest: one concerned projected enclosures on a Staffordshire manor belonging to his protégé-patron the earl of Suffolk (Blackstone was among three MPs charged with preparing this bill); another considered a petition from London merchants for an extension of the public wharfs, an issue already before the courts in which Blackstone would shortly be involved as counsel, while a third dealt with the improvement (or turnpiking) of the Wallingford-to-Faringdon road, which had intermittently engaged both Blackstone and his uncle Seymour Richmond since at least 1751.[69] Some were large, amorphous bodies like

---

[66] *H of P 1754–90*, iii. 96; Doolittle, 67; P. D. G. Thomas, 'Sir Roger Newdigate's Essays on Party, *c.* 1762', *English Historical Review*, 102 (1987), 392–400.

[67] Ibid. 399; Clitherow, xx. See below, Chapter 11.

[68] *CJ*, xxx. 1–200.

[69] *CJ*, xxx. 5–6, 7, 30, 38, 65, 86, 127–8, 132, 192; *Reports*, i. 581–90; *Letters*, 20–21.

the Committee for Privileges and Elections; others nominally included 'all the lawyers of the house', as did the committee on the Poor Law which Blackstone joined on 17 January 1765, and reported from five days later. Blackstone's report, advocating the consolidation of parishes into larger units for welfare purposes, formed the basis of a bill which he drafted with the lawyer MP Thomas Gilbert and others. Passing the Commons but rejected by the Lords, it was the precursor of what would eventually become a major piece of legislation, Gilbert's Poor Law Act of 1782. Such direct experience of the practical obstacles to statutory law reform may underlie a rhetorical question in book III of the *Commentaries*: 'who, that is acquainted with the difficulty of new modelling any branch of our statute laws (though relating but to roads or to parish-settlements), will conceive it ever feasible to alter any fundamental point of the common law'?[70]

Other committees on national issues to which Blackstone was named included one to examine the qualifications of proprietors of East India Company Stock (although generally showing little interest in Indian matters, he did join an opposition attempt in April 1767 to end the Chathamite administration's enquiry into the Company's territorial acquisitions), and another established to draft legislation enabling monies held in trust by Chancery to augment the salaries of that court's subordinate judicial officers.[71] Potentially wider significance attached to 'A Bill to enable Ecclesiastical Persons, and Bodies Politick, Corporate, and Collegiate, to exchange their Lands', presented to the House on 28 January 1765 by Blackstone and Richard Jackson, friend of Benjamin Franklin and agent for the colony of Connecticut. Their measure sought to provide legal machinery whereby landed property belonging to the established church, to university colleges, and to charitable trusts could be exchanged for lands of equivalent value held by lay persons, so that the holdings of both might be better improved or cultivated. Why Blackstone took this initiative is unknown, although it possibly reflected his previous experience as college estates steward and bursar. At all events, the bill did not meet with an easy passage, and after a series of committee meetings in February 1765 Blackstone sent an amended copy on 10 March to Thomas Townshend, member for Cambridge University, with a covering note which sought to allay concerns about the adequacy of safeguards

---

[70] *CJ*, xxx. 27, 30, 38, 76; *H of P 1754–90*, ii. 500; S. and B. Webb, *English Poor Law History Part I: The Old Poor Law* (1927; 1963), 171; *Commentaries*, iii. 267. Gilbert's bill was championed by the Bedford Whigs, and opposed by Bute's friends: P. Langford, *The First Rockingham Administration, 1765–1766* (Oxford, 1973), 54–5.

[71] H. V. Bowen, *Revenue and Reform: the Indian problem in British Politics 1757–1773* (Cambridge, 1991), 63; *CJ*, xxx. 38, 192.

against fraudulent or extortionate practices. This he evidently failed to do, since in the third-reading debate a week later Townshend opposed the bill 'as a matter of real danger to the Church'.[72] So did an Oxford colleague, George Hay, dean of the Arches, who (according to Harris) was 'set on by the Archbishop'. In response, Blackstone 'by espousing it and answering the above Gentlemen, shew'd Oxford not to have the same Apprehensions, as Cambridge and Lambeth'. But despite securing a comfortable majority of 113 to 95 when the house divided, Blackstone's bill lapsed in the Lords, doubtless thanks to the formidable voting power of the bishops.[73]

Blackstone's continued identification with the University of Oxford brought to his door in May 1765 Dr Samuel Musgrave, an accomplished Oxonian Greek scholar and physician, recently returned from Paris with a bizarre tale to tell. Recalling Musgrave as at best a distant acquaintance 'on a literary account at Oxford 5 or 6 Years ago', Blackstone was still sufficiently concerned by his accusations of conspiracy and corruption in high places, supposedly involving Bute, the Princess Royal, and the recent, still controversial peace treaty which had ended the Seven Years War, to draw up an immediate memorandum of their conversation. This he passed to Attorney General Norton at the House of Commons the same day, subsequently forwarding a copy with a covering letter, both of which eventually ended up in Bute's hands. Professing that he 'could give no Manner of Credit' to the charge that Bute (with whom he was evidently still in occasional contact) had been paid off by France for concluding the peace, Blackstone suggested that Musgrave was either 'part of some concerted Plan to raise a Party Clamour', or else mad—most likely the former.[74] This unsettling episode lacked any immediate consequences, for Musgrave was unable to get his claims taken seriously by anyone in a position to do anything about them. They attracted more attention when he revived them publicly in 1769, with the additional allegation that it was 'by the direction of Dr Blackstone' that he had 'waited on Lord Halifax, then Secretary of State'—who (of course) proved 'polite but evasive'. Musgrave was subsequently examined at the bar of the House of Commons, just before Blackstone gave up his seat; despite being found 'frivolous and unworthy of credit' by opposition as well as government members, his claims continued to enjoy some credence in quarters predisposed to believe the worst of

---

[72] Hampshire RO, 9M73/G714, 75.

[73] Ibid.; *House of Commons Sessional Papers of the Eighteenth Century*, ed. S. Lambert (Wilmington, 1975), xxi. 9–13; *CJ*, xxx. 65, 76, 129, 168, 186, 186, 222, 239, 259; *Letters*, 105 [where Thomas Townshend is mistakenly identified with his namesake, first viscount Sydney, MP for Whitchurch]. *LJ*, xxi. 84–5, 90, 101.

[74] *Letters*, 105–6, 191–3.

Bute. On this occasion Musgrave testified that Blackstone, 'much affected . . . in great agitation' had not only urged him to take his claims to the ministry, but 'sent three days after to know if I had been; for he said, "if you had not, I should think myself obliged, as a servant to the crown, to go and give it myself"'. Blackstone (who did not directly deny these details) may well have found himself perturbed and generally out of his depth when first confronted with the story told by Musgrave, someone he had known previously only as editor of Euripedes (and a go-between with Gerard Meerman). If a combination of *naiveté* and self-importance prevented him from dismissing Musgrave's account out of hand, further reflection (and perhaps Fletcher Norton's bluntly sceptical reaction) evidently induced a cooler view of the matter.[75]

Musgrave's revelations were an exceptionally dramatic and highly-coloured interruption to Blackstone's regular round of business. During the mid- to late 1760s he made considerable use of both public and private bills to advance projects designed to benefit the city and university of Oxford and the town of Wallingford, as well as other measures more narrowly concerning his Bertie clients. With a last-minute petition, 'hastily drawn up upon Memory' in January 1769 for a private act incorporating himself, Benjamin Buckler, and John Tracy as visitors of the Michel Foundation, establishing the statutes governing the foundation, and enabling the advantageous sale of a small portion of the Michel bequest, he also succeeded in bringing that troublesome and long-drawn-out affair to a satisfactory end. Coming after more than a decade of tedious wrangling, the favourable response of the provost and fellows of Queen's gave Buckler justified hopes that this act would be 'a Salve for all the old Sores, and that we shall be the most popular Visitors (in our College) of all the University'.[76]

Besides such largely local or regional initiatives, Blackstone took a leading role in drafting and promoting several reform bills of national significance. The first of these proposed what the legal historian Sir William Holdsworth characterized as 'radical reforms in the law relating to the administration of assets', by facilitating payment of creditors from the

[75] [W. Cobbett], *Cobbett's Parliamentary History of England* (1806–1820), xvi. 778, 782; [S. Musgrave], *An Address to the Gentlemen, Clergy and Freeholders of the County of Devon*, in *Cambridge Magazine* (1769), 339; *Gentleman's Magazine*, xl (1770), 93; Philip, 104; *Historical and Posthumous Memoirs of Sir Nathaniel William Wraxall*, ed. H. B. Wheatley (1884), i. 323, 325. Museum Meermano–Westreenianum, 257/53, Blackstone to Meerman, 13 August 1761.

[76] *Letters*, 141–2; Records of the Parliament Office, House of Lords, Main Papers, HL/PO/JO/10/7/301, 23 February 1769; Queen's College Archives, 5 M 87, 50143: Buckler to Blackstone, 1 February 1769; Doolittle, 34–5.

estates of their deceased debtors, including the real property of merchants and other traders, or in one version all persons. The whole subject doubtless had personal resonance for Blackstone, given his own father's indebtedness at his death and the consequent difficulties for his widowed mother, as well as for family members among Charles Blackstone's creditors. He appears to have drafted two bills in March 1767, following an unsuccessful attempt by another independently-minded MP, the merchant George Prescott, to promote a measure covering part of the same general ground. After scrutiny by Charles Yorke (the former attorney general), Blackstone's bills went through an intensive committee process over the next two months. This culminated in the third reading of an 'Act for the More Equal Payment of the Creditors of Persons Deceased', but although carried to the House of Lords by Blackstone on 19 May, it went no further. His other measure, 'for the more effectual relief of creditors out of the real estate of their deceased debtors', had its second reading in the lower house and was ordered to be printed on 25 May, but lapsed with the end of that parliamentary session on 6 June.[77] A similar fate met the bill against bribery and corruption in parliamentary elections introduced by the Chathamite MP William Beckford in January 1768, which Blackstone supported with amendments in committee before it was eventually dropped by its proponent.[78]

IV

This last involvement may seem difficult to reconcile with his role in tightening the earl of Abingdon's grip on the borough of Westbury. But Beckford's bill was primarily directed against buying and selling of individual votes by candidates and electors, rather than wholesale constituency manipulation by aristocratic proprietors and their professional advisors. Perhaps more to the point is the hint of some connection with the simultaneous Oxford electoral scandal, which arose from the disclosure that Abingdon and the duke of Marlborough had paid off the city's accumulated debt in return for the right to nominate its two parliamentary burgesses at the forthcoming general election. Blackstone possibly helped damp down the predictable furore in the Commons after disclosure of this deal by the

[77] *Letters*, 109; BL MS Additional 35879, fos. 372–90v; *CJ*, xxxi. 219, 295, 299, 344, 345, 352, 359, 362, 365, 368, 376, 383; *LJ*, xxxi. 606. Lambert, *Commons Papers*, 265–74, 275–82. W. S. Holdsworth, 'Gibbon, Blackstone, and Bentham', *LQR*, 52 (1938), 52–3.
[78] Warwickshire RO, CR 136B/2624 A1 (Newdigate's annotated copy of the printed bill); Thomas, *George III*, 184–5; *CJ*, xxxi. 545, 566–7, 583, 597–8.

231

two sitting members for Oxford, with hopes of obtaining an appropriate reward for himself. By mid-February 1768 his long-time academic antagonist Theophilus Leigh was retailing a current university rumour that 'the Citizens (lately Harass'd), will shew their Gratitude, at the next Election, to Dr Blackston'. But even if that gossip had some real foundation—as well it might, given Blackstone's close working relationship with Thomas Walker, Oxford's town clerk—his prospects of gaining one of the city's seats would scarcely have survived the subsequent revelation that it was the earl of Abingdon who, for reasons best known to himself, had encouraged the city's disgruntled MPs to go public.[79]

Leigh's speculation on the subject of Blackstone's political future (which made no reference to Westbury) arose in the context of a hard-fought campaign for the university's two parliamentary seats in the general election for George III's second parliament. Besides Sir Roger Newdigate, the candidates included three persons, all members of the previous parliament, with whom Blackstone had more than a casual acquaintance: Lord Fitzmaurice, his former pupil and Shelburne's younger brother, Dr George Hay, the civil lawyer of St John's College, and Charles Jenkinson, formerly Bute's private secretary, who was gradually rising in the service of the crown. Blackstone's role in this contest remains tantalisingly obscure. On the one hand his influence was now said to reach 'no further than the gates of All Souls'; on the other he was strongly suspected by Jenkinson's supporters of disingenuous double-dealing, ostensibly backing Jenkinson for the second place but encouraging his friends to canvass for Fitzmaurice, and possibly even bringing in Hay as a late candidate to further erode Jenkinson's vote.[80] The only hard evidence consists of a letter of 'Oxford news' written to Newdigate several weeks before the poll in which Blackstone quoted a wild overestimate of Hay's likely vote, plus the fact that, unlike his All Souls friends Buckler and Tracy, Blackstone himself ('to whose opinions', it was claimed 'they implicitly defer') actually voted for Hay (as well as for Newdigate, who was returned). Despite much heated speculation by committed partisans, no one seems to have noted the curious parallel between Fitzmaurice's withdrawal before the day of the poll, avowedly 'to preserve the Independency of the University' (thereby securing the return of the fifth candidate, Francis Page, a wholly unexceptional Oxfordshire Tory squire), and the abandonment of his campaign for the Oxford chancellorship in 1762 by Suffolk, another former Blackstone pupil (although

[79] Ibid; BL MS Additional 38457, fo. 148; *H of P 1754–90*, i.358.
[80] BL MS Additional 38457, fos. 60v, 69, 71v, 76, 84v, 101, 116, 122, 170–170v, 189v, 271, 323. Ward, *Georgian Oxford*, ch. 14.

of course this latter retraction lacked, from Blackstone's perspective, any such acceptable result). Leigh thought Fitzmaurice was 'put up . . . by one not much respected here', while after the election another Jenkinson partisan claimed to 'discern the Management of the Affair', referring darkly to Fitzmaurice's withdrawal, and doubts that 'a certain person has acted honourably'.[81] It seems likely that Blackstone's overriding priority was to ensure the return of Newdigate as sitting member, but then perhaps to do his part in resisting the claims of a candidate who might be represented as a ministerial threat to the university's traditional 'independence', and had not entirely lived down his past as an active adherent of the Whig 'New Interest' in the great 1754 Oxfordshire contest.

Yet if only because his time and energy were increasingly absorbed by other and more pressing concerns, Blackstone's role in the 1768 university campaign was almost certainly exaggerated by contemporaries (according to one leading participant, 'if I were to send you all the reports that spread in this place, I might fill ten sheets in a day').[82] Apart from the Botley Causeway and Swinford Bridge undertakings, together with further business concerning the Bertie estates and family, there is the evidence (as noted above) of a marked growth in his out-of-court legal practice from 1765 onwards. Completing his major publishing project was also a priority. While the first two volumes of the *Commentaries* were available within less than 12 months of each other (in November 1765 and October 1766 respectively), Book III did not make its appearance until June 1768. At 455 pages of text, plus a further 27-page documentary appendix, it was somewhat shorter than its predecessor (which ran to 539 pages, including both text and an appendix of illustrative deeds and instruments). But Book III's subject-matter, the various means available for 'the redress of private wrongs, by suit or action in courts', was considerably more demanding of both the author's legal knowledge and his expository talents.

The basic principles of land law, the main topic of Book II, had been set out nearly three centuries before in Thomas Littleton's standard student text. Despite numerous complexities subsequently multiplied by statute and judicial decision, the chief features of this body of legal learning were not so difficult for a clear-headed and diligent writer to elucidate and summarize, especially given that he had already published some of its central elements.[83] But civil procedure was a wholly different matter,

[81] BL MS Additional 38457, fos. 69, 76, 320, 321, 323; *Letters*, 133–4; Bodl. Gough Oxon. 80, *An Authentick Copy of the Poll . . . for the University of Oxford* (1768); Doolittle, 67–9. Above, Chapter 9, pp. 194–9.
[82] BL MS Additional 38457, fo. 189v.
[83] Cf. S. F. C. Milsom, *The Nature of Blackstone's Achievement* (1981), 5; above, Chapter 8, pp. 167–9.

because the medieval real actions were no longer directly relevant, while what would eventually become the substantive law of contract, torts, and so forth was still gradually emerging from a very complex assortment of procedural remedies. Blackstone frankly admitted that the 'great variety' of these last 'is apt at a first acquaintance to breed a confusion of ideas, and a kind of distraction in the memory: a difficulty not a little increased by the very immethodical arrangement, too justly complained of in our antient writers'. He nevertheless thought it necessary to provide some account of the old forms, as well as those in current use, 'apprehending that the reason of the one could never be clearly apprehended, without some acquaintance with the other', from which they had evolved by 'a series of minute contrivances'—even if 'it would be too irksome a task to perplex both the readers and myself with explaining all the rules of proceeding in these obsolete actions'.[84] Given the abstruse and disparate nature of much of Book III's technical subject-matter, Blackstone also found himself obliged to defend the common law at some length against standard criticisms of its intricacy, delays, and uncertainty, in passages either entirely new or much expanded from their Oxford originals. The peroration to one of these, which explains how the law's 'fictions and cir-cuities' have developed from 'the old feudal forms of action' as adapted to a 'more simple and commercial mode of property', deploys perhaps Blackstone's most famous and elaborately-crafted metaphor, that of 'an old Gothic castle, erected in the days of chivalry, but fitted up for a modern inhabitant. The moated ramparts, the embattled towers, and the trophied halls, are magnificent and venerable, but useless. The infer-ior apartments, now converted into rooms of convenience, are chearful and commodious, although their approaches are winding and difficult.'[85] Lastly, because his own practice had been primarily in King's Bench, he lacked familiarity with 'the very general and extensive jurisdiction' of the equity courts, especially Chancery. Blackstone understandably tackled this part of his task with considerable 'diffidence'.[86] His final chapter on equity procedure does indeed appear something of an afterthought, even though here, as elsewhere, he followed and expanded upon the basic plan of his lectures and their syllabus, the *Analysis*.

If the third volume of the *Commentaries* took 20 months to join the two books already published, it was no less warmly received by the review-ers (who were happy to focus on Blackstone's account of the various law

---

[84] *Commentaries*, iii. 265, 266, 271.
[85] Ibid., 267–8, 317–23, 325–30, 422–5.
[86] Ibid., 425, 429.

courts, bypassing the greater part of his treatise as 'mostly of a technical nature').[87] Sales revenue for 1768 also increased by nearly two-thirds over the previous year, which must have seemed ample retrospective justification for Blackstone's move of his London quarters north from Carey Street to a more fashionable address on the west side of Lincoln's Inn Fields. In 1762 the poet William Cowper, musing that 'every man may be rich if he will', claimed that he 'should not despair of a house in Lincoln's Inn Fields, with all its appurtenances'.[88] Blackstone's four-storied house, No. 55, was one of a pair built in the 1640s and damaged by fire in 1759, when occupied by Sir Thomas Denison, a puisne justice of King's Bench, who died in September 1765. Blackstone's tenancy of this 'Commodious Leasehold Dwelling House, with ample Offices in compleat Repair, two Coach Houses and Stabling for six Horses', for which he paid £120 a year, began some time between June and December 1767. The handsome residential terraces on the west side of Lincoln's Inn Fields, whose classical facades supposedly bespoke the architectural influence of Inigo Jones, still attracted wealthy aristocrats, as well as professional men; indeed the third earl of Abingdon had lived at No. 52, while Blackstone's surgeon-uncle Thomas Bigg occupied No. 40 (on the south side) from 1726 until he gave up his London practice in 1747. Blackstone's immediate next-door neighbours were the Sardinian ambassador (with his diplomatically-privileged chapel holding regular Roman Catholic services), and (from 1770) the banker MP Sir Walter Rawlinson; nearby lawyer residents included Eliab Harvey, John Morton, and Lord Chancellor Northington.[89] In short, this was an entirely appropriate London abode for 'a great and able Lawyer', his wife, and their still growing family.

---

[87] *Monthly Review* (December 1768), 465.

[88] *Annual Register for the Year 1768* (1769), 268–72. Appendix II below; *The Correspondence of William Cowper*, ed. T. Wright (1904), i. 18.

[89] *Survey of London: Volume III. The Parish of St-Giles-in-the-Fields (Part I.) Lincoln's Inn Fields*, ed. L. Gomme (1912), 52, 53, 71, 75, 79, 85–6, 102; LMA, ACC 1360/584/1; *Letters*, xxvi. J. Summerson, *Architecture in Britain 1530–1830* (Harmondsworth, 1970), 134, 162–4; Sheppard, *London*, 179.

CHAPTER II

'This Temper of the Times'[1] *(1768–70)*

D URING the two years immediately before he became a judge, Blackstone was frequently caught up in public controversy and debate, mostly arising from the application of his *Commentaries* to current political and social issues. Criticized by contemporary partisans and subsequent commentators as mere reflexes of careerist self-interest or obscurantist prejudice, his positions were seldom wholly consistent or straightforward. But they deserve to be assessed on their merits, as likewise his eventual promotion to the judicial bench in February 1770.

I

From the opening of George III's second parliament in May 1768, the *Commons Journals* tend to list no more than several names of MPs nominated to select committees, rather than (as before) a full roll call of committee membership. If only for this evidential reason, Blackstone appears conspicuously uninvolved in the legislative business of the House during his term as member for Westbury, at least by contrast with his level of activity in the previous parliament. On the other hand, during this same period of less than two years (fewer than 12 months' actual sitting time), he intervened in at least 11 debates (sometimes speaking more than once), whereas he is known to have delivered only 14 speeches over his first 7-year parliamentary term. To put these figures into perspective, more than half of all MPs in the later eighteenth century appear never to have spoken on public business. Indeed, the most complete record of Commons' debates over the three years 1768–70 includes speeches from only 142 of the total

---

[1] W. Blackstone, *A Reply to Dr Priestley's Remarks on the Fourth Volume of the Commentaries on the Laws of England* (1769), 27.

body of 558 members. Thus while Blackstone was by no means so tireless a parliamentary orator as, say, Edmund Burke, George Grenville, or Lord North, he was plainly a good deal more articulate than the average back-bencher, or even some leading ministers.[2]

Most occasions on which Blackstone addressed the Commons after May 1768 concerned the irrepressible John Wilkes. Back from self-imposed exile in France earlier that year, although still under sentence of outlawry, Wilkes's popular status as a martyr for liberty had gained him election at the top of the poll for the large Middlesex constituency on London's outskirts. This remarkable coup seriously embarrassed an already divided government, now under the de facto leadership of the duke of Grafton. Ministers generally agreed that Wilkes must not take his seat, even after his outlawry had been reversed on a technicality by Lord Mansfield's court of King's Bench. Yet excluding him from parliament plainly risked an even more serious outbreak of disorder and consequent bloodshed than had already accompanied his election and subsequent confinement to the King's Bench prison. That he was serving sentences for libels of which he had been found guilty back in 1764 in no way inhibited his legal and media campaign against the officials responsible for the general warrants which had led to his initial conviction. When parliament resumed after the summer recess in November 1768, Wilkes characteristically raised the stakes still higher by formally petitioning the House of Commons for redress of grievances, including the claim that the legal record of his case had been 'materially altered' at Mansfield's direction, and against his solicitor's objections, just before his trial.[3]

Having shown no previous signs of sympathy for Wilkes, Blackstone's contribution to the procedural discussion—'rather a conversation than a debate'[4]—after this petition was presented probably gave little comfort to Wilkes's supporters, but unfortunately no details of his speech survive. When the matter came to be formally heard by the House in late January 1769, Blackstone's hostility was more clearly revealed, as also its strong moral and religious underpinning. On 31 January 1769 he spoke three times, first on a procedural point, but then 'setting the house right about the nature of libels', he asserted that Wilkes was guilty of 'an impious libel, with intent to blaspheme the Almighty God'. His crime—in the

---

[2] H of P 1754–90, i. 97; Thomas, House of Commons, 229–31; Sir Henry Cavendish's Debates of the House of Commons During the Thirteenth Parliament of Great Britain. Vol. I. 1768–1770 (1841), xiv–xvi. For Rockingham's 'almost total and apparently insurmountable incapacity to speak in Parliament' (in his case, the House of Lords), see Langford, Rockingham Administration, 18–19.

[3] Thomas, John Wilkes, chs. 4–5; Cavendish, Debates, 45–7.

[4] Fortescue, Correspondence of George III, ii. 58–9 (Lord North to George III, 14 November 1768).

Essay on Woman—was indeed 'direct blasphemy . . . a vicious act, done with a vicious intention'.[5] Next day 'Mr Blackstone opened the debate' on Wilkes's accusation against Mansfield, with the assertion that he himself was 'totally unconnected with any party'. While that was let pass, Blackstone's formal resolution condemning Wilkes's 'groundless complaint' as an 'audacious aspersion, calculated to convey a gross misrepresentation . . . and to prejudice the minds of the people against the administration of public justice' did encounter opposition. One speaker tried to establish a disjunction between Blackstone's motion and 'what that gentleman has published' (presumably a reference to the discussion of 'amendments' in the third book of the *Commentaries*). Grenville suggested that the motion's imprecision meant 'it cannot be his own . . . he must have adopted it', and proceeded to offer a series of amendments designed to soften the force of Blackstone's words; most were accepted by the mover, before the amended motion was itself passed without a division.[6]

Horace Walpole characterized Blackstone's contribution on 1 February 1769 as 'a long obscure question', but made no such criticism of his role in the next day's debate.[7] This concerned Wilkes's provocative published claim that the previous year's 'horrid massacre', when a riotous crowd of supporters gathered outside his prison in St George's Fields, Southwark, was fired on by troops, resulting in at least six deaths, had been deliberately planned. Instead Walpole took pains to stress that 'even Dr Blackstone' opposed Attorney General William De Grey's motion to condemn Wilkes's words as a seditious libel. Blackstone actually managed to avoid directly opposing this motion, thanks to a procedural manoeuvre by the respected Yorkshire MP Sir George Savile, although he still felt it necessary to provide a detailed explanation of his reasons for 'voting against gentlemen with whom I have usually voted and shall hereafter vote'. His main point was that, while Wilkes's words were as 'unjust, scurrilous, and unworthy, as anything that ever fell from his pen', they were 'not the cause of the public' simply because directed at a minister of state, and so should be dealt with, if at all, by ordinary legal process: 'this House ought not to interpose'. Even the professional mantra added as awkward afterthought—'I do not recollect any precedent immediately bearing upon this occasion'—scarcely detracted from the good sense of this contribution.[8]

[5] Cavendish, *Debates*, 129. A. H. Cash, *John Wilkes* (2006), 130–131.

[6] *Cobbett's Parliamentary History*, xvi. 542; Cavendish, *Debates*, 131–3, 136–8. BL MS Egerton 217, fos. 14–19, 21–3; *Commentaries*, iii. 406–10. Fortescue, *Correspondence of George III*, ii. 81, misdates North's account of this debate to 4 rather than 1 February.

[7] Walpole, *Memoirs of George III*, iv. 65–6.

[8] Cavendish, *Debates*, 144; BL MS Egerton 217, fos. 87–8.

But if Blackstone here briefly parted company with the anti-Wilkes majority, he reverted to form on the substantive question of Wilkes's expulsion from the House, the main business of the following day (3 February 1769). According to George Grenville in the same debate, Blackstone spoke 'with a becoming zeal and indignation', and his 'opinions . . . joined to the serious manner in which he delivered them, seemed to make great impression on the House'. While Cavendish's notes suggest that 'Counsellor Blackstone' may have lost some of his audience when he 'enlarged a good deal upon libels and blasphemy', he evidently regained their attention with a powerful statement of personal religious faith as the grounds for his support of the motion: 'I hope I shall never be ashamed in this House to own myself a Christian. When I see all religion made a mockery and jest of, it behoves me to vindicate my God and my King.'[9] In the list of speakers for and against Wilkes's expulsion sent to George III next day by Lord North, the name of 'Dr Blackstone' appears immediately after those of the mover and seconder of the successful motion.[10]

Over the next two months Blackstone moved unsuccessfully on the disputed Cumberland election, offered mild opposition to the second reading of the Coventry Inland Navigation bill introduced by his friend Newdigate, and seconded the printing of the Oxford canal bill (having sought a 'Complete Copy . . . with the Amendments and new Clauses' from Thomas Walker several days before).[11] The final stages of the Botley and Swinford projects, as well as last-minute in-press tinkering with the fourth and final book of his *Commentaries*, may also have kept him away from parliament. But whether absent or present, he did not speak again on the still very current subject of Wilkes until the second-last day of the parliamentary session. On 8 May the House formally considered a Middlesex petition against the previous decision to award the seat to the second-placed candidate, Henry Luttrell, rather than the still-incarcerated Wilkes, now returned by the electors at no fewer than three successive polls. Asserting yet again his total independence of ministry, faction or party—'in this and every other question I have acted upon my own

---

[9] Cavendish, *Debates*, 153, 161–2.

[10] BL, MS Egerton 217, fo. 130; Fortescue, *Correspondence of George III*, ii. 80. For a garbled account, mistakenly attributed to the 17 February debate in which Blackstone is not otherwise recorded as speaking, see 'Diary of . . . Thomas Fry', ed. W. N. Hargreaves-Mawdsley (typescript, St John's College, Oxford, Munim. LXXXVI.D.8), 37: 'Blackstone made a Speech upon this occasion which was much ridiculed by Alderman Beckford . . . said that opposing the Gospel was opposing the common Law of the Kingdom'—which view seems actually to have been voiced by Serjeant George Nares: see Cavendish, *Debates*, 156.

[11] *Letters*, 140; Cavendish, *Debates*, 338, 414–17; Newdigate Diary, 13, 16 March 1769.

opinion without consultation'[12]—Blackstone attempted to set out the reasons why Wilkes was legally debarred from sitting and his opponent legitimately returned, notwithstanding the reiterated preference of the Middlesex electors. Reporting on the debate to his Irish friend Lord Charlemont, Edmund Burke classed him with the 'Lawyers for the Court' who argued in a 'bold and profligate' manner that 'the house had a power to qualifye or disqualifye without any other rule than their own discretion; and Blackstone went so far as to say "if he affirmed that we could make Laws, he could support himself by respectable authorities"'.[13]

The Commons had in the past expelled individual members, and even declared their incapacity for re-election. But the notion that by its mere resolution the House could effectively deprive free-born Englishmen of the right to choose their parliamentary representatives was undeniably disturbing. At a time of widespread economic distress, social unrest, and high political tension, and when the country could seriously be described as 'in greater danger, from popular tumults' than since Wat Tyler's rising,[14] the alternative nightmare of a corrupt government-controlled majority purging upright dissident MPs might not seem entirely fanciful.[15] Blackstone's contribution to this debate attracted wide attention, thanks partly to the subsequent speech of George Grenville, with whom he had occasionally allied himself in the past. For although Grenville's own administration initiated the original prosecution, this veteran politician now fully appreciated the danger of further fuelling Wilkes's cause by dogmatic insistence on the unbounded powers of the House with respect to elections. Grenville's position was foreshadowed in an earlier speech by his close follower Henry Seymour. Declaring himself 'a pupil' and admirer of Blackstone and his work, Seymour nevertheless confessed to 'much mortification today at what has dropped from him', then quoted 'some passages from the *Commentaries*' (presumably the second chapter of Book I, on the 'qualification of persons to be elected members of the house of commons'), before demanding: 'Has the House of Commons the power, at one blow, to cut off the franchises of eight millions of people?'[16] Speaking as a senior statesman towards the close of debate very early next morning, Grenville played adroitly on anti-lawyer sentiment, by doubting

---

[12] BL MS Egerton 217, fos. 337–8.

[13] *The Correspondence of Edmund Burke, Volume II*, ed. T. W. Copeland and L. Sutherland (Cambridge, 1960), 23.

[14] Cavendish, *Debates*, 152 (Lord Barrington, on conditions preceding the St George's Fields massacre).

[15] G. Rudé, *Wilkes and Liberty* (Oxford, 1962), ch. 6; Thomas, *John Wilkes*, 101–3.

[16] Ibid., 427. *Commentaries*, i. 169–70.

whether 'the law and usage of parliament' was 'a question for gentlemen of the profession'. He then remarked 'I greatly prefer the opinion given by the learned gentleman (Mr Blackstone) in his work on the laws of England to what fell from him this evening', before producing a transcript of 'restrictions and disqualifications' for election to the Commons enumerated over two pages of the *Commentaries*. This made no mention of expulsion and so could hardly apply in the case of Wilkes.[17] Having read out the list, Grenville slyly added '[t]he learned gentleman may have found reason to alter his opinion . . . I do not mean to press that point; but that opinion was one given upon great deliberation'.

II

Such studied restraint was not shown by all opponents of the ministry's stance on the Middlesex election. The issue continued to fill newspaper columns and generate pamphlets for months following parliament's dissolution on the day after this debate. The fiercest attacks appeared in the daily *Public Advertiser* as letters from the anonymous 'Junius', who on 22 June turned his acerbic attention to the lawyers who had supported Wilkes's expulsion. First noting that their 'profession is supported by the indiscriminate defence of right and wrong', while 'I have not that opinion of their knowledge or integrity to think it necessary that they should decide for me upon a plain constitutional question', he went on to devote particular attention to Blackstone, in terms which have been thought to point to 'a personal antipathy':[18]

Doctor Blackstone is solicitor to the queen. The doctor recollected that he had a place to preserve, though he forgot that he had a reputation to lose. We have now the good fortune to understand the doctor's principles as well as writings. For the defence of truth, of law, and reason, the doctor's book may be safely consulted; but whoever wishes to cheat a neighbour of his estate, or to rob the country of its rights, need make no scruple of consulting the doctor himself.[19]

---

[17] Ibid., 430.

[18] J. S. Watson, *The Reign of George III 1760–1815* (Oxford, 1960), 145.

[19] *The Letters of Junius*, ed. J Cannon (Oxford, 1978), 78 and n. The cheated neighbour was the duke of Portland, whose title to his Cumberland estates had been upset by Sir James Lowther on legal advice before the 1768 general election. Blackstone was one of three counsel signing an opinion for Lowther vis-à-vis the borough of Appleby, Westmorland, in May 1767, but evidence of his involvement in the Cumberland affair has yet to surface. Doolittle, 74; B. Bonsall, *Sir James Lowther and Cumberland and Westmorland Elections 1754–1775* (Manchester, 1960), 83–5, 108.

Blackstone wisely attempted no immediate answer. But a pamphlet by Sir William Meredith, the Rockinghamite MP for Liverpool, was a different matter. In his *Letter to the Author of the Question Stated*, dated 28 June and published anonymously the following month, Blackstone maintained that when it appeared 'in the dirty Channel of a News-Paper', the 'Charge of Inconsistence and Duplicity' could be 'deservedly left to perish without Reply, with the rest of the Lyes of the Day'. But once 'adopted by a Member of Parliament . . . when a Gentleman of Rank and Reputation does not scruple to own that Performance, it then becomes a Man's Duty to himself and to his Character, thus to vindicate (once for all) his Writings, and his Conduct'.[20] Meredith had followed a now familiar pattern, quoting the list of legal disabilities barring election as an MP from the *Commentaries*, then expressing a preference for 'the Thoughts of the Professor' over 'the Words of the Politician'. Yet Blackstone evidently found his approach less objectionable than that of Grenville, whom he accused of deliberately contriving to mislead the House, 'at the Conclusion of a Debate, after Midnight; in order to traduce the Integrity of a Man, for whom he professed a Friendship, and who deserved other Treatment from his Hands'.[21]

It is hard to believe that Grenville was more concerned to question Blackstone's personal integrity than to neutralize his formidable personal authority. But the latter's resentment at what he saw as betrayal 'by a Person, who (of all Men) should not have complained of Inconsistency with regard to Mr Wilkes' may have been exacerbated by uneasy consciousness of his own failure to respond appropriately at the time to both Grenville and Seymour. Yet even someone much quicker on his feet might have found difficulty in countering Grenville's charge of inconsistency so late in the day, especially given the *Commentaries'* bald statement that 'every subject in the realm is eligible of common right' for election to parliament. True, the preceding list of nine disqualifying conditions was prefaced by a general rider, that '[t]his depends upon the law and custom of parliaments'. But there is no suggestion that the list itself covered only those disabilities which were 'permanent, general, and applicable to whole Classes of Men', as distinct from 'temporary Incapacity, inflicted by the Censure of the House', to quote Blackstone's pamphlet reply to Meredith. His accompanying assertion, that to have 'mentioned as a general Class, "Persons incapacitated by a Vote of the House of Commons"' would be 'to

---

[20] [W. Blackstone], *A Letter to the Author of the Question Stated* (1769), 6–9.
[21] W. Meredith, *The Question Stated, whether the Freeholders of Middlesex lost their Right* (1769), 20–23; *Letter to the Author*, 8.

rank the Means of creating a Disability among the Disabilities created', seems little more than a debating point.[22]

The *Critical Review* happily declared that Blackstone 'has clearly eluded the charge of inconsistency' (not an unexpected conclusion, given the pro-administration stance of that journal).[23] But Junius strongly disagreed. His 18th letter, published on 29 July, addressed Blackstone and his pamphlet directly. This latter is oddly characterized as 'equally divided into an attack upon Mr Grenville's character, and a defence of your own', even though its two passing references to Grenville (quoted above) occupy barely one of Blackstone's twenty-four pages. But then Junius, whoever he was, showed 'habitual respect' for Grenville, whereas his treatment of Blackstone was consistently vituperative:

your justification of yourself is full of subtlety and refinement, and in some places not very intelligible. If I were your enemy, I should dwell, with a malignant pleasure, upon those great and useful qualifications, which you certainly possess, and by which you once acquired, though they could not preserve to you the respect and esteem of your country . . . but having no private resentments to gratify, I think it sufficient to have given my opinion of your public conduct, leaving the punishment it deserves to your closet and yourself.[24]

The day before this all-out assault appeared in the *Public Advertiser*, the same newspaper printed a purported extract from a recently-published pamphlet, under the title 'A Speech without Doors upon the Subject of a Vote given on the 9th Day of May, 1769'. Presented as an anonymous MP's justification of his support for seating Luttrell, despite the latter having received only a minority of the Middlesex vote, on the assumption that Wilkes was properly deemed ineligible by virtue of the House's resolution, this brief and cogent piece was almost certainly written by Blackstone. So Junius assumed, before cursorily dismissing it in his further letter to the *Public Advertiser* on 1 August, both as having appeared 'before Junius's letter'—which must mean that dated 29 July, addressed to Blackstone—and for taking as decided the very point at issue, about the legitimacy of Wilkes's exclusion.[25]

[22] Ibid., 5, 19, 20–21; *Commentaries*, i. 158–9, 169–70; from the fourth edition, after the words 'common right', this sentence continues 'though there are instances wherein persons, in particular circumstances, have forfeited that common right and been declared ineligible for that Parliament by a vote of the House of Commons, or for ever by an Act of the Legislature': *Commentaries . . .* (Oxford, 1770), i.176.

[23] *Critical Review*, 28 (July 1769), 70.

[24] *Letters of Junius*, 94–8.

[25] *Public Advertiser*, 28 July 1769; *Letters of Junius*, 91, 114–15.

Nor did matters end there, so far as Blackstone and Junius were concerned. A week later the *St James's Chronicle* carried an anonymous missive by one 'Publius', signed from the Middle Temple and addressing Junius on the subject of his 'Antiblackstonian Letter'. Disclaiming the role of 'formal Defender of the celebrated Commentator (who wants no such Defence)', Publius sought to demonstrate that Blackstone's distinction between disabilities affecting whole classes of persons, as distinct from specific individuals, was not 'framed and invented by Mr. B', as Junius had claimed. He then quoted a sentence on acts of attainder from the just-published fourth book of *Commentaries*, 'that I may help you the better to understand this whole Matter, and shew you, at the same Time, the Accuracy and Consistency of Mr B', before concluding with a parting jab: 'how prettily sometimes a Man may write, without being able to read'.[26] Junius (in the person of his auxiliary, Philo Junius) responded on 14 August, avoiding this specific point, but asserting that if Wilkes's expulsion did indeed disqualify him for future re-election, the matter was too important 'to be omitted in an accurate work treating of the law of parliament'. He then reverted to the safer ground of Blackstone's lamentable performance in the House, following the quotation of his own book against him:

The truth of the matter is evidently this. Doctor Blackstone, while he was speaking in the house of commons, never once thought of his Commentaries, until the contradiction was unexpectedly urged, and stared him in the face. Instead of defending himself upon the spot, he sunk under the charge, in an agony of confusion and despair. It is well known that there was a pause of some minutes in the house, from a general expectation that the Doctor would say something in his own defence; but, it seems, his faculties were too much overpowered to think of those subtleties and refinements, which have since occurred to him.

This 'brilliant little sketch of Blackstone's discomfiture' is cited by Junius's modern editor as one of his most enduringly effective passages.[27] If neither wholly accurate nor fair, although scarcely contradicted by his known and self-confessed inadequacy as a public speaker, its graphic portrayal of Blackstone's silent embarrassment seems to have passed unchallenged.

By way of final putdown, Philo Junius closed his letter with a warning: 'As to the Doctor, I would recommend it to him to be quiet. If not, he may perhaps hear again from Junius himself.'[28] Whether or not he paid conscious attention to this advice, Blackstone seemingly made no further

[26] *St James's Chronicle*, 8 August 1769. [27] *Letters of Junius*, xxviii, 98–9.
[28] Ibid., 115.

direct contribution to the continuing paper warfare over the Middlesex election—although it is hard to be entirely sure, since most participants preferred anonymity or pseudonyms. Indeed, besides the 'Speech out of Doors' and his response to Meredith's pamphlet, Blackstone has been credited with three more works defending Wilkes's expulsion and the election of Luttrell. In 1772, when his collected letters were edited for publication, Junius added as an appendix to his 14 August 1769 letter the five-page 'Postscript' to the Rev Nathaniel Forster's pro-ministerial *An Answer to a Pamphlet Entitled, 'The Question Stated . . . '* (1769), with a note that this text was 'supposed to be written by Dr Blackstone . . . in answer to Junius's Letter'. The attribution is plausible on stylistic grounds, and Forster was a near-contemporary of Blackstone's at Oxford; his *Answer* defends Blackstone's 'character, which has been attacked on this occasion with uncommon virulence', while maintaining that the 'power of expelling from the House' of Commons could hardly have been treated in Book I of the *Commentaries* 'under the head of qualification of persons to be elected into it'. Blackstone would have had no quarrel with the general line of Forster's tract, while its postscript is essentially a detailed refutation of yet another Junius letter published in mid-July 1769. That 'Letter XVI' was in turn largely devoted to attacking *The Case of the Late Election for the County of Middlesex*, a pamphlet which Junius claimed to contain the 'whole strength of the [ministerial] party'. This substantial work has been credited to Jeremiah Dyson, an expert on parliamentary procedure, as well as to Blackstone, but its real compiler was evidently the barrister Owen Ruffhead, and Junius made no attempt to father the piece on Blackstone.[29] Finally, in January 1770 Nathaniel Forster published, again anonymously, *A Defence of the Proceedings of the House of Commons in the Middlesex Election*. Theophilus Lindsey, the Unitarian Vicar of Catterick in Yorkshire, seems to have assumed that Blackstone was the author, perhaps on the strength of a brief notice in the *Monthly Review*, where (according to one 'Aristarchus', writing some months later in the *London Magazine*), it had been 'by implication attributed to Dr Blackstone', possibly with the encouragement of 'the printer . . . to quicken the sale of a very heavy pamphlet . . . but that it was not written by Dr Blackstone I can assure you . . . '.[30]

---

[29] Ibid., 99–105, 86–91. [N. Forster], *An Answer to a Pamplet Entitled, 'The Question Stated'* (1769), 9–13; Robert Bell's *The Palladium of Conscience* (Philadelphia, 1773) reprinted *The Case of the Late Election* under Blackstone's name, possibly for commercial reasons; BL MS Additional 38206, fo. 155.

[30] [N. Forster], *A Defence of the Proceedings of the House of Commons in the Middlesex Election* (1770); T. Lindsey to Francis, Earl of Huntingdon, 26 January 1770, *Notes and Queries*, 183 (1942),

The attribution of these various more or less fugitive publications to
Blackstone reflects his prominence in the Middlesex election controversy,
as also the transformation of his public image since 1762, when Wilkes's
North Briton depicted him as a doughty opponent of entrenched authority at the University of Oxford. While his speech and vote on 2 February
showed him to be no indiscriminate supporter of Grafton's administration, such nuances carried little weight in the feverish political atmosphere
of 1769–70, especially after Junius had singled him out for attack as a willing tool of government in its purported assault upon the constitution and
English liberty. Even earlier a Wilkeite 'Freeholder of Stanwell' named
Blackstone second in a list of five lawyer placeman MPs, servants of the
Crown whose 'Expectations of Preferment insure an intire Devotion
to the Ministry'.[31] Both sides in the Middlesex debate paid due deference to the authority of his *Commentaries*, and sometimes praised his
ability and learning. But as the opposition's toast to 'the first edition of
Dr Blackstone's *Commentary on the laws of England*' suggests, supporters of Wilkes generally tried to dissociate the author from his book. The
counter-argument, that if 'Blackstone is a prerogative lawyer . . . I should
think him less inclined to extend the powers of the House of Commons'
predictably gained no traction.[32] To cite his own rueful words, this was
'not an Age in which a Man who thinks for himself, and who endeavours
to think with Moderation, can expect to meet with Quarter from any
Side, amid the Rage of contending Parties'.[33]

III

Blackstone's standing with opponents of the court and other self-styled
friends of liberty had not been improved by the mid-year appearance of
the fourth and final book of *Commentaries*. This comprehensive account of
criminal law and procedure provided a relatively enlightened and humane
treatment of its subject-matter, not least in its introductory discussion of the
principles on which that law should be based, and the admitted shortcomings (or to use Blackstone's delicate phraseology, 'particulars, that seem to

64–5 (my thanks to Grayson Ditchfield for this reference); *London Magazine*, June 1770, 290–1;
Monthly Review, 42 (1770), 59.

[31] *St James's Chronicle*, 16 June 1768.

[32] *St James Chronicle*, 11 May 1769; *A Vindication of the Right of Election, Against the Disabling
Power of the House of Commons* (1769), 42; *London Chronicle*, 11 April 1769.

[33] [Blackstone], *Reply to Dr Priestley's Remarks*, 26–7; see further below, pp. 247–9, 257–8,
262–3.

want revision and amendment') of the law as it then stood, 'even with us in England, where our crown law is with justice supposed to be more nearly advanced to perfection'.[34] Yet the book's real virtues were soon overshadowed by a sharp reaction against its account of the legal status of Protestant Dissent, under the undeniably provocative chapter heading 'Of offences against God and Religion'. Within a month a rebuttal was published by the Nonconformist clergyman polymath Joseph Priestley, already a celebrated scientist, theologian and politico-religious radical, possibly egged on by his Wilkeite barrister friend John Lee.[35] Priestley's spirited rejection of 'most injurious reflections on that part of the community to which I belong' professed to be originally motivated by a concern that Blackstone, 'supposed to possess the confidence of the present ministry', might be taken as disseminating an official line, preparatory to establishing 'a system of civil and ecclesiastical tyranny'. It was entirely irresponsible 'in the present situation of public affairs', thus 'to irritate and disunite the subjects of this realm'. More to the point, Priestly bitterly resented Blackstone's various 'insinuations' against his co-religionists, represented with 'groundless rancour and unmerited abuse', not merely as 'peevish and opinionated', but also potentially disloyal subjects.[36] Priestley's objections were widely shared. While Owen Ruffhead in the *Monthly Review* regretted Blackstone's 'narrow and somewhat illiberal turn of mind in regard to Protestant Dissenters', the Independent minister Dr Philip Furneaux published early next year a series of seven *Letters* responding in detail to Blackstone's views, especially his contention that mere nonconformity to the Church of England remained a crime, notwithstanding the Toleration Act of 1689.[37]

Priestley's *Remarks* went through three English and no fewer than seven American editions.[38] His pamphlet is also significant as the first substantial published attack on the *Commentaries*, and the only one to which Blackstone ever responded in kind. Dated from Wallingford on

---

[34] *Commentaries*, iv. 3–4. Cf. L. Radzinowicz, *A History of English Criminal Law and Its Administration from 1750 Volume I The Movement for Reform* (1948), 345–51.

[35] *Remarks on Some Paragraphs in the Fourth Volume of Dr Blackstone's Commentaries on the Laws of England, Relating to the Dissenters* (1769). R. E. Schofield, *The Enlightenment of Joseph Priestley* (University Park PA, 1997), 215. For Lee's role, see *Theological and Miscellaneous Works of Joseph Priestley*, ed. J. T. Rutt (1817–31), i. 102, Priestley to T. Lindsey, 2 October 1769; this, however, seemingly relates to Priestley's 'Answer' of that same date (ibid. xxii.334), for which see further below, pp. 249–50.

[36] Priestley, *Remarks*, 303, 310–12, 320–3, 326.

[37] *Monthly Review*, 41 (October 1769), 295; Clark, *English Society 1660–1832*, 245–6. P. Furneaux, *Letters to the Honourable Mr Justice Blackstone concerning his Exposition of the Act of Toleration, and some Positions relative to religious Liberty, in his celebrated Commentaries on the Laws of England* (1769); see also W. Enfield, *Remarks on Several Late Publications relative to the Dissenters* (1770).

[38] Schofield, *Priestley*, 215n.

2 September 1769, Blackstone's *Reply* adopts a disarmingly moderate, even conciliatory tone. His previous policy 'with regard to the numerous Strictures which my Commentaries have excited, has been to neglect them intirely, if I thought them mistaken or trifling', but otherwise to 'correct my Mistakes in some subsequent Impression of the Book', and at all events not to 'dip myself in Controversy of any Kind'.[39] His reason for now breaking this rule was that 'an Author, of Reputation in the literary World, has very fairly subscribed his Name' to 'a very angry Pamphlet', in the process misrepresenting Blackstone's views on religious liberty. Nothing personal had been intended in the passages to which Priestley objected, since they were all 'written above fifteen Years ago', before Priestley himself had published anything. Indeed, the only one of his works Blackstone had read was the recently-published *History of Electricity* (1767), 'from whence I conceived a very favourable Impression of his Talents, as a *candid* and *ingenious* Writer'.[40]

Another mistaken supposition was that Priestley confronted 'a bigotted High-Church Man, and of a persecuting Spirit in Matters of religious Differences'.[41] This arose, Blackstone claimed, from misreading his text, which sought to explain the historical reasons why penal laws against Protestant Dissenters had been enacted in the later seventeenth century, not to endorse those 'Plans of Compulsion and Intolerance'. Yet he conceded that his words were 'somewhat incorrect and confused; and might lead a willing Critic to conclude, that a general Reflection was intended on the Spirit, the Doctrines, and the Practice of the Body of our *modern* Dissenters. A Reflection which I totally disapprove . . .'. Accordingly he undertook to amend the offending passage, so as 'to render it more expressive of that Meaning which I here avow'.[42] A series of changes made progressively to both the fourth (1770) and fifth (1773) editions deleted some derogatory phrases and added text to make it clear that no restraint should be laid upon 'rational and dispassionate Enquiries into the Rectitude and Propriety of our national Mode of Worship'.[43]

True, 'having made this Sacrifice to the Spirit of Truth and Moderation', Blackstone continued to insist that the Toleration Act failed to repeal the various pre-existing penal laws in matters of religion, as parliament might have done had it been intended to 'abolish both the Crime and the Penalty', rather than keeping them fully in force against Roman Catholics, anti-Trinitarians, and 'Persons of no Religion at all', and only exempting

---

[39] *Reply to Dr Priestley's Remarks*, 4.   [40] Ibid., 1, 5–6.

[41] Ibid., 6.   [42] Ibid., 7–8, 9–10.

[43] Ibid., 12.

from their rigour, under specified conditions, 'serious, sober-minded Dissenters'. While this issue plainly possessed emotional, symbolic, and some legal significance, Blackstone's position seems entirely compatible with Mansfield's dictum, in a celebrated case before the House of Lords in 1767, that 'there is no usage or custom, *independent of positive law*, which makes nonconformity a crime'.[44] The remainder of the *Reply* to Priestley is largely devoted to defending the claim (made originally in the first book of *Commentaries*) that the 1707 Act of Union between England and Scotland effectively prevented any change to the established religion of either kingdom, an issue on which Blackstone's views were further queried the following year by an anonymous pamphleteer, as well as by Furneaux, and even an otherwise sympathetic notice in the *Critical Review*.[45]

Blackstone ended his pamphlet with something like a resigned rhetorical shrug:

In this Temper of the Times, I am sensible that all Apologies are idle, and all Vindications useless. Yet I thought it a Duty to myself thus publickly to declare, that my Notions, in respect to religious Indulgence, are not quite so intolerant as Dr Priestley has endeavoured to represent them; especially as some Expressions of my own (not sufficiently attended to, when the Work was revised for the Press), may have countenanced such an Opinion in a superficial or captious Reader.[46]

Despite bridling slightly at this last characterization, and reasserting his own position on most of the substantive points, Priestley's brief *Answer to Dr Blackstone's Reply*, published as a letter to the *London Evening Post*, maintained a reciprocal civility and restraint. Thanking Blackstone for his 'genteel and liberal answer', Priestley admitted that his own tract, written 'in great haste', was 'not, in all respects, such as I now wish it had been'. Carefully distinguishing his sense of personal resentment at Blackstone's 'injurious representations . . . of the principles and practices of the Dissenters in general' from his regard for Blackstone as a writer, a man of 'sense, eminence, and worth', he added a final, more than formal, compliment: his own pamphlet 'was literally the creature of a day, and, figuratively speaking, its existence cannot be of much longer duration; whereas your "Commentaries on the Laws of England" will probably last as long as the

---

[44] Ibid., 11–12; W. Prest, 'The Religion of a Lawyer? William Blackstone's Anglicanism', *Parergon*, 21 (2004), 164–8; *Mansfield Manuscripts*, ed. Oldham, ii. 867 (italics added).

[45] *Reply to Dr Priestley's Remarks*, 15–24; *Commentaries*, i. 98, iv. 51; P. Furneaux, *Letters to the Honourable Mr Justice Blackstone* (1770) in *The Palladium of Conscience* (Philadelphia, 1773), 77–86; *An Objection Drawn from the Act of Union, Against a Review of the Liturgy* (1770); *Critical Review*, 28 (1769), 292–3; see also *The London Chronicle*, 28–30 September 1769, 313–14.

[46] *Reply to Dr Priestley's Remarks*, 27–8.

laws themselves'.[47] The republican antiquary Thomas Hollis felt that there was 'rather too much submission for the honour of having been noticed, in this letter'. But the indefatigably optimistic Priestley now set himself to compile a 100-page guidebook to Dissent, for the benefit of those fellow citizens 'who may entertain the same unfavourable ideas of Dissenters' as Blackstone had initially expressed, and subsequently disavowed.[48]

Blackstone's reference to 'numerous Strictures' on the successive volumes of his *Commentaries* may seem surprising, given the book's overwhelmingly favourable initial reception. Yet we have already seen that there was criticism of specific points of detail, some directly solicited by the author, 'whose commentaries were inspected in manuscript by most of the judges then on the bench', according to William 'Oriental' Jones, an Oxford student in the 1760s and subsequently as a practising barrister in London.[49] Blackstone's readiness to amend the text of successive editions as and when errors became apparent obviously made the *Commentaries* more useful to most readers. But such changes, especially on controversial topics, could also lead to charges of inconsistency, and worse. One leading example concerns the Evangelical anti-slavery activist Granville Sharp, who in the autumn of 1768 received 'a polite and affable reception'[50] when he and his brother called on Blackstone at his Lincoln's Inn Fields house. Sharp had already engaged Blackstone as one of his legal team defending a suit initiated by two West Indians over Jonathan Strong, originally brought to England as a slave, but saved by Sharp's intervention from being shipped back into bondage. Sharp also evidently secured Blackstone's agreement to review successive drafts of his treatise against slavery, which would be published in 1769. He had reason to think that Blackstone was sympathetic to his views. For in the first chapter of the first book of the *Commentaries*, dealing with 'The Absolute Rights of Persons', Blackstone wrote (following a judgment of Chief Justice Holt in 1706) that 'this spirit of liberty is so deeply implanted in our constitution . . . that a slave or a negro, the moment he lands in England, falls under the protection of the laws, and with regard to all natural rights

[47] J. Priestley, *An Answer to Dr Blackstone's Reply* (1769), in *Works*, ed. Rutt, xxii. 328–34.

[48] Ibid., i. 73n; Hollis referred to Blackstone as Priestley's 'jaco–proud adversary'. J. Priestley, *A View of the Principles and Conduct of the Protestant Dissenters, with Respect to the Civil and Ecclesiastical Constitution of England* (1769).

[49] Above, pp. 219–220; *Letters of Sir William Jones*, ed. Cannon, ii.609; D. Ibbetson, 'Sir William Jones as Comparative Lawyer', in *Sir William Jones 1746–94*, ed. A. Murray (Oxford, 1998), 19–20; *Letters*, iii–112.

[50] Gloucestershire RO, D3549 13/1/B25: Sharp to Blackstone, 4 October 1768 (copy, misdated 1765).

becomes *eo instanti* [from that instant] a freeman'.[51] However, the second (1766) edition of Book I changed the sentence following the word
'laws' by this addition: 'and so far becomes a freeman; though the master's
right to his service may probably still continue'. The same qualification
appears in the third (1768) edition, although from the fourth edition of
1770 onwards the word 'probably' is replaced by 'possibly'.[52]

By Sharp's own account, written some time after the event, immediately on learning of the first change to Blackstone's text, he 'sent his
Attorney to retain Dr Blackstone as one of his Counsel'.[53] Was this to
prevent Blackstone being fee'd by the West Indian slave-owners, or rather
in the hope of bolstering his original stance—'the learned Author having
been induced (as it is said) by the sentiments of the Chief Justice of King's
Bench to withdraw that opinion'? Most likely the latter, because when sent
a copy of Sharp's rebuttal of a legal opinion of 1729 on which slave holders
in England now relied, 'the Learned Commentator had no objections to
make to this answer, but only warned him that it would be "uphill work in
the Court of K[ing's] B[ench]"'.[54] Thereafter Sharp apparently engaged in
a protracted dialogue with Blackstone on the question of whether slaves
might legally continue in subordination to their masters after they arrived
in England, even if as servants or apprentices rather than mere chattels.

The inference that the *Commentaries'* apparent shift of position in 1766
reflected Blackstone's weakness in the face of pro-slavery pressure from
Mansfield seemingly originated with Sharp's early-nineteenth-century biographer, before being elaborated by modern scholars.[55] But while Mansfield
was certainly among the judges who provided Blackstone with corrections
for his second edition of Book I, any of their judicial brethren might legitimately have pointed to a contradiction between the initial postulate of the first
chapter, that slaves were freed simply by contact with English soil, and a
subsequent passage in chapter 14 ('Of Master and Servant'). Here, having
repeated that a 'slave or negro, the instant he lands in England, becomes
a freeman', Blackstone went on to assert that any 'right which the master
may have acquired, by contract or the like, to the perpetual service of John
or Thomas, this will remain exactly in the same state as before; for this is

---

[51] *Commentaries*, i. 123.
[52] F. O. Shyllon, *Black Slaves in Britain* (1974), 59–61.
[53] Gloucestershire RO, D 3549 13/3: 'An Account of the Occasion which first compell'd G. S. to study Law, & undertake the Defence of Negro Slaves', 7 (where the change is mistakenly ascribed to the third rather than second edition).
[54] Ibid.
[55] P. Hoare, *Memoirs of Granville Sharp, Esq.* (1828), i. 59; Shyllon, *Black Slaves*, 55, 63–4, 67–8; S. Schama, *Rough Crossings* (2005), 39–40. Mansfield was certainly capable of pressuring judicial colleagues to amend their publications: see [J. Disney], *The Life of Sir Michael Foster* (1811), 32.

no more than the same state of subjection for life, which every apprentice submits to for the space of seven years, or sometimes for a longer term'.[56]

Although the original documents are now missing, later copies of five letters Blackstone and Sharp exchanged between October 1768 and May 1769 survive. Sharp wrote the first two, which refer both to his law suit, and to manuscripts of his treatise on slavery, 'which I earnestly desire you to peruse, and to inform me whether you have any objection to what I wrote Concerning your own opinion on that head'. Only one letter is dated, but both appear to have been written early in October 1768.[57] Blackstone's reply on 11 October thanked Sharp for his 'Valuable Present of Books', and sought more time to consider his text, either a fortnight longer, or until the beginning of Michaelmas term in early November. There is then a gap of more than four months until Blackstone's letter of 20 February 1769, which appears to explain and justify a previous response (now missing) to Sharp's various 'Papers'. After thanking Sharp for 'the kind Attention you have shown to me, with regard to any Citations from my Commentaries', Blackstone continues:

My Books are now *Publici Iuris* [public law], and every Gentleman has a Right to make what Citations he pleases from them; nor can I reasonably be displeased at his doing so. I only desired not to have a passage cited from my first Edition as decisive in favour of Your Doctrine (Book I, Chap. 1) which I thought had been sufficiently explained and guarded by what followed in Chap. 14: but when I found it had been misunderstood both by yourself and others, I found it necessary to explain it more fully in my subsequent Editions. You are welcome to make what use you judge necessary of these corrected Editions; and also of another passage in Vol. II page 402, where the same Doctrine is occasionally hinted at. For you will observe, that I have never peremptorily said, that the Master *hath* 'acquired any Rights to the perpetual Service of John or Thomas or that the Heathen Negro *did* owe such Service to his American Master'. I only say that '*if* he did, that obligation is not dissolved by his coming to England and turning Christian'. It did not become me to pronounce decisively, on a Matter which is *adhuc sub judice* [still before the courts], whatever the Inclination of my own Opinions may be.[58]

The final paragraph addresses 'the nature of Villenage', something 'wholly distinct from Negro slaving', yet not altogether irrelevant, when 'how

[56] Oldham, *Mansfield Manuscripts*, ii. 1233–4; *Commentaries*, i. 412–13. The second edition omits the words 'by contract or the like': *Commentaries on the Laws of England* (Oxford, 1766), i. 424.

[57] Gloucstershire RO, D 3549 13/1/B25, Sharp to Blackstone, n.d., and 4 October 1768.

[58] *Letters*, 138–9. Cf. G. Sharp, *A Representation of the Injustice and Dangerous Tendency of Tolerating Slavery in England* (1769), 137–8: 'Nevertheless, in justice to Mr Blackstone, it must be remarked, that he hath not peremptorily said, that the master hath acquired any right to the perpetual services of John or Thomas . . .'.

little a matter will serve (in the humanity of the English Law) for an Evidence of Manumission'. On the other hand, since the common law did allow villeinage, the 'only Argument that can be drawn from it against you' is that 'Servitude' as such was not 'absolutely unknown to and inconsistent therewith'.[59]

An unsympathetic modern critic has termed this letter 'ingenious' but 'lamentable and unworthy', indeed a pronouncement 'in favour of slavery'.[60] That seems a harsh judgement, given the vague and unsettled state of English law with regard to slavery at this point, and to some extent even after Mansfield's qualified emancipist judgment in the great *James Somerset* test case of 1772. When Sharp first consulted Blackstone, the case law had long been 'confused and uncertain', with precedents 'not only badly reported but contradictory'.[61] So there were good grounds for caution in attempting to expound that law, quite apart from any author's natural desire to maintain internal consistency and avoid apparent contradictions. Blackstone was always anxious to get things right, and by no means impervious to argument. If (as evidently rumoured at the time) Mansfield did play some part in persuading him to change the text of his first edition, the manuscript Sharp presented to Blackstone in May 1769 (published later that year as *A Representation of the Injustice and Dangerous Tendency of tolerating Slavery*) may well explain why the fourth edition of the *Commentaries* (1770) downgraded the hypothetical continuance of masters' rights over the services of former slaves in England from 'probable' to merely 'possibly'. By the same token, following Somerset's case, Blackstone's fifth edition added the significant qualifications 'of right' and 'by general not by local laws' to his account of the obligations owed by 'the heathen negro' to 'his American master'. So, while Blackstone's support was doubtless constrained by his consciousness of the law's complexities, his expression of good wishes to Sharp for 'Success in his humane undertaking' need not be discounted as mere hypocritical rhetoric.[62]

IV

With the political climate still rancorous and unsettled over the summer and autumn of 1769, Blackstone's prospects of judicial preferment showed no perceptible improvement. All four volumes of the *Commentaries* had

---

[59] Ibid., 139. [60] Shyllon, *Black Slaves*, 66–7.

[61] R. Paley, 'After *Somerset*: Mansfield, slavery and the law in England, 1772–1830', in *Law, Crime and English Society*, ed. N. Landau (Cambridge, 2002), 168.

[62] *Letters*, 140.

now appeared in print to general applause, and having reached his late forties, their author could hardly be dismissed as too young or inexperienced for the bench. But although apparently on good terms with both chief justices and Chief Baron Parker,[63] he had lacked a powerful aristocratic patron since his break with Shelburne. Nor is there any reason to think that he was better known to, or regarded by, Lord Chancellor Camden than had been the case three years before. The bleakness of his prospects was captured earlier in the year, when an unfounded rumour of the duke of Grafton's imminent replacement as prime minister envisaged Blackstone as gaining the most minimal promotion, from Queen's solicitor general to Queen's attorney general.[64] However, the final breakdown of Grafton's tottering administration in January 1770 radically transformed the political landscape, and with it Blackstone's personal fortunes, especially after Camden vacated the key post of lord chancellor on 17 January 1770. Ten days later Grafton himself at last resigned, and the King immediately appointed Lord North as first minister in his place.

Despite enjoying the considerable practical advantage of leading his administration from the lower house, unlike his three immediate predecessors, North faced a parliamentary opposition more or less united on the Middlesex election issue, and backed out-of-doors by a strident national media and petitioning campaign. Several motions designed to negate the legitimacy of Wilkes's expulsion, by declaring that only an act of parliament, as distinct from a resolution of the House of Commons, could incapacitate any person otherwise eligible to stand for election as MP, were narrowly defeated or evaded by procedural manoeuvre. The most crucial of these, on 31 January, saw Blackstone take a characteristically individual if not idiosyncratic stand, asserting that the house was 'competent in the case of elections', but declaring his intention to abstain on the substantive issue, in so far as it involved the question of whether expelled members were thereby incapacitated from re-election. This was his last recorded speech as a Member of Parliament.[65]

Meanwhile Camden had been swiftly followed into opposition by his friend and Shelburne's protégé, Solicitor General John Dunning. So the sudden death on 20 January of Charles Yorke, after holding the chancellorship for just three days, left several politically sensitive legal posts vacant, in the face of 'a great want of able Men in the Law', and

---

[63] Writing to Alexander Popham in May 1767, Blackstone mentioned having 'dined today in Company with the three Chiefs, and some others of the Judges': *Letters*, 125. See also ibid., 112–113, 115.

[64] *Gazetteer and New Daily Advertiser*, 10 March 1769.

[65] Cobbett, *History of Parliament*, xvi. 802–3; Thomas, *Wilkes*, 104–6.

opposition taunts to the effect that a shortage of willing candidates meant North might have to take the seals himself.[66] He had previously complained of Dunning's lack of vocal support for the ministry in parliament, especially in relation to Wilkes's expulsion. Yet according to Clitherow, it was precisely at this point that the 'Offer of the Solicitor-Generalship, on the resignation of Mr Dunning . . . opened the most flattering Prospects' to Blackstone, who nevertheless refused the post, unwilling to burden himself with 'attendance on its complicated Duties at the Bar, and in the House of Commons'.[67] Clitherow's account is not supported by other sources; but nor was it queried by Blackstone's contemporaries, and North may have thought more highly than most of Blackstone's parliamentary abilities.[68] Following his refusal, the position continued unfilled for two months, before the appointment of Edward Thurlow, a future lord chancellor.

If Blackstone lacked the inclination as well as the fitness—both physical and psychological—to pursue the glittering prizes which a Crown law officer might reasonably anticipate, the alternative possibility of a puisne judgeship remained very attractive. In the first week of February the oldest of the sitting puisnes, Sir Edward Clive, was reported in the press as having 'on account of his age and infirmities, declared his intention of shortly resigning' from the court of Common Pleas; Clive was then in his mid-60s, but would survive only 15 months more.[69] A few days later, on Friday 9 February, 'William Blackstone esquire, King's Counsel and Solicitor-General to the Queen, kissed His Majesty's hand on being appointed one of the judges of the court of Common Pleas, in the room of Sir Edward Clive', who was to retire with a pension of £1,200.[70] On Monday, Blackstone was created a serjeant at law preparatory to being made judge; further press reports now had it that he was to replace Sir Joseph Yates in King's Bench, on the latter's transfer to Common Pleas.[71] So Blackstone, as he himself records, once again kissed hands on 16 February, and was 'appointed Judge of the Court of King's Bench, and received the honour of knighthood. And the same night, Mr Justice Yates resigned his office of Judge of the King's Bench, and he and myself were both sworn into our

---

[66] 'Diary of Thomas Fry', 51, quoting William Markham, dean of Christ Church; Cobbett, *History of Parliament*, xvi.806 (speech of Isaac Barré).

[67] Clitherow, xix.

[68] See above, pp. 225, 226, 239.

[69] *London Evening Post*, 3–5 February 1770: this news was printed as a 'Postscript', after an item recording Clive's appointment to ride the home assize circuit next Lent vacation. Sainty, *Judges*, 81.

[70] *London Evening Post*, 8–10 February 1770.

[71] *Middlesex Chronicle*, 8–10 February, 1770; *General Evening Post*, 10–13 February 1770.

respective offices before Lords Commissioners Smythe and Aston, at the former's house in Bloomsbury Square.'[72]

What underlay the formalities of this round of judicial musical chairs? There can be no doubt as to the unsettled state of the legal establishment at the beginning of Lord North's administration, with the office of lord chancellor placed in commission, after Sir Sidney Smythe (one of the two commissioners who swore in Blackstone) had declined taking the seals himself on grounds of age. Both Lord Mansfield and Sir Fletcher Norton were wrongly tipped as Camden's successor.[73] The King himself took a close interest in the matter, calling for and receiving reports from North on 29 and 30 January about his conversations with the two chief justices, Mansfield and Wilmot. These talks doubtless centred on the vacant chancellorship, but must have ranged more widely, given the interdependent nature of judicial appointments.[74] The barrister John Baker, who had retired to Horsham in Sussex after spending much of his life in the West Indies, heard from James Clitherow's brother a few years later that 'Judge Blackstone married Capt. Clitheroe's sister . . . the King insisted on his being Judge, contre le gré [against the will] of Lord Bute and others, who opposed it'. This is a more circumstantial version of James's assertion that 'early Knowledge of the Character, and Abilities of the Professor laid the first Foundation in his Majesty's Royal Breast, of that good Opinion and Esteem, which afterwards promoted him to the Bench'.[75] Even if calculated to impress his fellow dinner guests, Christopher Clitherow's tale was not inherently improbable, although Baker's recollection of it may have been somewhat garbled. Blackstone's role in both academic and parliamentary politics doubtless aroused Bute's enmity, but George III's break with his former tutor early in 1766 would have made the latter's views irrelevant after that date. Still, it is not hard to believe that others besides the much-maligned Bute had sought to keep Blackstone back—including Camden, and quite possibly Shelburne. In terms of George III's personal influence, it is notable that the judicial vacancy Blackstone filled was created by a resignation, rather than death in office. Whereas the lack of any regular superannuation arrangements kept most Georgian judges hanging

[72] *Reports*, ii. 681.

[73] *London Evening Post*, 10–13 February 1770; Blackstone, *Reports*, ii. 681. Smythe (b. 1705) was one year younger than Clive (b. 1704).

[74] Fuller reports to the king on the next judicial vacancy, in June 1770, reveal Mansfield providing detailed advice on preferred candidates, to which George responded by indicating his own preferences: *Correspondence of George III*, ed. Fortescue, ii. 126–7, 151–2.

[75] *Correspondence of George III*, ed. Fortescue, ii.126–7; *The Diary of John Baker*, ed. P. C. Yorke (1931), 320; Clitherow, xiii.

on until they themselves dropped, Sir Edward Clive was among the few favoured with a royal pension, quite possibly as an inducement to step aside in Blackstone's favour.[76]

Whether or not the King did actively encourage, or indeed demand, Blackstone's appointment, his promotion was inevitably condemned by opposition partisans. Horace Walpole, recounting the 'chief events' which followed 'Lord North's entrance into power', lists Blackstone's appointment among a series of changes in officeholders whereby 'the court found all their facilities of governing by corruption and influence return'.[77] With attacks on Blackstone's integrity still current nearly a year after the debates on Wilkes's expulsion, a new angle was provided by claims that North had engineered the resignation of Clive, an honest judge '(whose abilities may, perhaps, be somewhat impaired by age and infirmity)', so as to replace him with a 'c[our]t T[oo]l', who having 'so long, under cover, prostitut[ed] his abilities at the head of that wretched and abandoned herd of pamphleteers, hopes now to serve your l[ordshi]p in a more ample, and, at the same time c[orrupt] manner'.[78] However, North had mistaken Blackstone's character, for he 'never was actuated but by the most s[or]d[i]d avarice'; so far from having his ambitions gratified by becoming a judge, 'his expectations are at an end', and he 'the most ungrateful of men' might well turn against his patron. Thus 'Casca' in the *Public Advertiser* on the last day of February 1770.

This attack was promptly denounced in the paper's next issue as 'an ill-told fiction'; since 'the resignation was, as it ought and must have been, voluntary . . . Dr B[lackston]e deserved the place for his great and acknowledged merit; and that was his l[ordshi]p's sole motive for listening to his solicitation'.[79] This seems to be the only hint that Blackstone had actively sought judicial office in January 1770; what other candidates there may have been, if any, and precisely why Blackstone was at last successful remains a mystery, although broadly political considerations must certainly have played some part. Asserting that 'the railings of the opposition party . . . are become the mockery and scorn even of the mob', another correspondent fully agreed on Blackstone's unquestionable judicial abilities, while noting that Camden had also been 'charged with versatility in politics'. Casca responded nearly a fortnight later with the claim that 'at a

---

[76] Sainty, *Judges*, 58, n. 10; early reports of Clive's impending retirement spoke of his having 'a pension settled on him for life': *London Evening Post*, 3–5 February 1770; *Middlesex Journal*, 8–10 February 1770.

[77] Walpole, *Memoirs of George III*, iv. 147.

[78] *Public Advertiser*, 28 February 1770.

[79] Ibid., 2 March 1770.

Time when the public Suspicion is so justly roused and alarmed by such flagrant Invasions of the most delicate parts of the Constitution', it was absurd to suppose that 'simple Negation will be sufficient to invalidate a Truth, of which the Public have already been convinced'.[80] No doubt this was correct, at least so far as some sections of the public were concerned. As Dr Johnson's friend Mrs Thrale recalled, 'Party Matters run very high ... in the beginning of the Year 1770'.[81]

[80] Ibid., 13 March 1770.
[81] *Thraliana The Diary of Mrs. Hester Lynch Thrale . . . Volume I 1776–1784*, ed. K. C. Balderston (Oxford, 1942), 193.

CHAPTER 12

'At the Point He Always Wished For'
(1770–80)

THE medieval ceremonies traditionally associated with calls to the degree of serjeant at law had been largely abandoned by the time Blackstone went through the formalities prior to becoming a justice of King's Bench. But newly-called serjeants still distributed gold finger rings inscribed with a Latin motto or 'posy' to a long list of notables, legal dignitaries and office holders, professional associates, family, and friends. For his motto Blackstone chose a phrase derived from the poet Horace: 'Secundis dubiisque rectus', which may be roughly translated as 'whatever the circumstances, he is upright'.[1]

I

Although this was by no means his first public avowal of personal integrity, the recent charges of self-serving duplicity levelled against him in and out of parliament had been preceded by similar complaints during his Oxford days. Such allegations could easily be dismissed as the product of personal or political animus. But they evidently still rankled enough for Blackstone to signal, even before he took his oath of office, the intention to be what his brother-in-law memorialist would later characterize as 'an able, upright, impartial Judge; perfectly acquainted with the Laws of his Country . . .'.[2] Blackstone was initially intended to replace Sir Edward Clive on the court of Common Pleas, but following Chief Justice Wilmot's advice he evidently 'relinquished His Majesty's Nomination' in favour of Justice Yates,

---

[1] J. H. Baker, *The Order of Serjeants at Law* (1984), 105–6, 482.
[2] Clitherow, xxiv.

who wished to move from Mansfield's busy King's Bench to the relatively quieter Common Pleas. According to Blackstone, he made this decision 'only on account of poor Yates's representation of his infirm State of Health'. But there were suggestions at the time of 'some differences' between 'a chief and a puisne judge, in a certain court, which has made the latter's seat there uneasy to him'. Opposition and radical belief that Mansfield sought to replace the strict formality of English law with the discretionary justice administered in his native Scotland on behalf of an authoritarian government fuelled accusations that Yates left King's Bench because he could no longer stomach such activities, while Blackstone 'possessed of much less patience, and alike unable to continue in King's Bench' took the same course immediately after Yates's death.[3] The nature of Blackstone's relations with Mansfield is difficult to determine. Nearly 60 years later the aged Jeremy Bentham recollected a 'heartburning' between the two, claiming that his own *bête-noire* Blackstone found life as Mansfield's puisne like 'sitting in hot water'. Yet several months after Blackstone joined Mansfield's court they were described as two members of 'an inseparable triumvirate', who with Sir Fletcher Norton, the recently-elected speaker of the House of Commons, 'draw together on every occasion'.[4] This could be little more than politically-inspired speculation, especially after Norton's parliamentary defence of Blackstone against Grenville's attack in the previous year's debate on the expulsion of Wilkes.[5] Blackstone's relations with Mansfield may have cooled subsequently. But during the four months before Yates's premature death enabled Blackstone to take up his original preference for the less demanding venue of Common Pleas there is no sign of tension between the two, notwithstanding Blackstone's judgment in a case involving the Birmingham Canal company which joined him and Justice Willes in qualified dissent from Mansfield and the other puisne, Justice Aston. But then the court's internal dynamics would usually remain hidden, except to its members.[6]

A choice of Common Pleas over King's Bench was to some extent explicable in terms of judicial workload, since puisne judges in the three

---

[3] *Letters*, 142–3; *Independent Chronicle*, 14 February 1770; R. Morris, *A Letter to Sir Richard Aston* (1770), 56; Lemmings, *Professors*, 285–6; Oldham, *Mansfield Manuscripts*, i. 51–2; C. H. Fifoot, *Lord Mansfield* (Oxford, 1936), 171–5.

[4] Bentham, *Works* ed. Bowring, i. 248; *London Evening Post*, 7 April 1770. When Blackstone was created serjeant, Fletcher Norton was named as his 'patron' in the Common Pleas remembrance roll, together with the earl of Abingdon: Baker, *Serjeants*, 458.

[5] Cavendish, *Debates*, 431–2. The law reporter James Burrow commented that Blackstone's move to Common Pleas 'he was always understood to have had in View, whenever Opportunity should offer': *Reports of Cases adjuged in the Court of King's Bench* (1790), v. 2638.

[6] *Reports*, ii. 708–9.

Westminster courts all received the same base salary. Different volumes of business passing through each jurisdiction did however affect the amount received from fees, which might comprise a significant proportion (even a third or more) of a puisne's total income.[7] Against that financial consideration, Blackstone was on good terms with the scholarly John Eardley Wilmot, Chief Justice of Common Pleas, whose son's successful 1769 bid for an All Souls' fellowship he had assisted; he was also presumably the 'person much more able than myself in the guidance of a Law Education' whose views on that subject were outlined in a parental letter the year before.[8] So Wilmot senior's decision to retire from the bench in January 1771 possibly came as an unwelcome surprise, especially given that his successor was the ambitious Norfolk lawyer William de Grey, who had acted for the Whig 'New Interest' following the disputed Oxfordshire election of 1754.[9] However, having more recently preceded Blackstone in the office of solicitor general to Queen Charlotte, before serving successive administrations as solicitor and then attorney general, de Grey appears by now to have become a more or less apolitical legal functionary. There is no indication that he and Blackstone found it difficult to endorse each other's judgments, or to travel together on assize circuits, while in any case illness—mainly attacks of gout—often kept de Grey away from court.[10] Indeed many of the Common Pleas decisions recorded in Blackstone's posthumously-published law reports were the work of three and sometimes even only two puisne judges, 'absente de Grey CJ', who appears to have missed at least one hearing in nearly half of the 39 law terms between his appointment and Michaelmas 1779, when Blackstone's reports cease. Blackstone by contrast, although 'indisposed' for part of Michaelmas term 1771, participated in the court's work every succeeding term until Hilary 1778, when he was again absent for the hearing of several cases, with further bouts of illness in the following Easter and Trinity terms. So his own case notes—although far from complete, the most comprehensive record of proceedings in Common Pleas while he sat in that court—suggest that the 'many Interruptions by Illness' which according to Clitherow characterized the last ten years of Blackstone's life,

[7] Duman, *Judicial Bench*, 112–15.

[8] *Letters*, 45, 112–13, 115; Beinecke Library, O.S. c 43, Sir John Eardley Wilmot to John Eardley Wilmot, 20 April 1768, 26 June, 15 November 1769.

[9] Lemmings, *Professors*, 162, 199–200, 353; *Fifty Queries concerning the present Oxfordshire Contest* (Oxford, 1754), 23.

[10] Blackstone and de Grey took the Norfolk circuit together in the summer of 1776 (although de Grey did not attend, due to gout) and 1778, and had agreed to go on again in Lent 1780: *St James Chronicle*, 13 June 1776, 25 June 1778, 27 January 1780; Blackstone never shared a circuit with Mansfield: *Mansfield Manuscripts*, ii. 1493–1500.

had surprisingly little impact on this aspect of his judicial persona.[11] He also undertook a full share of duties at least twice a year at the Old Bailey criminal sessions for the city of London and Middlesex, and went out on circuit as an assize judge in the Lent and August vacations, something he seems to have done rarely, if at all, as a barrister. While taking all six circuits at one time or another during this decade, in the last four years of his life Blackstone was mainly commissioned on the Home and Norfolk, the two shortest circuits in travelling although not sitting time, given the crowded gaol calendars of London and its environs. Since the judges met to choose their own circuits by mutual agreement twice a year, this was presumably a matter of preference, doubtless reflecting Blackstone's deteriorating health and consequent reluctance to travel long distances; on 1 March 1777 a newspaper reported that he had not 'sufficiently recovered from his late Illness'—about which no more is known—to be in Aylesbury for the Buckinghamshire assizes, but 'proposes to set out tomorrow for Bedford, to hold the Assise for that County'.[12]

When first appointed to King's Bench, Blackstone had been the second-youngest judge in Westminster Hall (his colleague Edward Willes was some five months his junior). A year later the simultaneous retirement of Wilmot and Henry Bathurst's promotion to lord chancellor, followed immediately by the appointments of de Grey (b. 1719) as chief justice and George Nares (b. 1716) to join Henry Gould (also b. 1716) as puisne, left him no longer the most junior member of the Common Pleas quartet. But at 47 he was still the youngest, with the fewest years of practice at the bar, deficiencies for which his service as recorder of Wallingford, steward of All Souls College, and assessor of the Oxford Chancellor's court could hardly compensate. His publications demonstrated a formidably broad knowledge of English law as a system. Yet some lawyers might doubt the relevance of such an understanding to the daily work of judging, where cases so often turned on complex procedural points. Further, as late as November 1770 it was still being publicly claimed that Blackstone owed his promotion to 'espousing certain novel parliamentary tenets'.[13] While such politically-charged accusations could doubtless be shrugged off, they may

---

[11] *H of P 1754–90*, ii. 308; *Reports*, ii. 788, 790, 801, 1183–6, 1221; Clitherow, xxiii. J. Oldham, 'Underreported and Underrated: the Court of Common Pleas in the Eighteenth Century', in *Law as Culture and Culture as Law*, ed. H. Hartog and W. E. Nelson (Madison WI, 2000), 122.

[12] *The Proceedings of the Old Bailey, London, 1674–1834*: http://www.oldbaileyonline.org; TNA, C189/5–6; J. S. Cockburn, *A History of English Assizes 1558–1714* (Cambridge, 1972), 51–4; *St James's Chronicle*, 1 March 1777.

[13] Lemmings, *Professors*, 146–8; M. Lobban, *The Common Law and English Jurisprudence 1760–1850* (Oxford, 1991), 47–9; *Gazetteer and New Daily Advertiser*, 7 November 1770; the same journal had previously attacked 'W. B–l––ne, Esq' as 'The Time–Server': ibid., 26 January 1770.

have further determined Blackstone to distinguish himself sharply from the sleeping judges in the court of Common Pleas depicted by Hogarth some ten years before.

In fact, he turned out to be an exceptionally careful, conscientious, and well-respected judge. His own case notes show his judgments ranging between narrowly-framed technicalities (for example, as to whether a suit for 'criminal conversation' with the plaintiff's wife should be an action on the case, or alternatively for trespass—Blackstone notes that 'Master Burrows, at my instance, caused the roll to be searched, and found it to be an action of trespass and assault') to broad statements of public policy (for example, that discouraging foreigners from suing in the king's courts would 'ruin the national credit abroad, which is of the utmost importance to a trading country').[14] He occasionally reserved or respited judgment from assizes cases for the opinion of his colleagues, which might seem to corroborate the later story of William Scott, Lord Stowell, that 'more new trials were granted in causes which came before him on circuit, than were granted on the decisions of any other judge who sat at Westminster in his time. The reason was that being extremely diffident of his opinion, he never supported it with much warmth or pertinacity in the court above, if a new trial was moved for.'[15] But while his case notes are only a selection, they do not show Blackstone's decisions at sittings out of term being invariably reversed by motions for a new trial.[16] They do reveal him as quite capable of expounding his views on the law at length, even when in a minority, in what often read like miniature lectures, whether dealing with the writ of habeas corpus, the powers of the Exchequer, the doctrine of coverture, or the geographical limits of the East Indies.[17]

Some of his judicial brethren may have endured rather than welcomed these disquisitions; after Blackstone had spent a good six pages concurring with Justice Gould on the origins and nature of the privilege protecting officers of the court from militia obligations, Justice Nares, 'of the same opinion, declined going into the subject at large', merely pointing out that the legislature seemed to favour a money payment to personal service.[18] But civil relations were maintained, despite a 1776 land title case when the court found itself unable to agree (presumably split 2:2), on the evidential

[14] *Reports*, ii. 744 (*Melchart v Halsey*), 854 (*Batchelor v Biggs*).
[15] Ibid., 801 (*R. v Lennard*), 971–2 (*Smith v Eyles*); Prior, *Life of Malone*, 431–2.
[16] Cf. *Reports*, ii. 845 (*Howel v Handforth*); 1174–6 (*Henshaw v Pleasaunce and others*); 1299–1300 (*Aylett v Jewel*).
[17] Ibid., 745–6 (*Wood's Case*); 978–82 (*Scott v Shearman and others*); 1081–2 (*Hatchett and anr. v Baddeley*); 1287–9 (*Nicol v Verelst and others*).
[18] Ibid., 1124–31 (*Gerard's Case*).

requirements for a person claiming to be heir by descent (Blackstone, characteristically, seems to have been one of those maintaining that 'vague evidence of heirship' was insufficient). Later that term, in the absence of the chief justice, Blackstone and Gould held that a direction from Nares at a circuit trial had been mistaken, and 'Nares J. with great candour admitted the determination to be wrong'.[19] Gould, the court's longest serving judge, stated on another occasion (according to Blackstone's own notes) that his decision had been influenced by 'the reasons collected by my brother Blackstone (and which I have seen)'. Seeking to confirm details of a forgery case tried before Gould in the late 1760s, Blackstone sent him in April 1774 a deferential note of enquiry, written in the formal third person, and concluding as follows: 'Mr Blackstone hopes that he has not been too presumptuous in thus intruding a second time on Mr Justice Gould's goodness, which nothing but an anxiety to perform the task he has undertaken with as much accuracy as possible would have induced him to have done'.[20]

The nature of that task is unspecified, but it could well have been the drafting of a report on a criminal case tried before him during the Midland assize circuit in the recent Lent vacation. Such documents occasionally involved questions of law, as in the case of John Paty, 'a lad of eighteen years old' convicted of killing a mare and colt at Abingdon in September 1770. The Black Act of 1723 had made it a capital offence unlawfully to 'kill, wound or maim any cattle'; whether horses were cattle for this purpose was the question referred by Blackstone to all the judges assembled at Serjeants' Inn on the first day of the following Michaelmas term. They held that, since a seventeenth-century statute had made killing horses at night a felony, the Black Act merely extended that provision. So at the Berkshire assizes in Reading the following March young Paty was solemnly sentenced to death by Justice Ashurst—but then immediately reprieved for transportation to America. A petition from various JPs, clergymen, 'and many of the principal inhabitants' of Enborne, Berkshire, was subsequently presented on Paty's behalf. The secretary of state's office followed standard practice by referring this document to Blackstone as trial judge, to consider and report whether a free pardon was justified; evidently he did so recommend and Paty walked free, although his own notes of the case merely state that Paty was pardoned 'upon strong applications from the country'. (Blackstone's reservations about the ambit of the Black Act, voiced in a 1776 assize jury charge, were subsequently

---

[19] Ibid., 1099–1101 (*Roe on the demise of Thorne v Lord and others*); 1105 (*Smedley v Hill*).

[20] Ibid., 1089 (*Martin v Kersterton*); *The Polyanthea* (1805), ii.195 (my thanks to Emily Kadens for this reference).

given wide publicity when the remarks of 'this wise and upright Judge' appeared in the London press).[21]

Rather than addressing legal issues, most judicial reports on criminal trials were similar responses to petitions for clemency from and on behalf of convicted prisoners. Studies of the complex pardoning process have highlighted the crucial role of the judge's report after sentence in determining the eventual fate of those found guilty of felonies in eighteenth-century England.[22] Unfortunately the surviving documentation will not support a systematic study of Blackstone's responses to such petitions, nor enable us to compare his record for harshness or leniency with those of his judicial colleagues. His support in the fourth volume of the *Commentaries* for the principle of non-retributive but certain punishment proportional to the severity of the crime, as advocated by Cesare Beccaria's celebrated and recently translated treatise *On Crimes and Punishments*, suggests that he would have been predisposed to adopt a less severe approach towards crime and criminals than at least some of his judicial colleagues, perhaps most notably Mansfield.[23] It is true that on occasion he was prepared to let the full rigour of the law take its grim course, especially with those who appeared to be hardened recidivists lacking remorse or any prospect of rehabilitation. Thus on 28 August 1771 he told Thomas Walker, who had been enquiring about the fate of one John Morris, whom Blackstone had sentenced to death at the previous Wiltshire assizes for returning from transportation, that Morris (who was also charged with a fresh armed robbery) 'appeared on his Trial to be a bold artful Man . . . I saw nothing in him that made him an Object of Mercy'. These were the exact words used in his report on Morris, directed to the King via Lord Suffolk in the secretary of state's office some four weeks earlier; they must have sealed Morris's fate, since despite a blizzard of 'Letters and Expresses from Persons of Figure to whom he has got himself recommended', he was hanged at Salisbury a few days later.[24] An equally unforgiving attitude was shown to a renegade who 'positively unswore all he had sworn in Bow-Street' on being brought down from London to testify as a crown witness against his former companions in crime at the Maidstone Lent assizes in 1779:

Judge Blackstone for a considerable Time very solemnly reminded him of what he was about, but in vain; for he stuck to his last swearing, because he could not

[21] *Reports*, ii. 721–2 (*R. v Paty*); TNA, SP44/91/63 (3 May 1771). *Morning Chronicle and London Advertiser*, 14 March 1777.

[22] R. Ekirch, *Bound for America: the Transportation of British Convicts to the Colonies, 1718–1775* (Oxford, 1987), 33–45; P. King, *Crime, Justice and Discretion in England 1740–1820* (Oxford, 2000), ch. 9.

[23] Ibid., 224; D. Lieberman, *The Province of Legislation Determined* (Cambridge, 1989), 205–8.

[24] *Letters*, 146–7; TNA, SP37/8/132.

have the Reward, when his Lordship having read Waterman's Information, and seeing his present manifest and glaring Perjury, ordered him to the Bar, and the Witnesses to go immediately to the Clerk of the Peace, to have a Bill drawn against him.

In short order the unfortunate Waterman was indicted, tried, convicted, and sentenced to death with his fellow gang members: in passing sentence 'Justice Blackstone very pointedly remarked on his atrocious Conduct, and told him to prepare for Death, for he could not hope to receive Mercy'. At a subsequent trial for an attempted rape, Blackstone was reported as having 'summed up the evidence with great Accuracy, laying very heavy stress on the positive evidence of the Prosecuterix, though only a Child of about eleven years of Age'.[25]

Notwithstanding these instances of apparent judicial severity, most of the few cases where the outcome of Blackstone's report on a petition for clemency is known reveal a relatively compassionate approach. Lee Elkington, sentenced to transportation at the Oxford assizes in 1771, was pardoned on condition he joined the royal navy. Christopher Pearce, convicted at Salisbury in 1775 for 'cutting and stealing a Piece of Woollen Cloth' and sentenced to death accordingly, was first reprieved and then pardoned, on condition that he spend two years from the date of his conviction imprisoned in the gaol at Fisherton-Anger. This outcome resulted directly from Blackstone's statement of the case to George III, who was not only said to have approved 'very highly' of Blackstone's 'wise and judicious distinction . . . with respect to the Mercy for which you recommend this Convict', but also granted his pardon 'on the Conditions and in the Manner you have suggested'. A Devon forger, John Dormer, capitally convicted at Exeter on the same circuit, was also seemingly reprieved following Blackstone's favourable report, although the terms on which his sentence was commuted are unclear.

After the outbreak of hostilities with the American colonists put an end to transportation across the Atlantic, John Oram, sentenced at Cambridge in 1776 to transportation for horse-stealing, was recommended by Blackstone for mercy on condition of being sent to the house of correction 'to be kept at hard Labour for the Term of Three Years'. In 1777 the 20-year old servant Sarah Sunderland similarly received a five-year sentence in the Southwark house of correction after conviction before Blackstone for robbing her master and mistress; her sentence was possibly shortened following a later petition from an uncle on her behalf. Blackstone had been thinking about alternatives to American transportation for some time.

[25] *St James's Chronicle*, 15, 19 March 1779.

Two months after becoming a judge he prepared a draft amendment to the relevant statute, which would have clarified the reach of its provisions (following concerns foreshadowed in the fourth book of *Commentaries*) and enabled convicts to be transported to British possessions anywhere in the world. Despite possible scrutiny by a House of Commons select committee these clauses were not enacted; but direct experience of the increasingly inadequate sentencing options available to judges undoubtedly helped maintain Blackstone's active interest in the subject, and would eventually produce the major legislative initiative of his life.[26]

Civil as well as criminal cases were tried at assizes. They also required reports, provided by the presiding judge to the court from which the case had been sent for jury trial in the country by writ of *nisi prius*, if that judge sat in another Westminster jurisdiction. Five manuscript reports from Blackstone about King's Bench civil cases tried before him on the Home and Norfolk circuits in 1779 survive among the papers of Francis Buller, then recently appointed as a puisne judge in King's Bench. Since Blackstone would not be present when these cases came on in King's Bench, it was necessary to give reasonably full details of the evidence put to the jury, their verdict, and any question of law reserved for further consultation. His reports could be lengthy and elaborate, recounting his own investigations among relevant sources; for example, in a case concerning fees charged by customs officers, the printed *Journals* of the House of Commons and Malachy Postlethwayt's *Dictionary of Trade and Commerce*. A complex action over the disputed election of a canon of Chichester cathedral took up 11 pages, summarizing the evidence and arguments on either side, including precedents and by-laws reaching back to the sixteenth century, followed by his own directions to the jury. He did not complete this report until two weeks after the trial itself had finished.[27] He also furnished a written minority judgment to the House of Lords upholding the common law right of authors in the great 1774 copyright case of *Donaldson v Becket*, which (being sick at home with gout) was read on his behalf by Justice Ashurst. More informally, Lord Chancellor Apsley sought his advice on an application to suppress publication of a bookseller's abridgement of James Hawkesworth's semi-official three-volume *Account of the Voyages* of Captain Cook and others in the

[26] TNA, SP44/91 (Criminal correspondence and warrants), pp. 31, 371, 386, 391–2; SP44/93, pp. 120, 166; SP 44/94, 101; *Letters*, 141–2; East Sussex RO, SAS/RF 18/122–4; see further below, Chapter 13, pp. 296–301.

[27] LI, Dampier MSS, Buller Paper Books 51a (*Miller v Harwood*), 52 (*Doe on dem. Matthews v Jackson*), 81a (*Butcher v Easto*); J. Oldham, 'Eighteenth–Century Judges' Notes: How They Explain, Correct and Enhance the Reports', *AJLH*, xxxi (1987), 29–31, 35–6.

South Pacific; after spending 'some hours together', they agreed that such an abridgement was 'not an act of plagiarism . . . but an allowable and meritorious work'.[28]

Criminal trials generated more popular interest than civil suits, not least because the latter often involved complex questions of legal construction and interpretation. But at least one case fitting that description which did attract attention outside the legal profession, and in which Blackstone played a significant role, was what the *Annual Register* for 1772 termed 'the great cause of Perrin and Blake'. Besides the high material stakes, including a West Indian plantation reputedly worth £1,000 a year, *Perrin v Blake* pitted rationalist zeal against legal traditionalism, and Lord Mansfield against Sir William Blackstone. In Michaelmas term 1769 the court of King's Bench split 3:1 in a decision upholding a testator's clear intention to ensure that his estate remained in his family, rather than following an established rule of law dating back two centuries (the Rule in *Shelley's Case*) which the form of words actually used in the will had activated, thereby giving his immediate heir the right to sell the property. Justice Yates, the sole dissentient—Mansfield was not accustomed to minority judgments in his own court—maintained that privileging the presumed intention of a will over the legal sense of its words was to 'confound legal property by making titles obscure'. The case was then appealed by writ of error to the other eight judges sitting in Exchequer Chamber, who in February 1772 eventually reversed Mansfield and his colleagues by a margin of 6:2. Blackstone's lengthy judgment, which would be published after his death in the first volume of legal manuscripts edited by the scholarly Francis Hargrave, reiterated the dangers of departing from or disrupting 'those criteria which the wisdom of the law has established for the certainty and quiet of property'. He carried the bulk of professional and lay opinion with him on this crucial point of principle, which rejected judicial discretion where the law was already certain, however unsatisfactory the outcome might be in individual cases. It would not be surprising if Mansfield had allowed resentment of the major rebuff he and his court received in *Perrin v Blake* to affect his attitude towards Blackstone.[29]

Another civil case on which Blackstone and Mansfield differed arose from the political conflicts over the Middlesex election. John Horne,

[28] Rose, *Authors and Owners*, 155; *General Evening Post*, 19 February 1774; C. Lofft, *Reports of Cases Adjudged in the Court of King's Bench* (1776), 775 (*Curia Cancellaria, re Newbery*).

[29] *Annual Register 1772* (1773), 69–70; C. H. Fifoot, *Lord Mansfield* (Oxford, 1936), 171–6; W. Blackstone, 'An Argument in the Exchequer Chamber on giving judgment in the Case of Perrin and another against Blake', in *A Collection of Tracts Relative to the Law of England, from Manuscripts*, ed. F. Hargrave (1787), 513–78.

the radical clergyman of Brentford, founder of the Society of Supporters of the Bill of Rights, whom Blackstone must at least have known of via the Clitherow family, published several attacks on the ministerial office holder George Onslow, MP for Surrey. Onslow accordingly sued Horne for libel. The suit came for trial at Kingston-upon-Thames on 6 April 1770, towards the end of Blackstone's first assize circuit. It aroused sufficient public interest to attract the shorthand writer and bookseller Joseph Gurney, who produced semi-official reports of Old Bailey trials, and whose transcript 'Taken in Short-hand (by Permission of the Judge)' was subsequently published as a 48-page pamphlet. This verbatim account shows Blackstone (as the personified 'Court') accepting, after some discussion between Serjeants Leigh and Glynn, the latter's claim that any literal variation between Horne's published letter, and the version of that letter in the plaintiff's declaration, was sufficient to overthrow the latter's case:

Court. I own it is very nice, and should be glad if you could draw me a line, to get rid of so minute a nicety; but I take the law to be so settled.

Mr. Serjeant Leigh. The true line is, where there is an alteration of sense.

Court. I am afraid this will not do. That would let in a hundred altercations, whether the sense is or is not altered, and leave too much to the discretion of the judge . . . If you can draw me any rational line, at which I can stop, consistently with the rules of law, I would not consent to non-suit a plaintiff, in a cause of such expence and expectation, upon such an immaterial variation as this. It is as immaterial as possible, for the sense is not altered in the least. If I am wrong in it, can you put me in any method to set me right?

This Leigh could not do, but Blackstone gave his 'full consent' to a foreshadowed motion for a new trial, 'upon the ground of my being mistaken in point of law'.[30]

Onslow persisted with his suit, and a new trial duly granted by King's Bench was put down for the next assizes, this time in the safer hands of Lord Mansfield, with Horne facing additional counts of 'malicious and scandalous words spoken' at a meeting of Surrey freeholders the previous summer. Mansfield now made short work of Glynn's reference to Blackstone's opinion at the previous trial, asserting that 'with respect to the consequence of literal errors and omissions . . . the learned judge, who tried the former cause, hath since had his doubts'.[31] Having 'strongly

---

[30] *The Whole Proceedings in the Cause of the Action Brought by The Rt. Hon. Geo. Onslow Esq. Against the Rev. Mr Horne* (1770), 43–8; A. Stephens, *Memoirs of John Horne Tooke* (1813), i. 137–9.

[31] *The Genuine Trial Between the Rt. Hon. Geo. Onslow, Esq.; and the Reverend Mr John Horne . . . Before the Right Honourable Lord Mansfield* (1770), 26, 29.

urged the great impropriety, scandal &c of the various accusations' in his charge to the jury, Mansfield was doubtless gratified when they proceeded to award £400 damages to Onslow, even if only on the new counts, finding for the defendant on the original charges. But Horne, himself a former law student, was 'determined to appeal to a higher tribunal', in the shape of the court of Common Pleas. Here we have Blackstone's own report of the hearing, which began in November 1770 and was adjourned to the following term, when it was argued again, following the resignation of Chief Justice Wilmot and other changes in personnel. Finally the court delivered its unanimous judgment in April 1771, that the words complained of were not actionable, 'amount[ing] only to a charge of insincerity, and that only in the opinion of the speaker'.[32]

While Mansfield found Blackstone on the bench less than wholly deferential to political imperatives or his own opinions, he seems usually to have carried all or most of his Common Pleas colleagues with him. One exception was the 1773 case of *Scott v Shepherd*, celebrated by legal scholars because of its place in the development of the modern law of negligence. This action arose from a firework thrown inside a covered marketplace, putting out a young man's eye when it eventually exploded. Three of the four judges agreed that the unfortunate Scott had a valid case in trespass against the youth Shepherd who lit and first threw the squib— but Blackstone dissented, because he thought the wrong form of action had been used. Scott's injury did not result from the direct and immediate action of Shepherd, since the firework had been caught and thrown again by two other persons before Scott was hit; and 'where the injury is immediate, an action of trespass will lie; where it is only consequential, it must be an action on the case'. Yet in the very act of firmly endorsing the conservative principle that 'we must keep up the boundaries of actions, otherwise we shall introduce the utmost confusion', Blackstone showed himself to be struggling for a modern scientific answer to a fraught conceptual problem, employing the language of Newtonian physics to characterize the agents, instruments, and forces at work to produce Shepherd's injury.[33]

While cases such as this might not excite much interest outside the legal world, Blackstone appears to have enjoyed a higher public profile than his other judicial colleagues, with the exception of Mansfield himself. 'To Justice BLACKSTONE now direct your eye, | What other Justice can with BLACKSTONE vie?' demanded the popular poet

---

[32] *Memoirs of Tooke*, i. 140–3; Oldham, *Mansfield Manuscripts*, ii. 839–40; *Reports*, ii. 750–4.
[33] *Reports*, ii. 894–8; N. Swerdlow, 'Blackstone's "Newtonian Dissent"', in *The Natural Sciences and the Social Sciences*, ed. J. B. Cohen (1994), 205–34.

William Woty. A nephew of Sir Joshua Reynolds told his sister of a visit to Westminster Hall on Monday 23 January 1775 for the first day of Hilary term, 'to see the procession of the Judges, The Lord Chancellor, Lord Mansfield, Blackstone, etc. I think all the other ten Judges were present . . .'. Six months later Samuel Curwen, in temporary exile from Massachusetts, 'turned aside into the Hall, all the Courts being then sitting', and noted at the Common Pleas 'Judge Blackstone and Sarjant Glynn, and at the King's Bench Lord Mansfield and Sargent Wedderburne'; early next year he again walked through Westminster Hall and stopped briefly at the court of Common Pleas, where he saw 'chief Justice de Grey and his associates, one of whom was the famous Dr Blackstone'. Blackstone's fame, so far as Curwen was concerned, reflected his authorship of 'the well known Commentaries on the Laws of England', a work Mansfield had earlier reportedly said he would not suffer to be cited in his court, although it was 'of much utility to the public'. This was not a self-denying ordinance, since Mansfield had himself cited the *Commentaries* on the subject of judicial amendments even before Blackstone joined him as a temporary colleague, and his general ban, if ever there was one, had certainly been relaxed by 1774, when counsel referred to Blackstone's discussion of the colonial reception of English law without attracting adverse comment.[34] But if ill-feeling did indeed develop between Blackstone and Mansfield after the former became a judge, some resentment on the latter's part of the younger man's literary achievements and public standing could well have been at work.

Published reports of Blackstone's appearances on the bench, especially in prominent cases like the Horne libel trial, further boosted his image. When Sir John Fielding and another London magistrate were summoned to the Old Bailey sessions in October 1775 following the unauthorized release of a prisoner in their custody, a newspaper report distinguished between the demeanour of the two presiding judges, noting that while 'Justice Blackstone supported the Dignity of the Court; by treating the reverend Magistrate with the most courteous reciprocal Respect . . . . Baron Eyre, upon this Occasion, did not'.[35] The year before, when the court of

[34] W. Woty, *Poems on Several Occasions* (Derby, 1780), 27; *Sir Joshua's Nephew Being Letters Written, 1769–1778, by a Young Man to his Sisters*, ed. S. M. Radcliffe (1930), 32; *The Journal of Samuel Curwen Loyalist*, ed. A. Oliver (Cambridge MA, 1972), i. 27,113. *Lloyd's Evening Post*, 18 May 1770; 98 *ER* 350 (*R v Wilkes*); ibid., 1147 (*Atcheston v Everitt*); ibid., 865 (*Cause of the Island of Granada*); see also ibid., 1393 (*Gosling v Weymouth*) and J. Burrow, *A Series of Decisions of the Court of King's Bench upon Settlement-Cases* (1768), ii. 705 (*R. v Inhabitants of Nutley*).

[35] *St James's Chronicle*, 19 October 1775. Cf. *Morning Post and Daily Advertiser*, 18 September 1773, report on trial of General Gansel.

Common Pleas was treated to the rare antique spectacle of a trial of title by original writ of right before a Grand Assize of 16 jurors, 'upon the motion of Mr Justice Blackstone, order was made by the rest of the Judges, that the galleries of the Court be open for the admission of students of the several inns of Court'. But it seemed that the door-keeper 'meant to take advantage of the public curiosity' by charging an admission fee; whereupon Blackstone recalled an occasion 'when a gentleman, a counsel, had given a quarter guinea for admittance, the Court was about to commit the officer: but he added, I believe, on his asking pardon, and desiring to restore the money, at the intercession of the gentleman, the Court did not commit him'.[36]

II

Some sources give a less attractive impression of Blackstone's judicial persona. At supper with the topographer Daniel Lysons in 1793, the bookseller Joseph Farington learnt that 'Judge Blackstone' was 'a man of unpleasant manners'. The Surrey antiquary and solicitor William Bray similarly characterized 'the learned author of the *Commentaries*' as 'sour, morose and imperious'. Bray instanced a barristers' strike at the Bristol assizes, resulting from Blackstone's attempt to start proceedings at 7 a.m., despite being warned that most leading counsel had been held up by a protracted trial at Wells, the previous circuit town. Among those involved may well have been the barrister Francis Burton, who before leaving Oxford for the circuit in March 1771 told Dr Thomas Fry of St John's College that 'Judge Blackstone had given much offence to several of the Council [sic] by his rude behaviour to them, particularly Mr Skinner, whom he had frequently interrupted in the course of his pleading, in a very uncivil manner'.[37] Bray's close involvement with the Society of Antiquaries may have predisposed him to resent Blackstone's somewhat high-handed dealings with that body, while Fry was an old friend of John Wilkes, as well as a Whig and Low-Churchman. But there seems no reason to doubt the basic truth of these anecdotes, which gain further credibility from Clitherow's admission that his brother-in-law's 'rigid Sense of Obligation, added to a certain Irritability of Temper, derived from Nature, and encreased in his latter

---

[36] 98 *ER* 766 (*Tyssen v Clarke*).

[37] Surrey History Centre, Bray Family papers, G52/8/10/1. St John's College, Oxford, Munim. LXXXVI.D.8, 'Diary of Thomas Fry', ed. Hargreaves–Mawdsley, 65, 119, 120: 'Mr Skinner' was probably John Skynner, who practised on the Oxford circuit, or possibly Matthew Skinner, son of a former recorder of Oxford: *H of P 1754–90*, iii. 443; *HUO*, 101n.

Years by a strong nervous Affection, together with his Countenance and Figure, conveyed an Idea of Sternness'.[38] William Scott, Lord Stowell (who read law at Oxford in the 1760s) more bluntly recalled Blackstone as 'extremely irritable', however adding that 'he was the only man . . . he had ever known who acknowledged and lamented his bad temper'.[39] Whatever the discomfort of barristers targeted by angry outbursts from the bench, it is striking that Blackstone himself admitted and regretted a tendency to lose control. Such lapses would hardly help maintain the good order, decorum, and dignity to which he was otherwise so attached in his judicial persona, and which would increasingly come to be seen as a distinctive characteristic of English courts of law.[40]

In the 'Character' which concludes his brief life of Blackstone, Clitherow noted that the 'natural Reserve and Diffidence' which had marked his subject since childhood could appear 'to a casual Observer, though it was only Appearance, like Pride', especially after he became a judge, since he then thought himself obliged 'to keep strictly up to Forms (which, as he was wont to observe, are now too much laid aside) and not to lessen Respect due to the Dignity and Gravity of his Office, by any outward Levity of Behaviour'.[41] Blackstone certainly showed a consistent preoccupation with the minutiae of correct judicial behaviour. His first surviving letter after resigning from parliament on 9 February 1770, prior to appointment as justice of King's Bench a week later, concerned arrangements for the succeeding 'manager or adviser' to Lord Abingdon for the borough of Westbury, since 'it will be improper for me to appear any more' in that capacity. There is nothing to suggest that Blackstone retained any professional connections with the Bertie family or other former clients after he became a judge, unlike Chief Justice de Grey, whom his patron Viscount Townshend confidently expected to provide 'friendly attention to my Affairs' more than a year after assuming judicial office.[42] In August 1774, Blackstone expressed himself 'much obliged' to Lord Suffolk, almost certainly a former Oxford pupil and by now secretary of state in Lord North's ministry, 'for his Delicacy in not sending me an Official Letter' to accompany an application for clemency arising from the intervention of Dr Richard Kaye, royal chaplain and prebendary of York, on behalf of a prisoner convicted of sheep stealing and sentenced to seven years' transportation at the recent York assizes. The character witnesses for the

---

[38] Clitherow, xxvii.   [39] Prior, *Life of Malone*, 431.

[40] P. Langford, *Englishness Identified: Manners and Character 1650–1850* (Oxford, 2000), 158.

[41] Clitherow, xxvii.

[42] *Letters*, 141; BL MS Additional 50010, fo. 169, George Townshend to William de Grey, 2 August 1772.

accused had been unimpressive, while it appeared that 'he had clipped the Ears and plucked the Wool off the Sides' in order to remove the owner's mark, before selling the sheep in question as his own. Nevertheless Blackstone had no wish to 'obstruct the Royal Favor', should Lord Suffolk wish 'to oblige our Friend Dr Kaye', since it was not a 'Case of such very great Guilt or Notoriety that any Prejudice can result to the Public from granting William Birch a free pardon'.[43]

This done, however, there came a further request, relayed like its predecessor by William Eden, another Old Etonian ex-student from Oxford, now under-secretary in Howard's department, to arrange for Birch to be bailed forthwith, rather than kept in York Gaol until the next assizes. While avowedly happy to comply with these 'humane Wishes', Blackstone went on to elaborate an extensive justification for his action, based on the royal '[d]irections to admit him to bail, for the only purpose of pleading that Pardon when it shall be drawn out in the proper Forms—a Circumstance that rarely occurs', and a recent statutory provision authorising judges to order the immediate transportation of convicts. He further recounted how a 'desire to effectuate this Business in the most beneficial Manner for the poor Fellow, has induced me to assume *pro hac Vice* [for this office] an Attorney of this Town [Wallingford] as Deputy Clerk of Assise to draw the Recognizance . . . '. But finally, with a thought to the reaction of colleagues, he added that 'this Extra-Proceeding of mine must not, cannot, be drawn into Precedent for the future: For I myself, or any other Judge, might insist on being attended by the Clerk of Assise himself or his legal Deputy; and undoubtedly should do so, were these Applications, or could they be in their Nature, frequent'.[44]

This ponderous communication doubtless reflects lingering traces of a teacher–pupil relationship, as well as anxiety to dispel any possible hint of a readiness to sacrifice legal formalities at the bidding of a minister of state. A final example of judicial fastidiousness involved issues of decorum rather than strict rules of law. In January 1778, Blackstone commissioned the law printer and bookseller William Strahan, one of the partners who had acquired the copyright of his *Commentaries*, to sell a duplicate set of Viner's *Abridgement*, '23 volumes folio, well bound and nearly as good as new', which Strahan had previously told him 'would fetch a considerable Sum, I think You mentioned thirty or forty Pounds. Now, Sir, as this is a Matter that I cannot appear in or be named in with any Propriety, I have taken the Liberty to desire the Favour of you to avail Yourself of some Opportunity (which may frequently offer in Your Way) of disposing of

---

[43] *Letters*, 147–8.   [44] Ibid., 148–9.

these Duplicates for me'.[45] Whether concerned to avoid being associated with the sale of second-hand law books in general, or the work which had funded his Oxford chair in particular, Justice Blackstone was here as elsewhere expressing scruples, not abusing judicial prerogatives. We may recall his earlier avowal to 'have no such Attachments to Furs and Coifs, as to wish for the parade of a Judgeship . . .'. Rather than flaunting the majesty and power of his office, Blackstone saw himself as acting out a more principled determination, 'to maintain', as Book I of the *Commentaries* put it, 'both the dignity and independence of the judges in the superior courts'.[46] Yet such an agenda might easily be misconstrued, both by contemporaries and those later commentators who attributed to 'excessive caution and a scrupulous adherence to formalities' Blackstone's supposed 'reputation for being a painstaking judge, and nothing more'.[47]

---

[45] Ibid., 160–1.   [46] Ibid., 94; *Commentaries*, i. 238.

[47] Macdonnell, 'Blackstone', *DNB*; H. G. Hanbury, 'Blackstone as Judge', *AJLH*, 3 (1959), 1–27, is more sympathetic, but still rates Blackstone's judicial performance as only 'most workmanlike'.

CHAPTER 13

'Useful and Agreeable' (1770–80)

ON Blackstone's promotion to the judiciary, his brother-in-law recalled, he had achieved his ambition and 'might justly be said to enjoy *Otium cum Dignitate*' (dignified ease). But if release from the pressures of life at the bar and in parliament (to which, Clitherow tells us, 'he had a still greater Aversion') came as a relief, his judicial duties were not negligible, as we have just seen. Nor was his approach to what Clitherow terms 'the private Duties of Life' leisurely or relaxed.[1] Indeed the last ten years of Blackstone's life appear to have been only slightly less busy—and, in some respects, productive—than the preceding decades.

I

As Clitherow explained it, his subject had anything but an easy-going personality:

Being himself strict in the Exercise of every public and private Duty, he expected the same Attention to both in others; and, when disappointed in his Expectation, was apt to animadvert with some Degree of Severity, on those who, in his Estimate of Duty, seemed to deserve it. This rigid Sense of Obligation, added to a certain Irritability of Temper, derived from Nature, and encreased in his latter Years by a strong nervous Affection, together with his Countenance and Figure, conveyed an Idea of Sternness. . .[2]

That last unfortunate impression was widely shared. The poet-satirist Charles Churchill had depicted 'the scowling Blackstone' even while he was still 'Keeping the forwardness of youth in awe' at Oxford.[3] Serving on a Monmouth grand jury in the summer of 1770, Philip Thicknesse thought

---

[1] Clitherow, xx.   [2] Ibid., xxvii.
[3] C. Churchill, *Poems* (1769), ii. 226.

Judge Blackstone 'an ill looking sowre fellow', who 'did all he could to hinder the girls from *kicking up their heels*', presumably at the assize ball.[4] Even John Hall, the well-practised engraver who prepared a version of Blackstone's portrait by Thomas Gainsborough for the frontispiece of the eighth edition of the *Commentaries*, produced a likeness in which 'the Contraction of the Brows, and consequent Sternness of Look' were 'a little too marked', at least according to Lady Blackstone. Clitherow nevertheless insisted on the 'Virtues of his private Character . . . a chearful, agreeable, and facetious Companion . . . a faithful Friend; an affectionate Husband and Parent; and a charitable Benefactor to the Poor . . . '.[5] Such claims are difficult to verify, especially at this distance. But if Blackstone was not a particularly sociable person—even with the Society of Antiquaries, his involvement was desultory, half-hearted, and marred by controversy—he did possess the ability to inspire life-long affection.

Besides the four 'worthy friends'—John Tracy, Benjamin Buckler, Dick Bagot, and Alexander Popham—to whom he would leave mourning rings, Blackstone maintained contact with two more All Souls' contemporaries: the country clergymen George Bingham and Richard Graves. With Bingham, according to his son, Blackstone indeed 'kept up a correspondence . . . with a sincerity and fervour unaltered and undiminished to the last hour of his life . . . '; Graves celebrated their friendship in verse which betrays some consciousness of the gulf separating their respective talents and worldly status, and also evidently exchanged at least occasional letters with the man on whom the character 'Hortensius' in his novel *Columella* (1779) may be modelled.[6] It is not clear from the surviving evidence whether Blackstone's personal intimacy and political alliance with Thomas Winchester, vice president of Magdalen College, survived his departure from Oxford. Relations between Blackstone and Newdigate, seemingly closer and much better documented, remained strong throughout the 1770s, notwithstanding the death of Sir Roger's first wife, his subsequent protracted Italian sojourn, and remarriage in 1776; besides regular contacts in London during parliamentary sittings, there were family visits to Arbury involving the older Blackstone children, while the Newdigates stayed over a long weekend at Wallingford in July 1777, just after Oxford University's Encaenia. Their friendship even appears to have survived a widening difference of opinion on the religious subscription issue. Whereas Blackstone's closest Oxford friends

---

[4] P. Gosse, *Dr Viper* (1952), 143.   [5] *Letters*, 158; Clitherow, xxvi–xxvii.
[6] Doolittle, 97–99; Bingham, *Dissertations, Essays, and Sermons*, i. xxiii; Graves, *Euphrosyne*, i. 3–6,138,139; *idem, The Triflers*, 53, 58–9. Hill, *Literary Career of Richard Graves*, 84–85n.

Buckler and Tracy led the movement to scrap the requirement for under-graduates to subscribe to the Church of England's 39 articles, and in 1779 Blackstone himself was said to have 'revised' a bill proposed by a group of bishops to relieve Dissenting ministers and schoolteachers from the same burden, Newdigate remained throughout a committed opponent of any concession to non-Anglicans. Otherwise the two shared personal traits, political attitudes, and common interests in architecture, classical letters, and improvement (turnpikes for Blackstone, canals for Newdigate). His biographer characterizes Newdigate as possessing 'a humourless, self-righteous, and occasionally ill-tempered disposition', which might almost apply to Blackstone, except that he could make a joke, and occasionally shared one with Newdigate.[7] (A sardonic example supposedly 'related by Judge Blackstone' concerns a sailor who chewed tobacco with 'great unconcern' when sentenced to death for highway robbery, and on being told by the judge, 'piqued at the man's indifference' that he would go to hell, responded 'Then, my lord, I hope I shall have the pleasure of your company there'.)[8] Friends from legal or non-academic backgrounds were notably lacking, with the possible exception of Thomas Walker, town clerk of Oxford; but their association, founded on a shared professional involve-ment with the Bertie estates, may not have survived the divergent career and social paths of the two men after Blackstone became a judge and was knighted, despite having previously included both their wives.

While far from gregarious or sociable, Blackstone was plainly devoted to his wife, whose portrait he had painted by Gainsborough as a com-panion piece to his own, and also set in gold as an enamelled miniature on the lid of his tortoise-shell snuff box.[9] Sarah Blackstone, 'my dear Sally', remained almost continually pregnant throughout her first ten years of marriage, enduring a total of nine confinements between 1762 and 1771. Four boys and three girls survived infancy, with the first- and the last-born, both boys, dying young. Details of their upbringing are sparse, although we know that at least two Blackstone sons were sent to the classicist William Gilpin's progressive preparatory school at Cheam, until an outbreak of impetigo and a consequent falling-out between

[7] Lewer, 'Sir Roger Newdigate and Sir William Blackstone: the forgotten friendship'; Newdigate Diary, 30 August–3 September 1773, 4–6 July, 30 August–2 September 1777; *Letters*, 40–41, 82; *HUO*, 172, 175–9; G. M. Ditchfield, 'The Subscription Issue in British Parliamentary Politics, 1772–79', *Parliamentary History*, 7 (1988), 61–4; Prest, 'Religion of a Lawyer?', 156–7.

[8] Anon., *The Covent Garden Jester* (n.d. [1780?]), 24–5.

[9] The two portraits are listed as lots 524–5 in the catalogue of the Price sale, *BB*, 39; LMA ACC 1360/586/4, 'Sundries Sr W B'; the miniature of his wife may also have been one of a pair with the miniature of him now at Harvard (see Plate 17).

father and headmaster, which led the latter to conclude that 'Candour did not seem to be among Sir William's virtues'. Before this incident Gilpin had however returned home 'a very good little boy, and . . . an happier one' in December 1770.[10] This may have been Henry, the eldest surviving son, who nevertheless seems to have proved a considerable disappointment to his father, since in 1778 he recommended to Dean Lewis Bagot of Christ Church not Henry, but his younger brother James, as potentially worthy of a college scholarship. Henry, aged 16 at his father's death, was sent instead to Queen's College, where he took his bachelor's degree three years later and then disappeared from view, until his appointment as controller of customs at the port of St John's, Newfoundland, in 1797. Proving an abusive drunk, wife-beater, and comprehensive troublemaker, Henry lost this undemanding post after only two years, moved on to an equally unsatisfactory if slightly longer term as sheriff of the Three Rivers district of Lower Canada, but then secured the post of coroner of Quebec, where he remained until his death in 1825.[11] If Henry may have resisted his father's high expectations at some cost to his own psychological well-being, his younger brother James chose an easier path. Aged 13, and a pupil at Charterhouse, his father thought that 'he will not be deficient in either Genius, Application, or Prudence'. James accordingly entered Christ Church in 1781, and after graduating BA won an All Souls fellowship; he took his BCL in 1787, was called to the bar at the Middle Temple in 1788, and three years later, aged 28, became Vinerian Professor, subsequently further retracing his father's footsteps as DCL and principal of New Inn Hall. Unfortunately, no substantial achievement matched this formal replication of paternal awards and offices; if only 'Dr Blackstone had been a man of more energy and exertion', sighed Cyril Jackson, Bagot's reformist successor as dean of Christ Church.[12] Dr Blackstone did however manage to outlive his three brothers, who all died without acknowledged heirs (William having emigrated to North America with Henry, and Charles following Bigg family tradition as fellow of Winchester College and rector of Worting). This left James in possession of the family house at Wallingford, now grandiloquently renamed 'Castle Priory', although only part of his father's extensive library,

---

[10] For his side of the *contretemps*, see *Memoirs of Dr. Richard Gilpin*, ed. W. Jackson (1879), 133–4; Bodl. MS Eng. misc. d 378, p. 614.

[11] *Letters*, 151, 171; Philip, 119; W. R. Rendall, 'The Blackstones in Canada', *Illinois Law Review*, 16 (1921), 255–67.

[12] *Al. Oxon.*, ii.118; *MTAdmR*, iii. 398; H. G Hanbury, *The Vinerian Chair and Legal Education* (Oxford, 1958), 79–83; Nottingham University Library, Pl C 53/24, Cyril Jackson to duke of Portland, 25 September 1801.

following a Sotheby's sale in 1803 and despite his having bequeathed all but his 'meerly professional' law books 'in the nature of heirlooms' to be catalogued and retained at Wallingford.[13]

The hopes and expectations which burden the sons of famous men may weigh less heavily on their daughters. Nothing is known of the education of the three Blackstone girls, although on 22 January 1788 William informed his brother-in-law that he 'came to Town with Lady B on Monday last' and 'we have now cantoned out all our Young People at their respective Places of Education'; that choice of words suggests that the girls as well as the boys were sent away to boarding school. At this point Philippa, the youngest daughter, was nearly ten years old. Like her two sisters she would marry a clergyman, in her case the Rev Harry Lee, a fellow of Winchester College; her elder sister Sarah married Dr Thomas Rennell, Dean of Winchester Cathedral, while Dr William Cole, a classical scholar, master at Eton, and Vicar of Shoreham, Kent was the husband of the middle daughter, Mary, who in 1795 was the last of the Blackstone girls to marry.[14] As for their uncles and aunts, William seems to have been on closer terms with his elder brother Charles, who spent most of his life as a fellow of Winchester College, than with Henry, who after practising medicine in Reading and London for more than 20 years, chose to take orders and retire to New College, and the college-controlled Oxfordshire benefice of Adderbury, where he struck trouble with parishioners over tithes and rents before his death in 1778. Henry left no legacy to either of his brothers or their families, and there is no evidence of contact between them after their undergraduate days. Charles however wrote to his 'dear Brother' William 'most affectionately' in 1757, while William paid what was doubtless a family visit to Charles in Winchester in the summer of 1766, and named him with James Clitherow as executor of his will made in October 1778. On the grounds that Charles 'begins to be advanced in years and is situated at a considerable distance from me and my affairs', a codicil next month revoked this trust, but not the provision for Charles to be joint guardian of his sons with James Clitherow, and of his daughters with their mother. Sarah's other brothers and sisters with their spouses, plus four first cousins and William's own surviving uncles and aunts (the aged Seymour Richmond, Hannah, widow of the surgeon Thomas Bigg, and Richard Bannister, the widower who had married Mary Bigg's youngest sister), were all remembered by gifts of mourning rings, although the

[13] J. Burke, *A General and Heraldic History of the Commoners of Great Britain and Ireland* (1838), iii. 544; http://www.dangelnet/American/Blackstonenamecrest.html, accessed 6 February 2008; TNA, PROB 11/1061, fos. 102v–3; *LL*.

[14] *Letters*, 158; *Wither Family*, 149.

human realities which these tokens of extended family ties once represented are now lost to us.[15]

By the time Blackstone came to make what appears to have been his first and only will, he possessed a considerable property portfolio in and around Wallingford, including the George Inn, an island in the River Thames, arable and pasture fields, and several farms, with a total capital value of just under £15,000. Acquiring and managing these assets, plus a further £10,000 worth of mortgages and other securities (including large parcels of Botley, Brentford, Isleworth, Uxbridge, and Wantage turnpike bonds) was a major preoccupation during his 19 years of married life. Since all financial records have since disappeared, we can now only take James Clitherow's word for the 'uncommon Regularity in his Accounts' (no small praise, from that meticulous source). But surviving letters illustrate the formidable assiduity with which in 1772 Blackstone contested the claims of a titled Oxfordshire near-neighbour over his recently-purchased water and fishing rights, and the careful calculations he laid out in support of his proposal to release £7,000 from his marriage settlement in 1778, 'without tying up the £2,000 Turnpike Securities as I once proposed', so as to facilitate 'a very eligible Purchase of Lands which I have in my Contemplation'.[16]

None of this made Sir William Blackstone a landed magnate, nor even quite a country squire, as distinct from Wallingford's most distinguished inhabitant. The relative seclusion and substantial scale of his house, not to mention his office, social position, and frequent absences in London and on circuit, must have kept him at some distance from the town's everyday life. Nevertheless in 1774 John Robinson, general election manager for the North ministry, thought it worth asking Blackstone about candidates for the borough's two seats.[17] After becoming a judge his main documented involvement in local affairs was via the parish church of St Peter's, just to the north of his large garden. Having acquired the advowson shortly before the church reopened, he presented Samuel Viner (possibly a distant

---

[15] *Al. Oxon.*, i. 118; *Correspondence of Thomas Warton*, 198; *The Diaries of Sanderson Miller of Radway*, ed. W. Hawkes (Dugdale Soc., 41, 2005), 349. The 'Dr Blackstone' with whom Parson Woodforde caroused late at New College on 8 November 1774 was undoubtedly Henry: *Diary of a Country Parson*, ed. Beresford, i. 141–2. TNA, PROB 11/1041, fos. 154v–156; Queen's College Archives, 5 M 87, 125 (Charles to William Blackstone, 3 August 1757); *Letters*, 114–15; PROB 11/1061, fos. 105–105v; LMA, ACC1360/583/1.

[16] Doolittle, 99–103; LMA, ACC1360/585. 7–8; Clitherow, xxvi; *Letters*, 144–6, 158–60. See also Blackstone's letter to John Allnatt, 11 December 1777, about a purchase in Wallingford: New York Public Library, Montague Collection of Historical Autographs.

[17] *Parliamentary Papers of John Robinson 1774–1784*, ed. W. T. Laprade (Camden, 3rd Ser., xxxiii, 1922), 21.

descendant of the benefactor responsible for his Oxford Chair) to the rectory. In 1775 his own brother-in-law Richard Bethell (husband of Sarah's youngest sister) was ordained as curate, and henceforth appears as 'minister' in the parish registers, suggesting that Viner had become non-resident.[18] Fitting-out the rebuilt church with paved floors, stuccoed walls, near full-length plain-glazed windows, coffered ceiling, classically-proportioned plaster mouldings, and plain low pews was carried out, as the church-wardens minuted on 12 September 1767, 'according to Mr Taylor's plan this day produced by Mr Blackstone'.[19] Besides arranging for Robert Taylor (whose 'exceptional capacity for hard work' fortunately mirrored his own)[20] to add this relatively small job to his existing commitments on the Botley Causeway and Swinford Bridge projects, Blackstone served as churchwarden from 1768–70, while the work was completed and most of the necessary funds raised. The outcome was a modern, light, and airy interior, among 'the neatest and best adapted to this northern climate of any of our country churches', according to an early nineteenth-century observer. In the mid-1770s Taylor designed and constructed a contrasting neo-Gothic open-work steeple to complete the church, after some £500 had been raised, mostly by subscription from 'the Nobility, Gentry, Clergy & others residing at or in the Neighbourhood of Wallingford', as Blackstone reported. Local tradition has it that Blackstone also paid for an additional dial facing his house to be added to the clock installed at this time in the tower below the steeple. Finally at Easter 1778 he presented to St Peter's 'a Handsome Chalice, Paten and Plate of Silver double Gilt with proper inscriptions thereon'.[21] It seems very likely that among those who used this communion plate, sitting with or near Blackstone and his family in the front pew, was Dr Shute Barrington, the well-connected evangelical bishop of Llandaff, who began to stay regularly in the district from 1773, contributed to the spire subscription at the same rate as Justice Blackstone, and with his wife joined the Blackstones for Sunday dinner at Priory Place after church during the Newdigates' visit in 1777.[22]

[18] *Letters*, 134–6; Bodl. MS Arch. Pprs. Berks. d 10; Wilts. and Swindon History Centre, D1/51/5; D/1/20/1/2; D/1/14/1/16; *Al. Oxon.*, i. 104, iv. 1475, 1591; Berkshire RO, D/P 139/1/1; I am grateful for David Pedgley's help with this matter.

[19] Berkshire RO, D/P 139/5/2.

[20] H. Colvin, *A Biographical Dictionary of British Architects 1600–1840* (1995), 963.

[21] Berkshire RO, D/P 139/5/2 (St Peter's Churchwardens book), 2 November 1767, 5 April, 1768, 28 March, 20 May, 29 October 1769, 26 September 1775, 6 January 1777, 22 April 1778; I. Taggart, *St Peter Wallingford Oxfordshire* (1987), [2], [5].

[22] B. and D. Pedgley, *Crowmarsh: A History of Crowmarsh Gifford, Newnham Murren, Mongewell and North Stoke* (Crowmarsh, 1990), 51–2; Doolittle, 68, 104; Newdigate Diary, 6 July 1777; Hedges, *History of Wallingford*, ii. 402.

Blackstone's active involvement in refurbishing what was very much his own parish church reflects his undoubted passion for architectural project management. But its mainsprings were probably a generalized sense of civic and social obligation, mixed with what Clitherow termed his 'Ardour for Improvement', rather than any conscious attempt to express his fully internalized and seemingly unquestioning religious faith. No hint of either rational doubt or evangelical zeal disturbed Blackstone's calm belief in a benign and all-powerful, if somewhat remote Providence. This appears most clearly in the one surviving letter to 'my dear Love', which sought to calm Sarah's wifely fears following the news of a brother judge's collapse on circuit, by emphasizing that 'no Solicitude or Anxiety of Ours will hasten or retard the allwise Decrees of Him, who best knows what is fit for us, and whose Goodness will choose what is best'. Indeed, Blackstone's adherence to 'the great Truths of Christianity from a thorough Investigation of its Evidence', and regular 'Attendance on its public Duties' (as noted by Clitherow) suggest the sort of latitudinarian natural religion which subsequently gave the Hanoverian Church of England a bad name. Ironically enough, Victorian scholars cited Blackstone as a critic of precisely that tendency in Georgian churchmanship; but the original source of the words attributed to him cannot now be identified, and they are almost certainly apocryphal.[23]

More strictly charitable enterprises were less demanding of his time, although he served as a governor of Oxford's newly-established hospital, the Radcliffe Infirmary, alongside the earls of Lichfield and Abingdon, and also subscribed as a 'perpetual director' to the work of Dr William Hawes and his London-based Humane Society, founded in 1774 to promote measures for saving the victims of drowning.[24] A less socially inclusive initiative which he supported in 1779 was the association of Berkshire property-owners proposed by Bishop Barrington's brother William, former secretary for war, as a means of providing armed support for the magistrates in times of civil unrest. The bishop seems to have had several

[23] Clitherow, xviii, xxv; Prest, 'Religion of a Lawyer', 153–68; C. J. Abbey and J. H. Overton, *The English Church in the Eighteenth Century* (1887), 300: Blackstone 'had the curiosity, early in the reign of George III, to go from church to church, and hear every clergyman of note in London. He says that he did not hear a single discourse which had more Christianity in it than the writings of Cicero, and that it would have been impossible for him to discover, from what he heard, whether the preacher was a follower of Confucius, of Mahomet, or of Christ'. I am grateful to Barry Smith, Paul Langford, Lawrence McIntosh, Michael Roberts, and John Walsh for attempting to establish a provenance for this unreferenced citation.

[24] *Jackson's Oxford Journal*, 9 June 1770, 12 October 1771; *Reports of the Humane Society . . . 1777* (n.d., 1778?), 2; T. Francklin, *A Sermon Preached at St George's Bloomsbury . . . for the Benefit of the Humane Society* (1779), 25.

consultations with Blackstone, before forwarding his recommendations for 'circulating copies to the different markets and considerable towns of the Country', together with the assurance that the 'measure itself meets with my neighbour's highest approbation'.[25]

II

As for other activities favoured by the élite, field sports and outdoor pursuits in general did not appeal to Justice Blackstone. However unfortunate for the state of his physical health, his recreation was rather what Clitherow termed 'literary Retirement', in the library or study.[26] Elizabeth Harris, wife of the parliamentary diarist, whose son had attended Blackstone's lectures as an Oxford undergraduate, described for him a visit to their Salisbury house in July 1771 by the two assize judges, who:

> exprest great delight in our Garden Library etc. Your Friend Sr Wm Blackstone was highly pleased with the Books; his brother Naires is musical, so while Sr Wm was deeply engaged in a Book they with mutual consent left the room to repair to the music, and I left to Guard Sr Wm. He did not hear them go; some minutes after he took his Eye off the Book, and when he saw only me in the room he started, and asked what was gone of all the company and begd to [be] conducted to them.[27]

Besides hinting in an affectionate, amused, perhaps slightly patronising fashion at some social awkwardness and excessive concern for the proprieties, this anecdote provides a rare glimpse of Blackstone as bibliophile. James Harris was an accomplished classical scholar and philologist, whose library Blackstone might well have found absorbing. His own collection, dispersed by sale and otherwise after his death, cannot now be reconstructed, although his will carefully provided for the disposition of what was plainly a very extensive accumulation of books and manuscripts. The Codrington Library was to have the pick of the antiquarian law:

> my old manuscript Registrum Brevium, two antient manuscript Reports of Cases in the Starchamber, and another antient manuscript Treatise concerning ecclesiastical Courts; together with my old and curious Edition of Lyttelton's

---

[25] T. Hayter, *The Army and the Crowd in Mid–Georgian England* (1978), 73–4; BL MS Additional 73760, fos. 85, 88–90, 108–9.

[26] Clitherow, xx.

[27] Hampshire RO, 9M73/G1258/33, printed in *A Series of Letters of the First Earl of Malmesbury, his Family and Friends*, ed. J. Harris (1870), i. 234–5 (I owe this reference to the kindness of Rosemary Dunhill).

Tenures, printed by Lettou and Machlinia, and the Old Abridgment of the Statutes bound up therewith; another edition of Littleton printed by Tailleur at Roan; my old Edition of the Book of Entries; all Editions of the Statutes, in whatever Size or Language, printed previous to the Year 1660, and all the works of Mr Prynne, which I have already collected, or shall hereafter collect,

with the exception of items already held.[28] Then the eldest son 'who shall apply himself to the study and profession of the Law and shall reside in any of the Inns of Court for that purpose' by the age of 23 years was to receive 'all my printed law books' (except those already bequeathed to All Souls), 'including under that denomination only such Books as my Executors shall judge to be meerly professional and not any Books of General Antiquities or History'. If no son were to fulfil those conditions, the law books must be sold, and the proceeds added to his personal estate. The remainder ('except such as my Executors . . . shall consider as mere Rubbish and Lumber'), plus some domestic items (plate, linen, furniture etc.), which any executor thought 'proper to be preserved shall be catalogued and inventoried and shall be kept . . . as and in the nature of Heirlooms, so long as the law will permitt'.[29]

But if Blackstone's books were ever catalogued, before or after his death, any such list has either failed to survive, or remains in private hands. Instead we have only two auctioneer's catalogues from 1803 and 1845. Both sales included printed books and a few manuscripts from Blackstone's library, but these are listed indiscriminately with and largely indistinguishable from other items sold at the same time from the collections of his son James and the lawyer Philip Stanhope. American and British libraries hold a scattering of books bearing Blackstone's ownership signature or bookplate, and subscription lists yield details of a few more. There is also the collection of nearly 100 items transferred to Balliol College from New Inn Hall in 1887. But the overall dimensions, let alone the detailed content of Blackstone's library—or rather libraries, since he seems to have segregated his law books in London, keeping the rest at Wallingford—are no longer recoverable.[30]

The two sales catalogues purport to list some 6,700 volumes in total; even on the conservative assumption that as many as half did not belong originally to Blackstone, this would still leave an impressive collection. The quality of his books is no less noteworthy, for increasing disposable income enabled him to indulge his bibliographical interests. Whether or not the two incunabula listed in the 1845 catalogue (Homer's works printed

[28] TNA, PROB 11/1061, fo. 102.   [29] Ibid., fos. 102v–103.
[30] Chapter 4, pp. 36–9; *Letters*, 189.

at Florence in 1488, and a 1498 Aldine Press edition of Aristophanes) were originally his cannot be determined[31] but he certainly bequeathed four pre-1500 imprints to All Souls, including a copy of the first law book printed in England. Each is annotated with Blackstone's bibliographical comments, for example speculating that the *Old Abridgment* (which he had evidently acquired by 1765) 'being without Date, was printed before 1481, when Lettou began to put Dates, than after. And the partnership of Lettou & Machlinia was more likely to have been before their erecting separate Presses than afterwards.' In the 1760s Blackstone exchanged several letters on the early history of printing with the Dutch lawyer–antiquary Gerard Meerman, receiving in due course a presentation copy of his *Origines Typographicae* (1765), which incorporated material supplied from Bodleian Library manuscripts by 'that most humane and learned man [summae humanitas ac doctrinae vir] GUIL. BLACKSTONE'.[32]

Nor were his bibliographical interests wholly antiquarian; thus the final page of his copy of the first edition of Gilbert's *Historical View of the Court of Exchequer* notes 'Here follows in Edit. 1759 8 more pages belonging to this Chapter; and seven entire new Chapters, some of them extremely curious; which has made this Edition worth nothing, except to compare with the other when any Doubt arises; as both seem to be printed from surreptitious Copies of C[hief] B[aron] Gilbert's Work'.[33] A particularly striking and unexpected component of his collection is the 18 bound volumes containing 129 works by or associated with the seventeenth-century Presbyterian lawyer, controversialist, parliamentarian, and antiquary William Prynne, some evidently acquired from the library of another collector, James West, with further individual items added up to the last month of his life. Besides respecting Prynne's heroic labours among the records in the Tower after Charles II's restoration, Blackstone may well have admired his struggles against parliament's New Model Army and Cromwell's republic in the name of the ancient constitution and English liberties. The tally of some 200 published books and pamphlets written by Prynne also doubtless challenged his collector's instinct.[34]

---

[31] *BB*, 30. The Library of Congress holds a copy of Nicholas of Osimo, *Supplementum Summae Pisanellae* (Venice, 1479) containing a Blackstone bookplate, possibly inserted by the donor: Incun. 1479 .N52 1479b.
[32] Codrington: *Abbreviamentum Statutorum* (c. 1482), 3rd free end leaf, I.9.2 (Gallery). Museum Meermano–Westreenianum, 257/51–71; G. Meerman, *Origines Typographicae* (The Hague, 1765), ii. 25–6.
[33] Rare Book Room, Yale Law School Library: G. Gilbert, *An Historical View of the Court of Exchequer* (1738), 151.
[34] Codrington, SR 54 d 1–8; *Letters*, 182n, 189.

Blackstone himself continued to write and publish during the last decade of his life. Successive new editions of the *Commentaries* in 1770, 1773, 1774, 1775, and 1778 each incorporated textual revisions, as did the post-humous ninth edition published 'with the last corrections of the author' in 1783. What purports to be a third edition of *Tracts Chiefly Relating to the Antiquities and Laws of England* was printed at the Clarendon Press in 1771, although no second edition is known, and the contents of this finely-printed folio differ from those of the two-volume collection of *Law Tracts* published in 1762. Whereas that included the *Treatise on the Law of Descents*, now effectively incorporated into the second book of the *Commentaries*, the 1771 compilation reprints *An Analysis of the Laws of England*, which was reissued in the same year 'with a few alterations and improvements' as a *précis*, outline or abstract of the *Commentaries*, to which it claimed 'to correspond as exactly . . . as the former impressions were calculated to answer to the lectures then read by the professor'. This separate sixth edition of the *Analysis* appears to have been the first of Blackstone's legal writings not self-published, for the run of 1,000 copies produced at the Clarendon Press was charged to Daniel Prince, the Oxford bookseller. The *Tracts* of 1771 also include a new six-page 'Postscript' to the *Essay on Collateral Consanguinity*, responding to the 'Argument' of the legal anti-quary and barrister Edward Wynne, which had been successfully deliv-ered on behalf of his brother at the founder's kin appeal heard before Archbishop Secker in 1762, and subsequently published.[35]

Another addition, under the title *Observations on the Oxford Press*, was an edited version of the open letter to Vice Chancellor Randolph first published in 1758, omitting the angrier personal references, and updated with notes highlighting changes brought about as a result of Blackstone's successful reform campaign. A preliminary 'Advertisement' presents this document as a piece of contemporary history, which 'had it's effect: the grievances therein stated were redressed: and the Clarendon Press from that period began, and hath ever since continued, to do honour to the University, and the gentlemen appointed to conduct it'. But notwithstand-ing the vague suggestion that 'it might be useful to perpetuate certain facts therein stated, which were not always universally known', self-justification was surely a motive for adding this piece to what would be the last volume Blackstone himself brought out as author and publisher. That Justice Sir William Blackstone felt a need to perpetuate his contribution to the

---

[35] OUP Archives, OUP/PR/1/18/4, 309, 336, 361, 409; Eller, 3–8, 88–90, 97–99; *Tracts* (Oxford, 1771), 192–8; E. Wynne, *A Miscellany Containing Several Law Tracts* (1765), 143–77; above, Chapter 9, p. 187.

better regulation of Oxford University Press six years after resigning from its board of management is also suggestive of the extent to which the university maintained a hold on his heart and imagination. Appropriately enough, his very last surviving letter, written to Lewis Bagot when 'so weak that I can scarcely set pen to paper', addressed a matter of Press business and closed with wishes of success 'in this and all other your undertakings for the good of the University'.[36]

Besides editing and correcting his own previously-published work, Blackstone did manage some new writing during the 1770s, although nothing of book length. His second paper to the Society of Antiquaries took the form of a letter addressed in March 1775 to the legal antiquarian Daines Barrington (brother of his Wallingford bishop neighbour), and subsequently published in *Archaeologia*, the society's journal. An inscribed copper seal found on the demolition of a house in Oxford provided the pretext for a detailed legal-political history of the impact of statute law and judicial opinion on the jurisdiction of the church courts during the sixteenth and seventeenth centuries. Blackstone attributed the 'furious attack' of Prynne and his allies upon the bishops' use of their own seals to validate ecclesiastical court proceedings, rather than those of the Crown, to ignorance of the common law judges' 1606 opinion upholding the validity of these seals. Once this pronouncement became known in 1641, after Sir Edward Coke's papers confiscated at his death had been returned to his son, the bishops' critics immediately abandoned that part of their assault. Dr Samuel Pegge wrote from Derbyshire 'as an Associate with you in the Society of Antiquaries' to commend Blackstone's 'excellent observations on the ecclesiastical seal and the Controversies associated with it in the last volume of the *Archaeologia*', although only by way of introducing his own 'short disquisition' on an aspect of 'the old forest Law', in the (unfulfilled) hope that 'you will think it worth while, to send this letter to the Society'.[37]

While some readers of *Archaeologia* may have found the forensic style and largely non-archaeological content of Blackstone's paper little to their taste, other productions from his last decade enjoyed a wide audience. The second edition of Andrew Kippis's biographical dictionary includes a footnote of nearly 2,500 words to the article on Joseph Addison, in which Blackstone sought to vindicate that 'gentleman who was so amiable in his

---

[36] *Tracts*, 241–80; Blackstone's annotated copy from which the text was set is bound up in the volume now Bodl. MS Top. Oxon. d 387. *Letters*, 190; see also ibid., 154–7, 169–71.

[37] *A Catalogue of All Sir William Blackstone's Works*, 23–47, in *The Biographical History of Sir William Blackstone* (1782); Society of Antiquaries, Minute Book 14 (1775–6), 117–31; *Archaeologia*, 3 (1775), 414–25; Bodl. MS Add. c 245, 25.

moral character' from the charge of hypocritical double-dealing, levelled against him as 'Atticus' by his former friend, the poet Alexander Pope, in the *Epistle to Dr Arbuthnot*. Identified only as 'a gentleman of considerable rank, to whom the Public is obliged for works of much higher importance', Blackstone's authorship of this piece is attested by Richard Graves, who however professed himself unconvinced by his friend's quasi-judicial critique (that 'most exquisite chain of argument', according to a more sympathetic contemporary) of the case against Addison mounted by Owen Ruffhead in his 1769 biography of Pope.[38] Blackstone had certainly read and admired Addison since his own Charterhouse schooldays. But whereas that Augustan author's literary stocks were already in decline by the time Blackstone's note appeared, those of William Shakespeare continued to rise.

Blackstone strongly supported the burgeoning patriotic cult of the Bard. As early as 1746 he had drafted a series of 14 'Cursory Observations' on Thomas Hanmer's readings of doubtful passages in his recent edition of Shakespeare's plays; each questioned or rejected Hanmer's version and proposed his own alternative suggestion. He was later claimed to have been the 'learned correspondent' who supplied Samuel Johnson with an explanation for his 1765 Shakespeare edition of 'Cry Havoc, and let slip the Dogs of war' from *Julius Caesar*: 'in the military operations of old times, *havoc* was the word by which declaration was made, that no quarter should be given'.[39] Blackstone returned to his original 14 critical notes at some point in the 1770s, probably after acquiring and reading through the second edition of Shakespearean plays produced in 1778 by the veteran Johnson and his wealthy younger collaborator George Steevens, a work 'to which' (as he told Steevens in July of that year) 'I am indebted for the Renewal of a Pleasure which I had so often before experienced'. Once having established contact with Steevens, who was clearly delighted at the prospect of enlisting such an eminent assistant for his on-going editorial enterprise, Blackstone proceeded to forward what he modestly characterized as 'a few trifling Remarks which I made with my Pencil in the blank leaves of my Shakespeare'.[40] Their relationship blossomed over the following year, Steevens providing Blackstone

---

[38] A. Kippis, *Biographia Britannica* (1778–93), i. 56–8; Graves, *Triflers*, 59; J. Wooll, *Biographical Memoirs of the Late Revd Joseph Warton* (1806), 71. Cf. F. Atterbury, *Epistolary Correspondence* (1783–87), i. 86.

[39] T. E. Tomlins, 'Corrections of Shakespeare's Text, by Sir William Blackstone, &c', *The Papers of the Shakespeare Society* i (1853; 1844), 96–100; A. Sherbo, *Shakespeare's Midwives* (1992), 72–3, 85. Graves, *Triflers*, 58.

[40] *Letters*, 172.

with copies of Prynne's pamphlets for his collection, as well as enthusiastic and grateful feedback on his contribution, 'which confers the
highest honours our undertaking can receive' (with reference to the
accumulation of material for Edmund Malone's supplement to the 1778
Shakespeare). Blackstone for his part evidently relished the opportunity
to share his literary interests and knowledge with an appreciative and
informed collaborator. One May morning in 1779, a few days after the
end of Easter term, he even rode out to Steevens's house on Hampstead
Heath, to repay 'many Visits with which you have favoured me in Town'.
But 'being uncertain of meeting with you', it seemed best to leave a note
with the message 'that Poetical Criticism has gone on very slowly during
this last Fortnight of Business'. Yet it had still been possible to 'read over
the old Plays which you were pleased to send me'—presumably the edition promoted by Steevens of *Six Old Plays on which Shakespeare founded
his* . . . . (1779)—resulting in the enclosed 'Observation, if you think it
worth your Attention'.[41]

In May 1780, several months after his death, Blackstone's critical
notes were published in Edmund Malone's two-volume *Supplement to the
Edition of Shakespeare's Plays Published in 1778 by Samuel Johnson and George
Steevens*. Some editorial and authorial winnowing had reduced the longer and seemingly earlier version of two surviving drafts in Blackstone's
hand from some 140 notes, comments and suggestions to the 89 printed
by Malone. He had previously noted that Blackstone 'will not allow his
name to be affixed to them', but 'consented to let them be printed with
a particular mark'. This was a capital 'E', the last letter of his name, as
divulged in Malone's preface, which advertised these 'remarks of one of
the most eminent characters the present age has produced; a person whose
name will be revered, and whose works will be studied and admired, as
long as the laws and constitution of England shall have any existence',
with the assurance that publishing his identity 'will by no means diminish
the lustre of his reputation'.[42]

As we might expect, Blackstone's notes are informed by a remarkable
breadth of knowledge and learning. Legal lore is naturally prominent;
thus the phrase 'safe towards your love and honour' which concludes
Macbeth's welcoming speech to Duncan is explained, with a reference
to Littleton, as 'an allusion to the forms of doing homage in the feudal
times'. When in *King Henry VIII*, Catherine of Aragon tells Wolsey that

---

[41] Ibid., 178, 181–2, 184, 189–90; Folger, W.b. 51(1), (2), (3), Steevens to Blackstone, 4, 29 April,
3 May 1779.

[42] E. Malone, *Supplement* . . . *In two Volumes* (1780), iii–iv; Folger, W.b. 51 (1–12); *Historical
Manuscripts Commission, Twelfth Report*, App. X (Charlemont), i. 343–4.

'I utterly abhor, yea from my soul | Refuse you as my judge', readers are told that 'these are not mere words of passion, but technical terms in the canon law—*Detester* and *Recuso*', while in the opening scene of *Measure for Measure,* Duke Vicentio's assurance that his deputy is versed in 'the terms | For common justice' is glossed as 'the technical language of the courts. An old book called *Les Termes de la Ley . . .* was in Shakespeare's days, and is now, the accidence of young students in the law.'[43] Classical allusions and borrowings are also brought out, including an imitation of Terence's Latin in *All's Well that Ends Well,* while in *Henry IV Part II* the phrase 'Devour the Way' is said to be 'So, in one of the Roman poets (I forget which)—cursu consumere campum'—although Blackstone's original manuscript had 'Lucian, or Statius, or Silius Italicus'. One of Jack Cade's speeches in *Henry VI Part 2* triggers a reference to the *Origines Typographicae* (1765) of his Dutch correspondent Gerard Meerman, where it was cited 'to support his hypothesis, that printing was introduced into England by Frederic Corsellis, a workman from Haerlem, in the time of Henry VI'. The comment on Katherine's line 'That every thing I look on seemeth green' from the fourth act of *The Taming of the Shrew* reveals, not for the first time, an easy familiarity with scientific writing: 'Shakespeare's observations on the phenomena of nature are very accurate. When one has sat long in the sunshine, the surrounding objects will often appear tinged with *green.* The reason is assigned by many of the writers on optics.'[44] Youthful memories helped to explain 'Buz, Buz', Hamlet's response to the news from Polonius that the players had arrived: 'Buz used to be an interjection at Oxford, when anyone began a story that was generally known before'. It may have been still more recent experience with his own children which informs the gloss of 'like a parish top' from *Twelfth Night:* '"To sleep like a town top" is a proverbial expression. A top is said *to sleep,* when it turns around with great velocity, and makes a smooth humming noise.' Finally, in the same play Malvolio's mistaken recognition of his mistress's handwriting in the C's, U's, T's and great P's of the letter left for him by Maria leads Blackstone to conclude that 'I am afraid some very coarse and vulgar Appellations are meant to be alluded to by these capital Letters'—an observation not previously ventured in print, although subsequently endorsed by many editors. Indeed this particular textual elucidation evidently constitutes Blackstone's major lasting contribution to Shakespearean studies.[45]

[43] Malone, *Supplement,* i. 149–5, 216, 94.
[44] Ibid., 134, 187, 207, 133.
[45] Ibid., 354, 139, 140; Sherbo, *Shakespeare's Midwives,* 84.

III

Arguably the two most significant events in the last decade of Blackstone's life both occurred in the year 1776: publication of the American Declaration of Independence, and of Jeremy Bentham's *A Fragment on Government*. As an upholder of the Stamp Act, Blackstone was no friend to the American Revolution—in 1779 one of his last letters 'rejoice[d] at the fair Prospect of Success in America, which the last Accounts from thence have opened to Us'—while the *Commentaries* provided arguments and rhetoric for loyalists and supporters of the British government as well as the insurgent colonists. But Blackstone's clearly-stated emphasis on the authority of the law of nature and the absolute rights of individuals was of particular importance in formulating and defending the case for armed resistance to King George and his parliament. Edmund Burke pointed out to the House of Commons on the eve of the revolutionary war that 'they have sold nearly as many of Blackstone's Commentaries in America as in England'. In the new republic the book's influence continued to grow, with successive American reprints of the English text. In 1803, St George Tucker's five-volume edition incorporated notes and appendices on the developing body of American jurisprudence, state and federal. The *Commentaries* thus became and remained the basis of US legal education, hence moulding American legal thought and practice throughout the nineteenth century, and beyond.[46]

All this would scarcely have happened if Jeremy Bentham, Blackstone's most effective detractor, had enjoyed as much influence across the Atlantic as he did within his native England. We have already seen that even the first book of *Commentaries* attracted some less than favourable reviews, while the treatment of 'Offences against God and Religion' in the fourth volume provoked sustained protest and rejoinders from leading spokesmen for Protestant Dissent. Other criticisms followed. In 1772 an opponent of impressment for naval service suggested that the equivocal position adopted by the *Commentaries* on that subject reflected an authoritarian, pro-government bias. Next year Blackstone's claim that trial by jury secured English liberties was cited as 'one amongst the *innumerable* absurdities to be found in the Commentaries' (another was to speak of 'the *murder* of Charles I'). Around the same time James Burgh, a Dissenting school-master, lamented that 'a writer, whose admirable work will be read

---

[46] *Letters*, 186; D. R. Nolan, 'Sir William Blackstone and the New American Republic: A Study of Intellectual Impact', *New York University Law Review*, 51 (1976), 731–68. D. Kennedy, 'The Structure of Blackstone's Commentaries', *Buffalo Law Review*, 28 (1978–9), 205–379.

as long as England, its laws, and language remain, should be so sparingly tinctured with the true and generous principles of liberty'. Such views confirm John Horne Tooke's observation, looking back over his long career as radical activist, that 'when the *Commentaries* first made their appearance, they were esteemed so little friendly to freedom, as to be quoted on the side of power'.[47]

Neither a believer in the rights of man, nor friend to the American Revolution, the young Jeremy Bentham's differences with Blackstone sprang from very different and largely a-political roots. Although the *Fragment on Government* is generally cited as his first publication, it was preceded in 1774 by a translation of Voltaire's *Le Taureau Blanc* in two volumes, the first comprising a preface ('which just as well may be read afterwards') of 144 pages, largely devoted to ridiculing English law and legal institutions. Blackstone figures as a satirical butt, who 'seems to think, as far as he allows himself to *think*, it's the worst trick a man can get when he reads *law*: For which reason he has done all he can to break us of it'. A footnote refers to a passage in the *Commentaries'* fourth volume 'where he talks of the arrogance of setting up private opinion against public—Also Vol. i, ii, iii, & iv, *passim'*. The other two specific mentions of Blackstone's name focus on the same chapter, sending-up his pronouncements on blasphemy and witchcraft. The tone is largely playful, verging on burlesque, although with an occasional sharp edge, as with references to 'my grandmother and her pupil Judge Blackstone', and that Blackstone's 'grand concern is always orthodoxy'.[48]

Twenty-six years old and a non-practising barrister of Lincoln's Inn, Bentham then focused the full force of his formidable intellect on a serious and total refutation of Blackstone. Published anonymously in April 1776, *A Fragment on Government* consists of a preface condemning both commentator and *Commentaries* as muddled and malign. This is followed by five analytical chapters which focus on a mere seven pages from the section entitled 'Of the Nature of Laws in General' in the 'Introduction' to Blackstone's first volume. Amply demonstrating their shortcomings as legal and political philosophy, Bentham even attributed these intellectual inadequacies ('the universal inaccuracy and confusion') to his former teacher's ethical, personal, and social failings. Among the many 'capi-

---

[47] Above, pp. 219–20, 246–50; *The Rights of the Sailors Vindicated* (1772), 15–23; C. Crawford, *Letters from Academicus to Eugenius* (1773), 23–4; J. Burgh, *Political Disquisitions* (1774–5), i.186; Stephens, *Memoirs of Tooke*, ii. 437. Cf. J. Rayner, *An Inquiry into the Doctrine lately Propagated* (1769), 54.

[48] H. L. A. Hart, 'The United States of America', in *idem, Essays on Bentham* (Oxford, 1982), 52–67; *Bentham: Selected Writings of John Dinwiddy*, ed. W. Twining (Stanford, 2004), 11–12; *The White Bull, An Oriental History . . . faithfully done into English* (1774), i. xxix, lxii–lxiv, lxxxiii.

tal blemishes' of Blackstone's much-acclaimed work, there was a 'grand
and fundamental one, the antipathy to reformation': 'For indeed such an
ungenerous antipathy seemed of itself enough to promise a general vein of
obscure and crooked reasoning, from whence no clear or sterling knowledge could be derived; *so intimate is the connection between some of the gifts
of the understanding, and some of the affections of the heart*'. Here Bentham
seems to suggest that Blackstone's ill-nature, or misanthropy, was the root
cause of his resistance to the reform of flagrant legal and political abuses,
not only blinding him to their real nature, but encouraging attempts
at a sophistical defence of these evils. The point is driven home with a
social sneer, apparent in the adjectives 'ungenerous', and 'obscure'. One
need not be totally persuaded by recent scholarly emphasis on the social
construction of knowledge in early modern England to discern in this
passage something very like a refusal of epistemic credit to an author on
the grounds of his incivility.[49]

The interest aroused by Bentham's iconoclastic tract in legal and political circles seems to have turned around speculation about its authorship, and to have subsided immediately after his father divulged the
secret of young Jeremy's responsibility. What we know of Blackstone's
reaction to the attack comes largely from Bentham's own accounts to
several correspondents in Europe some two years later. He then claimed
that a copy of the *Fragment* had been sent to Blackstone by a bookseller,
who enquired whether, if the latter intended to reply, he might have the
honour of printing that rejoinder. The judge responded peevishly ('avec
assez d'humeur') that he would do nothing. According to Bentham, when
Lord Mansfield asked a similar question, Blackstone replied 'never, not
even if it had been better written'. 'He told Lord Mansfield that he knew
of what country I was, by my Scotticisms, and what is more, that I was
a Dr Gilbert Stuart'.[50] Bentham went on to assert that this misappre-
hension had induced Blackstone to send Stuart—whom he hardly knew,
other than through his *A View of Society in Europe* (1778), a work which
identified errors in two brief passages on feudal institutions in the second
book of the *Commentaries*—a letter full of the strongest praise ('pleine des
plus fortes éloges'). Like many of Bentham's recollections, this account
is not wholly trustworthy. The letter referred to is almost certainly that
printed in a posthumous second edition of Stuart's book, acknowledging
in polite but scarcely fulsome terms a presentation copy sent by the author.

[49] [J. Bentham], *A Comment on the Commentaries and A Fragment of Government*, ed.
J. H. Burns and H. L. A. Hart (1977), 394 [italics added]. Cf. A. Johns, *The Nature of the Book: Print
and Knowledge in the Making* (1998), 33–4, 167–8, 467–9, 561.

[50] Bentham, *Correspondence*, ii. 102–3, 148–9.

Blackstone does however accept the justice of Stuart's detailed criticisms, adding in characteristically self-deprecatory fashion 'I fear that an accurate inquirer may still find, in other parts of it, sufficient marks of what was really the case, that the book was not originally compiled with any view to submitting it to public inspection'.[51]

Bentham also provides two slightly different reports of Mansfield's reaction; to John Forster he wrote that since the *Fragment* appeared, 'Lord Mansfield has talked of Sir W. to a friend of mine under the name of poor Blackstone, and lamented that so much excellent matter as he was pleased to say, there is in my book, should be in a manner thrown away on such a subject'. The French soldier–*philosophe* François Jean de Chastellux was likewise told of Mansfield's reference to 'poor Blackstone', but with the addition that 'he delighted at the expense of his colleague' ('c'est beaucoup réjoui aux dépens de son confrère').[52] Of course these accounts need not have been mutually exclusive, but the element of possible ambiguity in the first is absent from the second. It is also interesting that neither in the *Fragment* nor this correspondence does Bentham mention his attendance over several years at Blackstone's lectures as an Oxford undergraduate. Indeed a draft covering letter to accompany a presentation copy of the *Fragment* for the great *encyclopédist* Jean d'Alembert insists that not only was there 'nothing of a personal, nor party nature' in his attack, but that 'I do not even have the honour to be known to the person whose book (for it is only the book) is the object of my own'.[53] While these protestations may have been consciously and formally correct, it does seem at least possible that Bentham's fierce (and as it would turn out, life-long) antipathy towards his former lecturer is not fully explicable in ideological or intellectual terms.[54] For Blackstone represented an ideal paternal authority figure, a man outwardly cold, formal, and remote, against whom Bentham could with good conscience displace some of the frustration, rebelliousness, and resentment which he carefully avoided expressing directly to his own biological father.

Blackstone chose not to answer Bentham's uninhibited assault on his book and himself as 'a bigoted or corrupt defender of the works of power'.[55]

[51] Ibid., 149; G. Stuart, *A View of Society in Europe, in its Progress from Rudeness to Refinement* (1778), 343, 344–5, 347; *Letters*, 194–5.
[52] Bentham, *Correspondence*, ii. 102–3, 148–9.
[53] Ibid., 116.
[54] Cf. Posner, 'Blackstone and Bentham', 589–97; J. H. Burns, 'Bentham and Blackstone: A Lifetime's Dialectic', in *Empire and Revolutions*, ed. G. Schochet *et al.* (Washington DC, 1993), 261–77; *Fragment*, ed. Burns and Hart, xx–xxiv.
[55] Ibid., 398.

However, the preface to the eighth edition of the *Commentaries* includes an additional paragraph, written in 1777 and published the following year, defending this decision, on the grounds that:

> no sooner was the work completed, but many of its positions were vehemently attacked by zealots of all (even opposite) denominations, religious as well as civil; by some with a greater, by others with a less degree of acrimony. To such of these animadverters as have fallen within the author's notice (for he doubts not but some have escaped it) he owes at least this obligation; that they have occasioned him from time to time to revise his work, in respect to the particulars objected to; to retract or expunge from it, what appeared to be really erroneous; to amend or supply it, when inaccurate or defective; to illustrate and explain it when obscure. But, where he thought the objections ill-founded, he hath left and shall leave the book to defend itself: being fully of opinion, that if his principles be false, and his doctrines unwarrantable, no apology from himself can make them right; if founded in truth and rectitude, no censure from others can make them wrong.[56]

Bentham was doubtless right to suppose that his tract was 'glanced at' in this (as he claimed) 'angry Preface', which he also termed 'a bad-tempered paragraph directed against me under the name of *zealot* . . .'. Yet measured against his own savage attack on Blackstone's mind and morals, the latter's response seems remarkably restrained.

IV

Even as Bentham was spruiking the merits of his *Fragment* around the French intelligentsia in the spring and summer of 1778, he found himself involved in a major project of moral and social improvement, championed by the very man whom he had portrayed to d'Alembert as 'the sworn enemy of all reform'. We have already seen that Blackstone's interest in the subject of criminal punishment, doubtless encouraged by his early reading of Beccaria, and evident in the fourth book of the *Commentaries*, appeared in a parliamentary context as early as April 1770, when he sent Fletcher Norton (as speaker of the House of Commons) draft clauses of minor amendments to the original transportation act of 1719.[57] These changes were intended to sanction the transportation of both women and those convicted of petty

---

[56] Balliol College Library, 1550.i.21, W. Blackstone, *Commentaries on the Laws of England* (Oxford, 1775), ii–[iv], holograph addition, with struck-out passage referring to 'genteel apology from his warm, but not uncandid, correspondent' (i.e. Priestley): see Plate 18.

[57] *Letters*, 141–2; see Chapter 12, pp. 266–7.

larceny (thereby closing a potential statutory loophole already identified in the *Commentaries*),[58] and also to provide for transportation to destinations other than America, a provision not enacted until 1779, when it became the first clause of what Blackstone variously referred to as the Convict, Hard Labour or Felons bill, but has come down to us as the 'Penitentiary Act'. The statute 19 George III, c. 74, 'An Act to explain and amend the Laws relating to the Transportation, Imprisonment, and other Punishments, of certain Offenders' has been described as 'the most forward-looking English penal measure of its time'.[59] Extending over no fewer than 12 printed pages in the *Statutes at Large*, its 74 clauses are primarily concerned to establish a better alternative to transportation, based on the premiss set out in its fifth clause, that 'if many Offenders, convicted of Crimes for which Transportation has been usually inflicted, were ordered to solitary Imprisonment, accompanied by well-regulated Labour, and religious Instruction, it might be the Means, under Providence, not only of deterring others from the Commission of the such like Crimes, but also of reforming the Individuals, and inuring them to Habits of Industry'.[60]

Blackstone played a pivotal role in the complex history of the Penitentiary Act from 1775 or 1776 onwards, preparing and promoting successive drafts, both outside and (via the lobbying of key MPs) within parliament. Whereas his former pupil William Eden has been regarded as prime mover in the passage of the measure by virtue of his parliamentary persona and ministerial connections, Blackstone was the indispensable 'great promoter of the design' (according to the prison reformer John Howard's first biographer writing in 1792), and at very least its 'joint Father'—his own words to Eden, in December 1778.[61] Earlier that year Eden had himself disclaimed 'any Praises given to the Draft' of the proposed Hard Labour bill which preceded the Penitentiary Act, 'because those praises are chiefly due to some of the Judges, and particularly to One whose Commentaries on the Laws of England place Him at the Head of English Writers'. Ironically enough, the source of that praise,

---

[58] *Commentaries*, iv. 363n.

[59] S. Devereaux, 'The Making of the Penitentiary Act, 1775–1779', *Historical Journal*, 42 (1999), 405.

[60] [O. Ruffhead], *Statutes at Large from Magna Carta to the 25th Year of the Reign of George III, inclusive* (1786), viii. 58.

[61] Devereaux, 'Penitentiary Act', 411, 433. G. C. Bolton, 'William Eden and the Convicts, 1771–1787', *Australian Journal of Politics and History*, 26 (1980), 30–40. J. Aiken, *A View of the Character and Public Services of the late John Howard Esq.* (1792), 107; *Letters*, 173, 183–4: on 11 May 1778 Blackstone referred to his 'Experience of 4 years' with penal reform bills, and to having first undertaken a draft of the 'Convict Bill in 1776 by a Command which I could not decline, signified to me by the late Earl of Suffolk'. George III's interest in penal reform is not otherwise recorded: cf. Black, *George III*, 432.

and Eden's correspondent on this occasion, was none other than Jeremy Bentham. Bentham hailed the draft as a 'capital improvement . . . in penal legislation', on discovering to his surprise that it had been before the House of Commons in one form or another for the past two years.[62] He then sent copies of his own 'Observations' on the draft to all the judges, receiving a reply only from Blackstone, who was 'extraordinarily civil to me', stating ('after a few thanks and epithets of commendation') that 'some of my observations (he believed) had already occurred to the patrons of the Bill, and many more well deserved their attention'. In May 1778 Blackstone forwarded to Bentham a printed copy of the bill as it had emerged from the Commons' committee chaired by another of his protégés, Alexander Popham, together with a further set of explanatory notes on its contents. (When recounting these events to various correspondents, Bentham speaks of Eden as having drafted the actual bill, although Eden himself in his note to Bentham quoted above took responsibility only for the accompanying 'Preface', reserving credit for the draft specifically to Blackstone, in conjunction with other unnamed judges).[63]

Besides drafting successive versions of what eventually became the Penitentiary Act, Blackstone seems to have taken personal responsibility for keeping the very busy Eden on task, before and after the latter's trip to America between March and December 1778 on an abortive peace mission (for which, remarkably enough, Eden even seems briefly to have contemplated Blackstone himself as a possible candidate 'from the Law Line').[64] Over much the same period he also enlisted Eden's assistance in a hard-fought campaign to compensate the puisne judges for the impact of successive land tax increases on their take-home pay, which likewise required parliamentary approval for some additional expenditure, even as the continuing American hostilities weighed ever more heavily on the government's budget. Both matters ('the Businesses that have lately employed our joint Attention', as Blackstone termed them in a note on 4 March 1778) caused him considerable anxiety and frustration. On hearing that his own well-intentioned proposal for a 'small Extension of the Plan' previously announced by Lord North to raise the judges' salaries was likely to sink the whole proposal, he complained bitterly of this 'Return, which I should not have expected for the Pains I have lately taken, and am at all times ready to take, where I think it can be of public Service.[65]

---

[62] Bentham, *Correspondence*, ii. 91; J. Bentham, *A View of the Hard–Labour Bill* (1778), ii–iii.

[63] Bentham, *Correspondence*, ii. 90–92, 103–4, 116, 122–4, 149–50.

[64] B. F. Stevens, *Facsimiles of Manuscripts in European Archives Relating to America, 1773–1783* (1889–98), iv. 374.

[65] *Letters*, 164–6.

To his friend Popham, who seems to have proposed a further amendment to the administration's bill forbidding the sale of posts in the legal
bureaucracy, he confided a weary belief that 'all the pompous Professions
of Lord North are intended to end in Nothing . . . I have seen so much
Tergiversation in the professed Patrons of this Measure, that I am quite
sick of it'.[66]

Next year, when the independent Yorkshire back-bencher Sir George
Savile introduced a new private member's bill in place of one which had
lapsed at the end of the previous parliamentary session, he shared with
Eden his scepticism about North's rumoured uneasiness on this score:
'I cannot conceive that Lord N. is very anxious about losing the popularity
due to such an Arrangement. If so, he has had marvellous Self denial for
these seven Years past, in declining to bring it forward himself.'[67] To help
ensure the passage of Savile's bill he wrote on the same day (25 February)
to three MPs of his acquaintance—Eden, Sir Roger Newdigate, and
William Strahan—seeking their support. But the matter dragged on over
the next two months, and it was not until 1 May that he was able to send a
brief note to Newdigate, expressing thanks 'for Your early and authentick
Intelligence of what passed last night in the Committee' and 'the grateful Sense of my Brethren (I am sure) as well as myself to Yourself and all
other of our Friends who supported our Interests last Night'.[68] As enacted,
the Judges' Salaries Augmentation bill of 1779 raised the annual salary of
each puisne judge in the central courts by £400, an outcome from which
Blackstone, like his colleagues, would have derived direct personal benefit
had he lived a little longer. He seems to have regarded their cause as a simple matter of comparative wage justice, embodying the same compensa-
tory principle which already operated in the case of the two chief justices,
as well as the Welsh and Scottish judges. But it also possibly carried some
constitutional significance in his mind, with respect to the separation of
powers, and the independence of the judiciary; hence his remark that 'the
Judges equally disdain being made the Tools of Opposition, as they do
being the Slaves of Ministry', made in the context of North's attitude to
Savile's motion.[69]

Supporting a major innovation in English penal practice, whereby
terms of imprisonment in purpose-built institutions, 'experimen-
tal Houses of Confinement and Labour, which I would wish to call
Penitentiary Houses', became an alternative sentencing option for

---

[66] Ibid., 168–9; cf. Devereaux, 'Penitentiary Act', 426.
[67] *Letters*, 177.   [68] Ibid., 182.
[69] 19 Geo. III, c. 65; *Letters*, 177.

convicted criminals, alongside death and transportation, involved no such obvious self-interest. But it similarly required the expenditure of a good deal of emotional and nervous energy. Blackstone's latest draft bill, 'thrown together' in April 1779, 'with as much Accuracy as many Distractions of my official Duty in Term time and other Avocations allow'—including presiding at the high-profile murder trial of Rev James Hackman, for shooting the earl of Sandwich's mistress—was subject to major and potentially fatal amendment at the hands of Sir Charles Bunbury and his followers in the House of Commons. Their changes 'totally Repugnant to all the Ideas which I have so long been forming on the subject' meant, according to Blackstone, 'that the Bill as at present garbled is none of mine'; hence his declared intention of 'totally abandoning it at present, and perhaps for ever'.[70]

Fortunately Eden's parliamentary manoeuvres saved the essential elements of Blackstone's measure, which became law in July 1779. Its framer then pressed on to ensure that 'the first Step to be taken in order to effectuate the main Purposes of the Act' should indeed be taken, by 'the Appointment of three Supervisors', who were to determine the site of the proposed penitentiaries and then to obtain plans and estimates for their construction. After politely expressing his 'hope . . . You have got proper Persons in Your Eye for this Service', Blackstone went on to state his own preference, that 'Mr Howard (the Gentleman who has taken so much laudable Pains upon the Subject of Prisons) could be prevailed on to be One; and some sensible (but not expensive or finical) Architect to be another; and any Man of Sense and Integrity, but zealously a Friend to the general Design, to be the third'. Eden was further urged not to let the whole scheme founder despite the inevitable distraction of the American war:

We must rely upon You to press the Matter home upon Administration; so that, notwithstanding the great national Objects which must now be the principal Employment of their Thoughts, they may spare one Half Hour in making this Appointment by the Privy Council; else a total Stop must be put to the Progress of this Business, which has cost its Wellwishers so much Anxiety and Time.[71]

Blackstone remained in touch with Eden 'on the Subject of the Convicts' during the autumn of 1779, detailing his own lengthy 'Correspondencies

---

[70] Ibid., 180, 183–4. Devereaux, 'Penitentiary Act', 429–32. *Walpole Correspondence*, xxiv. 459–60; *The Genuine Trial, Life and Dying Words of the Rev. James Hackman* (1779), 17–18; N. A. M. Rodger, *The Insatiable Earl* (1993), 124–5.

[71] *Letters*, 185–6.

and Negotiations with Sir Charles Bunbury in Suffolk, and through his Channel with Dr Fothergill at Buxton, and with Mr Howard, whose indefatigable spirit sends him everywhere, to complete his History of Prisons'.[72] The Dissenter Howard did not wish to serve without the Quaker Fothergill, and Fothergill 'at first totally declined'. After 'personal Conference' at Wallingford, and a further meeting in London, both agreed to accept the nomination, but objected to 'Mr Taylor, or any Architect, whom they thought they should rather *employ*, than *consort* with'. Nevertheless, on 10 November Blackstone still felt it possible to congratulate 'You and myself on the fair Prospect of seeing this Business well afloat', and a week later was able to forward 'three very eligible Names' for appointment as supervisors. Indeed it appears that the fate of the Penitentiary Act preoccupied Blackstone even on his deathbed, when he reportedly turned to the Quaker physician John Fothergill, and asked '"*what progress we had made in the penitentiary houses?*" The Dr answered, "that we had paid all possible attention to the opinion of others respecting a situation, that we must soon be obliged to request the opinion of our judges concerning it". "*Be firm in your own*", was all he was able to say, as he soon departed for a better life.'[73]

Blackstone's last letter to Eden, on 10 November 1779, had wished him 'Health and Spirits to support the fatigues of what I doubt will be a troublesome [parliamentary] Session'. Within three months, Blackstone himself was dead. How far the frustrations and pressures of the previous 12 months hastened his demise is impossible to say. Positive evidence of any significant decline in health or vigour during the 1770s as compared with the 1760s is lacking, although according to Clitherow 'many Interruptions by Illness' marked his brother-in-law's last decade, with the gout now joined by a 'nervous Disorder', which frequently 'brought on a Giddiness or Vertigo'. His obesity was doubtless allied to high blood pressure, and possibly diabetes; but after suffering 'a violent Shortness of Breath' around Christmas, he recovered and visited Oxford in the second week of January. To the young barrister William Jones, who had recently been attending John Hunter's London anatomy lectures, he 'seemed very much out of order; he thinks his complaint is the gout in the stomach; but to me it seems a violent concussion of the whole nervous system'. On returning to London for the beginning of Hilary term, Blackstone 'was seized with a fresh Attack, chiefly in his Head, which brought on a Drowsiness and

[72] *Letters*, 187–9.
[73] *The Beauties of Biography* (1792), ii.35; this account is confirmed by Aiken, *A View of the Character*, 109.

Stupor'. In his last surviving letter of 3 February 1780, for which he was 'obliged to employ my Wife as a secretary', Blackstone excused a belated reply to Lewis Bagot of Christ Church on the grounds of having been 'so roughly handled by an asthmatic disorder and the Physicians who have undertaken to cure it, that though getting better I am still so weak that I can scarcely set pen to paper'. But his optimism was misplaced: 'The Disorder increasing so rapidly, that he became at last for some Days almost totally insensible, and expired on the 14th of February 1780, in the 56th year of his Age.'[74]

[74] *Letters*, 188, 190; Clitherow, xxiii; *Letters of Sir William Jones*, ed. Cannon, i.338.

Chapter 14

Conclusion

O<small>N</small> 22 February 1780, following a service conducted by Bishop Barrington, Sir William Blackstone was buried in the family vault he had been licensed to construct under the east end of St Peter's Church, Wallingford. Within a month, it was announced that Lady Blackstone would receive a pension of £400.[1] William Eden, concerned that her husband had left an estate of less than £15,000 to support 'a widow and eight children', was evidently responsible for arranging this last royal favour. Despite having 'latterly seen much of his private Worth', Eden frankly admitted to no 'personal acquaintance with Lady B', and indeed slightly exaggerated the size of her remaining family (seven children, not eight, survived their father's death). So he prudently sought further advice as to their circumstances. Perhaps in recognition of the extent to which Blackstone had latterly abandoned the High-Church Anglicanism of his youth, or at least come to accept a more relaxed attitude towards religious heterodoxy, Eden approached his own friend John Lee, a prominent Yorkshire barrister, Rockinghamite MP, and Unitarian, as a potential source of information. While accepting that Lee might know no more of the family's 'internal state' than he did, Eden was 'certain that the K. will feel anxious to do so right a Thing, whenever the facts are sufficiently before him'.[2] As it happened, George III's bounty was enjoyed by the widowed Sarah Blackstone for only a little over three years, since she herself died in June 1783, before reaching the age of 50.[3]

---

[1] *Jackson's Oxford Journal*, 26 February 1780; *Annual Register for 1780* (1781), 202.
[2] William L. Clements Library, Lee Papers, Vol. 1, 39, 25 February 1780. For Lee's Unitarianism, see *Enlightenment and Religion*, ed. Haakonssen, 152–4, 183, 191.
[3] LMA, ACC 1360/585, 56.

Apart from a few conventionally eulogistic obituaries, there is little record of contemporary reaction to Blackstone's death.[4] The Royal Chaplain Dr Richard Kaye mentioned in a postcript the passing of 'my old Friend Sr Wm Blackstone, who has been invariable in his regard' and the diary of a future chief justice recorded Blackstone's death as that of 'a most learned judge'. William Jones announced that his next publication would begin with 'an éloge on Blackstone; he was, indeed, an excellent man, an incomparable judge, and, in my opinion, one of the best writers in our language'.[5] But the most substantial tribute came, after some delay, from his former colleagues at All Souls College, who agreed in December 1780 that 'a Statue be erected to the memory of Sr W Blackstone deceased'. Warden Tracy accordingly commissioned the sculptor John Bacon to produce a life-size image ('that of about five feet, seven inches') in statuary marble, showing Blackstone, seated, in judicial dress. Tracy eventually contributed £100 towards the total cost of £539; another £50 'to perpetuate the Memory of my late dear Friend' came from the estate of Benjamin Buckler, by virtue of a codicil added to his will just before he himself died on Christmas Eve 1780.[6] Originally placed in the college dining hall, where his lectures had been first delivered, the statue was then moved to the chapel, and finally in 1872 reached the Codrington Library, where it now remains.

Well before Bacon's handiwork was completed and delivered, James Clitherow had fulfilled an obligation as his deceased brother-in-law's executor by publishing two volumes of his case notes. Sales of these *Reports of Cases Determined in the several Courts of Westminster Hall from 1746 to 1779: Taken and compiled by the Honourable Sir William Blackstone* eventually added some £1,187 to the value of his estate (which actually totalled around £25,000 in 1781), while Clitherow's biographical preface provided an indispensable source for all future accounts of Blackstone's life.[7] This text gained further currency with the appearance in 1782 of *The Biographical History of Sir William Blackstone*. Yet despite its promising title, the 'Gentleman of Lincoln's Inn' who figured as author of this work had done little more than embroider verbatim quotations from

[4] LMA, ACC 1360/585 has two pasted-in newspaper cuttings, one from *Jackson's Oxford Journal* (see n. 1 above), the other unidentified; see also *The Gazetteer and New Daily Advertiser*, 15 February 1780.

[5] Nottingham University Library, PwF 6056, Kaye to Portland, 'Wednesday night'; G. T. Kenyon, *The Life of Lloyd, First Lord Kenyon* (1873), 52. *Letters of Sir William Jones*, i. 345: Jones to Althorp, 18 February 1780.

[6] Neill, 'Blackstone, Oxford, and the Law', 296–7; Codrington, Warden's MS 22/4, fo. 414v.

[7] LMA, ACC 1360/586/2/7; Doolittle, 100.

Clitherow's preface with his own mannered and pedantic commentary.[8] Admitting 'that very few particulars are to be met with in this History, that have not been already communicated to the Public', the anonymous compiler sought to justify his enterprise as a means of making Clitherow's 'Memoirs' available to a wider audience than could readily afford a copy of Blackstone's *Reports*.[9] Including preface, dedication, list of authorities, extensive footnotes and index, the *Biographical History* managed to spin out Clitherow's 31 pages to more than six times that length. Bound up with an equally diffuse *Catalogue of Sir William Blackstone's Writings*, plus a *Nomenclature of Westminster Hall* listing the names of judges, King's Counsel and serjeants at law from 1746–79, 'being the whole Time, in which Sir William Blackstone attended the Courts of Justice', this whole overblown production appeared under the auspices of a bookseller-printer specialising in 'popular and ephemeral literature'.[10] Yet even while reinforcing the status of Clitherow's 'Memoirs' as the standard narrative account of Blackstone's life, the *Biographical History* also pointed, perhaps not entirely inadvertently, towards another, markedly less favourable perspective on its subject.

Notwithstanding his avowed impartiality, Clitherow would hardly have written anything other than a respectful eulogy. But after repeating his words of praise on Blackstone's 'generosity, without Affectation, bounded by Prudence and Economy', the *Biographical History* used a footnote to suggest that the booksellers of London and Westminster were less persuaded of 'Sir William Blackstone's Generosity, as an Author at least' (possibly a reference to Blackstone's shrewd dealings with respect to the original self-published editions of his *Commentaries*, and other professional writings).[11]

---

[8] One of the British Library's three copies (shelf-mark 276 k 1) has a title page annotation identifying this person as 'Dr Douglas', which may explain other attributions of the work to 'D. Douglas'. However, no possible 'D. Douglas' appears in the membership records of Lincoln's Inn, as H. I. Whitaker (a former librarian of that society) pointed out in a note included in the second copy of the *Biographical History*, now at the Yale Law School Library. Whitaker's candidate was Sylvester Douglas, later Lord Glenbervie, the Scottish-born parliamentary reporter, barrister, and politician. But a preface to *The Nomenclature of Westminster Hall* bound up with the *Biographical History*, claims that 'the Compiler of this Nomenclature attended the several courts of justice himself, in and from Trinity term 1750 . . . ' (xviii). This rules out Douglas, who was only born in 1743. Another possibility is John Rayner, the erratic antiquarian-minded attorney, solicitor, and 'Gentleman of the Inner Temple', who published at least eight historical and legal treatises between 1758 and 1786: Langford, *A Polite and Commercial People*, 664–5. My thanks to Guy Holborn and Simon May for help with this puzzle.

[9] *Biographical History*, x–xi.

[10] H. R. Plomer, C. H. Bushnell and E. R. McDix, *A Dictionary of the Printers and Booksellers . . . in England, Scotland and Ireland from 1726 to 1775* (Oxford, 1932), 25.

[11] *Biographical History*, 95.

Further, Clitherow's guarded reference to Blackstone's irritability is pointed and particularized with an anecdote recounting his 'passion . . . instantaneous and violent' in reaction to a '*familiar* manner of accosting him (as he was pleased to term it)', when 'in the course of conversation, and out of pure respect' for his recently-conferred DCL degree, a 'certain bookseller, now deceased' happened to address him as 'Doctor' (instead, presumably, of calling him 'Sir'). The subsequent footnote goes so far as to suggest that not only 'those who did not know him' regarded Blackstone as ill-natured, but also '*some, who did*'.[12]

These comments may have comforted Blackstone's detractors. But no more than Clitherow does the *Biographical History* refer to the slashing attack on Blackstone and his *Commentaries* by Bentham's *Fragment on Government*. Indeed, there is little trace of that work's influence on attitudes to Blackstone and his writings immediately after the latter's death. In 1780 the reclusive barrister Manessah Dawes did however defend Blackstone against the *Fragment's* charges of being 'a professed champion for *religious intolerance*, and openly setting his face against civil reformation', as supported by no more than an anonymous author's opinion. While possibly making one think twice about the merits of the *Commentaries*, in the end his 'critical display of ingenuity, adding nothing to the reader's instruction or information', encouraged admiration for, rather than condemnation of, Blackstone's labours.[13] Here again the author seems to disappear behind his book. Less than three years before Blackstone's death it was remarked that, although 'his Writings are now greatly admired and read even by those who have no Business to make Law their Study, he is it seems for all that very unskilful in producing his Knowledge for the purposes of Conversation'. An accompanying anecdote, relating Blackstone's silence during some 'Law Talk', reports the remark of the veteran Serjeant William Davy, that 'he must sell out of the Stocks before he can give you change for a Guinea'.[14]

An equally irreverent attitude was shown by Horace Walpole, who confessed in May 1780 to have 'laughed at Dr Blackstone', whom young William Jones had 'quoted as an advocate for the rights of learning' when seeking Walpole's support for his candidacy to succeed Sir Roger Newdigate as MP for the University of Oxford. This perhaps foreshadows Edward Gibbon's sardonic announcement in 1789, after bemoaning 'what delays and difficulties do attend the man who meddles with legal and

[12] Ibid., 96–7 (italics in original).
[13] M. Dawes, *An Essay on Intellectual Liberty* (1780), 84–5.
[14] *Thraliana*, i. 150.

landed business', that 'the elderly Lady in a male habit who informed me that Yorkshire was a register County is a certain Judge, one Sir William Blackstone, whose name you have possibly heard of'.[15] But the final metamorphosis, from Commentator to old woman, awaited Jeremy Bentham's 1809 outburst about talk of 'balance' in relation to parliamentary reform—'never will it do: leave that to Mother Goose and Mother Blackstone'.[16] Unfortunately for Bentham and those of a like mind, Blackstone's book was not so easily brushed aside. Indeed, during the later eighteenth and early nineteenth centuries demand for successive editions, abridgements, and translations of the *Commentaries* seemed almost inexhaustible, notwithstanding continued criticism by Bentham and his followers, Dissenters, Irish patriots, commonwealthsmen, political radicals, reformers, and others who objected to Blackstone's emphasis on the supremacy of parliament, together with various judges, jurists, practitioners, and authors of legal treatises. Thus the French commentator Alexis de Tocqueville was expressing an entirely conventional—if never uncontested—view when, 100 years after Blackstone began his Oxford lectures, he termed him 'an inferior writer, without liberality of mind or depth of judgment'.[17]

Because Blackstone's posthumous reputation was inextricably and unsurprisingly intertwined with that of his *Commentaries*, tracing its vicissitudes over the past two centuries would involve examining the reception and influence of that book not only in Britain, North America, and Australasia, but much of Europe, Africa, and Asia as well. The aim of this biography has been rather to tell the story of Blackstone's life and work in his own time, while recognizing the *Commentaries* as still his major claim to fame, if by no means his sole noteworthy accomplishment. Sheer lack of evidence obscures a large part of that story, especially in its domestic settings, with family and friends. But more than enough survives to revise some established views and preconceptions, as well as to suggest additional contexts and perspectives, which in turn may help to inform future discussion of the *Commentaries*.

To begin with, the notion of Blackstone as arch-conservative, 'always found to be a specious defender of the existing order of things' according to the eleventh edition of the *Encyclopaedia Britannica*, should not have survived Holdsworth's enumeration of the *Commentaries'* readiness to criticise numerous aspects of the legal and political status quo, and

[15] Walpole, *Letters*, xxix. 36; *The Letters of Edward Gibbon*, ed. J. E. Norton (1956), iii. 170.
[16] Bentham, *Works*, ed. Bowring, iii. 450.
[17] Lobban, *The Common Law and English Jurisprudence*, 56–9; *Memoir, Letters and Remains of Alexis de Tocqueville* (Cambridge, 1861), ii. 223 (I am grateful to Keith Thomas for this reference).

Milsom's demonstration of both the difficulty and momentous consequences of his achievement in that book.[18] But to their insights may be
added the distinctly radical nature of Blackstone's activities and attitudes
outside the *Commentaries*, most notably as an educational and administrative innovator at Oxford University during the 1750s, together with his
efforts to implement a fundamental measure of penal reform in the late
1770s. A committed advocate of material and moral improvement, a reader
of Newton, and of Priestley's scientific writings, Blackstone was no blind
adherent of traditional ways—even in matters architectural, as witness the
octagonal neo-gothic spire he was responsible for commissioning for his
parish church. His politics were Tory, which until 1760 meant opposition
(never Jacobite), embodying a principled commitment to independence,
personal as well as institutional (in the case of the university). His parliamentary record is almost as confusing to historians as it was to contemporaries, partly because he followed no single leader or faction. To the
extent that Blackstone's Tory loyalties reflected his Anglicanism, they may
well have moderated as his youthful antagonism towards Dissent gradually softened. More broadly, however much Blackstone disliked the House
of Commons' rough-and-tumble, or deprecated ill-drafted legislation produced by ill-educated legislators, his emphasis on parliament's unfettered
sovereignty tended to both complement and legitimize the vast expansion
of parliamentary governance which has characterized the later modern
British state.

Far from being (in the words of one recent work of historical reference)
'insular, little touched by the spirit of the Enlightenment', Blackstone
surely qualifies as a leading representative of the English manifestation
of that European movement, or mood, in so far as 'improvement' was
'the core element in the British Enlightenment'.[19] That is certainly how
he was seen by at least some contemporaries, like the London journal which in 1779 named Blackstone with Montesquieu, Beccaria, and
Voltaire as a quartet who 'have echoed to each other, "This enlightened
age. This eighteenth century"'.[20] Insular only in the sense that he does
not appear to have travelled beyond England, possibly for financial reasons, Blackstone's range of interest and intellectual reference was far from
parochial. While evidently not possessing conversational French, he

---

[18] *Encyclopaedia Britannica* (1911), iv. 25–6; a handy conspectus of comments for and against the
Commentaries is provided by S. Allibone, *A Critical Dictionary of English Literature* (1908), i.197–8.
HEL, xii. 728–9 ; Milsom, 'The Nature of Blackstone's Achievement'.

[19] *Who's Who in British History Beginnings to 1901* (1998), i.113; P. Borsay, 'The Culture of
Improvement' in *The Eighteenth Century 1688–1815*, ed. P. Langford (Oxford, 2002), 184.

[20] *The Literary Fly*, no. 8 (6 March 1779).

wrote and read in that language, and the celebrated Parisian *avocat* Élie de Beaumont, Voltaire's pro-protestant ally during the Calas affair, was happy to count Blackstone among 'mes amis' when they met for dinner at Lord Mansfield's in November 1764. Blackstone had previously questioned de Beaumont about the practice of French courts in ransom cases, and they possibly discussed a French translation of the *Commentaries* in 1775. An equally significant European contact was the bibliophile Gerard Meerman, pensionary of Rotterdam, who (like de Beaumont a few years later) was granted an honorary doctorate in law when he visited Oxford in 1759, quite possibly on Blackstone's initiative; between 1761 and 1768 they corresponded on the history of books and printing, and exchanged copies of their respective publications.[21]

Unlike most Continental *philosophes*, their British counterparts were not characteristically irreligious or secularist in outlook. Blackstone's orthodox Anglican faith, and conspicuous lack of sympathy for Protestant Dissent (at least until his latter years), did not therefore automatically disqualify him from identification with the cause of enlightened progress. But these attitudes may have made for an unbridgeable gulf with the more sceptically-minded, such as Bentham and Gibbon.[22] It has been suggested that the 'Church of England in the first half of the eighteenth century perhaps reached the zenith of its allegiance'.[23] Blackstone's commitment to that church and interest in matters of religion are amply evidenced by his undergraduate reading and writing (most notably *The Pantheon*), various involvements with his Wallingford parish, his letters of condolence to a widowed cousin and of comfort to an anxious wife, the concern to vindicate his God and his King in the face of what he took to be Wilkes's blasphemies, his hopes for religious instruction as a potential means of rehabilitation in the new 'penitentiaries', as well as many passages in his Oxford lectures and the published *Commentaries*. All these point to a Christian belief which, if not particularly demonstrative, was a good deal more than merely formal or nominal. Another expression of religious faith may be found in Blackstone's sense of duty, whether to his college, his university, his family, or his King (who in the person of George III

[21] 'Un Voyageur Français en Angleterre', 103; *Letters*, 152; J. van Heel, 'From Venice and Naples to Paris, the Hague, London, Oxford, Berlin . . . The Odyssey of the Manuscript Collection of Gerard and Johan Meerman', in *Books on the Move*, ed. R. Myers *et al.* (2007), 91–2.

[22] Blackstone subscribed for two copies of the translation by his former Charterhouse teacher William Salisbury of J–B. Bullet's *History of the Establishment of Christianity* (1776), with accompanying 'strictures on Mr Gibbon's account of Christianity': ibid., iv.

[23] W. M. Jacob, *Lay People and Religion in the Early Eighteenth Century* (Cambridge, 1996), 19.

shared a similar ethos of service—as well as an obsession with time and punctuality).[24]

While it is generally agreed that Blackstone's prose style is one of the *Commentaries'* great strengths, even admirers find it difficult to defend the originality or precision of his theoretical reasoning. Blackstone's forte was plainly not philosophy. Indeed, notwithstanding his multifarious academic, bibliographical, historical, literary, and scholarly interests, it was primarily as a practical man of business and an organizer, someone who delighted in bringing order out of chaos, an expositor and a writer of great clarity and power, that he made his mark. He cannot exactly be said to have created an intellectual discipline, let alone to have been an original thinker armed with a single great idea. But he was a great educational innovator, who can be credited with founding the common law as an academic subject, as well as propounding an ecumenical model of liberal education in words which have scarcely lost their meaning or relevance: 'For sciences are of a sociable disposition, and flourish best in the neighbourhood of each other: nor is there any branch of learning, but may be helped and improved by assistances drawn from other arts'.[25]

Despite his academic persona, and the fact that he spent nearly half his lifespan as an undergraduate, fellow, professor, and head of house at the University of Oxford, Blackstone's practical experience of law and legal institutions was rather larger and more varied than has been commonly supposed. A somewhat disdainful critique of his *Reports* in the *Monthly Review* commented that 'as a pleader, as a senator, and as a judge, Sir William Blackstone was certainly respectable; but not the greatest of his time'.[26] This actually seems quite a fair assessment, if qualified by the observation that Blackstone was fated to serve only a ten-year term as puisne justice in the court of Common Pleas, as against Chief Justice Mansfield's 32-year dominance of King's Bench. Blackstone's judicial reputation may have suffered some continuing damage from the English bar's traditional condescension towards the supposed mere scholar or academic; it is conceivable that he was better regarded as a judge by non-lawyers than some members of the profession.

Unlike Mansfield, Blackstone was no relaxed public performer. Nor was he the easiest man to get along with, especially in his maturer years. An awkward combination of diffidence, reserve, committed diligence and drive, lack of physical grace and social graces, some insensitivity to the feelings of others (not least when minding what they might well have

---

[24] Black, *George III*, 148–9, 184, 427.   [25] *Commentaries*, i.33.
[26] *Monthly Review* 67 (July 1782), 5.

considered their own business) coupled with oversensitivity to personal slights, real or imagined, were among his less attractive qualities. The anxious quest for preferment on which he embarked in the 1760s, while scarcely atypical of the times, and at least partly motivated by concern to provide for his recently-acquired wife and growing family of children, is hardly a pretty or inspiring sight. But at least it betrays more humanity than might be suggested by monumental images of a bewigged and titled judge, in which the person is overwhelmed by the trappings of office. We should also note that the remarkable energy which Blackstone continued to expend even in the very last years of his life was, on the whole, then as before, devoted to projects other than personal aggrandizement. While doubtless ambitious, Blackstone did have a strong sense of obligation to others. In an age dominated by patronage he was also something of a meritocrat, who not only owed his personal success very largely to his own efforts, but sought to extend that principle more widely, as in his attempts to restrict the role of founder's kin at All Souls. By the same token, if much of his praise for the constitution, government, laws, and polity of Hanoverian Britain inevitably strikes modern ears as excessively complacent and hyperbolic, it is sobering to consider that the liberties which Blackstone celebrated as 'the Absolute Rights of Individuals'—not just of 'every Englishman'[27]—can by no means be taken uniformly for granted today, even in those societies which continue to depend upon the inheritance of the common law.

---

[27] *Commentaries*, i. 117, 123.

APPENDIX I

Blackstone's earliest known composition
(see pp. 24–5 above)

To the Rev: Mr Hotchkis
Sir:
Who can forswear your Nuptials to relate
And speak the Pleasures of so blest a State
A Love so constant and so true, a Flame,
To future Ages must be told by Fame:
Hers, like the Vestal Fire does ever burn:
Yours, like the glowing Ashes in an Urn.

No sordid Avarice was in your Love:
Beauty it was, not Gold, your Hearts did move:
Your Spouse a Nymph of chast Diana's Train;
Whilst you Minerva's Empire do maintain.
Thrice happy You! Now blest with such a Fair,
With whom the Queen of Love e'en dreads Compare.
Thrice happy Lady! blest with such a Man,
In whom, Goodnature and sound Learning reign.
Thrice happy Pair! both in each other blest,
Whom Virtue join'd with Goodness does invest.

Thus *Cattieuchlanian Tame with Isis join'd   *for Buckinghamshire.
Equals swift Eurus, rivals ev'ry Wind.
And pleasantly they join and mix their Stream,
And Each of Each, and both desirous seem;
Thence briskly flow, ambitious now to pay
A larger Tribute to the sov'reign Sea.
And as the Thames does, nourish ev'ry Plant,
And feels †Augusta as its Visitant;   †London.
So does your Influence with Learning feed
Her Chartreux Sons, her tender growing Breed:
With these may I be fortunate to share
The ampler Influence of your learned Care!

Hence I acceptance of my Lines desire
A Boy in Praise, unskill'd to turn the Lyre.

Foemina nunc docto pulcherrima juncta Marito est,
Tunc omnes monstrent Gaudia magna sua.

Tama velut, postquam Spatium iam voluerat amplum,
Obliquas Lymphas Isidis addit Aquis.

Vos quaerat faustos aque Fortuna secunda
Ac fruitur placidis Thamesis altus aquis.

W^m. Blackstone.

Source: 'Manuscript Poem', Lot 3, Sale 621, Freeman/Fine Arts of Philadelphia, Inc., 16 December 1993 (photocopy kindly supplied by Bill Cooper).

a. *James Clitherow's summary of Blackstone's annual income from All Souls College*

Sir W B's Acct of profits of All Souls Fellowship annually

Year		Amount	Liveries	Extra as Bursar
1744	chosen prob.	7: 17: 0	4	
1745	LLB Burs deput	57: 0: 8½	4	
1746	D° Dean	49: 1: 9½	2	
1747	D° Bursar	129: 19: 2¾	3¼	56: 5
1748	D° Dean	60: 7: 9¾	3	
1749	D° Cas. pos.	41: 4: 2¾	3¼	
1750	Dr Dean	59: 15: 5	3	
1751	Dr Bursar	156: 10: 4	4½	67: 13: 6
1752	Dr Cas.pos.	58: 6: 9	4¾	
1753	Dr	73: 8: 10½	4⅜	
1754	Dr	75: 8: 9	3½	
1755	Dr riding Burs	71: 16: 7¾	3	
1756	Dr	87: 10: 9½	2½	
1757	Dr cust Joc	83: 13: 2	4¾	
1758	Dr	85: 2: 3	4½	
1759	Dr	99: 19: 3½	5	
1760	Dr	63: 13: 0¼	3	
1761	"	54: 13: 5¼	2½	
1762	pt of a yr	5: 12: 1¼		

1 yr prob:
17 yrs fellow
<u>1 yr Quota</u>
19   1312: 1: 7

Besides which Chambers & Commons 12: 3: 0 a yr

Source: LMA, ACC 1360/586/1 (Clitherow Papers, Blackstone Trust, vouchers etc.).

b. James Clitherow's summary of Blackstone's earnings from his lectures and the Commentaries

20 Oct. 1758 chosen Vinerian Professor but before that he began his Law Lectures viz. 1753 gained by them as by his Books

1753	116. 0. 6
1754	226. 16. 0
1755	111. 6. 0
1756	I presume he did not read
1757	138. 12. 0
1758	247. 16. 0
1759	201. 12. 0

Then begins his Professors Salary	200 li a year
A present from the Prince of Wales	200. 0. 0

1760 Exclus of salary	258. 6. 0
1761	266. 14. 0
1762	340. 4. 0
1763	239. 8. 0
1764	237. 6. 0
1765	203. 14. 0
1766	4. 4. 0

Professorship I suppose then quitted because recd only 180 -pt of a yrs Salary

rec'd by Sale of his *Commentaries*

1765	380. 18. 2
1766	1598. 2. 4
1767	938. 11. 0
1768	1521. 8. 8
1769	2200. 16. 2
1770	1679. 11. 5
1771	1160. 9. 3
1772	3008. 4. 7
Copyright	2000. 0. 0
	14,488. 1. 7

Source: LMA, ACC 1360/586/5 (Clitherow Papers, Blackstone Trust, vouchers etc.).

Bibliography

PRIMARY SOURCES

1. Manuscript

Bedfordshire and Luton Archives and Records Service
R 3/266 (Davis and Reymers)
L30/14/333/32 (Thomas Robinson)

Beinecke Library
Osborn MS Files X–Z, 16549 (Charles Yorke)
O.S. c 43 (Sir John Eardley Wilmot)

Berkshire Record Office
W/Ac1/1/2 (Wallingford Corporation Common Council Book)
W/JQS/1 (Wallingford Sessions Book)
W/FA/C/1 (Wallingford Chamberlain's Receipt Book)
D/P 138/1/2 Wallingford St Mary parish register)
D/P 139/1/1 (Wallingford St Peter parish register)
D/P 139/5/1, 2 (Wallingford St Peter, Church Wardens' book)
D/P 139/11/1 (Wallingford St Peter, Poor Law Assessments)
D/EB/E1 (Seymour Richmond)
D/EH/T1; D/ESt/L2/3 (Deeds, settlement, evidence)

Bodleian Library
MS Auct. V. 2.4.31 (Charles Morton)
MS Ch. Wilts. c2 359 (Westbury)
MS Dep. b 48, fos. (Rowney Noel)
MS Eng. misc. a 23, fos. 26–31 (Clarendon proofs)
MS Eng. misc. d 578, p. 614 (William Gilpin)
MS Library Records e 554–5, 558–60 (Day books)
MS Rawlinson C 518 ('The Beginner's Advice towards the study of the Common Law')
MS Top. Oxon. b 177 (Bertie papers)
MS Top. Oxon. c 209 (Tracy and White papers)
MS Top. Oxon. d 378 (Thomas Walker and Earl of Abingdon's Trustees)
MS Top. Oxon. d 387 ('Controversial Papers relating to the Delegacy of the Press')
MS Top. Wilts. c 5 (Westbury)
MS D.D. All Souls b 15 (Miscellanea)
MS D.D. All Souls b 114 (Commons Book)

MS D.D. All Souls c 245 (box marked 'Terriers'), Bundle S (Edgeware rental)
MS D.D. All Souls c 255–6 (buildings)
MSS D.D. All Souls c 263 (bursars' accounts)
MS D.D. All Souls c 266/21 (appointment as steward)
MSS D.D. All Souls c 311–313 (compotus and expenses rolls)
MS D.D. All Souls e 266 (New Titling Book)
MSS D.D. All Souls e 21–38 (Song books)
MSS D.D. All Souls e 330–1 (Wine and cellar books)
MSS D.D. Bertie (earls of Abingdon)

British Library

Additional 17870 (Queen Charlotte's accounts); Additional 21507 (William Freke); Additional 28670 (Walter Bigg); Additional 35587 (Charles Viner); Additional 35636 (Charles Yorke); Additional 38457 (Charles Jenkinson); Additional 38838 (Thomas Bever notes); Additional 50010 (William de Grey); Additional 73760 (William Barrington)
Egerton 217 (parliamentary debates, 1769)

Codrington Library

MS 36 (Warden Niblett's Notebook)
MS 300 (i) (Dissertation on the Accounts)
MS 300 (ii–xxxvi) (Lecture notes, 1761–2)
MS 333 ('Elements of Architecture')
Acta in Capitulis 1707–53, 1753–1800
Appeals and Visitors' Injunctions
Library Minute Book
Steward's Books, 1742–48, 1754–60
Warden's MS 11 (Absence Book)
Warden's MS 17 (Philip Bliss notebook)
Warden's MSS 22–31 (Thomas Wenman's History)

Cornwall Record Office

R/5444, 5447 (Rashleigh)

East Sussex Record Office

SAS/RF 18/122–4 (Rose Fuller)

Exeter College, Oxford

Blacow transcripts

Folger Shakespeare Library

M.a. 11 (John Parnell)
W.b. 51(1), (2), (3) (George Steevens)

Free Library of Philadelphia
Hampton L. Carson Collection: Suffolk to [George Grenville?],
   3 December 1763

Getty Research Library
Special Collections, MS 89022 ('Abridgement of Architecture')

Gloucestershire Archives
D3549 13/1/B25, 13/3 (Granville Sharp)

Guildhall Library
MS 11,316/70 (St Michael Quorn, land tax)

Hampshire Record Office
9M73/G708–16 (James Harris)

Inner Temple Archives
CHA/2/1, 5/2 (Chambers' accounts)

Jesus College, Oxford
RE 6 (Bursar's Register 1713–1851)

Lambeth Palace Library
Secker Papers 6 (Founder's kin appeals)

Law Society, London
BLA/V61A, 2 vols. (Thomas Bever)

Lincoln's Inn Library
Dampier MSS, Buller Paper Books 51a (assize reports)

London Metropolitan Archives: City of London
ACC 1360/580–8 (Clitherow)
ACC 1876/G, PS (Charterhouse)

Magdalen College, Oxford
Liber Compotus, 1757–69
MSS 476 (Thomas Winchester); MSS 655b (Suffolk)

Middle Temple Archives
1/MPA/6–7 (Parliament minutes)
3 /BAL/1 (Bar ledger)
K10 (Parliament Book)

Morrab Library, Penzance
MOR/Bor/2E (William Borlase inward letters)

Museum van Het Boek/Museum Meermano–Westreenianum, The Hague
257/51–71 (Blackstone-Meerman correspondence)

New York Public Library
MSS and Archives Section: Montague Collection of Historical Autographs
(Blackstone to John Allnat, 11 December 1777)

Northamptonshire Record Office
Dolben and Langham (Cottesbroke) papers

Nottingham University Library
Portland papers

Oxford University Archives
Chancellor's Court papers, 1751–9
Hyp/A/60, 72 (Chancellor's Court)
NEP/Subtus/Reg Bg, Bh (Convocation registers)
NW/4/7 (*Bateman's case*, opinion)
NW/4/9 'Blackstone's Case of the Power of Convocation . . .'
SP/C/11 (Pomfret gift)
SP 70 (Book of Admission to Study Civil Law)
V/3/1/1, 12; V/3/2/1; V3/5/1–16 (Viner bequest)
WPα/22/1 (Blackstone drafts)
WPα/22/2 (annotated papers re university constitution)
WPα/22/3 ('Mem[orand]da concerning the Press')
WPα/23/6 (Chancellor's court procedure)
WPα/57/12 (Chancellor's Court rules)
WPβ (Vice Chancellor's compotus 1735–1768)

Oxford University Press Archives
Orders of the Delegates of the Press, 1761–5
OUP/PR/1/18/4 ('Account for Printing 1747–1780')
OUP 5/1/1 (Extracts of charters, etc.)

Oxfordshire Record Office
JXXVI/a/1 (lecture notes, 1758–9)
MS D.D. Par. Oxford St Ebbe's c 12 e
CH/L. II/1 (Deed of separation)

Pembroke College, Oxford
9/1/71–6 (Buttery books, 1738–44)
40/5/2 (College register)
62/1/13/1–5 (Themes)
4/4/1 (Caution money accounts)

Private collections

a. Francis Markham: (John Loveday correspondence)
b. Antony Taussig: (Willes to [Niblett], 23 November 1750; 'Friendship, an Ode';
   Shelburne to Blackstone, 11 September 1762)

The Queen's College, Oxford
5 M (Michel Foundation)

Records of the Parliament Office
HL/PO/JO/10/7/301 (House of Lords, Main Papers)

Royal Institution of Cornwall
BLP/1/49, 50 (William Jackson)

St John's College, Oxford
Munim. LXXXVI. D.8 (Thomas Fry's diary, ts., ed. W. N. Hargreaves-Mawdsley)

Somerset Archives and Record Office
DD/WY/183 (Alexander Popham)

Surrey History Centre
G52/8/10/1 Bray papers

The National Archives, Kew (formerly Public Record Office)
C11 (Chancery pleadings)
C33/389–402 (Chancery decree and order books)
C189/5–6 (Circuit fiats)
E161 (Exchequer: King's Remembrances, minute books)
KB21/36–7 (King's Bench crown side rule books)
KB125/149–153,156–61 (King's Bench pleas side rule books)
PROB 3, 11 (Wills etc.)
SP 37 (State Papers Domestic)
SP44/90–94 (Criminal petitions and reports)
T1/434/124 (Window tax)

University College London
MS Add. 120 (John Wilkinson)

Warwickshire Record Office
CR 136 (Sir Roger Newdigate)

Winchester College Muniments
330a, 8542c, 13360, 20631, 23205 a–b (correspondence and opinions)

Wiltshire and Swindon History Centre
D1/51/5 (Clergy book)
735/5 (Chilton Foliat register)

2. Printed

Newspapers and periodicals
Annual Register
Critical Review
Gazetteer and New Daily Advertiser
General Evening Post
Gentleman's Magazine
Jackson's Oxford Journal
Lawyer's Magazine, or Attorney's and Solicitor's Universal Library
Lloyd's Evening Post
London Chronicle
London Evening Post
London Magazine
Middlesex Chronicle
Monthly Review
Morning Post and Daily Advertiser
North Briton
Public Advertiser
St James Chronicle

Books and pamphlets

Anon., *A Dramatic Piece: By the Charter-House Scholars: In Memory of the Powder-Plot* (1732)
_____, *A Letter to the Rt. Hon. Henry Lord Viscount Cornbury* (1751)
_____, *An Authentick Copy of the Poll . . . for the University of Oxford* (Oxford, 1768)
_____, *An Objection Drawn from the Act of Union, Against a Review of the Liturgy* (1770)
_____, *A Petition having been propos'd in the last Convocation* (Oxford, 1758)
_____, *A Series of Papers on Subjects the most Interesting to the Nation in General, and Oxford in Particular* (1750)
_____, *A Vindication of the Right of Election, Against the Disabling Power of the House of Commons* (1769)
_____, *Dr Blackstone having desired the Authors of a Paper dated November 20, "to maintain their Accusations"* [Oxford, 1758]
_____, *Epicedia Oxoniensia in Obitum Celsissimi et Desideratissimi Frederici Principis Walliae* (Oxford, 1751)
_____, *Fifty Queries concerning the present Oxfordshire Contest* (Oxford, 1754)
_____, *Informations and Other Papers Relating to the Treasonable Verses* (Oxford, 1755)

_____, *Rules and orders relating to Charterhouse And to the Good Government thereof* [1748?]

_____, *The Beauties of Biography*, 2 vols. (1792)

_____, *The Biographical History of Sir William Blackstone, Late One of the Justices of Both Benches. A Name, as celebrated at the Universities of Oxford and Cambridge, as in Westminster-Hall. And A Catalogue of all Sir William Blackstone's Works, Manuscript, As Well as Printed. With a Nomenclature of Westminster-Hall. The Whole Illustrated with Notes, Observations and References. Also, A Preface and Index to Each Part. By a Gentleman of Lincoln's-Inn* (1782)

_____, *The Catalogue of Graduates &c. in the University of Oxford . . . 1735 to October 10. 1747* (Oxford, [1747?])

_____, *The Catalogue of Graduates &c in the University of Oxford, . . . 1747. to . . . 1760* (Oxford, [1760?])

_____, *The Genuine Trial, Life and Dying Words of the Rev. James Hackman* (1779)

_____, *The New Oxford Guide* (Oxford, 1759)

_____, *The Polyanthea*, 2 vols. (1805)

_____, *The Rights of the Sailors Vindicated* (1772), 15–23

Aiken, J., *A View of the Character and Public Services of the late John Howard Esq.* (1792)

Alcock, T., *Some Memoirs of the Life of Dr Nathan Alcock, Lately Deceased* (1780)

[Almon, J.], *A Letter Concerning Libels* (1764)

[Amhurst, N.], *Terrae-Filius: Or, the Secret History of the University of Oxford, in Several Essays*, 2 vols. (1726)

Atterbury, F., *The Epistolary Correspondence . . .*, 4 vols. (1783–87)

Ayliffe, J., *The Antient and the Present Estate of the University of Oxford*, 2 vols. (1714)

[Baker, J.], *The Diary of John Baker*, ed. P. C. Yorke (1931)

Bassett, F., *The Case of a Gentleman, Unjustly deprived of his Vote* (1759)

Bearcroft, P., *An Historical Account of Thomas Sutton Esq; And of His Foundation in Charter-House* (1737)

[Bentham, J.], *A Comment on the Commentaries and A Fragment of Government*, ed. J. H. Burns and H. L. A. Hart (1977)

_____, *Works*, ed. J. Bowring, 11 vols. (Edinburgh, 1843)

_____, *Correspondence*, ed. T. L. S. Sprigge, 12 vols. (1968–2006)

[Bingham, G.], *Dissertations, Essays, and Sermons*, ed. P. Bingham, 2 vols. (1804)

[Blackstone, W.], *A Case for the Opinion of Counsel* [Oxford, 1759; OUA WPα 22/2(10)]

Blackstone, W., *A Discourse on the Study of the Law* (Oxford, 1758)

_____, *A Letter to the Author of the Question Stated* (1769)

_____, *A Reply to Dr Priestley's Remarks on the Fourth Volume of the Commentaries on the Laws of England* (1769)

_____, *A Treatise on the Law of Descents in Fee-Simple* (Oxford, 1759)

_____, *An Analysis of the Laws of England* (Oxford, 1756, and later edns)

Blackstone, W., 'An Argument in the Exchequer Chamber on giving judgment in the Case of Perrin and another against Blake', in *A Collection of Tracts Relative to the Law of England, from Manuscripts,* ed. F. Hargrave (1787)

_____, *An Essay on Collateral Consanguinity, Its Limits, Extent, and Duration; More particularly as it is regarded by the Statutes of All Souls College in the University of Oxford* (1750)

_____, *A Question having been started, with regard to the Power of Congregation* [Oxford, 1758: Bodl. Gough Oxon. 96 (51)]

_____, *Books recommended as proper to accompany this course* [Oxford, c. 1758; Bodl. Vet. A5 a.15 (44)]

_____, *Commentaries on the Laws of England,* 4 vols. (Oxford, 1765–69, and later editions)

_____, *Considerations on the Question, Whether Tenants by Copy of Court Roll According to the Custom of the Manor, Though not at the Will of the Lord, Are Freeholders Qualified to Vote in Elections for Knights of the Shire* (1758)

_____, *Dissertation on the Accounts of All Souls College, Oxford . . . Presented to the Roxburghe Club by Sir William Anson* (1898)

_____, *Dr Blackstone finding himself personally charged* [Oxford, 1758; Bodl. Gough Oxon. 96 (38)]

_____, *In Michaelmas Term next will begin A Course of Lectures on the Laws of England* [Oxford, 1753; Codrington Library]

_____, *Law Tracts,* 2 vols. (Oxford, 1762)

_____, *Oxford 30 Dec. 1758. Copies of the Opinions of three very eminent and learned Gentlemen* . . . [Oxford, 1758; OUA WPα/22/2(3); Bodl. Gough Oxon. 96(61)]

_____, *Oxford, 18 June 1759. The Vinerian Professor gives this public Notice* [Oxford, 1759; Bodl. Gough Oxon. 96 (40)]

_____, *Present Draught. Proposed Amendments* [Oxford, 1759; OUA WPα/22/2(5)]

_____, *Proposals for a Course of Lectures; Scheme of the Course; Books recommended* [Oxford, 1754, 1760, 1764; Bodl. G. A. Oxon. b. 111 (50), (55b–c)]

_____, *Reports of Cases Determined in the several Courts of Westminster-Hall, from 1746 to 1779 . . . with a Preface Containing Memoirs of His Life,* ed. J. Clitherow, 2 vols. (1781)

_____, *Short Remarks on a Paper dated June 30, 1758* [Oxford, 1758; Bodl. Gough Oxon. 96 (29)]

_____, *Some Doubts having arisen with regard to Mr VINER's Intentions* [Oxford, 1758; Bodl. Gough Oxford 96 (14, 15)]

_____, *That it may be the more readily apprehended* [Oxford, 1758; Bodl. Gough Oxon. 96 (33)]

_____, *The Great Charter and the Charter of the Forest, with other authentic Instruments* (Oxford, 1759)

_____, *The Letters of Sir William Blackstone 1744–1780,* ed. W. R. Prest (Selden Soc., Supp. Ser., Vol. 14, 2006)

Blackstone, W., *The Members of Convocation are desired seriously to consider the following*. [Oxford, 1758; Bodl. Gough Oxon. 96 (52)]

____, *The Pantheon: A Vision* (1747)

____, *The Vinerian Professor is extremely concerned* [Oxford, 1761]

____, *To obviate the Mistakes of an Explanatory Paper* [Oxford, 1759; OUA WPα /22/2 (12); Gough Oxon. 96 (49)]

____, *To the Reverend Dr Randolph, Vice Chancellor of the University of Oxford* (Oxford, 1757)

____, *Tracts, Chiefly Relating to the Antiquities and Laws of England* (Oxford, 1771)

[Blackstone, W., Furneaux, P., *et al.*], *The Palladium of Conscience* (Philadelphia, 1773)

The Correspondence and other Papers of James Boswell relating to the Making of the Life of Johnson, ed. M. Waingrow (1969)

Boswell's Life of Johnson, ed. R. W. Chapman (Oxford , 1960)

[Buckler, B?], *Elisha's Visit to Gilgal and his healing the pot of pottage symbolically explain'd: a Sermon Preached before the Warden and College of All-Souls on Friday the second of November 1759* (1760)

Buckler, B., *A Proper Explanation of the Oxford Almanack for this present Year MDCCLV* (1755)

____, *A Reply to Dr Huddesford's Observations Relating to the Delegates of the Press* (Oxford, 1756)

____, *An Examination of the Objections to the Resolutions . . .* [Oxford, 1758; Bodl. G A Oxon. b 19 (779) & Bodl. Gough Oxon. 96 (22)]

____, *A View of the Misrepresentations* [Oxford, 1758; Bodl. Gough Oxon. 96 (25)]

____, *Stemmata Chicheleana* (Oxford, 1765)

Burgh, J., *Political Disquisitions*, 3 vols. (1774–5)

Burke, E., *The Correspondence of Edmund Burke, Volume II*, ed. T. W. Copeland and L. Sutherland (Cambridge, 1960)

Burrow, J., *Reports of Cases Adjudged in the Court of King's Bench*, 5 vols. (1790)

Campbell, R., *The London Tradesman* (1747)

Sir Henry Cavendish's Debates of the House of Commons During the Thirteenth Parliament of Great Britain. Vol. I. 1768–1770 (1841)

Chapman, T., *A Further Inquiry into the Right of Appeal* (Cambridge, 1752)

Churchill, C, *Poems*, 2 vols. (1769)

[Cobbett, W.], *Cobbett's Parliamentary History of England*, 36 vols. (1806–1820)

Congreve, R., *Panegyrica Oratio Habita in Regio Hospitio Olim Domo Carthusiana* (1733)

The Correspondence of William Cowper, ed. T. Wright, 4 vols. (1904)

Crawford, C., *Letters from Academicus to Eugenius* (1773)

The Journal of Samuel Curwen Loyalist, ed. A. Oliver (Cambridge MA, 1972)

Dawes, M., *An Essay on Intellectual Liberty* (1780)

[de Beaumont, J-B-J. É], 'Voyages Anciens, Moeurs Pittoresques. Un Voyageur Français en Angleterre en 1764', ed. V. de Gruchy, *Revue Britannique*, Sept.– Nov. 1895

Defoe, D., *A Tour Thro' the whole Island of Great Britain*, ed. G. D. H. Cole (1927; 1724–7)

The Correspondence of Robert Dodsley 1733–1764, ed. J. E. Tierney (Cambridge, 1988)

[Dodsley, R., comp.], *A Collection of Poems by Several Hands*, 6 vols., ed. M. Suarez (1782, 1977)

[Forster, N.], *An Answer to a Pamphlet Entitled, 'The Question Stated'* (1769)

_____, *A Defence of the Proceedings of the House of Commons in the Middlesex Election* (1770)

The Pension Book of Gray's Inn, ed. R. J. Fletcher, 2 vols. (1901–10)

Foss, E., *The Judges of England*, 9 vols. (1848–64)

Francklin, T., *A Sermon Preached at St George's Bloomsbury . . . for the Benefit of the Humane Society* (1779)

Furneaux, P., *Letters to the Honourable Mr Justice Blackstone concerning his Exposition of the Act of Toleration* (1769)

The Correspondence of King George III from 1760 to December 1783, ed. J. Fortescue, 6 vols (1927–8)

Letters from George III to Lord Bute 1756–1766, ed. R. Sedgwick (1939)

The English Essays of Edward Gibbon, ed. P. B. Craddock (Oxford, 1972)

The Letters of Edward Gibbon, ed. J. E. Norton, 3 vols. (1956)

Memoirs of Dr. Richard Gilpin, ed. W. Jackson (1879)

Graves, R., *Euphrosyne: or, Amusements on the Road of Life* (1780)

_____, *Recollections of Some Particulars in the Life of the late William Shenstone* (1788)

_____, *The Triflers* (1806)

The Grenville Papers, ed. W. J. Smith, 4 vols. (1852–3)

Additional Grenville Papers 1763–1765, ed. J. R. Tomlinson (Manchester, 1962)

[Gurney, J.], *The Whole Proceedings in the Cause of the Action Brought by The Rt. Hon. Geo. Onslow Esq. Against the Rev. Mr Horne* (1770)

Tory and Whig: the Parliamentary Papers of Edward Harley . . . and William Hay, ed. S. Taylor and C. Jones (1998)

A Series of Letters of the First Earl of Malmesbury, his Family and Friends, ed. J. Harris, 2 vols. (1870)

Hartley, D., *Observations on Man* (1749, 1791)

Remarks and Collections of Thomas Hearne. Vol. VIII (Oxford Historical Soc., 1907)

Historical Manuscripts Commission, *Twelfth Report*, Appendix X (Charlemont 1745–83) (1891)

Hoare, P., *Memoirs of Granville Sharp, Esq.* (1828)

Holliday, J., *The Life of William Late Earl of Mansfield* (1797)

[Huddesford, G.], *Observations Relating to the Delegates of the Press* (Oxford, 1756)

____, *To the Reverend and Worshipful the Heads* (Oxford, 1756)

Humane Society, London, *Reports of the Humane Society . . . 1777* (n.d., 1778?)

Diary of an Oxford Methodist Benjamin Ingham 1733–1734, ed. R. P. Heitzenrater (Durham NC, 1985)

Calendar of the Inner Temple Records 1750–1800, ed. A. R. Roberts (1936)

The Jenkinson Papers 1760–1766, ed. N. S. Jucker (1949)

The Letters of Samuel Johnson Volume I 1731–1772, ed. B. Redford (Princeton NJ, 1992)

[Johnson, S.], 'An Account of the Life of Peter Burman', in *Gentleman's Magazine*, 12 (1742), 207

Jones, W., *Essay on the Law of Bailments* (1781)

The Letters of Sir William Jones, ed. G. Cannon, 2 vols. (Oxford, 1970)

Journals of the House of Commons (1742–)

Journals of the House of Lords (1767–)

The Letters of Junius, ed. J. Cannon (Oxford, 1978)

[Lewis, W.], *An Answer to the Serious Inquiry* [1752?]

Lipscomb, G., *The History and Antiquities of Buckinghamshire*, 4 vols. (1831)

The Registers of St. Vedast, Foster Lane, and of St. Michael-le-Quern, London. Volume i: Christenings, ed. W. A. Littledale (Harleian Soc., 1902), 267

Lofft, C., *Reports of Cases Adjudged in the Court of King's Bench* (1776)

Malone, E., *Supplement to the Edition of Shakespeare's Plays Published in 1778 by Samuel Johnson and George Steevens*, 2 vols. (1780)

Martin, C. T., *Catalogue of the Archives in the Muniment Room of All Souls' College* (1877)

Meerman, G., *Origines Typographicae*, 2 vols. (The Hague, 1765)

Meredith, W., *The Question Stated, whether the Freeholders of Middlesex lost their Right* (1769)

Register of Admissions to the Honourable Society of the Middle Temple, ed. H. A. C. Sturgess, 3 vols. (1949)

The Diaries of Sanderson Miller of Radway, ed. W. Hawkes (Dugdale Soc., 41, 2005)

An Eighteenth-Century Correspondence: being letters . . . to Sanderson Miller, ed. L. Dickens and M. Stanton (1910)

Morris, R., *A Letter to Sir Richard Aston* (1770)

[Mortimer, C. and Tracy, J.], *A Reply to Dr Huddesford's Observations* (Oxford, 1756)

The Correspondence of Sir Roger Newdigate of Arbury, Warwickshire, ed. A. W. A. White, (Dugdale Soc., 37, 1995)

Nicholls, J., *Recollections and Reflections, Personal and Political*, 2 vols. (1822)

Nichols, J., *Literary Anecdotes of the Eighteenth Century*, 9 vols. (1812–15)

[North, R.], *A Discourse On the Study of the Laws* (1824)

____, *The Lives of the Norths*, ed. A. Jessopp, 3 vols. (1890)

The Proceedings of the Old Bailey, London, 1674–1834: http://www.oldbailey online.org

Oldham, J., *The Mansfield Manuscripts and the Growth of English Law in the Eighteenth Century*, 2 vols. (1992)

First Minute Book of the Delegates of the Oxford University Press 1668–1756 (Oxford, 1943)

Philip, I. G., *William Blackstone and the Reform of the Oxford University Press in the Eighteenth Century* (Oxford, 1955)

Memoirs of Laetitia Pilkington, ed. A. C. Elias Jr., 2 vols. (1997)

Pointer, J., *Oxoniensis Academia* (1749)

Priestley, J., *Remarks on Some Paragraphs in the Fourth Volume of Dr Blackstone's Commentaries on the Laws of England, Relating to the Dissenters* (1769)

_____, *An Answer to Dr Blackstone's Reply* (1769), in *Works*, ed. J. T. Rutt, 25 vols. (1817–32), xxii. 328–34

Prior, J., *Life of Edmond Malone* (1860)

Letters of Richard Radcliffe and John James, ed. M. Evans (Oxford Historical Soc., 9, 1887)

Sir Joshua's Nephew Being Letters Written, 1769–1778, by a Young Man to his Sisters, ed. S. M. Radcliffe (1930)

Rayner, J., *An Inquiry into the Doctrine lately Propagated* (1769)

The Correspondence of Samuel Richardson, ed. A. L. Barbauld, 6 vols. (1804)

Parliamentary Papers of John Robinson 1774–1784, ed. W. T. Laprade (Camden Soc., 3rd Ser., 33, 1922)

Correspondence of John, Fourth Duke of Bedford, 3 vols. (1842)

The Diary of Dudley Ryder 1715–1716, ed. W. Matthews (1939)

'Parliamentary Diaries of Nathaniel Ryder, 1764–7', ed. P. D. G. Thomas (Camden Miscellany, 23, 1969)

Salisbury, W., *A Sermon Preached in Charter-House Chapel, On Monday, Dec. 12, 1737* (1738)

Salmon, T., *The Present State of the Universities* (1743)

[Scrope, R.], *Elisha's Pottage at Gilgal, spoiled by Symbolical Cookery at Oxford* [1760?]

[Scrope, R. and Nowell, T.], *A Dissertation upon That Species of Writing called Humour, when applied to Sacred Subjects* [1760?; Bodl. Gough Oxf. 131]

The Correspondence of Thomas Secker, Bishop of Oxford 1737–58, ed. A. P. Jenkins (Oxfordshire Rec. Soc., 57, 1991)

Sharp, G., *A Representation of the Injustice and Dangerous Tendency of Tolerating Slavery in England* (1769)

The Works in Verse and Prose of William Shenstone, Esq; Vol. III. Containing Letters to particular Friends (1769)

The Letters of William Shenstone, ed. M. Williams (Oxford, 1939)

The Correspondence of Adam Smith, ed. E. C. Mossner and I. S. Ross (Oxford, 1977)

Spring, T., *A Familiar Epistle from a Student of the Middle Temple, London, to his Friend in Dublin* (1771)

Stephens, A., *Memoirs of John Horne Tooke*, 2 vols. (1813)

Stevens, B. F. (ed.), *Facsimiles of Manuscripts in European Archives Relating to America, 1773–1783*, 25 vols. (1889–98)

Strype, J., *A Survey of the Cities of London and Westminster . . . to the Present Time*, 2 vols. (1720)

Stuart, G., *A View of Society in Europe, in its Progress from Rudeness to Refinement* (1778)

Taylor, J., *Elements of Civil Law* (Cambridge, 1755)

The English Reports, 178 vols. (Edinburgh, 1900–1932)

Thraliana The Diary of Mrs. Hester Lynch Thrale . . . Volume I 1776–1784, ed. K. C. Balderston (Oxford, 1942)

Memoirs, Letters and Remains of Alexis de Tocqueville, 2 vols. (Cambridge, 1861)

Tomlins, T. E., 'Corrections of Shakespeare's Text, by Sir William Blackstone, &c' (Papers of the Shakespeare Society, 1, 1844, 1853)

[Voltaire, F-M.,] *The White Bull, An Oriental History . . . faithfully done into English*, tr. J. Bentham (1774)

Oxford in 1710 from the Travels of Zacharias Conrad von Uffenbach, ed. W. H. and W. J. C. Quarrell (Oxford, 1928)

Vowell, J., *An Accommodation of the Matters in Dispute* (Oxford, 1757)

Walpole, H., *Memoirs of King George II*, ed. J. Brooke, 3 vols. (1985)

____ , *Memoirs of the Reign of George III*, ed. D. Jarrett, 4 vols. (2000)

The Yale Edition of Horace Walpole's Correspondence, ed. W. S. Lewis, 48 vols. (New Haven CT, 1937–83)

The Correspondence of Thomas Warton, ed. D. Fairer (1995)

Warton, T., *Theocrite Syracusii quae supersunt* (Oxford, 1770)

Waterland, D., *Advice to a Young Student* (1730)

Letter Book of John Watts: Merchant and Councillor of New York, January 1, 1762–December 22, 1765, ed. D. C. Barck (New York NY, 1928)

Wellins, C., *A Collection of Thoughts, Moral and Divine, upon Various Subjects* (Manchester, 1761; Exeter, 1764)

Wesley's Standard Sermons, ed. E. H. Sugden, 2 vols. (1921)

Whittock, N., *A Topographical and Historical Description of the University and City of Oxford* (1829)

Wilkes, J., *The North Briton*, 3 vols. (1763)

[Wilmot, G.], *A Serious Enquiry into some Late Proceedings in the University of Ox[for]d* (1751)

       [_____], *A Letter to _____ M.D.* (1752)

Wood, T., *An Institute of the Laws of England* (1720, 1734)

____ , *Some Thoughts Concerning the Study of the Laws of England in the Two Universities* (1708)

Woodeforde, J., *The Diary of a Country Parson*, ed. J. B. Beresford, 5 vols. (1924–31)

Wooll, J., *Biographical Memoirs of the Late Revd Joseph Warton* (1806)

Master Worsley's Book on the History and Constitution of the Honourable Society of the Middle Temple, ed. A. R. Ingpen (1910)

Woty, W., *Poems on Several Occasions* (Derby, 1780)

Historical and Posthumous Memoirs of Sir Nathaniel William Wraxall, ed. H. B. Wheatley, 5 vols. (1884)

SECONDARY SOURCES

1. Books

Abbey C. J., and Overton, J. H., *The English Church in the Eighteenth Century* (1887)

Allen, B., *Morrells of Oxford: the Family and their Brewery 1742–1993* (Oxford, 1994)

Andrew, E. G., *Patrons of Enlightenment* (Toronto, 2006)

Anon., *Blackstone and Oxford: an exhibition held at the Bodleian Library* (Oxford, 1980)

____, *Bibliotheca Blackstoneiana. A Catalogue of a Library of 4,500 Volumes . . . the greater part having been collected by the celebrated Judge Blackstone and Dr Blackstone of Oxford . . . Sold by Auction, by Mr. Price . . . 10th of Sept., 1845* (1845)

____, *A Catalogue of the Law Library of Philip Stanhope . . . To which is added the Reserved Part of the Library of the Late Justice Blackstone . . . Leigh, Sotheby, & Son . . . 1803* (1803)

Aston, T. (ed.), *The History of the University of Oxford: Volume V: The Eighteenth Century*, ed. L. S. Sutherland and L. G. Mitchell (Oxford, 1986)

Baker, J. H., *The Order of Serjeants at Law* (1984)

Bigg-Wither, R. F., *Materials for a History of the Wither Family* (Winchester, 1907)

Bill, E. G. W., *Education at Christ Church 1660–1800* (Oxford, 1988)

Black, J., *George III: America's Last King* (2006)

Bonsall, B., *Sir James Lowther and Cumberland and Westmorland Elections 1754–1775* (Manchester, 1960)

Borsay, P., 'The Culture of Improvement' in *The Eighteenth Century 1688–1815*, ed. P. Langford (Oxford, 2002), 183–210

Bowen, H. V., *Revenue and Reform: the Indian problem in British Politics 1757–1773* (Cambridge, 1991)

Brooks, C. W., *Lawyers, Litigation and English Society since 1450* (1998)

____, 'Litigation, participation, and agency in seventeenth- and eighteenth-century England', in *The British and their Laws in the Eighteenth Century*, ed. D. Lemmings (Woodbridge, 2005)

Burns, J. H., 'Bentham and Blackstone: A Lifetime's Dialectic', in *Empire and Revolutions*, ed. G. J. Schochet *et al.* (Washington, DC, 1993)

Burrows, M., *Worthies of All Souls* (1874)

Buxton, J. and Williams, P., *New College Oxford 1379–1979* (Oxford, 1979)

Carter, H., *A History of the Oxford University Press: Volume I. To the Year 1780* (Oxford, 1975)

Clark, J. C. D., *English Society 1660–1832* (Cambridge, 2000)

———, *Samuel Johnson* (Cambridge, 1994)

Clarke, M. L., *Classical Education in Britain 1500–1900* (Cambridge, 1959)

Cockburn, J. S., *A History of English Assizes 1558–1714* (Cambridge, 1972)

Cohen, R., 'The return to the ode', in *The Cambridge Companion to Eighteenth-Century Poetry*, ed. J. Sitter (Cambridge, 2001)

Colley, L., *In Defiance of Oligarchy: The Tory Party 1714–1760* (Cambridge, 1982)

Colvin, H., *A Biographical Dictionary of British Architects 1600–1840* (1995), 963

Colvin, H., and Simmons, J. S. G., *All Souls: An Oxford College and its Buildings* (Oxford, 1989)

Craske, M., 'Contacts and Contracts: Sir Henry Cheere and the Formation of a New Commercial World of Sculpture in mid-eighteenth-century London', in *The Lustrous Trade: Material Culture and the History of Sculpture in England and Italy c. 1700–c. 1860*, ed. C. Sicca and A. Yarrington (2000)

Craster, E., *The History of All Souls College Library*, ed. E. F. Jacob (1971)

Curley, T. M., *Sir Robert Chambers: Law, Literature and Empire in the Age of Johnson* (1998)

Davies, G. S., *Charterhouse in London* (1921)

Davis, J., 'Founder's Kin', in *All Souls under the Ancien Régime*, ed. S. J. D. Green and P. Horden (Oxford, 2007)

de Villiers, E., *Swinford Bridge 1769–1969* (Eynsham, 1969)

Dickinson, H. T. (ed.), *A Companion to Eighteenth–Century Britain* (Oxford, 2002)

Ditchfield, G. M., *George III: An Essay in Monarchy* (Basingstoke, 2002)

Doolittle, I., *William Blackstone A Biography* (Haslemere, 2001)

Duman, D., *The Judicial Bench in England 1727–1875* (1982)

Earle, P., *The Making of the English Middle Class: Business, Society and Family Life in London 1660–1730* (1989)

Ekirch, R., *Bound for America: the Transportation of British Convicts to the Colonies, 1718–1775* (Oxford, 1987)

Eller, C. S., *The William Blackstone Collection in the Yale Law Library* (New York NY, 1993)

Endelman, T. M., *The Jews of Georgian England 1714–1830: Tradition and Change in a Liberal Society* (Philadelphia PA, 1979)

Faber, G., *Notes on the History of the All Souls Bursarships and the College Agency* (p.p., n.d. [c. 1950])

Fifoot, C. H., *Lord Mansfield* (Oxford, 1936)

Foster, J., *Alumni Oxonienses 1500–1714*, 4 vols. (1891–2)

———, *Alumni Oxonienses 1715–1886*, 4 vols. (1887–8)

Fussell, P., *The Rhetorical World of Augustan Humanism* (Oxford, 1965)

Godley, A. D., *Oxford in the Eighteenth Century* (1908)

Gomme, L. (ed.), *Survey of London: Volume III. The Parish of St-Giles-in-the-Fields (Part I.) Lincoln's Inn Fields* (1912)

Gosse, P., *Dr Viper The Querulous Life of Philip Thicknesse* (1952)

Grassby, R., *Kinship and Capitalism: Marriage, Family and Business in the English-Speaking World, 1580–1740* (Cambridge, 2001)

Green, V. H. H., *The Young Mr Wesley* (1961)

Guest, I., *Dr John Radcliffe and His Trust* (1991)

Habakkuk, J., *Marriage, Debt and the Estates System: English Landownership, 1650–1950* (Oxford, 1994)

Hanbury, H. G., *The Vinerian Chair and Legal Education* (Oxford, 1958)

Harding, V., 'The changing shape of seventeenth-century London', in *Imagining Early Modern London . . . 1598–1720*, ed. J. F. Merritt (Cambridge, 2001)

Harris, R., *Politics and the Nation: Britain in the Mid-Eighteenth Century* (Oxford, 2002)

Hart, H. L. A., 'The United States of America', in *idem, Essays on Bentham* (Oxford, 1982)

Hawkins, E., *Medallic Illustrations of the History of Great Britain and Ireland*, 2 vols. (1885)

Hayter, T., *The Army and the Crowd in Mid-Georgian England* (1978)

Hedges, J. K., *The History of Wallingford*, 2 vols. (1881)

Hill, C. J., *The Literary Career of Richard Graves* (Northampton MA, 1934–5)

Hill, C., 'The Norman Yoke', in *idem, Puritanism and Revolution* (1958)

Holdsworth, W. S., *History of English Law*, 16 vols. (1922–66)

Hoppitt, J., *Risk and Failure in English Business 1700–1800* (Cambridge, 1987)

Hunt, M. H., *The Middling Sort: Commerce Gender and the Family in England 1680–1780* (1996)

Hyde, R., *The A to Z of Georgian London* (1982)

Ibbetson, D. J., 'Charles Viner and his Chair: Legal Education in Eighteenth-Century Oxford', in *Learning the Law*, ed. J. A. Bush and A. Wijffels (1999)

——, 'Sir William Jones as Comparative Lawyer', in *Sir William Jones 1746–94*, ed. A. Murray (Oxford, 1998)

E. F. Jacob, 'All Souls College', in *VCH Oxford*, iii

Jacob, W. M., *Lay People and Religion in the Early Eighteenth Century* (Cambridge, 1996)

Johns, A., *The Nature of the Book: Print and Knowledge in the Making* (1998)

Jupp, P., *The Governing of Britain 1688–1848* (2006)

King, P., *Crime, Justice and Discretion in England 1740–1820* (Oxford, 2000)

Kirby, T. F., *Winchester Scholars* (1888)

Jones, G., *The Sovereignty of the Law: Selections from Blackstone's Commentaries on the Laws of England* (1973)

Kemp, B., *Sir Francis Dashwood* (1967)

Langford, P., *Englishness Identified: Manners and Character 1650–1850* (Oxford, 2000)

Langford, P., *Public Life and the Propertied Englishman 1689–1798* (Oxford, 1991)

———, *The First Rockingham Administration, 1765–1766* (Oxford, 1973)

Lemmings, D., *Gentlemen and Barristers: the Inns of Court and the English Bar 1680–1730* (Oxford, 1990)

———, *Professors of the Law: Barristers and English Legal Culture in the Eighteenth Century* (Oxford, 2000)

——— (ed.), *The British and their Laws in the Eighteenth Century* (Woodbridge, 2005)

Levack, B., 'The English Civilians, 1500–1750', in *Lawyers in Early Modern Europe and America*, ed. W. Prest (1981)

———, 'Law', in *The History of the University of Oxford: Volume IV: Seventeenth-Century Oxford*, ed. N. R. N. Tyacke (Oxford, 1997)

Lieberman, D., *The Province of Legislation Determined* (Cambridge, 1989)

Lobban, M., *The Common Law and English Jurisprudence 1760–1850* (Oxford, 1991)

Lockmiller, D. A., *Sir William Blackstone* (Chapel Hill NC, 1938)

Macdonnell, G. P., 'Sir William Blackstone (1723–1780)', in *The Dictionary of National Biography*, ed. S. Lee, vol. 5 (1885)

Macleane, D., *A History of Pembroke College Oxford Anciently Broadgates Hall* (Oxford, 1897)

Macray, W. D., *Annals of the Bodleian Library, Oxford* (Oxford, 1890)

———, *A Register of the Members of St Mary Magdalen College, Oxford*, n. s. vol. 5 (Oxford, 1906)

McCormack, M., *The Independent Man Citizenship and Gender Politics in Georgian England* (Manchester, 2005)

McDonnell, M., *A History of St Paul's School* (1909)

———, *The Registers of St Paul's School 1509–1748* (1977)

McManners, J., *All Souls and the Shipley Case (1808–1810)* (Oxford, 2002)

McNamara, J., *Boston Manor Brentford* (Hounslow, 1998)

Mallet, C., *A History of the University of Oxford*, 3 vols. (1927)

Matthew, C., Harrison, B., and Goldman, L., *Oxford Dictionary of National Biography*, 60 vols. (Oxford, 2004)

Midgley, G., *University Life in Eighteenth-Century Oxford* (1996)

Milsom, S. F. C., *The Nature of Blackstone's Achievement* (1981)

Monod, P. K., *Jacobitism and the English people, 1688–1788* (Cambridge, 1989)

Moore, N., *The History of St Bartholomew's Hospital*, 2 vols. (1918)

Namier, L., *The Structure of Politics at the Accession of George III* (2nd. edn., 1957)

———, and Brooke, J. (ed.), *The House of Commons 1754–1790*, 3 vols. (1964)

Nangle, B. C., *The Monthly Review First Series 1749–1789* (Oxford, 1934)

Neill, P., 'Blackstone, Oxford, and the Law', in *All Souls Under the Ancien Régime*, ed. S. J. D. Green and P. Horden (Oxford, 2007)

Oldham, J., 'Underreported and Underrated: the Court of Common Pleas in the Eighteenth Century', in *Law as Culture and Culture as Law*, ed. H. Hartog and W. E. Nelson (Madison WI, 2000)

Oman, C. W., 'All Souls College', in *The Colleges of Oxford*, ed. A. Clark (1891)

Outhwaite, R. B., 'Marriage as business: opinions on the rise of aristocratic marriage portions in early modern England', in *Business Life and Public Policy*, ed. N. McKendrick and R. B. Outhwaite (Cambridge, 1986)

Paley, R., 'After *Somerset*: Mansfield, slavery and the law in England, 1772–1830', in *Law, Crime and English Society 1660–1830*, ed. N. Landau (Cambridge, 2002)

Pedgley, B. and D., *Crowmarsh: A History of Crowmarsh Gifford, Newnham Murren, Mongewell and North Stoke* (Crowmarsh, 1990)

Philip, I. G., *The Bodleian Library in the Seventeenth and Eighteenth Centuries* (Oxford, 1983)

Pocock, J. G. A., 'The Varieties of Whiggism from Exclusion to Reform', in *idem*, *Virtue, Commerce and History* (Cambridge, 1985)

———, *The Ancient Constitution and the Feudal Law* (Cambridge, 1987)

Pool, P. A., *William Borlase* (Truro, 1986)

Porter R., and Rousseau, G. S., *Gout The Patrician Malady* (1998)

Prior, J., *Life of Edmond Malone* (1860)

Quick, A., *Charterhouse: a History of the School* (1990)

Rashdall, H., *The Universities of Europe in the Middle Ages*, ed. F. M. Powicke and A. B. Emden, 3 vols. (Oxford, 1936)

Radzinowicz, L., *A History of English Criminal Law and Its Administration from 1750 Volume I The Movement for Reform* (1948)

Raven, J., *The Business of Books: Booksellers and the English Book Trade 1450–1850* (2007)

Reade, A. L., *Johnsonian Gleanings . . . Part V The Doctor's Life 1728–1735* (1928)

Reitan, E. A., *The Best of the Gentleman's Magazine, 1731–1754* (Lewiston NY, 1987)

Robson, R. J., *The Oxfordshire Election of 1754* (1949)

Robertson, C. G., *All Souls College* (1899)

Rodger, N. A. M., *The Insatiable Earl* (1993)

Rose, M., *Authors and Owners: The Invention of Copyright* (1993)

Rothblatt, S., *Tradition and Change in English Liberal Education* (1976)

Rudé, G., *Wilkes and Liberty* (Oxford, 1962)

Sack, J. J., *From Jacobite to Conservative* (Cambridge, 1993)

Sainty, J. C., *A List of English Law Officers, King's Counsel and Holders of Patents of Precedence* (1987)

———, *The Judges of England 1272–1990* (1993)

Schofield, R. E., *The Enlightenment of Joseph Priestley* (University Park PA, 1997)

Seaborne, M., *The English School: its architecture and organization 1370–1870* (1971)

Searby, P., *A History of the University of Cambridge Vol. III 1750–1870* (Cambridge, 1997)

Sedgwick, R., (ed.) *The House of Commons 1715–1754*, 2 vols. (1970)

Shapin, S., *A Social History of Truth: Civility and Science in Seventeenth-Century England* (1994)

Sheppard, F., *London, A History* (Oxford, 1998)

Sherbo, A., *Shakespeare's Midwives: Some neglected Shakespearean* (1992)

Shyllon, F. O., *Black Slaves in Britain* (1974)

Smith-Dampier, J. L., *Carthusian Worthies* (Oxford, 1940)

Squibb, G. D., *Founders' Kin: Privilege and Pedigree* (Oxford, 1972)

____, *Doctors' Commons* (Oxford, 1977)

Stein, P., *The Character and Influence of Roman Civil Law* (1988)

Stone, L., 'The Size and Composition of the Oxford Student Body 1580–1910', in *idem*, ed., *The University in Society Volume I* (Princeton NJ, 1975)

Suarez, M. F., 'The Production and Consumption of the Eighteenth-Century Poetic Miscellany', in *Books and their Readers in Eighteenth-Century England: New Essays*, ed. I. Rivers (2001)

Summerson, J., *Architecture in Britain 1530–1830* (Harmondsworth, 1970)

Sutherland, L.S., 'Pembroke College', in *VCH Oxfordshire*, iii

____, 'William Blackstone and the Legal Chairs at Oxford' in *Evidence in Literary Scholarship*, ed. R. Wellek and A. Ribeiro (1979)

Swerdlow, N., 'Blackstone's "Newtonian Dissent"', in *The Natural Sciences and the Social Sciences*, ed. I. B. Cohen (1994)

Taggart, I., *St Peter Wallingford Oxfordshire* (1987)

Thomas, P. D. G., *British Politics and the Stamp Act Crisis* (Oxford, 1975)

____, *George III: King and Politicians 1760–1770* (Manchester, 2002)

____, *The House of Commons in the Eighteenth Century* (Oxford, 1971)

____, *John Wilkes A Friend to Liberty* (Oxford, 1996)

Thomson, G. S., *The Russells in Bloomsbury, 1669–1771* (1940)

Tyack, G., *Warwickshire Country Houses* (Chichester, 1994)

van Heel, J., 'From Venice and Naples to Paris, the Hague, London, Oxford, Berlin . . . The Odyssey of the Manuscript Collection of Gerard and Johan Meerman', in *Books on the Move*, ed. R. Myers *et al.* (2007)

Venn, J. and J. A., *Alumni Cantabrigienses, Part I to 1751*, 4 vols. (Cambridge, 1923)

Ward, W. R., *Georgian Oxford* (Oxford, 1958)

Warden, L., *The Life of Blackstone* (Charlottesville VA, 1938)

Watson, A., *The Making of the Civil Law* (1981)

Webb, S. and B., *English Poor Law History Part I: The Old Poor Law* (1927; 1963)

Winstanley, D. A., *The University of Cambridge in the Eighteenth Century* (Cambridge, 1922)

Wordsworth, C., *Scholae Academicae Some Account of the Studies at the English Universities in the Eighteenth Century* (Cambridge, 1910)

Wrigley E.A. and Schofield, R. S., *The Population History of England, 1541–1871* (1981)

Yeo, R., *Encyclopaedic Visions* (Cambridge, 2001)

2. Periodical Articles

Baker, J. H., 'A Sixth Copy of Blackstone's Lectures', LQR, 84 (1968), 466

Baloch, T. A., 'Law Booksellers and Printers of Agents of Unchange', CLJ, 66 (2007), 389–421

Bolton, G. C., 'William Eden and the Convicts, 1771–1787', *Australian Journal of Politics and History*, 26 (1980), 30–40

Cairns, J., 'Blackstone, An English Institutist: Legal Literature and the Rise of the Nation State', OJLS 4 (1984), 318–60

Chrzanowski, S., 'Lady Blackstone's Cookery Book', *American Bar Association Journal*, 64 (1978), 371–3

Connors, R., '"The Grand Inquest of the Nation": Parliamentary Committees and Social Policy in Mid-Eighteenth-Century England', *Parliamentary History*, 14 (1995), 285–313

Cross, R., 'Blackstone v Bentham', LQR, 19 (1976), 516–27

Devereaux, S., 'The Making of the Penitentiary Act, 1775–1779', *Historical Journal*, 42 (1999), 405–33

Ditchfield, G. M., 'The Subscription Issue in British Parliamentary Politics, 1772–79', *Parliamentary History*, 7 (1988), 45–80

Doolittle, I. G., 'Sir William Blackstone and his *Commentaries on the Laws of England* (1765–69): a biographical approach', OJLS, 3 (1983), 99–112

____ 'William Blackstone and the Radcliffe Camera, 1753', *Bodleian Library Record*, 11 (1982), 47–50

____ 'Jeremy Bentham and Blackstone's lectures', *Bentham Newsletter*, 6 (1982), 23–5

Finnis, J. M., 'Blackstone's Theoretical Intentions', *Natural Law Forum*, 12 (1967), 163–83

Gibson, W., 'Bishop Gibson's Codex and the reform of the Oxford University Press in the Eighteenth Century', *Notes and Queries*, 42 (1995), 47–52

Gwyn, H., 'Pedigree of the Blackstone Family', *Gentleman's Magazine* (Sept. 1827), 224

Hagerty, G., 'Horace Walpole's Epistolary Friendships', *British Journal for Eighteenth-Century Studies*, 29 (2006), 201–218

Hanbury, H. G., 'Blackstone as Judge', AJLH, 3 (1959), 1–27

Harlan, R. D.,'Sales and Profits on Some Early Editions of Sir William Blackstone's *Commentaries*', *Papers of the Bibliographical Society of America*, 58 (1964), 156–63

Holdsworth, W. S., 'Gibbon, Blackstone, and Bentham', LQR, 52 (1938), 46–59

Kennedy, D., 'The Structure of Blackstone's Commentaries', *Buffalo Law Review*, 28 (1978–9), 205–379

Lemmings, D., 'Blackstone and Law Reform by Education: Preparation for the Bar and Lawyerly Culture in Eighteenth-Century England', *Law and History Review*, 16 (1998), 211–255

Munby, J. T. and Walton, H., 'The Building of New Road', *Oxoniensia*, 55 (1990), 123–30

Nolan, D. R., 'Sir William Blackstone and the New American Republic: A Study of Intellectual Impact', *New York University Law Review*, 51 (1976), 731–68

Odgers W. B., 'Sir William Blackstone', *Yale Law Journal*, 27 (1918), 599–618 & 28 (1919), 542–66

Oldham, J., 'Eighteenth-Century Judges' Notes: How They Explain, Correct and Enhance the Reports', AJLH, 31 (1987), 9–42

Posner, R. A., 'Blackstone and Bentham', *Journal of Law and Economics*, 19 (1976), 569–606

Prest, W., 'Common Lawyers and Culture in Early Modern England', *Law in Context*, 1 (1983), 88–106

____, 'Blackstone as Architect: Constructing the Commentaries', *Yale Journal of Law and the Humanities*, 15 (2003), 103–133

____, 'The Dialectical Origins of Finch's *Law*', CLJ, 36 (1977), 326–48

____, 'The Religion of a Lawyer? William Blackstone's Anglicanism', *Parergon*, 21 (2004), 153–68

Rendall, W. R., 'The Blackstones in Canada', *Illinois Law Review*, 16 (1921), 255–67

Saunders, D., and Hunter, I., 'Bringing the State to England: Andrew Tooke's Translation of Samuel Pufendorf's *De Officio Hominis et Civis*', *History of Political Thought*, 24 (2003), 218–34

Skinner, S., 'Blackstone's Support for the Militia', AJLH, 44 (2000), 1–18

Spurrier, L., 'Eternal Vows: Or a Faithless Old Swain', *The Berkshire Echo*, 21 (2002), 2

Thomas, P. D. G., '"Thoughts on the British Constitution" by George III in 1760', *Bulletin of the Institute of Historical Research*, 60 (1987), 361–3

____, 'Sir Roger Newdigate's Essays on Party, c. 1762', EHR, 102 (1987), 392–400

Underwood, M., 'The Structure and Operation of the Oxford Chancellor's Court', *Journal of the Society of Archivists*, 6 (1978), 18–27

Whibley, L., 'Dr Johnson and the Universities', *Blackwoods Magazine*, 226 (1929), 369–83

3. Unpublished Theses and Papers

Cannon, J. A. 'The Parliamentary Representation of the Borough of Chippenham, Cricklade, Downton, Hindon, Westbury, and Wootton Bassett, in Wiltshire, from 1754 until 1790', University of Bristol PhD thesis, 1958, 2 vols

Howard, A. J. 'Boston Manor and the Clitherow Family: a preliminary survey' ts., Guildhall Library, 1969

Howard, S. 'Biography and the Cult of Personality in Eighteenth-Century England', University of Oxford DPhil thesis, 1989

Lewer, A., 'Sir Roger Newdigate and Sir William Blackstone: a forgotten friendship', ts, 1995

Matthews, C., 'Architecture and Polite Culture in Eighteenth-Century England: Blackstone's Architectural Manuscripts', University of Adelaide PhD thesis, 2007

Rothstein, N., 'The Silk Industry in London, 1702–1766', University of London MA thesis, 1961

Simmons, J. S. G., 'List of All Souls Fellowship Candidates 1689–1914', ts, Codrington Library

Index